# Central Asia and South Asia

*Energy Cooperation and Transport Linkages*

## HIMALAYAN RESEARCH AND CULTURAL FOUNDATION

The Himalayan Research and Cultural Foundation is a multi-disciplinary research, cultural and development facilitative organization engaged in appraising and creating awareness about various issues related to the Himalayan and trans-Himalayan regions in South and Central Asia, or parts thereof connected with its environment, biodiversity, regional development, human resources, history, culture, art and literature, social structures, economies, human rights, peace processes etc., thus contributing to sustainable development and promotion of human, educational and economic advancement of the peoples of the region, besides preserving and enriching their rich and variegated cultural heritage. The Foundation has evolved as a vibrant national centre specialized on the Hindu Kush-Himalayan and trans-Himalayan regions in South and Central Asia. By means of its publications and activities, the Foundation has been providing a specialized input and expert analyses on a wide range of issues.

### *PUBLICATIONS*

BOOKS

***Afghanistan Factor in Central and South Asian Politics***
Edited by K. Warikoo (New Delhi, 1994), 73pp.
***Society and Culture in the Himalayas***
Edited by K. Warikoo (New Delhi, 1995), 316pp.
***Central Asia : Emerging New Order***
Edited by K. Warikoo (New Delhi, 1995), 352pp.
***Jammu, Kashmir and Ladakh : Linguistic Predicament***
Edited by P. N. Pushp and K. Warikoo (New Delhi, 1996), 224pp.
***Artisan of the Paradise : A Study of Art and Artisans of Kashmir***
By D.N. Dhar (New Delhi, 1999), 230pp.
***Gujjars of Jammu and Kashmir***
Edited by K. Warikoo (Bhopal, 2001), 317pp.
***Bamiyan: Challenge to World Heritage***
Edited by K. Warikoo (New Delhi, 2002), xviii, 313pp. 61plates.
***The Afghanistan Crisis: Issues and Perspectives***
Edited by K. Warikoo (New Delhi, 2002), xxvi, 523pp.
***Mongolia-India Relations***
By O. Nyamdavaa (New Delhi, 2003), 228pp.
***Child Labour Rehabilitation in India***
Edited by B. Zutshi and M. Dutta (New Delhi, 2003), 257pp.
***Mongolia-China Relations***
By Sharad K. Soni (New Delhi, 2006), xix, 328pp.
***Afghanistan: The Challenge***
Edited by K. Warikoo (New Delhi, 2007), 377pp.
***Drugs Production and Trafficking in Afghanistan***
By Deepali Gaur Singh (New Delhi, 2007), 380pp.
***Afghanistan: Challenges and Opportunities (set of 3 volumes)***
Edited by K. Warikoo (New Delhi, 2007), 1282pp.
***L. Berzenczey, Adventures in Central Asia: A Hungarian in the Great Game***
Edited by P.J.Marczell (New Delhi, 2007), 223pp.
***Cultural Heritage of Jammu and Kashmir***
Edited by K. Warikoo (New Delhi, 2009) 338pp.
***Cultural Heritage of Kashmiri Pandits***
Edited by S. S. Toshkhani & K. Warikoo (New Delhi, 2009) xxviii, 363pp.
**Rites and Rituals of Kashmiri Pandits**
S.S. Toshkhani (New Delhi, 2009) 237pp.
**Mongolia in the 21st Century: Society, Culture and International Relations**
Edited by K. Warikoo and Sharad K. Soni (New Delhi & London, Pentagon, 2010, 374 pp.)

JOURNAL
***Himalayan and Central Asian Studies***
(Quarterly being published regularly since 1997)

# Central Asia and South Asia

## *Energy Cooperation and Transport Linkages*

*Edited by*

K. Warikoo

Issued under the auspices of
HIMALAYAN RESEARCH AND CULTURAL FOUNDATION

PENTAGON PRESS

*Central Asia and South Asia: Energy Cooperation and Transport Linkages* / K. Warikoo (Ed)

ISBN 978-81-8274-555-1

First Published in 2011



*Published by*
PENTAGON PRESS
206, Peacock Lane, Shahpur Jat,
New Delhi-110049
Phones: 011-64706243, 26491568
Telefax: 011-26490600
email: rajan@pentagonpress.in
website: www.pentagonpress.in

*Typeset in Garmond 11pt by The Laser Printers*

*Printed at*
Guide Offset Printers, Delhi.

# Contents

# Preface

With Central Asia and the Caspian region having emerged as vital source of energy supply, there has been a new quest for alternative and shortest transportation routes to export oil/gas from this region to other countries, especially the South Asian countries. The Middle East being in a flux, particularly after the Iraq conflict, the ongoing Iran imbroglio and now the war in Libya, energy-importing countries have been diversifying their sources of supply. Whereas Europe is looking towards Russian supplies, Japan and China are keen to tap the Russian Far East, Siberia, Kazakhstan and the Caspian region for their growing energy needs. China needs to boost its energy consumption by about 150 per cent to maintain its economic growth rate. For India, with its huge demand for energy, Central Asia in its extended neighbourhood presents a potential source of energy. Being the sixth largest energy consumer in the world, India's crude imports are expected to double in a decade. Kazakhstan, which is the major oil/gas producing country in Central Asia, has its oil exports being routed through pipelines to Russia and China. Transport linkages are important to enter the energy market and integrate the region with other parts of the world.

In the case of India, it is facing logistic hazards due to lack of common border with Central Asian countries. Notwithstanding these constraints including strict visa regimes, inadequate banking facilities etc., India and Central Asian Republics have been maintaining close ties. India is also associated with CICA, SCO, and North-South Corridor. The North-South Transport Corridor, which was launched in the year 2000 by India, Russia and Iran with the projection of carrying cargo of 20 million tonnes by 2010, is also beset with certain problems on the ground. The North-South Transport Corridor seeks to restore the historic trade of conventional commodities between South Asia and Central Asia by facilitating faster and cheaper movement of goods from South Asia to Europe, and establishing a strategic transport link between Asia and Europe via Central Asia, Iran and Russia.

Two ancient concepts related to the region, i.e. Silk Route and Great Game have become quite relevant in contemporary times. Both these past experiences are valuable and explain to us the present situation in Central Asia, which now experiences a "New Great Game." In ancient times, the proximity between the two regions was based on the concept of geo-culture. The rise of economic ties gave rise to Silk Route. Later on geo-economics preceded geopolitics. The oceanic powers exploited the geopolitical concept for their own benefit. The concepts of heartland, World Island, rim land were used by colonial powers for their benefit. Whereas the geo-strategic significance of Central Asia and the big power interest in the region make it an area of great importance, there is need to engage in genuine partnership in the region in a spirit of non-hegemonic intentions.

Cross-border energy projects have two major problems – investments and vulnerability to supply interruptions. The challenges like sovereignty of the nations, political barriers, security of supplies, lack of a holistic approach to energy security, paucity of infrastructure etc. need to be met in order to develop the security aspect of energy cooperation and gradually bring it into the socio-economic dynamics in Central and South Asia. Apart from dialogues, knowledge sharing mechanisms and bilateral agreements to develop energy and transport linkages, a comprehensive universal framework is required to facilitate energy transit and trade by providing a level playing field to member countries. The establishment of a Pan-Asian gas supplies system passing through Asia connecting the source country and consumer countries would be beneficial for the region. Energy trade between Central Asia and South Asia needs to be dealt with on two parallel tracks – hydrocarbon trade and electricity trade. Energy security implies stable supply, developed market and secured transportation routes.

It is against this background that this book deals with all these issues related to energy and transport linkages between Central and South Asia. The book is based on the papers presented by eminent academics and specialists from India, Kazakhstan, Russia, China, UK and USA at an International Seminar at New Delhi organised by the Himalayan Research and Cultural Foundation in association with the Central Asian Studies Programme, School of International Studies, Jawaharlal Nehru University, New Delhi. Part I, which covers the broad theme of 'Energy Cooperation', comprising twelve chapters, deals with the geopolitics of energy resources in Eurasia, Caspian Basin, Russia's energy policy, Kazakhstan's energy strategy, China's energy initiatives in Central Asia, besides exploring the problems and prospects of India-Pakistan-Iran (IPI) and Turkmenistan-Afghanistan-Pakistan-India (TAPI) pipelines. Part II dealing with the subject of 'Transport Linkages', includes eight chapters which deal with the challenges of connectivity faced by landlocked states, Silk Route, Trans-Siberian Railway, North-South Corridor, India's options for land access to Central Asia and newly built Gwadar Port in Pakistan.

*K. Warikoo*

# Contributors

1. **Prof. Devendra Kaushik** is former Chairman, Maulana Abul Kalam Azad Institute of Asian Studies, Kolkata.
2. **Dr. Shirin Akiner,** who taught at the School of Oriental and African Studies, University of London, is an Associate Fellow of the Royal Institute of International Affairs, London and author of several books on Central Asia.
3. **Prof. R.G. Gidadhubli** is former Director of Eurasian Studies, University of Mumbai, Mumbai.
4. **Prof. P.L. Dash** is former Director, Centre for Central Eurasian Studies, University of Mumbai, Mumbai.
5. **Dr. Irina Morozova** is associated with the International Institute for Asian Studies, Leiden, the Netherlands.
6. **Bek Ali Yerzhan** is associated with Faculty of International Relations, Al-Farabi Kazakh National University, Almaty, Kazakhstan.
7. **Ms. Oxana Dolzhikova** is associated with the Institute of World Economy and Policy (IWEP) of the First Kazakhstan President Foundation.
8. **Ms. Yelena I. Rudenko** is associated with the Institute of Oriental Studies, Almaty, Kazakhstan.
9. **Dr. Xu Qinhua** teaches at the School of International Studies, Renmin University, Beijing (China).
10. **Dr. Nawal K. Paswan** is Assistant Professor, Central Asian Studies Programme, School of International Studies, Jawaharlal Nehru University, New Delhi.
11. **Dr. Savita Pande** is Professor, South Asian Studies, School of International Studies, Jawaharlal Nehru University, New Delhi.
12. **Dr. Mahesh Ranjan Debata** is Assistant Professor, Central Asian Studies Programme, School of International Studies, Jawaharlal Nehru University, New Delhi.
13. **Late Prof. Martin Glassner,** was Chairman, Department of Geography, Southern Connecticut State University, USA from 1982-1994. His major books

include *Access to the Sea for Developing Land-Locked States*, The Hague: Martinus Nijhoff, 1970; *Systematic Political Geography*, Fourth Edition, New York: John Wiley and Sons, 1988; *Political Geography*, Third Edition (with Chuck Fahrer), Hoboken, N.J.: John Wiley and Sons, 2003; *Geography against Development: A Case for Landlocked Developing Countries* (Editor), New York: United Nations, 2006.

14. **Avinoam Idan** is associated with the Centre for Advanced Energy Studies of the University of Haifa, Israel.

15. **Dr. Victor M. Mitypov** is Consultant at the Ministry of Finance, Republic of Buryatia, Ulan Ude, Russia.

16. **Prof. Marino Baldano** is Head, Department of History, Sociology and Ethnology, Institute for Mongolian, Buddhist and Tibetan Studies, Siberian Branch, Russian Academy of Sciences, Ulan Ude, Russia.

17. **Dr. Meena Singh Roy** is Research Officer, Institute for Defence Studies and Analyses, New Delhi.

18. **Dr. K. Warikoo** is Professor, Central Asian Studies Programme, School of International Studies, Jawaharlal Nehru University, New Delhi.

19. **Neeladri Chatterjee** is associated with the University of Delhi and Petroleum Conservation and Research Association.

19. **Cdr. Alok Bansal** is Executive Director, National Maritime Foundation, New Delhi.

20. **Dr. Mondira Dutta** is Associate Professor, Central Asian Studies Programme, School of International Studies, Jawaharlal Nehru University, New Delhi.

# PART I
# Energy Cooperation

# 1

# New Geopolitics of Hydrocarbon Resources
## *A Eurasian Perspective*

*Devendra Kaushik*

The Eurasian part of the world map got sharply transformed at the end of the 20th century. The formation of new independent states on the territory of this vast landmass in the wake of the disintegration of the USSR changed the geopolitical configuration in the two continents of Europe and Asia, radically altering many of our firmly rooted understandings about developments in West and Central Asia. The geopolitical changes following the collapse of the Soviet Union led to a qualitatively new situation, which gave rise to a new alignment of global forces.

From one side the end of the bipolar world which was based on the two opposing super powers – the USSR and the USA – led to an enhanced role of the United States, now trying to become an undisputed arbiter of international relations as the sole hyper-power. The wars in Afghanistan and Iraq are but links in the same chain. Their aim is not just global political hegemony but also access to important raw material resources. In fact, control of vital raw materials and mineral resources is the necessary means for attaining global political hegemony. So long as humankind does not discover new cheaper and more effective fuel, oil and gas will continue to be the basic factor determining the development of contemporary economies. It is thus understandable that the rich energy resources of the Caspian and Central Asian region should attract the attention of the United States. On the other side the unilateral world is also a relative and conditional notion. On the Caspian geopolitical field new actors have also appeared. Besides Russia which continues to make efforts to preserve its traditional influence in the region, the European Union has also deep stakes in the area because of its dependence on its energy resources. The neighbouring powers of Iran and Turkey, besides India and China are also interested in this region due to its geo-strategic location as well as rich hydrocarbon resources.

The intertwined nature of political domination and access to important natural resources was clearly brought out in the Carter Doctrine proclaimed in 1980 by President Carter in relation to the Persian Gulf Region and extended in 1997 by

President Clinton to the Caspian Region. President Carter established the Rapid Joint Task Force along with a network of US military bases in the Greater Middle East Region to protect the flow of oil from the Persian Gulf region. The process was accelerated by President Reagan in 1983 by transforming the Joint Task Force into the US Central Command on par with US European Command, Pacific Command and the Southern Command. The Carter doctrine began to be globalised under the Clinton administration. In 1997 Clinton told the visiting Azerbaijan President that the United States could not afford to rely on any single region for its energy supplies. "By facilitating Azerbaijan's oil export, we not only help Azerbaijan to prosper, we also help diversify our energy supply and strengthen our nation's security", Clinton was reported to have told Azerbaijan's President. He also extended this formulation to Kazakhstan, another promising source of petroleum, and to Georgia, a major transit country on the proposed pipeline from Baku to Turkey. Thus were established military ties between Pentagon and these countries leading to a significant US presence in the Caspian Basin. These ties were further utilized by President Bush Junior to facilitate US intervention in Afghanistan following 9/11. It is thus important to note that the military ties in the Caspian and Central Asian region were originally motivated by concern over the safety of energy supplies and the same are being used to counteract the threat posed by terrorism. The Carter Doctrine which has been a central objective of American foreign policy was further globalised by the National Energy Policy (17 May 2001) widely known as the Cheney Report. The policy called for greater diversity of oil production focusing upon South Africa, West Coast of Africa and the Caspian Basin. The US policy of anti-terrorism and oil protection has also been integrated. Georgia has been extended military assistance to protect Baku-Ceyhan Pipeline against sabotage and insurgent and terrorist attack. Azerbaijan too has been helped to develop and deploy a small navy in its Caspian Sea enclave and setting up of a US base in that country was also under active consideration.

The Trans-Caucasian and the Caspian region has been since antiquity well-known as a great migration route between the West as well as the East linking Europe and Asia. In the pre-Christian era the Indo-Aryan tribes are believed to have taken this route which was used much later by the Turks for migration in the reverse direction. In recent times the Nazi horde had planned to penetrate West, Southwest and South Asia. The 19$^{th}$ Century "Great Game" over Central Asia was mainly explained in terms of the strategic significance of this region because of its geographical location as the gateway to the Indian subcontinent and Persian Gulf. Even then the geographical or the geopolitical was but a façade and the leitmotif was the economy-driven imperialist rivalry between the two European great powers Britain and Russia. The Central Asian and Caspian region was before the discovery of sea route in the 15$^{th}$ century an important overland transit route between the East and West. It was through this region that pilgrims and traders passed on their way from China and India as well as from Europe to China and India. Greek Writer Strabo testifies to the flow of Indian goods along the Oxus, the Caspian Sea, Transcaucasia and further

West along the Black Sea Coast to Europe. The ancient route between the West and the East crisscrossing Central Asia and the Caucasus were known in the history as the Great Silk Route. A branch of the Silk Route also proceeded in the direction of the North through the Volga region. Free uninterrupted flow of culture and commerce was characteristic of the ancient Great Silk Route and no geopolitics was involved in its operation unlike the present oil and gas pipelines– its modern hi-tech version.

The Indian connection with Central Asia and Transcaucasia is pretty old. Archeological findings confirm the existence of close cultural and trade links between the peoples in the two regions as far back as the third millennium BC in the period of the Harappan civilization. These links continued to develop in the succeeding periods of history. There were Armenian trading posts in India and in ancient Georgia, Indian *Panchatantra* (didactic tales told through animals and birds) enjoyed great popularity. An Indian fire temple existed on the Caspian Sea coast near Baku which used to be thronged by a multitude of pilgrims from India throughout the 19th century. Incidentally, the Caspian natural gas burnt the fire in this temple. The Ossetians, one of the ethnic groups in Georgia and north Caucasia are closely related linguistically with the Indo-Aryan creators of the Vedas. A series of trade routes connected the Volga region with northern India via Transcaucasia (Derbent, Baku and Shemakha) and Central Asia. Indian gold coins from 14th century have been found in the Volga region near the village called Tenishevo which is indicative of the trade with the Golden Horde. In fact, a trade route between India and Russia had existed through Central Asia and the Caspian Sea since the 10th-11th centuries.

The British colonial power was conscious of the Indian historical links with Central Asia and the Caspian region and did not hesitate to exploit them to promote its strategic and geopolitical goals. During the World War I, it sent a contingent of Indian soldiers under General Malleson based in Meshed in Iran with the aim of preventing the Baku oilfields from falling into German hands. This military action in Central Asia and Transcaucasia by the British Indian authorities continued even after the end of the World War I. The British, however, failed in their mission to turn the scales against the Bolsheviks in the Civil War following the 1917 October Revolution in Russia.

The geostrategic location of the Central Asian and Caspian region in the centre of the West-East and North-South communication corridors has catapulted it into the vortex of a geopolitical struggle over its sizeable hydrocarbon resources which is sometimes called a "new round of the Great Game". But the US interests in the Caspian region are not motivated just by the need to protect the country from what is called "oil blackmailing" or to ensure the fulfillment of its growing energy demand. In fact, Washington is yet to overcome the "Cold War syndrome". It still continues to vigorously pursue the objective of marginalizing Russia in its "near abroad" and thus further consolidate its victory in the Cold War which it achieved through the disintegration of the Soviet Union. Caspian oil is looked upon by Brzezinski as the "best tool" for integrating the Central Asian and Trans-Caucasian countries into the world market and turning them away from Russia, thus for ever eliminating the possibility of post-imperial integration. America is busy creating more or less a new sphere of influence – the largest ever since the last one that appeared in the Middle East half a century ago.

Washington does not spare any effort to project its "genuine" interest in the development of the energy resources of the Caspian-Central Asian region. Yet strategic not economic leitmotiv remains crucial for its policies towards this region. Behind its interest in oil there lies a deep desire for controlling its flow to China and India, for isolating and marginalizing the influence of Iran and Russia – the two traditional players in the field. It is using Turkey as a proxy to expand its political, economic and military interests in Central Asia and Caucasia. Trying to orientate the oil transit routes towards Turkey, it desires to weaken Russia economically by ending its monopoly over the transport of oil to the West through its territory.

The United States wants oil to flow from Kazakhstan and Azerbaijan through the turbulent Caucasian region ending up at the Turkish Mediterranean port of Ceyhan even though it may be more expensive because of the long distances involved and more vulnerable due to a volatile situation prevailing in the areas through which the Baku-Tbilisi-Cehyan (BTC) pipeline has to pass. Though concerned about the environmental degradation threat to the Black Sea waters due to leakage of oil from tankers passing through the Turkish straits, it conveniently ignores a similar threat posed by the underwater pipelines to be laid in the Caspian Sea to bring Kazakh and Turkmen oil and gas to Baku. Similarly, while it wants Turkmen gas to flow to Pakistan and India through politically unstable Afghanistan, it objects to the flow of Iranian gas through the same route.

In this context one is reminded what Lord Curzon wrote in 1889 – "Turkestan, Afghanistan, Transcaucasia and Persia – to many these names breathe only a sense of utter remoteness or a memory of strange vicissitudes and of moribund romance. To me, I confess they are pieces on a chessboard upon which is played out a game for the domination of the world". Interestingly leading US strategic thinker Brzezinski has chosen the title *The Grand Chessboard* for his book which deals with the American moves on the Eurasian grand chessboard to perpetuate the global primacy of the United States.[1]

Washington has dexterously blended its supposed or real interest in the oil of the Caspian basin into its neo-imperial designs of world domination under the cover of fighting terror and tyranny. Energy provided to it one of the strongest synergy of interests between the sole superpower that has set its sight on the region as a strategically important land rich in mineral resources and the local ruling elite looking for assistance from other than Russian sources to bolster their shaky economies and overcome the poverty and underdevelopment of their countries. The United States dovetailed the Caspian region energy security issues to the global energy security discussion by projecting Caspian energy as an alternative to energy supply from the volatile Gulf region.

American political analysts have been developing the geopolitical structure of the "Greater Middle East" since the disintegration of the Soviet Union. The peculiarity of this model is that it adds to the traditional Middle East, new independent states in Transcaucasia, Central Asia and the Indian subcontinent, uniting them into a single macro region. Consequently the problems of the settlement of the Middle East proper dissolve into problems of the "Greater Middle East". The former Soviet republics in Central Asia and Transcaucasia increasingly act as the main US foothold in the new macro-region along with Turkey and Israel. The Georgian direction has also gained prominence in this concept.[2] Israel-Turkey-Georgia are assigned an important role in the Russian strategy of the United States. A new geopolitical configuration was sought to be formed through the so-called 'colour' revolutions in Ukraine and Georgia. The Caucasian and Central Asian region is being actively integrated with the West through the Partnership for Peace Programme of NATO. The US is training the Georgian armed forces and conducting with Ukraine joint naval exercises in the Black Sea. A plan is being mooted to post the US military personnel to protect the pipeline going to Turkey through Georgia.

The theoretical foundations of the US activism in the Caspian and Central Asian region and pursuit of a 'forward' policy reminiscent of the British power during the 19th century 'Great Game' were laid by Brzezinski, Security Advisor to President Carter. Stephen Blank is right in identifying him as a promoter of a "neo-Mackinderian scheme of a grand anti-Russian Eurasian coalition led by the United States and embracing Europe, Turkey, Iran and China". "This coalition", Blank writes, "seeks to obtain Eurasia's energy supplies and orchestrate a renovated global anti-Russian containment policy under US leadership."[3] More than a decade earlier American jurist Francis P. Sempa in his article published in 1987 called Mackinder the "grandfather" of the policy of containment propounded by Kennan. Sempa remarked: "most Americans might be startled to discover that current American foreign policy has its intellectual roots in concepts first formulated over 80 years ago by a British Geographer."[4]

Brzezinski lays emphasis on the fact that all through history Eurasia has been the centre of world power and that for the first time a non-Eurasian power has emerged not only as the key arbiter of Eurasian power relations but also as the world's paramount power.[5] "Eurasia is thus", writes the American scholar, "the chessboard on which this struggle for global primacy continues to be played and that struggle involves geostrategy – the strategic management of geopolitical interest".[6] American global hegemony which is dependent upon its preponderance on the Eurasian continent is viewed by Brzezinski as conducive for international stability. Samuel P. Huntington endorses his view in the following words: "The sustained international primacy of the US is central to the welfare and security of the Americans and to the future of democracy, open economies and international order".[7]

The Grand Chessboard of Eurasia has five geostrategic players and five geopolitical pivots. France, Germany, Russia, China and India are listed by Brzezinski as major active players, (Great Britain, Japan, Indonesia etc. though important states do not qualify as such). Ukraine, Azerbaijan, South Korea, Turkey and Iran play the role of critically important geopolitical pivots, though both Turkey and Iran to some extent – within their more limited capabilities – are also geo-strategically active.[8]

The master American strategists advocate the course of geopolitical pluralism in Central Asia and Caucasia instead of "mature strategic partnership" promised to Russia. Azerbaijan is viewed by him as an active "cork" controlling access to the "bottle" that contains the riches of the Caspian Sea Basin and Central Asian corridor for pipelines.[9] Kazakhstan and Uzbekistan are labelled as "shield" and "soul" for the region's diverse national awakenings. The future of Russia as envisaged by him lies in a loose confederation composed of a European Russia, a Siberian republic and Far-Eastern republics" with a decentralized political system based on free-market.[10] Interestingly, Ukraine and Georgia which have recently undergone regime changes through a colour revolution were listed among the five "geopolitical pivots" in Brzezinski's famous work.

Brzezinski's ideas continued to influence the policies of several American administrations. The US Secretary of State during the second term of President Clinton, Mrs. Madeleine Albright, who was a favourite student of his at the high-profile Wellesley Women's College where he taught, in her memoirs, fondly recollects how at a masquerade at the place of Brzezinski they both entertained the guests impersonating a horse. Brzezinski "was first pilot" and she his second, i.e., Brzezinski was head of the horse and Madeleine controlled its rear.[11] The geopolitical ideas of Brzezinski were faithfully implemented in the Balkans by his pupil State Secretary. She even tried to implement them to some extent in the Caucasus, though in her memoirs she displays a very poor knowledge about the region. Writing about her 1994 week-long trip to Caucasus, she relocates Moldova from the Carpathian to the Transcaucasian region and messes up Georgians with "a Slav nation like Poles and Czechs".

The Mackinderian geopolitics which got a fresh wind through the publication of Brzezinski's book gave an impetus to the resurgence of a Russian conception of geopolitics. The publication of Russian Communist Party Leader G.A. Zyuganov's book *Geografiya Pobedy: Osnovy Rossiiskoi Geopolitiki,* (Geography of Victory: Bases of Russian Geopolitics) which synchronized with the Publication of Brzezinski's book in 1997 was an important event in the re-emergence of geopolitics in Russia. On 18 December 1997, a special session of the State Duma Committee on Questions of Geopolitics under A.V. Mitrofanov was held to discuss this book. In his presidential speech Mitrofanov described the publication of the book as a "big political event". The leaders of the Communist Party of the Soviet Union in their days and the Communist Party of the Russian Federation subsequently never talked of geopolitics. In fact both geopolitics and genetics were shunned by them as "a prostitute girl of imperialism". Mitrofanov cited Zuganov to the effect that "a strong Russia, be it communist, democratic or monarchical, was not needed by the West". He also drew attention to an important quotation from Marx highlighted by Zuganov. Marx wrote: "Russia could not leave the mouth of river Neva into the hands of Swedes, it is the only natural outlet for its product for the north, similar is the case of mouth of the rivers Don, Dnieper, Buga and the Kerchenski Bay which cannot be left to the marauding Tartar nomads... The Baltic provinces by virtue of their geographical location are also naturally essential for this nation which possesses the country situated behind them... In other words Peter annexed all the territory which was required for the natural development of the country".

In Zuganov's view, Russia is the main continental force controlling the nucleus of Eurasia. Britain ruled for centuries over the Trans-oceanic territories, passing on the baton to the USA only after 1935.He analyses the main idea of Russian geopolitics first laid down by Filofei, a monk Pskov and followed in the doctrines of Stalin and Brezhnev. In his view all of them oriented towards the state self-sufficiency and creation around Russia of a "large space" comprised by strategic allies. "Hence, on account of our geographical location, our ideology was, so to say, to meet the enemy at distant steps. We strove to push ahead the space of our state as also of our allies in order to counteract that danger which was always characteristic for our state beset by perpetual problems created by our geographical condition. The nomadic hordes marched from the West and the South", writes Zuganov.

According to Mitrofanov, in 1453 AD, the Turks captured Constantinople, the capital of Byzantine, which was the second Rome. About the same time the Russian lands had been unified which enabled the transfer of the Centre of Orthodox Christian civilization to Moscow which was looked upon as the third Rome by Filofei. This gave birth to the idea of a universal mission of Moscow which has remained the basis of Russian geopolitics. Mitrafanov advocates the restoration of a bipolar world with Russia as the second pole on the basis of a sound understanding of Russian geopolitics. He ridicules the idea that the present day Russia has no economic resources to achieve this goal by posing a question to the Russian rulers – how a state possessing 25 per cent of natural gas and 20 per cent of the world's oil reserves not to speak of enormous stocks of gold, diamond and aluminum has a budget of 90 billion dollars? Russia, in his view as also of his several compatriots, was fully in a position to regains its lost global status if it corrects the course of its domestic policy by rooting out misgovernance and corruption.[12]

The birth of the Shanghai Five Organisation in April 1996 which was renamed as the Shanghai Cooperation Organisation (SCO) in June 2001 when Uzbekistan joined, brought a distinct change in the security scenario prevailing in the Central Asian region. This organization after making a significant contribution to the confidence building effort in Eurasia and improvement in its security environment through reduction in armed forces deployed in the border regions gradually evolved into a Eurasian regional organization over the years. After significant success in border delimitation and demilitarization the organization shifted its attention to elimination of religious militancy in the region. On 15 June 2001, the six states signed the convention against terrorism, separatism and religious extremism. They also decided to widen inter-state cooperation in diplomatic, commercial, military, technological and other fields for reinforcing regional security and stability. They committed themselves to cooperation in combating trafficking of drugs and arms, in fighting terrorism, religious extremism and separatism as also in resolving disputes over trans-border resources such as water, energy and transport infrastructure. At its Tashkent Summit held in 2004, the SCO took a decision to direct its activities towards economic cooperation and infrastructure development. China announced its decision to give $1 billion aid for development of trade in the region. For some time there remained certain misunderstandings among the member states of the SCO on account of establishment of two separate anti-terrorist centres under the Collective Security Treaty Organisation and the SCO in Bishkek and Tashkent separately. Before the June 2002 summit at St. Petersburg, which adopted the Charter of the SCO and Declaration of Heads of States of Members of the SCO, there arose some doubts and misgivings about Russia's Westward tilt on account of Russo-American Agreement in Moscow for reduction of nuclear arms and the Rome Declaration setting up the Russia-NATO Joint Council. However, these doubts were cleared after Putin addressed a press conference at the conclusion of his talks with the President of Finland Tarja Halonen. Putin declared that Russia continues to have "major interest in the East" and that China was one of "Russia's critical partners". Although the Foreign Policy concept adopted in 2000 under Putin gave priority to Russia's relations with the CIS and called Russia a Eurasian state, the Foreign Policy of Russia under Putin also emphasized the priority given by Russia to its relations with Europe. Through his various policy pronouncements Putin reiterated Russia's commitment to the goal of ensuring strategic stability in the world by establishment of a new global security system through a "permanent dialogue" with the United States. Putin also advanced the concept of a "stable arc" aimed at setting up a buffer zone separating the NATO in the West by the CIS Collective Security Treaty Organisation in the middle and SCO in the East with Russia's participation in both.

The main spirit behind the SCO is the growing realization among the Eurasian powers that regional security cannot be ensured through overseas structures located far from the territory. For this it is necessary that a group of neighbouring states in a region recognize themselves as a community in which their national identity is complementary rather than adverse to their neighbours. The SCO has particular focus on non-traditional issues such as environment protection, water management and cooperation in development of energy and transport, prevention of drugs and arms trafficking, organized crimes and tackling problems of migration and refugees.

Apprehensions have been expressed by western analysts about Russo-Chinese cooperation through the SCO lasting itself in the long-run. Thus, Martha Brill Olcott writes, "If Russia were to grow so weak that China would regard its influence as withdrawn, it seems inevitable that China would move to replace Russia. It might do so by military means or by economic means, which would be determined by nature of the vacuum China perceived to exist."[13] Similarly, Stephan Blank expects China not the United States to be the bigger rival of Russia in Central Asia for the trans-Caspian energy and influence.[14] Chinese scholars Wang Fushi and Wen Li have expressed the view that China is more important than India and Iran for the global strategy of Russia. China has, they write, a greater weight than India and Iran for a speedy development in the direction of multipolarity, a trend that has acquired prominence during the second half of the 1990s. In their opinion Russia is faced with the inevitable choice of developing and promoting a new type of relationship with China. Russia's relations with India and Iran will not "necessarily be as transparent and predictable, or play an important role in Russia's implementation of its strategy in world politics, as Russian-Chinese relations." Russia-India relations, according to them, are more of a regional than global significance for Russia's geopolitical strategy. These relations have changed since the disappearance of the Soviet Union. Russo-Iranian relations are also not viewed as crucial for Russian geostrategy on account of difficulties in international relations due to the rise of Islamic fundamentalism. It might have an unsettling effect on Russia's Muslim population and create complications in Russia's relations with the West. The Chinese scholars perceive difficulties for Russia in making a final strategic choice in favour of Asia since notwithstanding the fact that the bulk of Russian territory lies in Asia, there are ample statistics to show that Europe is the main agent of Russia's economic and commercial ties, as well as its source of foreign investment. The placing of accent on the great Asian nations as a response to NATO's Eastward expansion can only yield significant results in the future when Russia is able to make its strategic choice.[15]

Russia being a key state on the Eurasian landmass cannot drop out of the new round of the "Great Game" which is being currently played. It is a natural and compulsive player. Its present economic weakness notwithstanding, Russia has numerous strong reasons to maintain its special relationship with the Caspian-Central Asian states. The region is but the continuation of the Russian steppe. There are no physical barriers separating the two. Both have historical ties going to the remote past. Though the trade of Central Asia and Caucasus with Russia has been gradually declining, yet Central Asia still remains Russia's main trade and economic partners. In spite of the exodus of the Russian speaking population from Central Asia and Caucasia and the declining volume of trade, Russia by virtue of its historical links, geographical proximity and superior military strength remains a major power centre in Eurasia.

Russia's reassertive stance in Central Asia is likely to be strengthened in days to come. The importance of Central Asia and the Caucasian region in the foreign policy of Moscow increased tremendously in the aftermath of the massacre by terrorists in Beslan. Putin's address to the nation on 4 September 2004 signaled a change in Russia's perception of its adversary. President Putin minced no words in openly stating that Russia was under attack by powerful circles within the Cold War era adversaries of the Soviet Union, in whose hands terrorism "is an instrument wielded for the purpose of breaking the country".

Notwithstanding a certain firmness displayed by Russia in the aftermath of the Beslan massacre, Russian policy towards Central Asia continued to blow hot and cold. But,on the whole it remained both pragmatic and moderate. In his 21 February 2005 speech in Brussels, the US President George W. Bush categorically asserted his belief that "Russia's future lies within the family of Europe and the Trans-Atlantic Community". President Putin seemed to be heeding the above advice of President Bush when he declared in his April 2005 State of the Nation address that "Russia was, is and will ... be a major European power." He even went on to the extent of saying that "Russia should continue its civilizing mission on the Eurasian continent." This statement of his created a lot of misunderstanding not only in the Central Asian states but also in several Asian countries. However, to be fair to Putin it must be stated that what he had in mind was far from the colonial 'white man's burden' doctrine. To him this mission consists in ensuring that "democratic values, combined with national interests, enrich and strengthen our historic community." The same address it may also be mentioned urged upon Russia and other members of the CIS to draw "on the genuinely useful experience of our neighbours and also to share with them our own ideas and the results of our work". Nevertheless, the choice of the term 'civilizing mission' was not an appropriate one to say the least.

An insight into the thinking of the Putin administration on international relations can be gained from an important article by Foreign Minister Sergei Lavrov. Lavrov highlights the underlying principles of Russian foreign policy as "pragmatism, multi-vectorness, a consistent promotion of national interest without sliding into confrontation". The Russian Foreign Minister referred to a phenomenon of an "'Asian Face' acquired by globalization". He called upon the rejection of winner syndrome and insisted upon "complete equality and mutual engagement from the beginning, i.e, the joint analyses of threats, the joint elaboration of decisions and also their joint implementations". Stressing the reality of multipolarity as an optimal method of conducting world affairs, Lavrov underlined the increased significance of the energy factor in global politics which has been selected as a priority for Moscow's G-8 meet. The G-8 summit was expected to discuss this question not only in the Near East and Middle East perspective but also in the CIS space too.[16]

Under President Putin's direction, the Russian policy towards Central Asia was all set to move towards moderation based on pragmatism rather than confrontation. The holistic approach towards Central Asia became evident after the session of the Eurasian Economic Community at St. Petersburg in 26 January 2006. The accession of Uzbekistan to the Eurasian Economic Community and the integration of Central Asian Cooperation Organisation (CACO) into the Eurasian Economic Community (EEC) in general is a significant development. The St. Petersburg meet which decided to take joint action on creating a currency union by organizing an integrated currency market is a bold step in the direction of forging a Common Economic Space, covering Central Asia, Russia and Belarus. The EEC which now incorporates the CACO, will take steps in the direction of cooperation in the peaceful use of nuclear energy. Both Kazakhstan and Uzbekistan are rich in both hydrocarbon resources and raw material for nuclear energy. Putin's meeting with President Niyazov on the sideline of the EEC meet also discussed cooperation between Russia and Turkmenistan's energy resources. Both the heads of states expressed their strong desire to bring energy resources to Asia and Europe.

The year 2006 witnessed the reemergence of the old Cold War like situation with the numerous propaganda attacks by Washington on the Kremlin. The report of the US Council on Foreign Relations released on 5 March 2006 alleged that Russia's foreign and domestic policies had taken a reaction that hurt US's global interest. It reached the conclusion that a "US-Russian partnership is no more possible". Earlier, the Annual Human Rights Report of the US State Department strongly criticized the Russian leadership of President Putin for authoritarianism – by virtually stripping parliament of power, restriction on media, political pressure on the judiciary and harassment of some NGOs.

The 16 March 2006 White House Document called the "National Security Strategy" accused that Russia was making efforts to prevent democratic development at home and abroad and warned that this would hamper development of Russia's relations with the United States, Europe and its neighbours. The US Secretary of State, Ms. Condoleezza Rice speaking in Sydney in Australia went to the extent of expressing the hope that the Russian people "will find their voice to demand accountable, transparent institutions... and if necessary to change their government". The rekindling of the ambers of a new Cold War by Washington resulted in hardening of the Russian attitude towards the United States. This is reflected in two important articles published in the *Moscow News* by Foreign Minister Lavrov (cited above) and the Russian daily *Rossiskaya Gazeta* of 6 March 2006. Lavrov makes a strong plea for dumping Cold War style dogmatism. He declares that Russia will not play the role of "Frontline State" in the "Cold War" which is now between civilizations. He also made it clear to the United States that it would be naïve to expect from Russia a readiness "to be content... with the role of one being led."

This anti-Russian Cold War American posture has had little effect on the neighbouring Central Asian Republics. On the contrary, one sees unprecedented growth in their bilateral and multilateral relations with Russia. Kazakh President Nazarbaev's first ever state visit to Tashkent from 19 to 21 March 2006 was hailed as a major factor for stability in the region. During the summit, President Nazarbaev called for expanded contacts in "military and technical spheres". The most significant development was the Kazakh leaders public endorsement of the Uzbek President's handling of the 5 May 2005 Andijan event. Nazarbaev said that Karimov "defended the peace... not only of Uzbeks, but also Kazakhs, Kyrgyzs and Tajiks by confronting trained extremist groups in Andijan". Without mentioning the United States by name Karimov stated that "certain external forces were trying to achieve their far-reaching geopolitical goals without considerations of our national interest". Both Kazakhstan and Uzbekistan have established an Inter-State Council to develop a programme of economic cooperation.

International observers have pointed to the Russian hand behind the Kazakh-Uzbek rapprochement. The Tashkent visit of the Kazakh President was followed by his visit to Moscow on 5 April 2006. Speaking at a Duma session Nazarbaev expressed his confidence that we are on the threshold of founding Eurasian Union. He declared that Kazakhstan and Russia had agreed to establish a joint bank with a capital of $ 1.5 billion to finance projects within the Eurasian Economic Community. Nazarbaev also pointed out that Russia, Kazakhstan and Belarus have agreed to adopt 38 regulations concerning the Common Economic Space activity in the near future.

In the new millennium, Russia has not only increased its military cooperation with the Central Asian states (with the exception of Turkmenistan) and even gained some new bases in Kyrgyzstan and Tajikistan, it has also made significant advance in the direction of resurgence of its economic power, regaining the position of the former USSR in the global energy market. It is successfully using its new economic resources – its Soft power – to induce the Central Asian states to pursue a policy of closer economic and political cooperation. As a Western analyst Fiona Hill rightly observes, "... Russia's growing economy, the persistence of the Russian language as a *lingua franca* – the language of commerce, employment and education – for many of the states of the former Soviet Union, a range of new Russian consumer products, and a burgeoning popular culture spread through satellite TV, a growing film industry, rock music, Russian popular novels, and the revival of crowning achievements of the Russian artistic tradition have all made Russia a more attractive state for regional population than it was in the 1990s. Over the last several years, Russia has become a migration magnet for Eurasia. Millions of people have flooded into Moscow, St. Petersburg and other Russian cities from the South Caucasus and Central Asia in particular in search of work and a better life."[17]

Russia is increasingly harnessing its energy resources as an effective instrument. of its foreign policy. As a key element in its "post-imperial" (not neo- imperial) policy in Central Asia and the Caucasus, Russia is trying to reintegrate this region into a common energy complex with its active participation. At the St. Petersburg G-8 Summit, President Putin came out with his blueprint for a "world energy order". Putin's article in the *Wall Street Journal* indicated that Russia would not like to act as the United States' energy appendage. Of course, he would welcome cooperation with the West, but he clearly warned that "energy egoism is a road to nowhere".

The debate over the US policy in the Caspian and Central Asian region goes on endlessly with no sign of dilution in the aggressive stance of the neoconservative advocates of the 'forward policy'. Thus we have experts like Stephan Blank who write: "Given the stakes involved here, the disarray of Russian and of US strategies, and most crucially the fragility of the democratic statehood across the region, complacent Wilsonianism and talk of win-win outcomes seems unjustified even though economic forces are propelling American and other firms into the local energy sweepstakes. Economic forces may drive their actions and impel them to put pressure on their governments for political support. But it is of political decisions that will be made in many capitals regarding energy, not the economic forces acting on energy firms that will decide the issue. Geoeconomics still takes a backseat to geopolitics in the new great game."[18]

The NATO has also of late started flexing its muscles in the Caspian region. At the Third Annual Conference on Problems of Security and Regional Cooperation organized by the Kazakh Institute of Strategic Studies, the Kazakh-Russian University and the Friedrich Ebert Foundation in Almaty on 21 June 2005 the NATO representative in Central Asia Alexander Catranis stated, "Strategic and geopolitical frontlines are moving in the direction of the Caspian Sea, and to the deserts and mountains between Central Asia in the North and in India-Pakistan's disputed area of Kashmir in the South. NATO must be able to strike where the origin of the threat/risk is located, not where its effects appear. The new strategy is designed to achieve assurance, discussion, deterrence and defense against any potential adversary in any environment".[19]

There are of course some sane voices to be heard. Amy Myers Jaffe, Energy Research Fellow at the James A. Baker III Institute for Public Policy, Rice University, Houston and Robert A. Manning, Senior Fellow and Director of Asian Studies, Council on Foreign Relations, Washington DC, in their article argued that "the notion that Central Asian and Caucasian oil can be the panacea to long-term energy security in the West is misguided." They further wrote: "the dream that these newly independent states can both solve Western energy problems and give the West geopolitical advantages against Russia, Iran and China may be alluring to underemployed post-Cold War strategists and oil executives alike. But it is a chimera that could be counterproductive to the long-term interests of America and even NATO in Russia and Iran. It could also inadvertently draw the US into the complex ethnic conflicts in the region's unstable embryonic states, aptly dubbed as 'Eurasian Balkans' by Zbigniew Brzezinski".[20]

Russian scholar G. Chufrin is of the opinion that on the issue of Russian-US interaction in the Caspian Sea region the best strategy for both countries to pursue their national interest is to avoid unnecessary confrontation and seek instead some form of strategic understanding and cooperation. According to him the region is and will remain high on the agenda of both Russian and US foreign and security policy. Their national interests in the region are highly competitive but not necessarily incompatible or antagonistic – including in the economic area, although here the level of competition is understandably higher. The successful example of mutually beneficial commercial cooperation such as the construction of the pipeline from the Tengiz oil field in Kazakhstan to the Russian Black Sea port of Novorossiysk by the Caspian Pipeline Consortium in which Russian and US companies are the major shareholders is worth emulating. Chufrin recommends the continuation of the existing practice of exchanging views on the situation in the Caspian region between the US Department of State and the Russian Foreign Ministry. He emphasizes that neither Russia nor the USA could play a dominant role in the region unilaterally.[21]

Kazakh scholar M.T. Laumulin has expressed the growing anxiety of the policy making elite in his country over threat to political stability in the light of US policy of regime change through 'colour revolution'. While agreeing to the need for change in the ruling elite in an orderly way through consensus, he cautions against effecting these changes in a populist manner. He pointed to the persistence of North-South contradictions in Kyrgyzstan even after the regime change and warned that any change in Uzbekistan would affect other Republics as well. Alleging constant pressure on Kazakhstan from the United States not only for increasing the pace of democratization to ensure peaceful and legal succession of power but also for raising the supply of Kazakh oil to the BTC Pipeline, Laumulin sought a pause of 5 to 7 years for a stable economic development. In his presentation at the Third Almaty Conference on Security and Development he laid stress on stability "in the interest of all concerned players in the geopolitical game". He expressed the view that for cooperation between Russia and the United States, Washington must take into consideration the lawful interest of Moscow in the region and address latter's concern for strategic security. He also insisted that Washington should not engage in the one-sided game of changing regimes in the region which might be viewed by Russia as playing the game without rules. He also stressed that Russia must as well appreciate the concern about the worsening socio-economic situation and the growing outmoded character of several existing regimes. In his opinion, a consensus was also needed on reforms in countries close to Central Asia such as Afghanistan, Iran and Pakistan where the failure to effect reforms may have negative consequences for the region. The Kazakh scholar called for a dialogue between Russia, United States and the West on Central Asia. This dialogue should show due consideration for China's interest and of course the interest of the Central Asian states, their people and the elite under formation. In his view the emergence of Central Asian states as full subject of international politics depends on the change in the geo-political situation in the region in the 21st century which was not possible under condition of single power domination.[22]

In view of the expected increase in the demand for oil in the various parts of the world, the Caspian Sea and Central Asian region has acquired a great significance. In the next five years the world demand for oil is estimated to rise up to 30 per cent. The fastest growing economies of Asia – China and India are expected to raise Asia's dependence on oil import from the present level of 60 per cent to 80 per cent by 2030. India has joined China in the list of biggest Asian importers of oil which also includes Japan and South Korea. India which is now the sixth biggest oil importer in Asia, shows an annual 10 per cent growth of oil demand. Overall, Asia today accounts for 90 percent of the global growth in oil consumption. It is in Asia that the main energy market is being formed. Considering that Indonesia, formerly a major oil supplier, has now turned into a net oil importer, a fierce competition for oil in the Asia Pacific region is unfolding itself. Even the United States will be importing more than 70 percent of its energy requirements from abroad compared to 50 percent at present. China is the world's second (after the US) biggest oil consumer, accounting for almost half of the global consumption growth. India's oil demand will also double in the next 10 years. At present India ranks 6th in the world in terms of energy demand. According to a policy paper prepared by B.K. Chaturvedi, India's Petroleum Secretary, India's existing oil import dependence of 69 per cent will further go up in future to about 80-90 per cent. This calls for vigorous follow up measures to improve energy security particularly by raising the share of equity oil in it. In the field of its demand for gas, the situation is not so bad in India thanks to a better domestic resource base. There are possibilities for supplies from Iran, Bangladesh, Myanmar and Central Asia.

At the Golden Jubilee celebrations in Jakarta of the first Afro-Asian Conference, India's Prime Minster Dr. Manmohan Singh drew attention to the need for close cooperation between the oil producers and consumers in Asia and Africa. He said, "While our continents include both major producers and consumers of energy, the framework within which we produce and consume energy is determined elsewhere". Asian oil demand was reported to have reached a record high level of 216 million barrels per day in 2003. It grew to 380 million barrels a day by the year 2005. The local production, as per estimates of the US Department of Energy was hardly eight million barrels daily. [23] This increased oil demand of Asia was expected to be met by the development of new oil fields in Russia's Eastern and Western Siberia regions. Russia has made a commitment to supply oil to China through construction of an oil pipeline from Angarsk (near Irkutsk) to Daqing in China. To ensure its supply of oil from Kazakhstan, China has completed construction of a 1240 km. long pipeline at a cost of 800 million dollars. This pipeline extends from Atasu (North West Kazakhstan) to Alashankou (Xinjiang). With a capacity for 50 million tons annually, it would be transporting 20 million tons in 2015 reaching its peak of 50 million tons in 2035. In his meeting with China's President Hu Jintao, the Kazakh President Nazarbaev suggested that Russia might use this pipeline for its oil supplies to China. Russia could easily do that by using its already functioning old pipeline from Omsk to Chardzhou in Turkmenistan, which passes through Atasu from where the newly constructed pipeline to China starts.[24]

The present writer has been advocating the opening up of an overland route from India to Central Asia through the Xinjiang region of China which will give yet another option for reaching Central Asia besides the already operational Bandar Abbas Sea and railroad route through Iran and the still problematic route through Afghanistan. India has only to join the Tibet-Xinjiang road built by the Chinese through the disputed Aksai-Chin territory of Ladakh in their possession. Tajikistan, Kyrgyzstan and Kazakhstan are known to be taking keen interest in using the Chinese built Karakoram Highway to gain access to the Pakistani port of Karachi. Tajikistan has already linked its city of Kharog in the Pamir region with the Karakoram Highway. The distance from Kharog to Karachi via Islamabad is roughly 3,200 kilometers. From Kharog to the Indian port of Kandla through Ladakh and Himachal Pradesh it works out to about 3,800 kilometers. This route through Aksai-Chin in Ladakh has definite advantage over the Karakoram route because of its lower height and better climatic conditions. It was for this reason that British trader R.B. Shaw and British Commissioner of Jullundur, Sir Douglas Forsyth, preferred it over the latter. This route which was known as the Chang Chenmo route was quite popular with the Indian traders engaged in trade with Central Asia. The present writer first made a proposal for reopening this route at the International Conference held in Delhi in July 1999 to mark the 90$^{th}$ birth anniversary of noted Tajik scholar Bobojan Gafurov. In this conference, which was inaugurated by the then Prime

Minister Atal Behari Vajpayee, Dr. Farooq Abdulla, then Chief Minister of Jammu and Kashmir, reiterated this demand before the three Chinese delegates participating in the conference. In 2006, the Chairman of the Xinjiang region of China, Ismail Tiliwandi, during his visit to India, proposed the construction of a direct pipeline from China to India. He also supported the export of hydroelectric power from Kyrgyzstan to India through this route. India's former Petroleum Minister M. S. Aiyar proposed the extension of Iran Pakistan- India gas pipeline across northern India and Assam to the Chinese province of Yunnan. Both Central Asia and India as well as China stand to gain by the fruition of these projects for overland transit for energy because of close proximity between them – one of the world's biggest oil producing region and one of the biggest energy markets. If these projects materialize, it will be a big testimony to the success of multilateral cooperation between India, China, Russia and the Central Asian Republics. Atasu in North-West Kazakhstan (the starting joint for pipeline to China's Alashankou in Xinjiang) if joined by Russia's Omsk-Chardzhou pipeline passing through this place will also open up the possibility of Russian and Kazakh oil reaching India through the Xinjiang region of China. The countries of the Eurasian region must carry forward their cooperation into the energy sector to ensure energy security to India and China. Geoeconomics of cooperation must prevail over geopolitics of exclusion.

It is gratifying to note that despite an overdose of pragmatism and deficiency of visionary inputs in the policies of Putin's Russia, Hu Jintao's China and India headed by UPA coalition under Man Mohan Singh and a geopolitically oriented hegemonistic United States, a network of transport and communication infrastructure has taken shape which can be gainfully harnessed for the advantage of all the concerned powers.

## ENDNOTES

1. Z. Brzezinski, *The Grand Chessboard: American Primacy and its Geo-strategic Imperatives,* New York: Basic Books, 1997.
2. Yelena Bondareva, "Georgia – Forward Line in "Greater Middle East", *Russian Analytica,* Vol. 2, September 2004, pp. 119-26.
3. Stephen Blank, "Every Shark east of Suez: great power interests, policies and tactics in the Trans-Caspian Energy War" *Central Asian Survey,* Vol. 18, No. 2, 1999, pp.149-84.
4. Francis P. Sempa, "Geopolitics and American Strategy: A Reassessment" *Strategic Review,* Spring 1987, pp. 27-38.
5. Brzezinski, op. cit, p. XVIII.
6. Ibid, p. XIV.
7. Samuel P. Huntington, "Why International Primacy Matters?" *International Security,* Spring 1993, p. 83.
8. Brzezinski, op. cit, pp. 37-41.
9. Ibid, p. 129.
10. Ibid, p. 202.
11. Madeleine Albright, *Madam Secretary,* Miramax Books, 2003.
12. *Geopoliticheskie Tsennosti I Interesy Rossiiskoi Federatsii,* Stennogramy, Rassherennykh Zasedanii Komiteta Gosudarstvennoi Dumy Po Voprosom Geopolitiki, 1996-1998, gody, Moscow, 1998 pp. 70-3.

13. Martha Brill Olcott, *Kazakhstan: Unfulfilled Promise,* Washington DC, 2002, p. 234.
14. Blank, op. cit, pp. 153-81.
15. Weng Fusi and Wen Li, "Russia's Geopolitical Problems in the face of NATO's Enlargement to the East", *Far Eastern Affairs,* Vol.1, 2000, pp. 18-24.
16. Sergei Lavrov, "Russia in Global Politics", *Moskov skiye Novosti (Moscow News),* 3 March 2006.
17. Fiona Hill, *Energy Empire: Oil, Gas and Russia's Revival,* The Foreign Policy Centre, September 2004, p. 3.
18. Blank, op. cit, p. 179.
19. Alexander Catranis, "NATO'S Role in Central Asia", *Trtia Almatinskaya Konferentsya Po Voprasam Bezopasnosty I Regionalnogo Sotrudnichestva,* KISSI, Almaty, 2005, pp. 70-7.
20. Amy Myers Jaffe and Robert A. Manning, "The Myth of the Caspian Great Game: The Real Geopolitics of Energy", *Survival,* Vol. 40, No. 4, 1998-99, p. 112.
21. Gennady Chufrin, "The Caspian Sea Region: Towards an Unstable Future", in Gennady Chufrin (ed.) *The Security of the Caspian Sea Region,* SIPRI, OUP, pp. 342-3.
22. M.T. Laumlin, "New Political Factors and Geo-politics of Central Asia", see no. 19, pp. 17-21.
23. *The Wall Street Journal,* 23 March 2004.
24. Dinara Kalieva, "Geopolitika Nefterprovodnykh Kommunikatsii v Kaspiiskom Regione", *Analytic,* No. 2, 2005, pp. 13-20.

# 2

# Asian Energy Projects in Caspian Basin

*Shirin Akiner*

## Asian Economies and Asian National Oil Companies

The energy[1] needs of Asian consumers will undoubtedly play a role of increasing importance in global geopolitics. If current rates of growth are maintained, as seems likely, China, Japan and India, and to a lesser extent Malaysia and South Korea, will increasingly be competing for control of hydrocarbon resources in oil and gas provinces around the globe. Beyond question, the most dramatic change in recent years has been in the huge increase in China's energy needs. In the period 1990-2008, China's oil consumption almost quadrupled, reaching 7.8 million barrels per day (b/d). It was estimated that by 2010 it would reach 8.2 million b/d 2010.[2] China had 16 billion barrels of proven oil reserves, but domestic production was not expected to rise above some four million bbl/d in the near future. The shortfall would thus be made up in imports, bringing China into competition with the two other large net importers of oil, the USA and Japan. The situation with gas was similar. By 2007, China's gas consumption had reached 2,490 billion cubic feet (Bcf), 25 percent above the level in 2006.[3] This outstripped annual domestic production, which stood at 2,446 Bcf. For the first time in almost twenty years, China was forced to turn to imports to cover the deficit. In mid-2006, the country imported almost 140 Bcf of liquefied natural gas (LNG).[4] Thereafter the volume of imports continued to grow steeply. In other Asian countries there have also been sharp rises in energy consumption over the past decade, particularly in South Korea (especially of gas) and in India.

Foreign energy companies are active in most Asian countries and in some cases, play a dominant role. However, the national oil and gas companies fulfill a unique role in the energy strategy of these countries.[5] Created by national governments to develop their own resources as well as to safeguard long-term energy supplies, these companies engage in exploration and production operations at home and increasingly, abroad. Most are still state-owned. In China, the three giants are the China National Petroleum Corporation (CNPC), the China Petroleum and Chemical Corporation

(Sinopec – China's second largest petroleum and gas producer) and China National Offshore Oil Corporation (CNOOC – China's third largest petroleum company). In Malaysia, there is the state-owned Petroleum National Berhad (Petronas), a well-established, highly successful company, with a diversified portfolio that spans a large part of the globe. In the Republic of Korea, and more recently in Vietnam, state oil and gas companies have also been expanding their activities domestically and overseas.

In recent years there have been some moves to reduce state control of the energy sector in order to introduce greater competition and thereby to enhance efficiency. In Japan, in 2001 the government decided to break up the monolithic Japan National Oil Corporation (JNOC), enabling private and semi-private companies to participate in the energy sector. Indonesia, too, embarked on a policy of liberalization in 2001, though this was pursued less vigorously than in Japan. To a lesser extent, a similar trend is to be observed in India, where state oil and gas companies remain the major players,[6] though the private sector is beginning to play a significant role. Yet in all these countries, whatever the precise nature of the ownership of the oil and gas companies – state, private or some form of public-private partnership – their operations are closely aligned to the national energy strategy. Thus, in a loose sense, they are collectively termed 'national oil companies' (NOCs), as opposed to Western-dominated 'international oil companies' (IOCs).

Compared with IOCs, the NOCs are in many ways at a disadvantage. They are newer, smaller and have more limited financial and technical resources. However, they do have some advantages. The special relationship that they have with their governments makes it possible for them to offer benefits that go far beyond the provisions of any specific deal. The IOCs cannot match – and would not wish to compete – with this broad spectrum political and economic engagement. Chinese companies in particular are able to offer prospective partners incentives such as the provision of attractive development and investment packages in non-energy sectors, as well as preferential trade deals. Moreover, they are not necessarily under the same constraints as IOCs to make robust commercial decisions, since the primary consideration is to serve the longer-term national security agenda rather than to promote the viability of the company. Requirements to observe transparency and disclosure may also be more flexible and less strictly applied in some NOCs. These comments do not apply to all NOCs, some of which adhere to the same business principles as IOCs. Nevertheless, most NOCs are generally able to 'add value' to a commercial relationship by leveraging inter-governmental links. The personal intervention of senior political figures is often a key factor in driving forward large deals. In the developing world this multi-facetted approach, drawing on political, economic and socio-cultural assets, can play a major part in ensuring the success of a project.

## Post-Soviet Caspian Developments

The Caspian basin, the newest oil province in the world, is still far from fully explored. In the early 1990s there was excited speculation that this region might prove to be as rich in hydrocarbon reserves as the Persian Gulf region. By the end of the decade, a more sober assessment of the region's resources had emerged. In 2005, it was estimated that the Caspian Sea region had proven (economically recoverable) oil reserves of some 48 billion barrels, equalling around 4 percent of total world proven reserves; estimated additional 'possible' (yet to find) reserves were very much larger, but the probability of such finds was only around 50 percent and moreover, if they did materialise, they would not necessarily be economically recoverable. Caspian gas reserves were estimated at 257 trillion, with additional 'possible' reserves of up to 293 trillion cubic feet; this would probably contribute some 3 percent of world output.[7] Nevertheless, even at this level, they would still be of strategic importance to the overall global energy balance.[8]

During the Soviet period, the Caspian basin was closed to the foreign investors. The situation changed dramatically after the disintegration of the Soviet Union at the end of 1991. However, there were still many obstacles to be overcome. Some of these were to do with inadequate infrastructure, particularly the restricted number of export routes. Technical issues such as these were gradually resolved as new pipelines were built and modern technology was installed. The problem that proved to be the most difficult to resolve was the legal status of the Caspian Sea.[9] For centuries there had only been two littoral states, Iran and the Russian Empire, later the USSR. These two state entities had applied a condominium-type model of joint use and joint sovereignty to the Caspian Sea.

After the disintegration of the Soviet Union, three new littoral states emerged – in addition to the Russian Federation (hereafter, for brevity, 'Russia') and Iran, there were now Azerbaijan, Kazakhstan and Turkmenistan. There was no unanimity between these five states as to the type of legal regime that should apply to the Sea (whether it should be subject to the law of the sea, of frontier lakes, of a condominium or of some other regime). Russia and Iran favoured a continuation of the condominium-type model, arguing that the Sea should be treated as an 'indivisible reservoir', the object of common use by all the littoral states, to be utilized with the agreement of all. The three other states favoured some form of division. A joint Special Working Group of representatives of the littoral states was created in 1996; it convened on a regular basis and provided a mechanism through which outstanding issues could be resolved. By 2009 considerable progress had been made, but there was still no final *de jure* agreement on the legal status of the Sea. Nevertheless, it was accepted that the littoral states had *de facto* established territorial rights to the areas off their coastlines (surface waters and seabed), thus in effect creating national sectors.[10]

## Asian Participation in Caspian Exploration and Development Projects

Given the massive rise in the energy needs of the industrializing Asian economies, it is inevitable that they should seek to increase the volume of their oil and gas supplies. This is partly achieved through imports. However, Asian NOCs are also actively pursuing investment in overseas exploration and production projects, expanding their holdings in oil and gas fields in Asia and Africa. Over the past decade, they have also been steadily building up a presence in the Caspian basin. In the early 1990s, IOCs dominated the development of the Caspian oil and gas sector. Ten years later, a growing number of Asian NOCs were acquiring stakes in regional projects. This was almost wholly driven by east and south Asian countries. West Asia – the Middle East – was poorly represented in the Caspian basin at this stage. A few export-oriented projects were linked to Iran (natural gas delivered by pipelines from Turkmenistan, crude oil from Kazakhstan).[11] The attempts of Iranian state companies to join international exploration and development consortia in Kazakhstan, however, were thwarted by US pressure.[12] In Turkmenistan, Iranian involvement was initially complicated by rival claims to jurisdiction over offshore areas in adjacent sectors of the Sea; these issues were resolved relatively quickly, but nevertheless, progress towards implementing projects was slow.[13] Arab companies were even more cautious. In 2009 there were only two Arab projects in the region: the Cheleken offshore contract area in the Turkmen sector of the Caspian operated by the Dubai-based Dragon Oil plc;[14] and a joint venture to develop an offshore field in the Kazakh sector of the sea in which Abu Dhabi's Mubadala Development Company was a partner.[15] Further projects were under discussion, though, and it seemed possible that Middle Eastern investment in the Central Asian energy sector in the future would increase.

By contrast, by 2010 NOCs from China, Japan, Malaysia, India, the Republic of Korea (South Korea) and Vietnam, were all active in the Caspian basin. Below, the main acquisitions made by NOCs from these countries are charted.[16]

*China*: China is the lead Asian country in the Caspian basin today. Historically, the bulk of China's energy supplies came from the Middle East. This was a cause of unease on two counts. Firstly, there were concerns over the level of political risk in the Middle East. Secondly, oil from the Middle East was shipped through the Straits of Hormuz and Malacca, a line of supply that could, in a crisis, be vulnerable to US pressure.[17] Such considerations prompted China to explore other options. The contiguity of the Caspian basin, albeit located at some considerable distance from Chinese industrial centres, made it an obvious focus of attention.

China's first significant bid to access Caspian energy came in 1997, when, despite strong competition from US companies, the government of Kazakhstan awarded the China National Petroleum Company (CNPC) exclusive negotiating rights for a contract to develop the Uzen field (the country's second largest onshore oil deposit, after Tengiz). However, for technical reasons, CNPC was unable to implement the project and later withdrew. This, though, was a temporary setback: subsequently, CNPC secured a majority shareholding in the Aktobe field in north-west Kazakhstan. This provided China with a foothold in the Caspian basin. There were no immediate attempts to acquire new interests. Rather, the following years were a time of consolidation and establishing relationships.

In 2005, China was ready to make a step change in its activities in the region. In March that year, Sinopec and China National Offshore Oil Corporation made an ambitious bid to buy into the Kashagan project. This mega-structure in the Kazakh sector of the Caspian Sea was discovered in July 2000.[18] Located in the northern part of the Caspian Sea, some 75 km south of Atyrau, it proved to be one of the largest oilfields in the world.

A multinational consortium was formed to develop the project. In February 2001 the Kazakh government specified that the company would have to meet five obligations, including a commitment to commence oil extraction in 2005. However, the extraordinarily difficult technical and environmental conditions in the Kashagan field resulted in numerous delays. It was impossible to meet the agreed deadline. The government responded by imposing massive fines. It also demanded a radical overhaul of the management structure, including a larger role for KazMunaiGaz, the Kazakh state oil company. In October 2008, the agreed start-up date for commercial production was postponed until 2013 at the earliest.[19]

Meanwhile, the consortium underwent several changes in the partnership structure. In 2001, TotalFinaElf (later Total), Royal Dutch/Shell, ENI, ExxonMobil and the BG Group (formerly British Gas) held shares of 16.7 percent each, while US-based Phillips Petroleum Company (ConocoPhillips from 2002) and Inpex (Japan) held 8.3 shares of percent. Two years later, BG decided to sell its stake and Sinopec and CNOOC each tried to acquire one-half of its holding. Negotiations appeared to have been concluded successfully, but at the last moment, the other consortium partners exercised their pre-emptive rights to buy the BG shares, thus locking the Chinese companies out of the deal. KazMunaiGaz bought one-half of the BG Group's stake; the remainder was sold to other project partners.[20]

The Kazakh government strongly supported the Chinese bid to join the Kashagan consortium; according to some reports, President Nursultan Nazarbayev himself had helped to broker the deal and was angered by the consortium's failure to accept it.[21] In October 2005, another Chinese company, CNPC, made a bid for Canadian-listed Petrokazakhstan (formerly Hurricane Hydrocarbons). This was significant, because PetroKazakhstan was the third largest oil producer in Kazakhstan, with holdings that included 12 oilfields, exploration licences in six areas and the Shymkent refinery. Despite stiff competition from India's Oil and Natural Gas Corporation (ONGC), the Chinese company acquired it for $4.2 billion, apparently with the backing of the Kazakh government. The Kazakh-Chinese relationship was strengthened in July 2006, when CNPC sold a 33 percent stake in PetroKazakhstan to KazMunaiGaz; as part of this deal, the Kazakh state company gained equal rights in the management of the Shymkent refinery. This series of transactions was mutually beneficial, since it gave the Kazakh government greater control over domestic oil supplies, but also increased China's hydrocarbon holdings in Kazakhstan.

A further Chinese acquisition in Kazakhstan was made in 2006, when China's state-controlled International Trust and Investment Corporation (CITIC), a multi-sector conglomerate, made a bid worth over US $2 billion for Nations Energy (NE). In December that year the deal was finalised for a reported price of US $1.9 billion. The chief asset of this Toronto-listed company (headed by Indonesian Hashim Djojohadikusumo) was the Karazhanbas oilfield in western Kazakhstan. It had been acquired by NE in 1997 and by 2005 was producing production 41,000 barrels per day; with modern technology it was estimated that output could be increased considerably. At the time, this deal was the third largest overseas oil acquisition made by a Chinese company.

Yet another Kazakh acquisition was made in April 2008, when two Chinese companies, CNPC and PetroChina (China's largest refiner after Sinopec), together with KazMunaiGaz, jointly bought MangistauMunaiGaz (MMG) from Indonesia's Central Asia Petroleum for $3,300 million. MangistauMunaiGaz was Kazakhstan's biggest independent oil producer, with proven and probable crude reserves of 370 million barrels and about 41.8 bcm of gas-in-place; in addition, MMG had rights to explore and develop 15 oil and gas fields in Kazakhstan. Its crude output in 2008 stood at 40 million barrels.

Kazakhstan remained the main focus for China's energy projects. Some attempt was made to secure deals in Azerbaijan. This was welcomed by the Azerbaijani authorities,[22] but although in June 2003 Sinopec joined a consortium to develop the Pirsaat field, located some 70 km south of Baku (recoverable reserves estimated at 1.5 million tonnes), there was little further progress. A more fruitful relationship was China's engagement with Turkmenistan. In July 2007 CNPC signed a landmark Production Sharing Agreement (PSA) with TurkmenGaz, the Turkmen state gas company, to develop the Bagtyarlik gas fields. Located in eastern Turkmenistan, on the right bank of the Amu Darya River, this territory had not yet been fully explored but it was estimated that the deposits might contain up to 1.7 bcm of recoverable gas reserves. A noteworthy aspect of this deal was that it was the first time the Turkmen authorities had granted a foreign company permission to conduct onshore exploration and production operations. The significance of this field was that it was to provide gas for the Central Asia-Pipeline from Turkmenistan to China (see below). In August 2009, PetroChina bought CNPC's share in this project, paying $1,190 million for the right to develop these deposits.

***Japan***: Japanese companies were also active in the Caspian basin. Like China, Japanese interest was driven by the need to seek additional energy suppliers. This was highlighted in 1997, when Prime Minister Hashimoto launched his 'Eurasian Diplomacy' policy and singled out the Caspian basin as one of its target areas.[23] Companies such as Itochu, Marubeni, Mitsui and Komatsu had been participating in engineering and infrastructure projects in Azerbaijan, Kazakhstan and Turkmenistan since the early 1990s, but towards the end of the decade, they began to acquire stakes in oil exploration and development projects. The lead corporations in these ventures were Inpex and Itochu. Inpex bought into the offshore Kashagan project in the Kazakh sector of the Caspian Sea (see above), while Itochu joined the Azerbaijan International Operating Company – the consortium that was developing the Azeri-Chirag-Guneshli (ACG) field off the coast of Azerbaijan – acquiring a 10 percent stake. There was some Japanese involvement in other projects in Azerbaijan, generally in partnership with SOCAR. However, the results were largely disappointing, failing to yield commercially viable quantities of petroleum. At the time of writing there has been no direct Japanese involvement in exploration and development projects in Turkmenistan; discussions about an oil concession have so far been unsuccessful.

*Malaysia*: Malaysian involvement in the Caspian basin began in the mid-1990s. Petronas signed its first agreement with the Turkmen government in 1996. This was a 25-year PSA covering the exploration and development of three large offshore petroleum and gas deposits: Barinov, Livonov and Shafag. According to the terms of the PSA, 60 percent of the revenue was earmarked to cover extraction costs, 40 percent to be shared equally as profit. By 2005, Petronas was producing nearly 800 tonnes of petroleum and 500 bcm of natural gas each day from the offshore Ovez and Makhtumkuli fields. In 2006, Petronas began commercial production of oil at the Dyarbekir field (part of the same contract area); by mid-year, it had extracted some 40,000 tonnes of oil. Future prospects looked good and Petronas was justifiably confident that the PSA would continue to be mutually beneficial for the partners.

*India*: Indian interest in Caspian energy developed more slowly. In 1997, the Oil and Natural Gas Corporation (ONGC) secured a license to explore a 10,000-sq km area in the Pavlodar basin (north Kazakhstan). However, there was little further activity until June 2002, when Prime Minister A. B. Vajpayee attended the Summit meeting of the Kazakh-sponsored Conference on Interaction and Confidence-Building Measures in Asia. During his visit he publicly stressed the importance of Caspian basin energy supplies for India. He concluded an agreement for the acquisition of stakes in a number of oil and gas fields, to be developed by the Indian conglomerate ONGC Videsh. In 2005, ONGC's subsidiary, ONGC Videsh Ltd (OVL), signed a memorandum of understanding with KazMunaiGaz to undertake joint exploration in the Caspian Sea, with the aim of identifying opportunities for collaborative ventures. Other Indian companies (including OVL) were reportedly seeking to acquire stakes of some five percent in the Azerbaijan's ACG fields and Shah Deniz.[24] However, these negotiations moved slowly and at the time of writing, no concrete developments were as yet taking place.

*Republic of Korea*: The Republic of Korea became actively interested in the energy resources of the Caspian basin some years after India had begun to take soundings in the region. However, it then moved rapidly from negotiations to implementation. Its first venture was launched in Kazakhstan in February 2005. It was undertaken by a consortium headed by the state-run Korea National Oil Corporation (KNOC), and included SK Corporation, Korea's largest petroleum refiner. The Korean consortium signed agreements with KazMunaiGaz to develop a crude petroleum project in the offshore Zhambyl field. In 2006, KNOC also embarked on a project in Uzbekistan, becoming one of five partners in a multinational consortium comprising Uzbekneftegaz (Uzbekistan's National Oil and Gas Company), Lukoil

Overseas (Russia), Petronas (Malaysia) and the China National Petroleum Corporation. All five members held equal shares in the venture. Seismic surveys and the drilling of two exploratory wells were carried out in April 2007.

*Vietnam*: The most recent Asian NOC to become involved in exploration and development projects in the Caspian basin was PetroVietnam, which in August 2008 signed its first cooperation deal with the Uzbek state oil and gas country to acquire hydrocarbon assets in the country.

*Indonesia*: Indonesia's exposure to the Caspian region was still very perfunctory, with no indication of long-term interest.

## Asian Investment in Caspian Export Facilities

*Kazakh-China Oil Pipeline*: Initially, the newly independent Caspian states were dependent on the old Soviet pipeline network for export faculties. Gradually, however, other routes were developed.[25] One of the most important post-Soviet destinations for Kazakh oil was China. In 1997, Kazakhstan began sending crude petroleum to China by rail. Later that year, the Canadian-owned PetroKazakhstan (see above) registered a joint venture with a Kazakh company to complete the construction of a rail transhipment terminal on the China–Kazakhstan border.

The ultimate aim was to build a transcontinental pipeline that would stretch from the Caspian to the Dushanzi refinery in Xinjiang (western China), and from there to link into the Chinese domestic network. In the 1990s, the scale and cost of this massive venture were so daunting as to make the project seem no more than a fantasy. However, it had political backing in the two countries at the highest level. Rather than attempting to carry out the whole project in one operation, it was decided to undertake it in two phases. The first would link central Kazakhstan to the Chinese border; the second phase would extend the line westwards to the Caspian. This was a wise decision, since much of the work consisted in linking up segments of the pipeline network that already existed within Kazakhstan itself. By 2002, the construction of the Atyrau–Kenkiyak segment of the pipeline had been completed. In 2004, the final stage of this first phase, the construction of the cross border connection between Atasu on the Kazakh side to Alashankou on the Chinese side, was commenced. This was finished in December 2005 and in mid-2006 the pipeline became fully operational. It had a capacity of 10 million tonnes per annum and could deliver oil from Kazakh fields as well as Russian oil from the west Siberian oilfields to the Chinese network.

In August 2007, during President Hu's visit to Kazakhstan, CNPC signed an agreement with KazMunaiGaz for the inauguration of the second phase of the project, an extension of over 700 km westward to the Caspian Sea. It would double the pipeline's capacity to 20 million tonnes of crude oil per year. Work on the Kenkiyak–Kumkol segment (estimated project cost $1,000 million, with initial transportation capacity of 10 million tonnes per year) was launched in December 2007. Kumkol was already connected to Atasu, thus this was the final link in the trans-Kazakhstan-China oil pipeline. Completed in record time, it was put into operation in July 2009. The Kenkiyak–Kumkol segment (capacity 200,000 b/d) also gave CNPC access to its newly-acquired MangistauMunaiGaz assets (see above).

*Kazakhstan-China Gas Pipeline*: The idea of a Kazakhstan–China gas pipeline, to follow the Kazakhstan–China oil pipeline, was first mooted in 2003, during a visit by President Hu to Kazakhstan. This was to form part of a larger trans-Central Asia project stretching from Turkmenistan, across Uzbekistan and Kazakhstan, to China's north-western Xinjiang region. CNPC, the lead company on the Chinese side, agreed deals with the state oil and gas firms of Turkmenistan, Uzbekistan and Kazakhstan, giving them 50 percent stakes in their respective segments of the pipeline (see below). In July 2008 work began on the construction of the 1,300-km Kazakhstan–China segment. It was to be built in five stages, with the first gas shipments scheduled for 2011.

*Azerbaijan BTC Oil Pipeline*: In Azerbaijan, the priority was to construct new export pipelines for the transport of oil and gas from the Azeri-Chirag-Guneshli fields and Shah Deniz to world markets. Japanese Inpex and Itochu formed part of the BP-led multinational consortium (apart from Azerbaijan's SOCAR, other shareholders included US Chevron, Norwegian Statoil, Turkish TPAO, Italian ENI, US ConocoPhillips and French Total) to construct the Baku-Tbilisi-Ceyhan (BTC) oil pipeline from the Baku terminal in Azerbaijan to the Turkish terminal of Ceyhan on the Mediterranean coast. The construction of the gas pipeline from Baku to the eastern Turkish city of Erzurum, which followed a parallel route, was undertaken by the same consortium and launched slightly later. The BTC project was controversial owing to a number of environmental concerns. There were also serious technical problems to be overcome. This raised the cost significantly (contributing to a 30 percent budget overrun – the final cost was estimated at over US$ 4 billion), but nevertheless, the pipeline was completed in early 2005 and commissioned the following year.

Kazakhstan had intermittently expressed interest in an underwater link to Baku, and in 1998, concluded an agreement with three Western companies (Royal Dutch/ Shell, Mobil and Chevron) for a feasibility study on parallel petroleum and gas pipelines under the Caspian Sea to Azerbaijan. It was not until late 2002, however, that serious negotiations began on the construction of a petroleum pipeline from the Caspian port of Aktau to Baku. In June 2006, Kazakhstan agreed to join the BTC project. Yet, there were strong environmental objections to this project, particularly from Iran and Russia, and it was unlikely that it would be implemented in the near future.[26]

*Indian Projects and BTC*: In 2005, the Indian Oil Corporation, Bharat Petroleum and Hindustan Petroleum began exploring ways of importing crude from Azerbaijan for processing in Indian refineries and were considering, as one of the possible options, making use of the BTC pipeline to transport petroleum to Ceyhan for on-shipment through Israel or the Suez Canal. To date these plans have not progressed.[27]

*Central Asia-China Gas Pipeline:* The genesis of this project dates back to 1992, when Mitsubishi Corporation and CNPC began to undertake feasibility studies regarding the construction of a trans-Asian gas pipeline. In 1997, Mitsubishi formed a consortium with Exxon (subsequently ExxonMobil Corporation) and CNPC to develop a pilot project to construct a pipeline linking gas fields in Uzbekistan and Turkmenistan, via Kazakhstan and mainland China, to a terminal on the Yellow Sea, with the possibility of on-shipment to Japan and eventually South Korea. The project was technically viable, but the distance to the Pacific coast (over 6,000 km) and the difficult geographic conditions made it extremely costly (preliminary estimates suggested a bill of US $9,500 million). It was deemed a visionary, but unrealizable, idea and soon ceased to be discussed as a serious proposal.

Unexpectedly, the project was resuscitated by the late President Niyazov. During his visit to Beijing in April 2006 he concluded an agreement with President Hu Jintao on the supply of Turkmen gas to China, to be sourced from the Bagtyarlik gas fields mentioned above. This would require the construction of a pipeline that would stretch from eastern Turkmenistan (190 km) via Uzbekistan (550 km), and across Kazakhstan (1,300 km) to Horgos, the border crossing between Kazakhstan and China; from there it would feed into China's domestic network for delivery to cities such as Shanghai and Hong Kong. It was an immensely complex undertaking, technically as well as politically. Nevertheless, it was implemented with extraordinarily speed. Immediately after the agreement had been concluded, a working group was established to finalize the route and to draft the necessary inter-governmental documents.

Construction of the Turkmen section of the pipeline began in August 2007. The following year, CNPC began construction of a gas-purification plant (annual capacity 5 bcm) close to the Turkmen Bagtyarlik gas fields, to prepare gas for pumping into the new pipeline. The entire project was completed on schedule in less than two years. On 14 December 2009, in the presence of the presidents of Turkmenistan, China, Uzbekistan and Kazakhstan, the formal valve-opening ceremony was held at Samandepe (eastern Turkmenistan), the starting point of the new pipeline.[28] It would carry some 5 bcm in 2010, and at least 13 bcm in 2011. A linking pipeline from western Kazakhstan, scheduled for commissioning in 2011 (as mentioned above), would provide an additional 10 bcm per annum. By 2013, operating at full capacity, the Central Asia-China pipeline would supply 40 bcm annually to China, 30 bcm from Turkmenistan, the remainder from Kazakhstan.

*TAPI*: The project for the construction of oil and gas pipelines from Turkmenistan's eastern gas fields to Pakistan via Afghanistan, with a possible extension to India, was originally proposed in the early 1990s by Bridas, the Argentinean company that was one of the early pioneers in Turkmenistan. However, major contractual disagreements arose between Bridas and the Turkmen government and as a result, Bridas ceased operations. Subsequently, the US petroleum company Unocal and its strategic partner, the Saudi Arabian company Delta Nimir, took up the project and in May 1997, signed a memorandum of agreement with the Turkmen government for the construction of a pipeline from Turkmenistan to Pakistan. A consortium was created that included Japan's Itochu Corporation, Korea's Hyundai and Pakistan's Crescent Group. In December 1997, at the invitation of Unocal, an official Taliban delegation visited the US for talks on the on oil and gas exploration and pipeline projects.[29] However, by this time the security situation in Afghanistan was deteriorating and by the end of 1998 the project had been shelved indefinitely.[30]

After the US-led military intervention in Afghanistan in October 2001, hopes for a more peaceful and prosperous future began to revive. In May 2002, the Presidents of Afghanistan, Pakistan and Turkmenistan met in Islamabad and agreed to pursue the project; the Asian Development Bank provided funding for a feasibility study. The project was given new impetus when in April 2008 India formally joined the steering committee of the pipeline, now renamed the Turkmenistan-Afghanistan-Pakistan-India pipeline (TAPI). A framework agreement was signed by the oil and gas ministers of the four countries. The proposed pipeline (estimated length 1,680 km) is intended to deliver 90 million cubic metres of gas a day (mmcmd). Afghanistan's share would initially be around 5.0 mmcmd, rising to 14 mmcmd in the third year; the remainder would be divided equally between India and Pakistan. The gas would be supplied from the Dauletabad field in Turkmenistan. A draft framework agreement was prepared for the consideration of the governments of participating countries.[31] However, the project then stalled again.

*Northeast Asian Gas and Pipeline:* Another, yet more ambitious, plan was proposed by the Tokyo-based Northeast Asian Gas and Pipeline Forum (members include Japan, China, Russia, the two Koreas and Mongolia).[32] This envisaged the construction of two natural gas trunk lines for East Asia. The southern one would connect Central Asia, northwest China and Shanghai. This was an imaginative, but highly problematic, project. Leaving aside obvious financial and technical difficulties, the biggest hurdle was the need to create a robust framework for regional cooperation and coordination. At the time of writing (2010), there was little evidence of genuine political will to achieve this among the potential partners.

## Role of the Shanghai Cooperation Organisation (SCO)

The Shanghai Cooperation Organisation (SCO) was formally established in June 2001. It originally comprised six members – China, Kazakhstan, Kyrgyzstan, Russia, Tajikistan and Uzbekistan – but later accepted four observers – India, Mongolia, Pakistan and Iran. Many Western analysts saw this organisation chiefly in terms of a rival to Western interests, particularly in the energy sphere.[33] However, although the SCO had many important regional functions, as of 2010, it still played a minimal role in energy issues. In Shanghai, in June 2006, at the fifth-anniversary SCO Summit, Russian President Putin proposed the creation of an SCO 'Energy Club';[34] three years later, despite ongoing discussions on this project, it had still not taken concrete form. Meanwhile, bilateral arrangements continued to develop. As indicated above, China's involvement in the Caspian basin began before the SCO had been formally established and continued seamlessly beyond the creation of this body.

China's share in Kazakh energy, though steadily increasing, was still relatively small. Chinese involvement in Uzbekistan, another SCO member state, was even more limited. By contrast, the US and European majors continued to dominate the Kazakh energy sector and there was no likelihood of this changing in the foreseeable future. Russia, too, played an important role in the development of the oil and gas resources of Kazakhstan, likewise of Uzbekistan.[35]

Looking beyond SCO, Chinese companies were active in Turkmenistan and Azerbaijan, neither of which were members of the SCO. As indicated above, other Asian countries that were represented in the Caspian basin in 2010 were Japan, Malaysia, India and South Korea. Of these, only India had observer status in the SCO. Thus, while membership of the SCO might conceivably facilitate energy cooperation between member states, in practice, projects were going ahead on the basis of bilateral economic complementarities, notably China's need for energy, and the Caspian states' need to find new markets.

## Asian Involvement in the Caspian Region: Prospects and Challenges

The developments described above indicate that Asian interest in the energy resources of the Caspian basin is natural and indeed inevitable.

The main reasons are as follows:

1. The Asian 'economic miracle' has created a rapid rise in energy consumption. This, in turn, requires new energy supplies. The Caspian basin, with its large, still under-exploited, resources is an obvious focus of attention.
2. The Caspian basin, located between South and East Asia, represents a pivotal juncture in transcontinental trade routes, hence its hydrocarbon resources are instinctively regarded as 'Asian'.
3. Transcontinental pipelines create political synergies. In the case of pipelines that directly link two countries, without crossing the territory of any other states, as is the case with the Kazakhstan-China pipelines, the bond is even stronger.
4. The possibility of external interference, whether military, political or economic, is virtually nullified. This is particularly attractive to countries (notably China, but also Japan) that fear that threats to their energy supplies might be used by the US to exert political or economic pressure.
5. Caspian oil and gas developments provide good commercial opportunities for Asian investors. Also, Asian energy companies have relevant managerial and technical skills, long experience of working in energy projects in other parts of the world and are thus well placed to take advantage of the opening up of the Caspian region.
6. There is no single pattern to Asian involvement in the Caspian basin. Some projects are directly related to the energy needs of their home country (e.g. Chinese ventures), but in other cases, the incentive is primarily commercial (e.g. Petronas activities in Turkmenistan). Japanese companies generally

prefer partnership in multilateral consortia, partly because they are larger (e.g. the Kashagan mega-project) and partly because the shared risk lowers commercial exposure. The few fields in Azerbaijan that Japanese companies have attempted to develop alone, or in partnership with local partners, have to date yielded disappointing results.

Asian involvement in the Caspian region is not, however, without some constraints and potential dangers:

1. The distances from oil and gas fields to prospective Asian markets are immense and the routes run across difficult and inhospitable terrain, with extreme climatic conditions. Thus, the cost of construction, likewise of maintenance, is very high. This slows down the pace of development.
2. Caspian oil and gas may be attractive as an alternative source of energy for Asian customers, but it is not always economically and technically competitive when compared with other supplies. For example, the Russian Far East is in some ways a more promising option for China than the Caspian basin.
3. Common energy needs could serve as the foundation for regional alliances and foster interdependencies. However, they could also lead to hostility. In mid-2003, for example, Japanese government officials were warning of 'an imminent energy war' with China.[36] The immediate trigger for this anxiety was Sino-Japanese competition over drilling rights in Iran. There are likely to be more such incidents in the future. India, too, is now joining the competition for oil and gas. Political goodwill, as well as skilful diplomacy will be needed if energy rivalries are to be held in check.

## Conclusions

To summarise the findings of this paper, in the mid-1990s there was virtually no Asian involvement in oil and gas projects in the Caspian basin. A decade later, Asian NOCs were not only active in the region but were set to increase substantially their share in the development of the Caspian energy sector. However, to put this into perspective, Asian exploration and development projects were smaller, riskier and often technically more difficult to execute than those that were being developed by IOCs.

Regarding export pipeline construction, apart from a small pipeline from Turkmenistan to Iran, the first new oil and gas pipelines were built by consortia of IOCs; Japanese companies had a small share in some of these projects. The later pipelines, however, were built by China (Kazakhstan-China and Turkmenistan-China). Psychologically, if not actually materially, these oil and gas pipelines running eastwards changed the balance of perceptions: the Asians suddenly seemed to be 'winning' the competition for energy supplies. In particular, the launch of the Turkmenistan-China gas pipeline caused alarm, prompting one European analyst to comment that it was 'Game Over' in Central Asia for the West.[37]

The situation was not so simple, however. The Central Asian states welcomed Asian involvement in the region. Firstly, the Central Asians understood the need to diversify their outlets, as well as their partners. Secondly, they recognized the growing strength of Asian markets and were eager to link into this process. Yet this did not mean that they were turning their backs on the West. Quite the contrary – it was precisely by maintaining a balance of interests that they would benefit most fully from their resources. Thus, while the Asian NOCs were a welcome presence in the Caspian basin, the region would remain open to investment from companies around the world. Moreover, for the foreseeable future the market would continue to be dominated by the larger, wealthier and technologically more advanced US and European majors. Far from 'the game being over', new synergies and patterns of cooperation were likely to emerge. The energy sector in Central Asia was highly dynamic, constantly evolving and developing. Thus, it was futile to attempt to make categorical long-term predictions. Rather, it was a region where trends were fluid, still in the process of formation, and therefore requiring ongoing observation and analysis.

## ENDNOTES

1. The term 'energy' in this paper is used with reference to the oil and gas projects. However, it should not be forgotten that uranium and rare earths are also becoming important components of the energy mix. To date, these sectors have attracted far less attention from foreign investors, public or private. However, this is now changing. In particular, Chinese, Japanese, and to a lesser extent Indian companies are already establishing long-term partnerships with Central Asian producers.
2. U.S. Energy Information Administration (EIA), *Short-Term Energy Outlook July 2009*: http://www.eia.doe.gov/China Oil Energy Data Statistics and Analysis.mht.
3. EIA, *Short-Term Energy Outlook*, July 2009: China Gas Energy Data Statistics and Analysis.
4. Ibid.
5. Here the term 'Asian' is used with reference to south, south-east and east Asia, unless otherwise specified.
6. Notably, the Oil and Natural Gas Corporation (ONGC), the Indian Oil Corporation (IOC), and the Gas Authority of India Ltd (GAIL).
7. Estimates encompass Azerbaijan, Kazakhstan, Turkmenistan, Russia and Iran, but not Uzbekistan.
8. B.A. Gelb, *Caspian Oil and Gas: Production and Prospects,* CRS Report for Congress, updated 8 September 2006, pp. 1-2; EIA, *Caspian Sea Region: Survey of Key Oil and Gas Statistics and Forecasts,* July 2006; T. Adams, 'Caspian energy development', in *The Caspian: Politics, energy and security*, ed. S. Akiner, RoutledgeCurzon, London/New York, 2004 (hereafter *The Caspian*), pp. 90- 106, esp. 92-93.
9. A. Granmayeh, 'Legal history of the Caspian Sea', in *The Caspian*, pp. 17-47.
10. S. Akiner, "Politics of Energy in the Caspian Sea Region: Legal Status", in *Eastern Europe, Russia and Central Asia 2010,* Routledge, London, pp. 15–26.
11. In 1997, Iran launched a 200-km pipeline (capacity 10–12 bcm per year) connecting Korpeje, near Turkmenistan's south-western gas field, to the Iranian gas distribution system at Kurtkui (J. Roberts, 'Pipeline Politics', in *The Caspian,* pp. 86-87). In January 2010 a new pipeline from south-eastern Turkmenistan to Iran was inaugurated that at peak capacity would deliver up to 14 bmc annually of Turkmen gas ('Iran, Turkmenistan launch

new gas pipeline', *PressTV*, 29 December 2009). Iranian crude oil 'swaps' with Kazakhstan were initiated in 1996 (see M. Jafar, 'Oil, politics and the new "Great Game"', in *The Caspian*, pp. 204-205.
12. Granmayeh, *op. cit.*, pp. 24-25.
13. Granmayeh, *op. cit.*, p. 25.
14. The oil and gas producer Dragon Oil was originally based in Dublin and London; in 1999 the Emirates National Oil Company became the major shareholder and the headquarters of the company moved to Dubai. A production sharing agreement (PSA) for a 25-year term for the exploration and development of the Cheleken field was signed with the Turkmen government in November 1999. In February 2009, Dragon Oil announced that the Cheleken field contained proved and probable reserves of 645 million barrels of oil and condensate (*Irish Times* online, 10 February 2009).
15. Other partners were KazMunaiGaz and ConocoPhillips; the joint venture was created in June 2009.
16. The following sections draw on the annual survey given in S. Akiner, 'Politics of Energy in the Caspian Sea Region', *op. cit.*, pp. 15–26.
17. S. Akiner, 'Achievements, new concerns, future prospects', in *The Caspian,* pp. 391-92; Akiko Fukushima, *Co-operation for Peace and Stability in the Caspian Sea/Central Asia Region* (paper presented at the Seventh Annual Seminar on Central Asia and the Caucasus, Tehran, June 1999).
18. In 1993 the Caspian Shelf Consortium (comprising Agip, BG, BP, ExxonMobil, Royal Dutch/Shell Statoil and Total) was created to explore a new offshore area in the Kazakh sector of the Caspian Sea. The discovery of Kashagan was the result of several years of exploration undertaken by this group.
19. 'Kashagan to be operated by all', *Upstream Online*, 7 October 2008.
20. Jafar, *op. cit.*, pp. 214-15.
21. It was widely believed that Kazakh President personally backed the Chinese bids. The Kazakh authorities announced the withdrawal of the Kashagan consortium's pre-production VAT exemptions shortly after it was confirmed that the offer of the Chinese companies had been rejected. It is possible that this was mere coincidence, but some analysts linked the two events, suggesting that displeasure over the failure of the deal had influenced the Kazakh decision ('Kazakhstan Ends Tax Break after China Cut from Project', *Ambo News*, vol. 81, no. 95, 19 May 2003; see also *RFE/RL Business Watch*, 17 June 2003).
22. President Heidar Aliev publicly welcomed the prospect of Chinese engagement in Azerbaijan ('Azerbaijan Wants Chinese Investment', *Xinuha News Agencies COMTEX News Network*, 24 February 2003; AFP, 4 June 2003).
23. For a detailed analysis of Japanese policy in the Caspian region, including its energy policy, see R. Drifte, 'Japan's Eurasian diplomacy: power politics, resource diplomacy or romanticism?', in *The Caspian*, pp. 278-94; see also R.H. Dekmejian and H.H. Simonian, *Troubled Waters: The Geopolitics of the Caspian Region*, I.B. Tauris, London/New York, 2001, pp. 146-49.
24. In July 1999, BP Amoco (created through the merger of BP and US Amoco) announced that gas resources of some 400 bcm had been discovered in the offshore prospect of Shah Deniz; this was the first confirmed discovery of new energy resources in the region since the dissolution of the USSR.
25. For a discussion of the politics of the various projects, see J. Roberts, 'Pipeline Politics', in *The Caspian*, pp. 78-91.
26. S. Akiner, 'Achievements, new concerns, future prospects: Environmentalist objections to the Baku-Tbilisi-Ceyhan pipeline', in *The Caspian*, pp. 383-88.
27. For an overview of Indian gas needs and regional pipeline projects see R. Kandiyoti,

*Pipelines: Flowing Oil and Crude Politics*, I.B. Tauris, London/New York, 2008, pp. 87-96.

28. 'China president opens Turkmenistan gas pipeline', *BBC News Channel*, 14 December 2009.
29. 'Afghanistan: Afghan Taleban say Ready for Gas Pipeline Accord', *Reuters Business Briefing*, 4 January 1998.
30. G. Canzi, 'Turkmenistan's Caspian resources and its international political economy', in *The Caspian*, pp. 189-90.
31. *BBC Monitoring Central Asia*, 31 May 2008.
32. Drifte, *op. cit.*, p. 289.
33. S. Blank, 'The Shanghai Cooperation Organization and its Future', *The Central Asia-Caucasus Analyst*, 22 May 2002.
34. A. Matusov, 'Energy Cooperation in the SCO: Club or Gathering?' *China and Eurasia Forum Quarterly*, Vol. 5, No. 3 (2007), Central Asia-Caucasus Institute & Silk Road Studies Program, pp. 83-99.
35. Kazakhstan and Russia are both members of the Eurasian Economic Community (EurAsEC). It was launched in 2001 by Belarus, Kyrgyzstan and Tajikistan; in January 2006, Uzbekistan formally acceded to the organisation but withdrew in 2008. The primary aim of the EurAsEC is to further economic cooperation between member states.
36. 'Oil-thirsty China and Japan Battle on Drilling', *The Times*, 21 July 2003.
37. A. Bonzanni, 'For the West, "Game Over" in Central Asia', *World Politics Review*, 8 January 2010.

# 3

# Energy Resources of Central Asia and Geopolitics of Pipelines

*R.G. Gidadhubli*

The Central Asian Republics (CARs) of the former Soviet Union have been in the process of transition from the former socialist system to market economy. During the past two decades, after the Soviet disintegration, these states have made considerable efforts in this process of transition. In this regard, it may be worthwhile to examine the following – the importance of the energy sector in the task of economic transition; advantages and benefits they have received in economic development and the problems and constraints they have experienced in their task.

## Importance of Energy Resources for the CARs

The Central Asian Republics have been endowed with resource potentials such as hydrocarbon resources, non-ferrous and precious minerals, chemicals, agricultural products such as raw cotton and so on. So far as hydrocarbon resources are concerned, huge potentialities of oil and natural gas in Kazakhstan and natural gas in Turkmenistan and Uzbekistan, hydro-electricity in Tajikistan and Kyrgyzstan were fairly known during the Soviet era. But in comparison to the resource potentialities in other parts of the former Soviet Union such as East and West Siberia, Volga-Ural regions of Russia, in Azerbaijan, the share of the CARs was relatively moderate. For instance, the share of the CARs was 16 per cent in the total estimated reserves of 57 billion barrels of oil in the former Soviet Union. In 1991, out of the total production of about 10 million barrels of oil per day, the CARs contributed less than 7 per cent. So far as the potentiality of natural gas is concerned, the CARs were identified as promising areas in the former Soviet Union. At the same time, the energy sector of the CARs as of the USSR as a whole suffered from certain constraints-the shortage of modern technological equipments; low level of productivity; high cost of production and so on. Under Mikhail Gorbachev's policy of *Perestroika*, a beginning was made when Western technology was being acquired in the country. In the development of the Tengiz oil field in Kazakhstan, former Soviet Union sought the collaboration of Chevron company.

In the aftermath of the Soviet break-up, there was great interest in the energy sector of the CARs by leading Western powers and international companies. In fact, hype was created in the West and that Turkmenistan was called the 'Kuwait of the 21st Century'. There were even speculations as to whether Central Asia could be an alternative to the Middle East. However, it was stated by some energy experts that Central Asia was an additional rather than an alternative source of hydrocarbon resources for the West. In a recent study, Frederick Starr and Svante Cornell have opined that although the Caspian oil and gas reserves account for about five per cent of global reserves, they are quite significant for the region and for world energy market. In 2001, the US Energy Information Administration reported that the Caspian Sea region had 34 billion barrels of proven oil reserves and 235 billion barrels of possible oil reserves. The proven oil reserves were estimated to be about one-fourth of that of the Middle East. Similarly, proven natural gas reserves of the Caspian region including that of Uzbekistan were estimated to be about 243 trillion cubic feet. Among the five Caspian Sea states, Kazakhstan and Turkmenistan besides Azerbaijan possess the lion's share of energy resources.

There are several factors, which have contributed to make the energy sector important for the CARs. Firstly, in the aftermath of the Soviet break-up, as the CARs were struggling to recover from the shock and bring about transition, the interest of the Western countries in general and that of the USA in particular in the energy sector of Central Asia played an important role for the leadership of these countries. Secondly, the entry of some energy companies such as Chevron, Exxon, Mobil etc. in the task of exploration and exploitation of energy resources of Central Asian region benefited the CARs in getting not only modern technology but also much needed investment in the energy sector. Thirdly, the leadership of these countries realized that energy resources had a ready market, unlike for other commodities, in the world and hence exporting oil and natural gas would bring much needed hard currency for cash-starved Central Asian countries. Fourthly, during the Soviet era, the CARs were relatively less developed economically as compared to other former Republics such as Russia, Ukraine, Baltic Republics etc. Hence, there was limited choice for the leadership of the CARs but to depend upon the energy sector for generating resources for economic survival and development. Fifthly, unprecedented rise in the prices for oil and natural gas in the international market has made a qualitative difference to the importance of energy resources both to the CARs as supplier of these products and to the countries, which have a demand for the Central Asian energy resources.

To take advantage of growing demand for energy resources in the world and rising prices for oil and natural gas, particularly since the last few years, Kazakhstan and Turkmenistan, which among the CARs are endowed with rich energy resources, have intensified their efforts to explore and exploit their energy resources in their respective shelfs in the Caspian Sea. For instance, in 2001, the Agip Kazakhstan North Caspian Operating Company (AGIPKO) began its appraisal programme by drilling wells in the East Kashagan field. In 2003, seismic survey work was initiated over 1,600 sq. km area to get a more precise estimate of the size of Kashagan since reserve estimates in this area varied between 8 and 50 billion barrels of oil. The significance of Kashagan lies in the fact that analysts believe the Kashagan oil field to be the largest single oil field discovered in the past two decades.

Similarly, Turkmenistan started intensive development work on six onshore and two offshore oil-gas fields in 2001. As a result of intensive exploration in Amu Darya onshore zone of Eastern Turkmenistan, it was estimated that this region contained over one billion barrels of oil and 1.765 trillion cubic meters of natural gas. Uzbekistan also undertook exploration work in the last decade and it was reported that out of 171 discovered fields, 73 were providing hydrocarbons. With these efforts, the Central Asian countries were able to increase the production of oil and natural gas significantly after they gained independence. Several Western, Russian and Chinese oil companies have been actively operating in Central Asia, particularly in Kazakhstan contributing to the rapid increase in the energy estimates and production of the CARs and enhancing the economic importance of the energy sector.

## Geopolitics of Pipelines

The CARs are landlocked countries and hence the transportation of oil and natural gas to world markets has been a major problem. During the Soviet era hydrocarbon resources of these states, which were the republics of the former USSR, were transported both for domestic consumption of the country as well as for export. Pipelines were laid in the past by the central planners taking into consideration to supply oil and gas in the domestic market and demand for exports to world markets. At any rate, these republics did not have much say in the matter since all decisions were taken at the central level. The centralized planning authorities had laid the pipelines for transporting oil and natural gas produced in Central Asian Republics as well as in Azerbaijan, which were linked to the pipeline network passing through the Russian Federation. A small quantity of oil was also transported through the Iranian pipelines. After the CARs became independent countries, they have been required to deal with the problem of transportation of oil and natural gas. Since the existing pipelines were passing through Russia, the CARs had to depend upon Russia for exporting their energy resources to world markets. Russia has, therefore, acquired great international significance both to the Central Asian countries, which are keen to export their energy products to foreign countries including the Western countries, which have great demand for oil and natural gas produced by the CARs. According to some analysts, from its own national interest Russian firms such as Rosneft, Lukoil would get preference over others from Central Asia etc. Moreover, there were technical considerations involved since there was capacity constraint on the pipeline network of Russia, which could transport only about 130-140 million tons of oil per year. This was inadequate to meet the growing needs of both Russia and the Central Asian states to export oil to global markets. In view of these political and technical considerations, the leaders of Central Asian states and Azerbaijan considered that these independent countries would be at a disadvantage in their efforts to export oil and natural gas produced in their own countries. Apart from this, it was realized that diversification of export options was necessary for these states and hence felt need for having additional pipelines.

In view of all these considerations, a beginning was made in the 1990s to lay additional pipelines in order to link the Central Asian countries with the outside world to meet the growing needs of these foreign countries. Several countries along the Caspian Sea basin strove to develop their oil and natural gas reserves, attracting interest and investment from numerous international energy companies.

## Caspian Pipeline Consortium (CPC)

In order to meet the needs of the CARs to increase opportunities for exporting their energy products, the Caspian Pipeline Consortium (CPC) was formed, which was independent of the Russian government pipeline Transneft. This pipeline was designed to transport oil from the Tengiz oil field in the Caspian Sea to Novorossiysk Port on the Black Sea. Under Boris Yelstin's policy of economic reforms and liberalization, the USA supported the CPC project to enable Kazakhstan to export oil to the West. Several private firms including some foreign companies such as EXXON had share in this project. Russia has 24 per cent share in the CPC project, while Chevron has 15 per cent, Mobil 7.5 per cent. Under the then prevailing conditions of low prices for oil in the international market in the 1990's, some analysts opined that this project was considered to be not very profitable. There were delays in the completion of this project even as it was crucial for Kazakhstan's economy. Kazakh Prime Minister, Q. Tokayev stated in May 2001 that Russia was taking a 'negative attitude' which caused this delay. It appears that Russia and Kazakhstan had to sort out some differences on matters relating to customs duty to be paid to Russia, the quantum of oil transported through the pipeline and so on. Moreover, Russian policy makers contended that on the 'terms of the use of the pipeline' agreement, besides Russia and Kazakhstan the foreign companies, which were using the pipeline should also be party to the agreement. There were also other constraints and disadvantages that Kazakhstan faced in exporting oil through CPC. Firstly, this pipeline passed through North Caucasus, which was affected by volatile Chechen militant activities. Secondly, the pipeline ended at Novorossiysk on the Black Sea port. Some experts opined that this sea was having heavy traffic problems as tankers had to pass through the congested Bosphorus Strait. Thirdly, as the pipeline passes through Russian territory, some Russian firms wanted priority for themselves over foreign firms to export oil to world markets. Some political groups even expressed the view that the CPC could be a competitor to Russian oil exporters. As opined by Starr and Levante, Kashagan oil field will produce about 450,000 barrels of oil per day by 2010, which can eventually increase up to 1.2 million barrels per day. Hence, Kazakhstan will anyway require an additional pipeline. In the opinion of Western energy experts, Kazakhstan can even consider a parallel pipeline to CPC, to transport oil into the BTC pipeline or export to China. Each of these options offers opportunities and challenges to the policy makers of Kazakhstan.

Many of these issues and problems, which were prevailing in the last decade have been sorted out and resolved by the leaders of both Russia and Kazakhstan. As stated above, Russia has been one of the important partners in the 1,580 kms long CPC pipeline. The CPC was completed despite some delays and Kazakhstan was able to export about 28 million tons of oil per year. More significant is the fact that Vladimir Putin, with larger geopolitical and geo-economic policy considerations, even tried to bring Kazakhstan closer to Russia in the energy sector. This is evident from the fact that during Kazakh President's visit to Moscow in April 2006, Putin agreed to increase the quantum of oil exported through the CPC from the existing 28 million tons to 67 million tons per year. Nazarbaev expressed his satisfaction and stated that this agreement with Putin would help Kazakhstan to increase the oil export in the near future. Thus Putin seems to have shown one-upmanship over the strategic options proposed by the Western experts.

## Multiple Pipeline Policy: Conflict of Interest between Russia and the West

While Russian policy makers, in their own national interest, wanted to continue their control over the pipeline network, the CARs decided to create additional and or alternative routes for exporting oil and natural gas to Western markets. Thus the concept of Multiple Pipeline Policy (MPP) emerged in the early 1990's. The USA in particular and the West European countries in general have actively supported the Multiple Pipeline Policy in Central Asia. The objective has been to enable the CARs to provide alternative routes to export energy resources and diversify the market for their products. Moreover, the West has geopolitical interest in containing monopoly position of Russia over the marketing of energy resources of Central Asian countries. Hence Mann, a leading US energy expert stated in July 2006 that "Our pipeline policy – a policy of anti-monopoly – is changing the landscape of Eurasia in an important and welcome way," But from their own national interest, Russian policy makers have consistently opposed the MPP since it would reduce Russia's influence over the Central Asian region and create rivalry among major energy players in the world.

Notwithstanding such conflicting views, the CARs pursued their own national interest in promoting alternative pipelines for exporting oil and natural gas to world markets. Thus Baku-Tbilisi-Ceyhan (BTC) pipeline project was initiated, which connected Baku in Azerbaijan on the Caspian Sea passing through Georgia linking the Turkish port of Ceyhan. Initially some critics considered that this BTC pipeline project was not viable on various grounds. Firstly, as this project would cost about $ 4 billion, it was considered to be economically not sound at the prevailing low prices for oil in the international markets. Secondly, the pipeline passed through several mountainous regions and hence technically hazardous. Thirdly, the pipeline which passed through Autonomous Regions inhabited by ethnic groups which were politically sensitive-Meshketia, Javkati etc. in Georgia and the region was facing ethnic violence and conflicts and hence unsafe. Despite such criticism the contentions of which were not fully convincing to the initiators of the project, it was implemented. BTC pipeline was not only bypassing Russia, that it would link the Caspian Sea with the Mediterranean Sea, hence providing direct access to world energy markets. The BTC pipeline was inaugurated in May 2005 and Kazakhstan Foreign Minister, Kasymzhomart Tokayev evinced considerable interest in exporting oil through this pipeline initially through tankers up to Baku and by laying pipelines in the future. He even supported the proposal of constructing underwater pipeline linking Kazakhstan's port of Atyrau and Baku.

## Trans-Caspian Pipeline

In 1997, a proposal was made to lay Trans-Caspian pipeline, which would pass through the Caspian Sea bed. This pipeline would enable Kazakhstan and Turkmenistan to export oil and gas from their oil and gas fields via Baku for the Western markets. The USA offered to provide funds for a feasibility study of the 'Trans-Caspian Pipeline Project' as a part of the policy of promoting multiple pipeline networks from the Caspian Sea to the Mediterranean bypassing Russia. Even as the concerned Central Asian countries and Azerbaijan were initially interested in this project, there were critics who opposed it. For instance, Russian experts opined that this undersea pipeline was environmentally hazardous as this region is known for 'hyperactive geo-dynamic conditions', and hence technically not sound. Moreover, the cost of the project was high and under prevailing low international prices for oil and gas in the 1990's it was considered economically not viable. It appears that after almost a decade, in 2006 the US policy makers took renewed interest in this project. In January 2006, the US Deputy Secretary of State, Matthew Bryza during his visit to Turkey resuscitated this proposal. As observed by Bhadrakumar, the Trans-Caspian pipeline was also part of the policy option, which was offered by US Vice President, Dick Cheney during his visit to Central Asia in May 2006. As the head of the Jamestown Foundation think-tank put it, Cheney was 'flexing US muscles a little bit ... planting a big American flag in Central Asia'.

Russia, which had opposed this proposal in the past, repeated its objections. Moreover, the Russian gas giant Gazprom added a new dimension to this issue. In the last few years, Gazprom has entered into long term deals with Turkmenistan and Kazakhstan. This policy measure shows how the Russian government and the energy giants are working in tandem to achieve the country's interest. In the present context, this policy measure seems to benefit the Central Asian countries as well. Firstly, it is economically beneficial for both Turkmenistan and Kazakhstan. Secondly, the leaders of both Kazakhstan and Turkmenistan do not want to antagonize Russia. Thirdly, it has been pointed out that Trans-Caspian pipeline needed the cooperation of all the Caspian states, including Russia and Iran, who have opposed it. Thus it appears that both Kazakhstan and Turkmenistan have diplomatically expressed their reservation on the US proposal. Thus as of now this project appears to be still far from reality. Overtime this proposal may again become a realistic possibility.

According to some US policy makers, the CPC pipeline from Tengiz to Novorossiysk on the Black Sea, the BTC pipeline from the Caspian Sea to Ceyhan on the Mediterranean and proposed Trans-Caspian pipeline are all indicators of the "signal successes" of the Multiple Pipeline Policy that the United States has pursued and encouraged in the Central Asian region.

## US Policy towards the CARs

Ever since the disintegration of the USSR, the USA in particular and the Western countries in general have been actively pursuing their political and economic policies towards the Central Asian region. For the policy makers of the West, the availability of abundant energy resources in the Central Asian region offered an opportunity to put the development of the energy sector in the centrestage to serve their own geopolitical and geoeconomic objectives. According to some analysts, the West was guided by several considerations. Firstly, being guided by their own interest, strong support to the leaders of the CARs to ensure political sovereignty, independence and political stability was a prime consideration for the Western powers. Secondly, the Western powers considered that the genuine interest of the Central Asian countries would be served if they follow Western type of political democracy and build democratic institutions in their newly independent states as a part of their transition from the former socialist system. Thirdly, to achieve geopolitical interest, the West was keen to restrict Russia's sphere of influence on Central Asia and specifically contain Russia's monopoly over the energy sector of Central Asia. Fourthly, the West considered it necessary to extend support to the CARs in their task of economic stability in their countries. Hence economic assistance and support both from several international institutions and from individual countries to the CARs was to a great extent guided by this consideration. Investment by the Western countries in the development of the energy sector of the CARs was intended to be a part objective.

These objectives of the west are evident in the views of a few top US officials expressed at the hearing of the House International Relations Sub-Committee on 25 July 2006. Some of the experts opined that ever since the Soviet disintegration, the USA has been committed to helping the countries of Central Asia develop strong, democratic institutions and create "win-win" solutions in developing energy resources. With regard to the energy sector of the Central Asian region, energy expert Mann stated that the challenge for the USA was to help the Central Asian region achieve greater economic independence by expanding its export options through a regional East-West Energy Corridor consisting of multiple pipelines. Lana Ekimoff, the Director of the US Department of Energy's Office of Russian and Eurasian Affairs, who also testified at the Sub-Committee, stated that by 2010, countries in the region are expected to export up to four million barrels of oil and 680 million cubic meters of natural gas per day. It was pointed out that though the availability of Caspian oil and gas though modest as compared to that of the OPEC, it helped to diversify global energy supply, which ultimately contributes to global energy security. Ekimoff further added that the full potential of the region's energy resources remains unknown.

## European Union and the CARs

West European countries have taken interest in the MPP of Central Asian region. Some part of their energy imports at present comes from the CARs through Russia. The European Commission Strategy Paper (1999) spelt out its Programme for "Central Asia 2002-2004". The Paper elaborated common problems and shared challenges of Central Asia. It also stated that the objective of the EU is to support the CARs in making more sustainable use of natural resources of Central Asia including oil and natural gas of the region. During the last decade, the EU provided assistance of over $ 944 million to all the five CARs for their economic development including the development of the energy sector. As compared to USA, the European Union has been a late entrant in the scene. Andris Piebalgs, the EU Energy Commissioner, who visited Central Asia in May 2006 admitted "...but it's true that we have neglected the potential of this region for quite a substantial time...". The EU policy makers feel that Central Asia can be an important source of energy and can meet about 10 per cent of the demand of natural gas in the future. From the perspective of the EU, Kazakhstan will play an important part by virtue of the potentiality of energy resources including uranium. Andris Piebalgs has opined that Kazakhstan has created favourable investment climate by following economic reforms, which is an additional factor in its favour. Turkmenistan would be the next country with huge natural gas resources, which is attracting the EU interest, as opined by the Energy Commissioner.

Even at present, oil and natural gas of Central Asia reaches Europe through Russia. But some EU members have encountered difficulties since Russia has refused to sign a transit protocol allowing outsiders access to the pipeline network of Russia. Even if this problem is sorted out, there will be need for additional pipelines for meeting the energy demand of the EU from Central Asia. The EU is interested in more reliable routes and hence, promotes pipeline projects from the Caspian Sea to Azerbaijan and Turkey to Europe. In addition to the BTC pipeline, which has become a reality in 2005, the EU seems to be interested in Trans-Caspian Pipelines, which will give the CAS a wider choice of exporting their energy resources to west Europe. As stated by the EU Spokesman, feasibility studies are being financed by the EU. He even emphasized that private companies should invest in building the pipelines. In view of this, the west European countries in general and the EU in particular are likely to play an important role in the energy sector of Central Asia in the years to come.

## China and Central Asia

China has been playing an important role in the Central Asian region in general and in the energy sector in particular. With consistently high economic growth during the last couple of decades, China's demand for energy resources has increased annually at the rate of about 10 million barrels over the next 10-15 years. In order to meet this huge demand for energy, China has been actively seeking alternative sources of supply in the Middle East, in Africa etc. During the past decade or so, the Chinese leaders have paid special attention to enter the Central Asian energy sector. Mutual exchange of visits by the leaders of China and the CARs, particularly after the Soviet break-up, created cordial political relations among them. Further the creation of the Shanghai Cooperation Organization (SCO) has strengthened China's political and economic ties with the CARs. China has made huge investment in the energy sector of Kazakhstan, Turkmenistan for exploration and exploitation of oil and natural gas in these countries. China's CNPC has been one of the major players in this regard. Even when the energy prices were low in the 1990's, the Chinese leaders proposed pipeline routes over thousands of kilometers for transporting oil and natural gas from these countries. This was part of the Chinese strategy to bring the CARs closer economically. This is evident in the remark of Yi, a senior Chinese Commerce Official made in October 2006 on the occasion of two-day Business Development Forum of Central Asia Regional Economic Cooperation (CAREC). He stated that China's 'Go West' strategy and policy was intended to develop economic cooperation with its neighbours in Central Asia. As a result of this policy, trade between China and the CAREC countries increased from $ 1 billion in 1997 to 9.8 billion in 2005, nearly 10-fold increase in about eight years. This included trade in energy products. In turn 'Orientation Towards China' was also in the interest of the CARs as stated by the Turkmen President who was spelling out strategies and approaches for meeting the needs of the 21st Century. He was specifically mentioning the role of China with regard to the main directions of transportation of oil and natural gas pipeline projects of Turkmenistan and Kazakhstan. For instance, a major pipeline project was 2,880 km. long pipeline from Aktybinsk in Kazakhstan to Xinjiang in eastern parts of China which would cost over 3.5 billion dollars. Thus there is mutuality of interest between China and the CARs.

Another important development in this regard is the fact that during the last decade, China and Russia have come closer in developing their political and economic relations with Central Asia. This includes the energy sector. To some extent, this is a part of the policy of Russia and China in containing the growing influence of the United States in the Central Asian region. Hence as opined by many analysts, there is 'Great Game rivalry' between Russia and China on the one hand and the USA on the other in the energy sector of Central Asia. Russia has pursued the policy of tapping energy resources of Central Asia to be exported to China through the Russian pipelines. Apart from this, Russian policy makers and Russian companies have evinced interest in participating in the energy projects in Central Asia including exploration, production and transportation of oil and gas to China. While cooperating with the CARs in the energy sector to meet the rapidly growing market of China, Russia is also concerned about the aggressive policy of China in Central Asia and about the big energy projects between China and the CARs, which may affect Russia's influence in the Central Asian energy sector in the long run.

## Conclusion

From the above account, it may be stated that the Central Asian countries, particularly Kazakhstan, Turkmenistan and Uzbekistan are well endowed with hydrocarbon resources. After gaining independence, these states have given considerable attention to the development of their energy sector as there was ready demand for these products in the world markets. Moreover, by exporting oil and natural gas, they were able to earn much needed hard currency for survival and economic development. But the CARs being landlocked countries have faced considerable difficulties in exporting energy products since the prevailing pipelines laid during the Soviet era were passing only through Russia. This monopoly position provided the Russian policy makers political leverage to influence the policies of the CARs. From their own national interest, the Central Asian countries proposed to expand the scope for exports to world markets by creating additional pipelines. The USA and the Western countries have extended strong support for Multiple Pipeline Policies, which has been consistently opposed by Russia. Thus, there has been conflict of interest between Russia and the West on the issue of pipelines making Central Asia as the scene of "Great Game" rivalry. During the last decade, China has also been actively pursuing its 'Go West' policy, which also involves energy sector of the CARs. In pursuing their energy policies, the Central Asian leaders have to strike a delicate balance in serving their national interest while not antagonizing the big powers. Energy exports under prevailing conditions of unprecedented rise in the prices for oil and natural gas have brought huge economic benefits to the CARs. At the same time, from long term perspectives, it is necessary for the Central Asian leaders to use petro-dollars to diversify and broaden the base of their economies rather than depending only upon the energy sector.

# 4

# Yin and Yang of the Caspian Conundrum

*P.L. Dash*

Nineteen years down memory lane since independence, there have been numerous, grand, pipeline proposals in all possible directions from Central Asian and Caspian regions. A cursory look at many of them leads one to believe as if true globalization is materializing in pipeline connectivity. However, a thorough perusal of many a pipeline proposal leads one to despair not exactly about the fluctuating assessment of oil and gas reserves in the region, not necessarily about the true intentions of multinational companies venturing two steps and backing out one from the prospective oil fields, not entirely about lack of political commitments in pursuing the pipeline dreams; but certainly about the worrisome bickering and mutual hostility wrecking the countries of the region to disappointing fragmentation rather than genuine globalization. The USA vies to elbow out Russia from the Caspian by choosing alternative routes of gas and oil transportation. Crucially located Iran is sidestepped like a stepchild. Russia pursues its policies gingerly relative to its former Republics to sustain its own national interest and provide a lifeline to her southern security zone. Turkmenistan cries foul of others, but pursues a complex policy of 'positive neutrality' in consonance with what it considers her national interest. Azerbaijan and Kazakhstan are virtually hijacked by Russia through bilateral deals, thus complicating the Caspian scenario as never before.

Be that as it may, the five littoral states of the Caspian have been locking horns among one another how to divide the Caspian hydrocarbon resources. They debate, discuss and determine the Caspian legal status that remains so far undefined. What has been famous in history as the "Caspian Sea" has indeed been treated as a "Lake" and regulated by Russia and Iran for navigational and other purposes for most part of history because Central Asian states as we see them today did not exist then. The post-Soviet appearance of three other independent, coastal sovereign states has dramatically altered the Caspian scenario. Efforts are afoot to treat the sea as a sea; and not as a lake. On this issue, most littoral countries most often differ, very often dither on a decision and quite often postpone the cardinal issue of territorial delimitation of the water zone accessible to each of them. Equally problematic are the 'islands of disputes' that continue to threaten the emerging contours of bilateral and multilateral ties. The intricate debates over the years require a detailed study that constitutes the subject matter of this study.

## Delimitation Proposals

Since the Soviet disunion, nearly half a dozen proposals for delimiting the Caspian coastal zone and sea shelf sharing have been afloat. And all of them are basically flawed by their inconsistency; hence unacceptable to all or some of the littoral states. As a result Caspian countries have been vacillating a great deal from time to time with sway of events gradually unfolding. A cursory look at all these delimitation proposals leads us to the following conclusions. First, the 1940 Soviet-Iran agreement on trade and navigation fixed a 10-mile fishing zone for each coastal country, underscored that the Caspian was "jurisdictionally considered a Soviet-Iran sea with rights of each country to maintain fleet."[1] This arrangement continued until the Soviet collapse. The new post-Soviet situation demanded a novel approach that would suitably accommodate the aspirations of sovereign littoral states of the Caspian region.

Secondly, in the aftermath of the Soviet collapse, the so called "two nation theory" was replaced by a new reality of "five nation theory". Increasing demand pointed to re-division of the sea as per national sectors by applying the 1982 Law of the Sea Convention. Application of the Convention would define the Caspian as a lake or a sea – open, closed or semi enclosed. Following the example of Titicaca border lake division – the only lake shared between Peru and Bolivia with a 12-mile access zone from the coast – there were demands for 12-mile access zone. In 1992, the Russian Foreign Ministry declared the Caspian as a closed sea with 12-mile access zone for each coastal country. However, such a proposal could not sustain and fizzled out in the intense debate of how to define the Caspian with outlets to navigable Volga through the port of Astrakhan.

Third came the demand from Iran for a 20-mile territorial waters as access zone from the coast for fishing and the rest to be considered properties of five countries. This was initially supported by Russia, but when Iran put forth demand for another 20-mile as exclusive economic zone, hectic diplomacy began among other Caspian countries to scuttle the Iranian plan. The idea of 20-mile or 20+20 mile had longevity of less than two years. Without any support, it met with a slow demise. Iran has also been demanding equitable distribution of the sea and its resources among all five coastal states.

The fourth proposition for a 45 mile zone from the coast was suggested by Evgeny Primakov in Ashgabat in November 1996 on the territory of neutral Turkmenistan. The same month it was followed by Azerbaijan within the framework of national sectors for determining a 45-mile exclusive jurisdiction for exploration of mineral resources. A breadth of 45 miles around the sea would be thus the exclusive zone from the coast of each country and rest of the sea be treated as transnational zone for joint holding. Prime Minister Primakov apparently made this as his personal suggestion; and by early July 1997, Russia and Azerbaijan were already in agreement with each other to explore the sea shelf on the Azerbaijani zone. However, when such activities extended beyond 45 miles, Russia and Azerbaijan had differences and exchanged diplomatic notes.[2]

The fifth proposal for delimitation of the Caspian was aired by a special working group on Caspian formed by all five countries. The meeting was held in Baku in February 2003. Its job was to work out a Convention that would finally regulate the activities of littoral states in the Caspian. The convention addressed three topical questions: territorial waters for sovereign use by each country, a defined fishing territory for each country; and the open sea zone. The Convention proposed that the breadth of sovereign "territorial water limits of each country ought not exceed 15 nautical miles (1 nautical mile = 1.852 kilometers) from the coast, and this should be demarcated as the state border with the neighbors. The division of the Caspian shelf would, however, be determined by the principle of national, sectoral division of the Sea from its borders for all economic activities including exploration of hydrocarbons.[3] A conflict resolution mechanism, common to all five states, would be in place to resolve mutual disputes, as and when they arise. By now, however, all these delimitation proposals seem to have outlived their utility because a tangible solution has been evading all littoral countries primarily because concerned countries have been acting too selfish in the façade of their national interests.[4] The only tangible outcome has been confidence building by continuing dialogue in and around the Caspian problem.

## The Models

Aside from these five mile zone proposals, there are two other significant propositions floating around for a solution, none of which seems viable in the present context. First, Kazakhstan favors a division of the sea into national sectors, thereby defining borders of the sea by stretch of the sea coast in possession of each country. By virtue of such division, Kazakhstan expects to get the lion's share of the coastal zone and sea shelf because it has the longest stretch of Caspian coastline. Russia comes the second. Russia has wooed Kazakhstan in this effort in the past years with a view to retaining their control over roughly 60 percent of the sea, leaving the rest 40 percent of the sea to other three littoral countries, which they grumble to accept. Such a proposition virtually negates the 45-mile idea and consigns all mile zone proposals to the dustbin of history. Much as it addresses the Kazakh national interest, national sectoral division fails to address the common problem concerning the legal status and perpetuates the seeds of discord, simmering beneath the hydrocarbons of the sea. Secondly, the Russian attitude is too rigid and inconsistent to be viable. In the name of national interest, Russia has been shifting sides from one idea to the other as if it could control most of the sea as it did through Soviet years. It has negotiated with all countries all mile zone ideas on table. It has insisted on segregating Iran to 13 percent of the sea area south of Astara-Hasankuli mean line. It has signed agreements with Kazakhstan for division of national sectors of the sea. It has sided with the 45-mile idea of Primakov and eschewed it the moment it felt there were no takers. It has rejected Iran's proposal for an equal distribution of the sea and its resources. An analysis of all these manipulative diplomacy by Russia tends us to draw one conclusion: Russia has been consistently pursuing a course to assure 12 mile sovereign territorial water zone for each country, assigning the rest of the sea to joint control on paper; and de facto control by Russia. Russia's bullying tactic is unacceptable to other countries.

Thirdly, Russian approach to determine the Caspian legal status is important for a variety of reasons. Russia is the only country that has developed pipeline system for oil and gas transportation across the former Soviet space. Azerbaijan, Russia and Kazakhstan have agreed, for their sake of convenience, to use the Russian pipelines for oil and gas export. Turkmenistan also exports its gas through Russia. The only country left out in the whole game is Iran. In a real sense, Russia wishes her domination to continue and rejects innovative ideas of laying cross-country pipeline system that would connect Caucasian and Central Asian arteries of the Soviet era with emerging pipeline structures in southern or eastern direction. In order to bypass Iran, Russia and the US have a common approach; In order to bypass Russia all countries of the Caspian plus the US are unanimous.

The countries are thus facing a bewildering puzzle of grouping and regrouping in the sway of events that sweep their region. While oil diplomacy and politicking continue to make the Caspian status inconclusive, inevitable tie-ups are precipitating a national crisis for all in the region. Often all these countries fail to understand that what they consider national in content in the aquatic zone of the Caspian has in fact transnational character. This identity crisis of the Caspian pipeline politics, loaded with heavy doses of national interest, overwhelms the scenario with a basic feeling of insecurity, resulting in various unwelcome groups, who endeavor to assert their presence in the Caspian. Group one is littoral states, group two is non-littoral countries, group three is non-Russian states, group four is interested foreign powers, group five is closed and distant neighbors and group six are those who target long term oil market and commerce in the area. The political, diplomatic and strategic interplay of all these half a dozen groups would finally determine the shape of things to come in and around the Caspian in the years to come.

For the present, by crystallizing the above discussion to substantive conclusions, we have an inconclusive array of debatable propositions. First, the National Sector Model, initially argued forcefully by Azerbaijan and then followed by Kazakhstan has withered away over the years, equally forcefully enforcing Russian predominance on the two proponents of this model. As a result, many bilateral and trilateral arrangements have emerged: In March 1998, Azerbaijan and Turkmenistan signed a joint communiqué on the 'middle line principle' to divide and exploit the sea although the communiqué did not settle their disputes over contesting oil fields of Azeri Chirag and Kyapaz. In July 1998, Kazakhstan and Russia signed a bilateral agreement for division of the bottom of the Sea on the principle of 'modified middle line'. A few months later Russia and Azerbaijan followed suit. Thus, a trilateral arrangement ensued in May 2003 between Russia, Azerbaijan and Kazakhstan that dealt with some issues of mutual demarcation; but did not entail a final solution.

The Condominium Model, favored by Russia that provided for joint and sovereign territorial zones for each country, failed to satisfy the ambitious overtures of littoral countries. It clashed with the Egalitarian Model of division adduced by Iran. Iran's insistence on equal division of the sea is fiercely contested by Russia. Although Russia agrees to Iranian idea of treating the Caspian as a lake, major differences are eminently discernible on division of the sea. Thus contending propositions and clashing interests, ownership issues of on-sea oil fields and mutually acceptable territorial delimitations are some of the impediments raising roadblocks for resolving the legal status dispute of the Caspian. In July and September 2003, when littoral states met in Moscow and Ashgabat respectively, hopes ran high about a resolution, but all endeavors petered out, when status issues were sidestepped and technicalities overwhelmed the discussions. The legal status thus remains debatable without any feasible solution in sight. Russia's preeminent position in the Caspian, military or otherwise, vis-à-vis other littoral states and its manipulative diplomacy with individual Caspian states is another stumbling block to overcome before any final settlement of the legal status is arrived at.

## Why Russia?

Russia comes to the forefront of energy politics again and again in Eurasia for a number of reasons. First, the country's very Eurasian existence, spanning over eleven time zones makes it all pervasive. Secondly, its enormous reserves of oil and gas make it a prominent energy power in the world. Thirdly, Russia's preeminence in Central Asia and the Caucasus, particularly after its five day war with Georgia speaks for itself as a credible transit partner in all feasible routes and pipelines across the north for supply of energy to Europe. Fourthly, Russia's efforts to bolster the communication corridors from north-south transport passage to Eurasian continental bridge is as much a laudable acquiescence of emerging realities as it is demonstrative of resilience on the part of an oil major to adapt to the transformed regional geopolitics. In the backdrop of all these, what Russia indeed intends to do is to "raise tenfold its oil and gas export to Asia in upcoming 10-15 years."[5]

In the global energy matrix, Russia's position remains irreplaceable. Russia's estimated oil reserves stand at 44 billion tones – roughly about one fifth of the world's total. After years of post-Soviet slump, the country's oil production has once again picked up. Among the several handicaps facing Russian oil industry are efforts at reasserting centralized governance of the energy sector, exclusive state control, excessive orientation toward export, irrational use of oil revenues by the state, improper planning for further exploration and extraction of new fields, intensive use of existing oil wells and gas fields and many other related problems. Privatization has faltered on way to success. After nearly two decades of difficulties associated with an extraordinary transition, the government has once again come back as a major oil manager as in the Soviet era. In early August 2006, Russian oil giant Yukos had gone bust. For many years on, oil tycoon Mikhail Khadorkovsky has been languishing in jail. The Putin regime had consistently tried to regain government control over the oil industry that was privatized earlier. The hike of a single dollar in oil price pushed up Russian GDP by 0.5 percent, hence the country has immensely gained from oil price spike the world over in 2008, when a barrel of oil touched \$150. Demand for oil has put Russia once again in the oil map of the world as a giant producer whose name remains untarnished. The higher the price of oil, the better it is for Russia. Russia occupied in 2002 the second place after Saudi Arabia in oil reserves of the world. Its proven oil reserves are certainly 12 to 13 percent of the global oil reserves.[6]

For decades, India and the former Soviet Union had close political, economic and military relationship. They were in a sense considered best of partners. India had been importing oil from the former Soviet Union for many, many years. However, most of the oil was Iraqi oil, coming to India and other countries as the result of a swap deal the former Soviet Union had with Iraq to exchange arms and weaponry for oil. The deal was beneficial for both: the Soviet Union had a client state to buy arms, India was cutting cost and time to get oil and meet her energy requirements. The deal had thus mutual benefits. The first Gulf war in 1991 had ended this arrangement partially and the dethronement of Saddam Hussein in 2003 had severed this channel of oil procurement forever. The post-Soviet roadblocks in Indo-Russian relations are now largely episodes of yesteryears. Under the Putin dispensation and since, both countries have begun once again looking to the future with crimson hopes. India's energy dependence on Russia has in fact never ceased. In the whole scheme of things that go with India's postulations for ensuring energy security, Russia continues to remain for India a long standing trade partner and reliable oil supplier. You talk of Sakhalin, Russia figures. You talk of the Caspian states, Russia figures too. You talk of the North-South corridor, Russia comes as a domineering partner. You talk of transporting hydrocarbons via Iran, Russia comes as a leading supplier. You talk of getting oil and gas from anywhere in the post-Soviet space, it will pass across Russian built pipeline arteries of the Soviet era to the first available terminal for export because Russia continues to maintain these internal pipelines in most post-Soviet states. It seems as if Russia is intrinsically and perpetually linked to regional energy security system. Since Russia is likely to remain a leading world player in the energy market in the changing context of a globalizing world order, the traditional, mutual goodwill between India and Russia stands a good deal in India's favor. What India needs is to maintain an energy alliance with Russia with a view to ensuring her future energy security.

Russia further continues to figure in Indian strategic planning in view of her defence dependence. India continues her military and strategic cooperation with Russia despite the fall and swell of post-Soviet years. The strategic parameters of this cooperation are inevitably linked to issues of India's energy security because oil is as much the locomotive of economic growth as it is essential for overall security. This intrinsic linkage would precipitate mutual energy cooperation between the two countries in the years to come. However, both India and Russia face in this sphere of cooperation tangible impediments from other competitors afield in the area. Several new energy poles have appeared in the scene, both consumers and producers. They include the US, the biggest consumer of energy pegged at 29 percent of the world total, Russia, the second largest producer of oil and largest producer of natural gas, Japan, a sizeable consumer, OPEC members, who are the biggest oil suppliers, Caspian littorals and Norway as emerging suppliers, upcoming economic powers such as China and India, and possibly other poles of East Asia yet to emerge. In this configuration of new energy poles, Russia, OPEC, Caspian littorals and Norway remain suppliers, while rest are consumers. In this globalizing new energy poles that would unify a consumer-producer alliance, India's sustainable energy alliance with Russia would have a pivotal role to play amidst economic and geo-strategic jockeying of all these players in the very periphery of India and Russia.

Napoleon Bonaparte once exhorted: "if you wish to know the policy of a country, look at the map". He apparently meant that regimes come and go, leaders rise and fall, ideologies flourish and perish, histories lead or mislead depending on how it is interpreted. However, what never withers is geography. It is this geography that makes incumbent upon India to sustain Russia in friendship, because it is a country whose geography is vast. Whether it is oil import by India from Sakhalin or gas import from the Caspian littoral countries, Russia is evidently in picture and could always offer India a helping hand in her energy security. Russia's political proselytizing in the Caspian region, her post-Soviet friendship with Iran despite US opposition, her loss of face and money in Iraq after the American conquest and her help to the young leadership in Syria are ample evidences to suggest that albeit a dilapidated power struggling to regain her lost glory, Russia remains a credible partner for India's energy security. Although her position in India is not exactly that feeble, India's recent closeness to the US after signing of the civilian nuclear deal has begun to cast a pall of gloom in certain circles in Russia and India. Yet Russia was standing stoic behind that deal. Putin's Russia has been grappling with the change in geo-politics and gradually accosting the course to respecting the rights of every sovereign country to pursue security and foreign policies of its choice.

That Russia was back to reasserting its global power status in West Asia and Caspian region was evident when Putin extended an invitation to the Hamas leader, Mahmoud Abbas, to visit Moscow in the aftermath of his victory in Palestinian elections. Around that time, *Iran Daily* wrote: "...it did not cost anything and it put Russia back on the map of the Middle East. While the whole world was still puzzled and confused with the Hamas victory, Putin used the sharp scalpel of unemotional logic and made the first move of a new game." Putin had in fact politically and diplomatically outwitted many world leaders, who never expected such an adroit diplomatic step. But he actually assuaged the gravity of the Hamas victory by extending a mediatory platform by Russia in the Middle East peace process, should there ever be a stalemate. The subsequent escalation of Israel-Palestine relations is indicative of the deepening Middle East crisis, where Russia would clearly have a paramount role to play in the peace process. The development of West Asian events since the American involvement in democracy building in Afghanistan and Iraq reminds us that the name of the game is "New Great Game". It is replayed with Britain being replaced by the US; and other actors, willy-nilly, taking sides with any of the powers. India's position once again is not exactly the same as it was under the British Empire. India is free to pursue her policies with Russia and the US with equanimity. In terms of immediate energy security, dependence on Russia remains exclusive, in the medium term, quest for alternative energy sources would prod India to seek as much of US technological help as possible; and in the long term energy collaboration, both Russia and the US would mirror on the radar of India's quest for energy security.

From specific oil rich areas in the post-Soviet space to overall regional geopolitics in West Asia and Middle East, including energy politics, the Russian presence is pervasive. Earlier it was subdued, after Georgian episode it is reassertion. It would gather momentum as Russian economic growth gathers steam. In energy politics, there is no way one could elbow out Russia from this space. Therefore, Russia must remain in the Indian scheme of things as a credible partner of regional geopolitics and energy supply in the years to come. The endowment of abundant hydrocarbon reserves on the part of Russia, and mutuality of interests and commonality of views between the two countries on many burning issues of international conduct are what drive India to Russia to cooperate in various areas of significance. The process of globalization has emancipated India from the shackles of barter based Rupee-Ruble trade. Commercial considerations and economic prospects of having a viable market in India would provide as much credible incentive to Russia to sustain alliance with India as the factors of energy and security dependence would prod India to maintain credible alliance with Russia.

## Defining Indian Interest

Roughly 10 percent of the world's population in richest countries uses more than 45 percent of the world's energy, while 20 percent of the population in poorest countries uses less than 5 percent of the energy. India with her billion plus population is among the poor, but emerging countries; so is China. Two out of every six people live in these two countries. Their sheer size – one third of the world total – and economies inclining to sustained growth over a decade would make them major consumers of energy. India's per capita energy consumption is just 7 percent of the world average, which is a fraction of the US per capita consumption. The present energy consumption pattern in India is dependent for 36 percent on coal, 36 percent on traditional sources, 17 percent on oil, 7 percent on gas and 4 percent on hydro and nuclear power. With an upward looking economy, maintaining a sustained growth of 6 plus percent in the last 12 years, and still growing despite a world meltdown, the energy consumption pattern is likely to undergo a sea change in upcoming decades. Estimates suggest that the current 70 percent import dependence on oil is likely to shoot up to 90 percent by 2020. It is also opined that by 2020 China and India put together will consume 60 percent of the world oil output. While options such as shift in the supply pattern and energy saving measures will be adequately addressed, renewable, wind and bio sources of alternative energy production will assume significance in addition to the current hydel, hydro, nuclear, oil and gas pattern. India's import dependence is sure to surge in view of its low domestic production. So would surge the quest for places from where alternative energy could be procured.

Here three vital energy rich areas come to picture – West Asia, Caspian/Central Asia and the Russian Federation. All five Caspian littoral states would assume significance in this regard in the upcoming years because they are located in and around Central Asia. Therefore, emerging pipeline structures in various directions from these energy rich regions to the energy-poor areas, where India is located, have been discussed threadbare in recent years. The Caspian region provides an opportunity now than never before because there are three independent actors like Azerbaijan, Kazakhstan and Turkmenistan, besides Iran, who could serve as energy suppliers to the Indian market, in addition to Russia. High potential coupled with their geographical contiguity makes neighborhood syndrome a phenomenon of mutual dependence.

In any of the possible propositions of laying a surface pipeline from the gas fields of these countries to any destination in South Asia, the political and ethnic volatility of Pakistan and Afghanistan are the major roadblocks to be cleared. For example, a pipeline from Iran or Caspian countries via Iran has to pass through Pakistan. But Pakistan remains ethnically volatile and politically disturbed. Decades of economic grievances of the Beluch against Islamabad are compounded by years of neglect that has deprived the local tribes any say in the matter of governance on their native soil. A case in point was Islamabad's decision to develop the Gwadar deep seaport on the Arabian Sea as a viable and proximate sea-surface link for piping Central Asian and Iranian gas first to Pakistan, and then to India and beyond. The decision was taken without consulting the Beluch that resulted in widespread protests. The outcry of the locals was valid for three reasons. First, land of the local tribes was appropriated at a pittance by non-resident Pakistanis, who were eager to invest in infrastructure. However, in practice, the land shuffled hands quickly for pecuniary gains by the selfsame investors, neither bringing any benefit to the locals nor helping in betterment of the economic predicament of local tribes; nor creating viable infrastructural amenities. Secondly, the problems persisted because Gwadar is a gold mine and the locals did not have land documents nor ownership papers, thus falling easy prey to foreign land buyers, who profiteered out of each deal signed. The overwhelming apprehension of resettlement of outsiders, the memory of the settlement of Afghan refugees and fresh onslaught by non-resident Pakistanis threatened the locals with a demographic imbalance. They feared that the ongoing influx would render the "local tribes to Red Indians of Beluchistan". In expression of their anger against the Gwadar project, the locals had killed a Chinese engineer engaged in development of the port that had elicited state repression on them. Finally, the locals had a genuine grievance. From the Sui gas field of Beluchistan, 6,000 million cubic feet of gas is pumped out daily to adjacent Punjab, Sindh and other far off places in Pakistan, while locals shiver in freezing winter in interior Beluchistan. They simply demanded their rights to live better. All these would tell negatively on the future of gas pipeline projects to India, whether from Turkmenistan or Iran. The gang rape of Shazia Khalid, a lady doctor in Sui hospital, by an army Captain and his accomplices, had sparked outrage in Sui. The resultant protest by the leaders of the Bugti and Mengal tribes snowballed into choking the gas pipeline to the entire country and Musharraf's threat to suppress the protest was nothing but indicative of the resentment the locals have against the centre and vice versa.[7] The killing of the Bugti leader further complicated the tenuous centre-state relationship. Thus from the worries of Waziristan in the north to the sorrows of Sui in the South, Pakistan's vulnerability to ethnic tensions laden with bellicose irredentism provide too awesome a prospect for laying pipelines. This could only be countered by mutual economic dependence for development of a network of regional energy security system for the benefit of all. The supplier countries could reap the benefits of their sale, the buyer countries would get energy for their development and economic growth, the transiting countries would benefit through tariff revenues; and the region would surely inch toward prosperity.

The other worrisome aspect that impedes easy flow of Caspian gas via Iran is the Iran-Libya sanction act of the US that imposed sanctions on non-US companies investing in Iranian pipelines. Iran has thus been passing through the horn of a dilemma: US companies are not permitted to invest in Iran, non-US companies elicited punitive US sanctions should they venture to invest in Iran and countries around Iran considered various options to see Iranian gas flow to them. As a result of bilateral and trilateral efforts, two distinct possibilities had emerged in the past decade. In 1997, Iran and Turkmenistan completed the Karpedze- Kurt Kui gas pipeline at a cost of $190 million, linking the two countries. This first ever southward looking line is on a swap arrangement to which Kazakhstan subsequently joined that made it a trilateral artery of Caspian, Iranian and Turkmen gas supply to South Asia. Should ever this line be connected to the Jamnagar facilities of the Reliance in India, it would be an ideal cross country connectivity. Perhaps dependence on gas for economic prosperity would one day tide over political volatility and mutual hostility.

The second venture of benefit to India from this area emanated from Turkmenistan. In December 2002 Turkmenistan, Afghanistan and Pakistan had signed a trilateral agreement to seek investors to finance a venture of 3.5 billion dollars pipeline construction. However, in July 2003, the Asian Development Bank, the main supporter of this pipeline, called for further feasibility study, thereby delaying its construction. The ADB has once again picked up threads to construct this pipeline. Besides these two cross country ventures that ultimately would benefit

India, some 1,800 miles of pipelines are planned from Turkmenistan in the eastern direction that would pass via the mountain ravines of Kyrgyzstan and Tajikistan and through the Kazakh steppe to China. India may thus expect connectivity from China anywhere into Indian territory via Tibet.

As promising gas and oil fields of the Caspian and Central Asian region would reach out in search of equally promising markets worldwide, there is likelihood of a web of inter-locking oil and gas fields with multiple outlets from the fields of production to needy markets. Over the next 10 to 15 years, the demand for oil in Europe will grow approximately by one million barrels a day, while in the East, it will be 10 million barrels a day. Thus the first generation market across Europe is saturated with little or no possibility of sale of gas or oil from this region. The second generation market is steadily growing and unfolding in the East, particularly with China and India emerging as alluring markets. One pipeline that deserves mention here is Atasu-Alatau Kazakh-Chinese pipeline of 613 miles that connects Atasu, a small hamlet in Karaganda oblast of Kazakhstan with Alatau in Chinese Xinjiang.[8] This Kazakh-Chinese joint venture, built at a cost of $850 million, was scheduled for completion by December 2005, but got delayed that has now been completed. Kazakhstan is looking forward to supply its gas and oil to the southern market too, right up to India and beyond.

An Indian analyst had suggested 8 innovative ways of providing an energy security cordon across Central Asia that would serve Indian interest despite the region remaining hostage to political volatility.[9] Filtering Caspian from her overall Central Asian analysis as an important and alternative source of India's energy security, one could deduce that Caspian engagement with energy diplomacy has left a strong regional imprint in the neighborhood, affecting regional economies in general and emerging markets in particular. India must, therefore, find a way of continuous engagement with the Caspian states, foster a lasting relationship through investment partnership and joint exploration of natural resources. In this regard, the following avenues are open to India in the years ahead.

First, India must prioritize her objectives vis-à-vis all Caspian states. In order of priority, Kazakh oil and Turkmen gas are of utmost importance to India. Within the existing pipeline framework, they could flow to India with little efforts via Iran. Iran remains the country of north-south connectivity, and India, Iran and Russia have already been exploring the possibility of strengthening a regional north-south transport corridor for mutual benefits. Efforts must be made to make this a viable transport route of continuous engagement of the Caspian states. Secondly, after engaging these three countries- Kazakhstan, Turkmenistan and Iran in pipeline politics and regional diplomacy, India and Russia, as initiators of the north-south corridor, could attract Azerbaijan, thus making a platform of total involvement of all concerned countries in Caspian energy politics, including their exploration and transportation.

Thirdly, a landmark law called Energy Charter Treaty (ECT) is in force effective April 1998 to which Central Asian countries are signatories. This treaty guarantees to protect investment in "exploration, extraction, refining, production, storage, surface transport, transmission, distribution, trade, marketing or sale of energy materials or products and not discriminate against investors from member countries."[10] The treaty in other words provides an opportunity to India to venture into the field of direct investment in oil fields of the Caspian. The ONGC is active in a number of countries such as Russia's Shakhalin-I, southern Iraq's Tuba, Vietnam's Nam Con San and in acquiring overseas oil equity and shares. It has similar involvement in collaboration with Canadian and Turkish oil companies in Sudan, Libya and Myanmar. However, in the case of Caspian, it has been less forward looking, only bidding a minority stake in Kurmangazy oil field in Kazakhstan that finally went to China. Time is ripe for India to actively and aggressively engage itself in possible oil ventures of all five Caspian states and some concrete steps have been taken with Kazakhstan in this regard in January 2009, when Nursultan Nazarbaev was India's guest on the Republic Day.

Fourthly and finally, for ensuring energy security, India could work out a pipeline option with China – possibly a sub-line forging out southward from the main line running from Central Asia to mainland China. It could also work out with Kyrgyzstan and Tajikistan for supply of hydro electricity anywhere across the origins of Amu Darya and Syr Darya. In this regard, Tajikistan is the country India must keep in mind. Amu Darya is an exotic river, originating from various mountains in Tajikistan and Wakhan Corridor in Afghanistan. From Wakhan Darya in Afghanistan to Pyandzh along Tajik-Afghan and Tajik-Uzbek borders, where the river meanders to assume its name to Amu Darya, it is not only fed by numerous forceful tributaries where there are places with great hydroelectric potential. Indian experience in electric grid-connecting could be offered to source energy from Central Asian Amu Darya to India. Although it may sound as exotic an idea as Amu Darya itself, it is a feasible proposition in view if the vast experience India has in grid connectivity across the Indian subcontinent, an experience that could be shared with Central Asia to sell electricity to India which has a peak shortage as high as 20 percent and base load shortage of 13 percent. Similarly, Kyrgyzstan, possessing the origin of the Syr Darya along with its numerous tributaries, has enormous hydro power. The short distance between India and these two Central Asian countries could make it worthwhile to replicate the grid experience on a virgin field. While Central Asian countries are fighting over how to share their river waters, India could extend a helping hand not only for solving their river disputes, but also sharing the experience of water sharing and electricity generation.

## ENDNOTES

1. Alimamed Nuriev, *Zarkalo*, Baku, 15 October 2003. Reprinted in *Russia and the Muslim World*, No. 2, 2004, p. 157.
2. Ibid., p.161.

3. E. Makhmudov, Obsudzaetsya Status Kaspia, *Zerkalo*, Baku, 27 February, 2003, See also *Russia and the Muslim World*, No. 5, 2003, p. 230.
4. Stefan Wagstyl, Russia plans Tenfold rise in Oil and Gas Exports to Asia, *South Asian Financial Times*, Dubai, 11 September 2006, p. 1.
5. Yury K. Shafranik, Russia in a Multi-polar Energy World, *World Affairs*, Spring 2006, pp. 42-43.
6. Avnery-News.co.il, *Iran Daily*, 9 March 2006, p. 7.
7. Mariana Baabar, Belochistan between Gas and Guns, *Outlook*, 31 January 2005, pp. 20-22. Also see, Baluchi Press, *The Economist*, London, 22 January 2005, p. 54.
8. Aleksandr Gordievskii, Kazakhstan Postabit Neft v Kitaiu, (Kazakhstan supplies oil to China) *Russia and the Muslim World*, No. 9, 2004, pp. 211-214.
9. Sudha Mahalingam, "India-Central Asia Energy Cooperation", in *India and Central Asia: Advancing the Common Interest*, Edited by K.Santhanam and Ramakant Dwivedi, IDSA and Anamaya Publishers, New Delhi, 2004, pp. 137-140.
10. See Roggenkamp in T. Walde (Ed.), *The Energy Charter Treaty: An East- West Gateway for Investment and Trade*, Kluwer Law International, London, The Hague,1996, pp. 510-511.

# 5

# Russia's Energy Policy in Central Asia
## *Imperatives for India*

*Irina Morozova*

The post-Cold War world system spurred ahead the globalization of markets and increase of poverty, created opportunities for regional economies' growth and conditions for exclusion of other regions from high-tech global development. Neo-liberalism of the mid-1970s challenged the nation-state and opened the door for various non-state actors to the new, more acute multi-level competition for the access to resources and markets. The present globe-local geo-political game is being held between states, transnational companies, international organizations and financial markets, as well as various criminal, half legal and local groups.

The emerging new globalizing energy market is supposed to diminish dependency on the stock exchange trading oil and gas, OPEC, TNCs and the major producing as well as consuming countries. Although a few energy-producing centers/regions (Middle East, the Russian Federation, Central Asia, and Latin America) actively develop and a number of exporting states open their national resources for foreign investments, the tendencies for monopolization remain. The largest energy consuming countries, predominantly the USA, tend to increase its influence on energy markets, creating energy security power projections. The appearance of new big consumer countries and regions in Asia, such as India, China, South-East Asia, can significantly influence the trajectories of oil and gas supply routes. The interdependency of the producing and consuming world centers is emphasized by experts on energy political economy; however, the inevitability of the multi-polar energy world[1] is arguable. India is commonly recognized as a huge emerging energy consumer that needs to meet the demands of its rapidly increasing population and economic growth.

India clearly demonstrates intentions to diversify its energy supplies (nowadays the country largely depends on the Middle East) and gaining stable and profitable position in the Asian energy market (in competition against other Asian 'giants').

**Table 1: Current and Prospective Population and Economic Growth of India**
(in comparative perspective)

| Country | Population (total) 2005 | Population growth (annual %) 2005 | Population growth (%) 2006-20 | GDP (current US$) 2005 | GDP in PPP (in US $ tm) 2020 | GDP growth (annual %) 2005 | GDP growth (%) 2006-20 | GNI per capita, Atlas method (current US $) 2005 |
|---|---|---|---|---|---|---|---|---|
| India | 1.1 billion | 1.4 | 1.6 | 785.5 billion | 6.5 (3rd place in the world) | 8.5 | 5.5 | 720.0 |
| China | 1.3 billion | 0.6 | 0.8 | 2.2 trillion | 14 (2nd place in the world) | 9.9 | 5.1 | 1.720.0 |
| Japan | 128.0 million | 0.1 | n.a. | 4.5 trillion | n.a. (4th place in the world) | 2.7 | n.a. | 38, 980.0 |
| Germany | 82.5 million | –0.0 | 0.2 | 2.8 trillion | 2,5 (5th place in the world) | 0.9 | 1.5 | 34, 580.0 |

**Source:** World Bank, UN, Deutsche Bank Research *Formel-G.*

The predicted future energy consumption rates are generally very high. At the same time, the share of oil and, especially gas, in primary energy use in India is difficult to predict. Firstly, considerable percentage of India's population may continue relying on traditional, non-commercial sources of energy.[2] Secondly, the underdevelopment of India's domestic distribution infrastructure will hold back the increase of the gas share in the country's energy sector, despite the prognosis of tripling the demand by the year 2020. Although natural gas is a potential 'clean' alternative, coal is likely to remain the primary commercial fuel in the total energy supply in India.

Crude oil and oil products are the main imported energy resource. The imported oil accounts for 70 per cent of the need for consumption and is about to reach 75 per cent in 2006[3]. India's dependency on imported crude oil is likely to increase against the poor domestic production, mainly because of the lack of knowledge and experience necessary for exploration and investments into development of oil fields. The government is making effort to diversify its energy imports, searching for renewable resources and nuclear power. However, the share of these resources in the energy imports is rather minor.

**Table 2: Current and Prospective India's Oil and Gas Demand**
(in comparative perspective)

| Country | Oil demand (million barrels per day) | | | Gas demand (bcm) | | |
|---|---|---|---|---|---|---|
| | 2002 | 2010 | 2020 | 2002 | 2010 | 2020 |
| OECD North America | 22.6 | 25.5 | 28.7 | 759 | 866 | 1002 |
| OECS Europe | 14.5 | 15.3 | 16.3 | 291 | 585 | 705 |
| Russia | 2.7 | 3.1 | 3.6 | 415 | 473 | 552 |
| India | 2.5 | 3.4 | 4.5 | 28 | 45 | 78 |
| China | 5.2 | 7.9 | 10.6 | 36 | 59 | 107 |

**Source:** *World Energy Outlook 2004*, pp. 82, 130.

The most intriguing question, however, is whether the demand continues growing with the same high rate as predicted. What political-economic conditions may boost the production and flow of hydrocarbon into the country or slow down energy demand and supply? History has already proven the unreliability of many energy prognosis. The most illuminating case is the disintegration of the USSR that radically changed the already existed state of the market and created new ones. The development scenarios of the new growing Asian economies, such as India and China, are still open to various interpretations. In case of Turkey, for instance, the energy demand is growing much slowly than was previously envisaged,[4] especially at the stage of lobbying for the construction of pipeline systems from Azerbaijan to Turkey via Georgia.[5]

However, despite all empirical skepticism, India's need to import hydrocarbons and diversify its suppliers is evident and India is carefully searching for new suppliers outside the Middle East. Central Asian energy resources and, above all hydrocarbon reserves of the Caspian Sea, therefore, attract attention.

## India's Search for Energy Security in Russia and Central Asia

In a long term perspective, India is not a new player in Central Asia. Through centuries, the two regions influenced each other by means of migrations, cultural exchange and trade relations. In modern times the Indian peninsula and Central Asia occurred to be zones for Western colonial expansion. While Dutch and British colonial administrations in India were running Ost-Indian companies (that are compared by some scholars with contemporary TNCs), Central Asia was a ground for the well-known Great Game between Great Britain and the Russian Empire. A century later, when the post-Soviet Central Asia re-emerged as a geopolitically heterogeneous region with various international and local actors involved in 'New Great Game', India being one of them, became a vital participant in the competition for Central Asian natural resources.

Russia is the key power that India meets in Central Asia and, taking into account the positive legacy of Indo-Soviet relations, a potentially friendly partner. However, whether or not and how fast India gains access to the Central Asian gas and oil to a great extent depends not only on the success in negotiations with Russia and Russian energy companies, but clearly on the abilities of all parties involved to balance interests and profits.

To assess India's interests in Central Asian gas and oil and perspectives for joint development (together with Russia and other states) of the region's energy resources, one has to take into consideration a number of key issues about the current state of the Central Asian and Russian energy sector. The abundance of hydrocarbon resources in Central Asia may be a myth. The amount of oil and gas reserves in Central Asia and the Caspian region can be noticeably exaggerated for political purposes. None of the Central Asian states sits in the list of the top ten countries with proven oil reserves.[6] None of them on its own can develop into a really competitive and sufficient oil and gas exporter without proper co-operation among each other. Control over Central Asian resources and energy exports forms the key interest of Russia.

In 1990, the so-called transition economies (including the former USSR) were producing more gas than in 2002.[7] Russia still has not entirely recovered form the drastic fall in energy demand and production that happened at the very beginning of the 1990s. Still, remaining the third largest energy consumer in the world, Russia has to meet its energy needs by restructuring and reforming the energy sector and industry and securing both domestic energy needs and exports. The state budget growth after 2000 (as well as in former decades) is largely supported by profits gained from gas and oil exports. According to the World Bank, oil and gas alone contribute a quarter of Russia's GDP.[8] The sensitivity of Russia's production on world gas and oil prices, costs and taxes is alarmingly high, and the economic growth is disputable against the perspective of lowering the prices in the second part of the decade.[9] In case of maintaining high rates of economic growth Russia predicts to stop increasing its energy exports already by 2012-15.[10] In the short-term, oil and gas production is expected to grow, albeit at a slower pace. So far, what are the means to maintain and increase production? How Russia can influence the prices in the world oil and gas market?

The exploration drilling in the countries of the former Soviet Union accounts just for 4 per cent from the whole number of new field wildcats wells drilled during the period 1993-2002. This could be explained and justified by the high seventh place that Russia occupies among top ten countries with proven oil reserves.[11] At the same time, standing on the tenth place of the list the USA is actively exploring new fields (together with Canada and Mexico 61 per cent of new field wildcats).[12] The newly opened oil stock exchange in St. Petersburg is deemed to diminish Russia's dependency on OPEC by introducing its mechanisms of price-making.

The strong state regulatory function in relations with the TNC, state possession of the control shares in the TNCs and the blocking shares in Gazprom are listed in the government's Energy Strategy document called "Energy Strategy of Russia for the period to 2020,"[13] adopted by the Russian parliament in August 2003.

Most criticism on Russia's energy policy, coming from the West, is directed to the lack of market mechanism in the formation of domestic and export prices, conservative fiscal policies, absorption of windfall revenues by the government and smooth spending, non-liberal business climate, especially for the foreign investors. The on-going competition in the energy deal between Russia and the EU culminates at Russia's refusal to sign the EU Energy Charter. One of the documents of the Energy Charter is Transit Protocol, according to which Russia has to give access for free gas transit from Central Asia to Europe, while European pipelines do not fall under the force of the Protocol.[14] Russia's government intends to keep the pipeline monopolies, Transneft and Gazprom, in state hands. In addition to the rhetoric on Russia's national interests, former President Putin emphasized Russia's intentions to diversify its energy exports to Asia. The diversification is clearly elaborated in the Energy Strategy stating that: Russia is going to meet its new customers in the east and in the south.[15] The first target is East Asian market, namely Japan, Korea and China. Russia's energy strategy towards South Asia and primarily India is less focused for a number of reasons we will discuss further.

As we mentioned before, there is little exploration going on of the new gas reserves in Russia, since developing these new fields, according to the *World Energy Outlook*, is more costly enterprise than the development of the existing fields that used to be in the 1970s. The Russian Energy Strategy prioritizes "the overall involvement of Central Asian states into the Russia's fuel-energy balance of hydrocarbon reserves (especially natural gas)."[16] From Russia's perspective, the former Soviet pipeline system and infrastructure should not be divided, but integrated and serve as a "motor for integration processes within the Commonwealth of Independent States (CIS)". By declaring responsibility and paying for the debts of the USSR, Russia, above all, approves its economic interests to develop and exploit Central Asian hydrocarbon reserves in co-operation with the governments and companies of these Republics.

The exports of crude oil, gas and refined products from Central Asia are limited by a lack of transportation and terminal capacity. Currently Gazprom is a full monopolist of the Soviet gas pipeline systems. It has a monopoly on all gas exports outside the CIS. The company signed long-term agreements with Central Asian states (Turkmenistan, Uzbekistan, Azerbaijan, Kazakhstan) to transit gas. Over 1 tcm of region's gas reserves of 8 tcm have been sold.[17] Although the agreements are profitable for Central Asian states, as well as for Russia,[18] Gazprom has also restricted Central Asian national gas companies' access to its transmission system.

Caspian littoral states are constrained against diversification of their transmission system to the south, above all, due to the lack of decision on the legal status of the Caspian Sea. Iranian side is still holding back the solution, promoting the idea of equal division of the seabed among all the five Caspian states, so each of them would receive 20 per cent (at the time of the former USSR's existence Iran possessed 13 per cent). Azerbaijan and Turkmenistan are still disputing this proposal of Iran. Russia's policy on the status of the Caspian Sea improved during the last few years. Moscow signed bilateral treaties on the division of the seabed with each Caspian state excluding Iran.

Russia's plans in the Caspian region became more pragmatic in general. Yeltsin's disorientated policy towards Central Asia and the course on demilitarization of the Caspian Sea supported by the young Russian liberals went into the past after the inauguration of Vladimir Putin. The Russian 'concept of national security' includes the preservation and strengthening of Russia's positions in Central Asia and the Caspian Sea, and above all, Russia's military presence in the region.

The current Russian/Central Asian pipelines system is oriented almost fully towards the European consumer. While at the western cost of the Caspian Sea, the operating Baku-Tbilisi-Ceyhan and prospective Baku-Tbilisi-Erzurum bring Azeri and partly Kazakh hydrocarbon to Turkey (to be transported further to Europe) and the "Blue stream" delivers Russian gas under the Black sea to Turkey, most of Central Asian states – Turkmenistan, Uzbekistan and Kazakhstan are still at preliminary stage of developing and diversifying their exports. Similar to the Russia's energy policy in Asia, Central Asian states consider East Asian market first. China, as the direct neighbor that increases its investments into the regional economies, is viewed as a potential partner for co-operation.

## China Entering Central Asian Energy Market: New Competition for India?

By all means, China is interested in the region's natural resources and above all the hydrocarbon reservoirs of the Caspian Sea. China National Petroleum Corporation (CNPC) has already entered Kazakhstan energy market. Among other activities, it invested $4.3 billion in Aktyubinsk oil company and $1.3 billion in a joint venture with the Kazakh firm KazMunaiGaz to develop Uzen field on the Caspian Sea coast. Uzen project came within the 1997 deal with Iran, according to which Uzen oil produced by CNPC would move across the Caspian to a refinery near Teheran, while China will receive an equivalent amount of Iranian crude oil that Iran will export from its Gulf coast.

There have been a number of variants of hydrocarbon supplies from Central Asia to China. All of them serve the interests of a particular Central Asian country. At the beginning of 1990s China started investigating opportunities and costs to construct a great pipeline system from Turkmenistan to Xinjiang. In April 2006, the President of Turmenistan S. Niyazov signed a "Framework agreement" with his Chinese counterpart about the conditions for a prospective contract on the construction of this pipeline system. Ashgabat boasts to supply 30 billion cubic meters of gas since 2009, even at the expense of other export contracts already signed with Gazprom and RosUkrEnergo.[19]

Kazakhstan in its turn negotiated with China gas supplies of 8 to 10 billion cubic meters already in 2008 with the increasing amount of 30 billion cubic meters annually by 2030.[20] Kazakhstan is currently promoting a few gas routes to China.[21]

Central Asian oil and gas companies come into a competition with the Russian ones. Natural gas and oil flows from Siberia were an alternative to the "Silk Road" options. Despite the skepticism about the prospective Chinese-Russian projects, the bilateral agreements were signed in 2006. Nevertheless, the bilateral agreements between China and Russia signed under great endorsement of both governments do not necessarily signal China's priority choice for Russian hydrocarbons. These agreements are not yet long-term contracts, but the signs of intentions to launch such contracts. Currently the supplies of Russia's oil account just for 5 per cent of the general volume of Chinese oil import.

China is the second regional player that India has to catch-up with in Central Asia (and the first one in South and South-East Asia). The Indian state company Oil and Natural Gas Corporation (ONGC) tried to compete with the China National Petroleum Corporation (CPNC) for obtaining shares of the Canadian oil company PetroKazakhstan Inc. that had its assets in Kazakhstan. However, the shares were sold to the CNPC in August 2005. In that situation the government of

Kazakhstan was concerned to strengthen its control over the foreign capital in the national energy market and introduced additional amendments to the law that allowed the state to block the sales of foreign companies' shares.[22] The CNPC had to sell 33 per cent of the newly purchased shares to the Kazakh state oil company "KazMunaiGaz". Although India has less arguable historical legacy in relations with the Central Asian states than China (territorial disputes alone could be mentioned in this respect), the latter has been remarkably successful in developing bilateral relations with these countries. India is still not in the top 10 of the list of the main foreign investors into Kazakh economy and its fuel-energy sector, and the ONGC lags behind ChevronTexaco, ExxonMobil, Agip, Maersk, Hurricane Hydrocarbons, Oman Oil, CNPC and Lukoil (the latter has recently demonstrated tendencies to increase investments into Kazakh energy sector).

Nevertheless, ONGC, even lagging behind CNPC, has invested 3.5 billion US dollars in overseas exploration since 2000. The Russian Far East has become an attractive field for these investments. Most Russia's domestic investments go to the already operating fields in West Siberia. However, in not too distant future attention is likely to shift to less mature basins, including East Siberia and the Far East. Development and production costs for these projects will be considerably higher because of the less developed infrastructure, harsh geological and operating conditions. The average investment needed per barrel of capacity is higher than in most other parts of the world.[23] The knowledge factor is, in addition, convincing to call for partners for joint development and exploitation of oil fields. If participation of Shell and BP brings innovative technology to develop gas reserves at the Kovykta field near Irkutsk, as well as Sakhalin-1 and Sakhalin-2 projects, investments to the eastern dimension of Russia's energy policy are brought by Asian governments concerned. ONGC currently possesses 20 per cent shares in the investment consortium of Sakhalin-1 project. The Indian government expresses its interests to achieve a broader involvement of Indian national economy into the joint projects of developing hydrocarbon reserves with the Russian counterpart,[24] namely entirely state-owned Rosneft.[25]

## Towards Euro-Asian Economic Cooperation?

India's geographic position does not provide an opportunity to tap Central Asian resources easily. The presence of Afghanistan, Iran and Pakistan with all local and global conflicts that surround these states standing between India and Central Asia considerably slows the progress of Indo-Central Asian cooperation in the spheres of economy, energy and transportation. Most of the suggested routes of pipeline systems demonstrate new power blocs and projections rather than carefully assessed economic profitability. The prospective Trans-Afghan pipeline is supposed to supply Turkmen gas via Afghanistan to India is backed by the USA. The instable Afghanistan is unlikely to be a reliable partner in such a deal, not mentioning Indo-Pakistan tensions. By controlling Turkmen transportation corridors and signing long-term contracts with S. Niyazov, Russia weakened Turkmen part in the negotiation process over this pipeline. At the same time, Russia would like to participate and involve Turkmenistan in the Iran-Pakistan-India natural gas pipeline system project. The World Bank and Japan's Sumitomo Mitsui Banking Corporation expressed certain willingness to finance the project[26] (convincing example of multi-level competition, in which the interests of the states do not necessarily correspond with the gains by transnational companies and international financial organizations).

India-Pakistan dispute over Kashmir is still a stumbling block for economic co-operation, although some progress has been made since 2004, reviving hopes for the "peace pipeline". At the same time both countries have developed pipeline projects with Iran and China bypassing each other. Hence, the ONGC suggested a project "Energy Highway", imagining Russia-China-India pipeline, stretching from Russia through Turkmenistan, Uzbekistan and Kazakhstan, to Chinese Xinjiang, entering India via Ladakh, crossing "the India-China portion of the militarized Line of Control"[27] to supply gas to Northern India. For any observer such a project looks unfeasible. Bilateral Indo-Iranian and Sino-Indo-Iranian co-operation in energy sector is more realistic (the development of Iran's Yadavaran onshore oilfield or the port Chabahar).

In its geopolitical competition with the great neighbors – Iran and China – India applies for Russia's influence. Co-operation in energy sector between the two states has increased recently, as well as in the nuclear power sector. Russia, India and Iran are also promoting the idea of a north-south oil and gas pipeline systems and transportation corridors to connect Europe and Asia (which might be perceived as a competition for the US-led East-West Corridor through Baku, Tbilisi and Ceyhan). For better cooperation with China, India initiated Asia Energy Alliance.

In a broader geopolitical sense, India's prospective membership in the Shanghai Cooperation Organization (SCO), in which India currently has a status of Observer, may draw a new configuration out of this China-Central Asia-Russia alliance, transforming it into a super continental Euro-Asian association. The thought of the famous Russian politician E. Primakov about 'strategic triangle' of Russia, China and India might be realized. From Primakov's point of view, such a triple union could become a "second center" of regional Eurasian integration (the first center is the European Union). However, in spite of the fact that these three states on the international arena support each other's internal problems (Chechnya in Russia, Xinjiang in China, Kashmir in India), at the same time their interests are not alike, as also in Central Asia.

## ENDNOTES

1. See, for instance, Y.K. Shafranik, *Oil Industry in the System of Russia's National Economy and Geopolitics* (Moscow: NP, 2004).
2. *World Energy Assessment Overview: 2004 Update*, p. 26.
3. "The Energy Game" in *Heartland: Eurasian Review of Geopolitics*, November 2005.
4. *World Energy Outlook*, 2004, p. 313.

5. Brenda Shaffer, "From pipedream to Pipeline: A Caspian Success Story", *Current History*, vol. 104, no. 684 (October 2005), pp. 343-346.
6. *World Energy Outlook* 2004, p. 91.
7. Ibid, p. 138.
8. World Bank, 2004.
9. *World Energy Outlook*, 2004, p. 290.
10. *Osnovnye polozheniya energeticheskoi strategii Rossii na period do 2020 goda [Main statements on the energy policy of Russia by 2020]* (Moscow: Ministry of Energy of the Russian Federation, 2001), pp. 88-89.
11. *World Energy Outlook*, 2004, p. 91.
12. Ibid., p. 98.
13. Ibid., pp. 8, 55.
14. Dmitry Butrin, "Economic Charter Above All: Germany and France want Russia to keep to Europe's Energy Rules", *Kommersantú*. No. 192, 13 October 2006.
15. *Osnovnye polozheniya energeticheskoi strategii Rossii na period do 2020 goda [Main statements on the energy policy of Russia by 2020]* (Moscow: Ministry of Energy of the Russian Federation, 2001), p. 89.
16. Ibid., p. 90.
17. *World Energy Outlook*, 2004, p. 169.
18. Boris Antsifero, *"Okno v Evropu" dlya Kazakhskoi nefti* ("Window to Europe" for Kazakh Oil), *Gazeta.kz*, 17 June 2002.
19. A. Karavaev, "Turkmeniya – poteryannyi almaz iz korony 'Gazproma' " ("Turkmenistan – a lost diamond from the crown of Gazprom"). *Agentstvo Politicheskih Novostei Kazakhstana*, 11 May 2006.
20. Alfa Bank. Ezhednevnyi obzor rynka aktsii. (*Daily review of stock market.*) 22 March 2006. http://www.alfacapital.ru/attach/1/19/08/ABDaily_2006_3_22.pdf
21. G.G. Rakhmatulina, From her article published in *Sbornik materialov mezhdunarodnoi konferentsii "SOC i problemy bezopasnosti v Tsentral'noi Azii" (Collected materials of the international conference "SOC and security problems in Central Asia")* Almaty, October 2005. http://www.kisi.kz/site.html?id=3403
22. "Delo" No.1, 19 October 2005.
23. Ibid., p. 304.
24. *Ministr energetiki Indii posetil OAO "NK "Rosneft-Sakhalinmorneftegaz""* (Minister of Energy of India visited OAO NK Rosneft-Sakhalinmorneftegaz) http://business.zontik.ru/text.php?id=1792
25. Russia has limited and would put even more restriction on the foreign corporations' development of gas fields on the territory of the Russian Federation. The recent version of the law "On resources" identifies all fields with hydrocarbon reserves not less than 75 billion cubic meters as strategic ones and participation of a Russian oil company is obligatory. http://www.nazenergy.ru/arch.htm
26. Chietigj Bajpaee, "India, China locked in Energy Game", *Global Economy*, 17 March 2005).
27. "The Energy Game" in *Heartland: Eurasian Review of Geopolitics*, November 2005.

# 6

# Kazakhstan's Energy Strategy

*Bek Ali Yerzhan*

Strategy-2030 visualizes the future development of Kazakhstan. The strategy outlines following long term priorities of Kazakhstan's development: national security, internal stability, economic growth, education, health and welfare of citizens, energy resources, infrastructure (communications and transport) and professional state employees.

The energy resources are put as fifth long term priority. It includes (a) long term partnership with international oil companies. The partnership implies investments, hi-tech, employment, professional training, ecology, social programmes and transparency; (b) creation of pipeline systems for oil and gas exports in order to lessen Kazakhstan's dependence, have monopoly over consumer prices and diversified transportation routes; (c) long term partnership with world powers and strengthening of Kazakhstan's role as world oil supplier, which implies international legal, political, economic as well security support of Kazakhstan; (d) development of internal energy infrastructure, self sufficiency, internal pipelines, and modernization of current processing plants and construction of new modern refineries; (e) use of energy revenues for development and future generations. It implies smart investment of petrodollars in education, human resources and creation of various development institutions.[1]

Kazakhstan is one of the oil rich countries in the world. Kazakh President Nazarbayev visualizes Kazakhstan to become one of the top ten energy exporters in the world by the year 2012. With proven oil reserves of 9 billion barrels and probable reserves of upto 29 billion barrels, Kazakhstan is Central Asia's energy titan. By 2015 Kazakhstan would produce 120-150 million tons of oil and 30 billion cms of gas. The existing and emerging energy transit routes make it a potentially valuable ally to both Asia and Europe and to the United States as well. Kazakhstan offers an alluring prospect of supply diversification for countries overly-dependent on the Persian Gulf region or Russia.[2]

Apart from its significant oil and gas resources, Kazakhstan with its 25 per cent share of the world reserves has all the necessary foundations for uranium industry.

Thus, like many resource-rich nations, the Kazakh economy is driven primarily by its energy industry which accounts for a third of government revenues and more than half of the country's export earnings. Most of the foreign direct investment is also targeted at developing its oil and gas fields or in the construction of pipelines to take this energy to global markets. However, Kazakhstan's ability to harness its hydrocarbons for accelerating its growth will critically depend upon its ability to diversify all round economy of Kazakhstan and attract investments and to rapidly expand its access to global energy markets. For instance, Caspian offshore oil development requires 150 billion dollars.[3]

A substantial part of Kazakhstan's reserves are located in the Caspian Sea whose legal status is yet to be determined. 75 explored oil fields having 1 billion tons of oil) are located in Atyrau oblast, Western Kazakhstan. 39 oil fields with 846 million tons of oil are now under development. 7 oil fields are under preparation for development. 24 oil fields with 50 million tons of oil are under supplementary exploration. Tengiz (800 million tons of oil), Korolevskoe (30.5 million tons), Kenbai (30.8 million tons) are regarded to be the largest oil fields in Atyrau oblast. Maghystau oblast comes after Atyrau oblast with 70 oil fields. 27 fields are actively being developed. Uzen, Zhetybai, Kalamkas, Karazhanbas are regarded to be the largest oil fields in Manghystau oblast.

Kashaghan (Western Kazakhstan oblast) and Zhanazhol (Aktobe oblast) are regarded to be the oil fields with prosperous future. Kashaghan, the last major oil find anywhere in the world in a quarter of a century and termed the 'elephant' field, commenced production in 2008. Kashaghan reserves are estimated to be 7 billion tons. Kashaghan, north-eastern part of Caspian offshore is located about 75 kms to south-east of Atyrau. By 2015 only Kashaghan oil field is expected to yield 3 million barrels a day, which is equal to what Iran is extracting now.

In 2004, Kazakhstan produced approximately 1.22 million barrels a day of oil of which its own consumption was 224,000 barrels daily, thus making available approximately one mbd for exports. For the first half of 2005, Kazakhstan exported an average 1.1 million barrels daily in three directions: northward through the Russian pipeline system and rail network; westward through the Caspian Pipeline Consortium and in barges to Azerbaijan and southward through swaps with Iran. Kazakhstan also exported approximately 30,000 barrels a day eastward to China via the Alashankov rail crossing in 2005.[4] The growth of oil extraction and the introduction of BTC and Atasu-Alashankou pipeline is expected to increase production and export of oil.

Kazakhstan is also home to substantial gas deposits. The country produced 20.49 bn cm of gas in 2004. Production grew 36 per cent year-on-year in the first eight months of 2005 to 17.44 bn cm. Kazakhstan plans to increase production to 50 bn cm a year by 2010 and to 80 bn by 2015. Gas exports are entirely routed through Russia. However, Kazakhstan now wants to build a gas pipeline to China for which it has signed a preliminary agreement with that country. Kazakhstan is also open to the idea of linking up this proposed gas pipeline to supplies from Turkmenistan and Uzbekistan as well.

The rich oil reserves, new explorations and Kazakhstan's initiatives on attraction of investments have evoked interest of foreign countries as well as international companies in the region, especially the Caspian Sea. The huge amount of investments has flown into the region. Kazakhstan attracted 80 per cent of all investments in the whole of Central Asia.

When oil from all the fields begins to flow at full capacity, Kazakhstan will need to strengthen its export capacity and processing capabilities. This will require more export pipelines, processing plants and a diversified customer base as well. After all, security of markets is as much a concern for the suppliers as security of supply is to the buyer. The issue is not only economical but also geopolitical.

The processing incapability of Kazakhstan increases its dependence on Russia. In this regard, Kazakhstan's strategy is to modernize existing processing plants, participate in joint ventures and construct new modern plants. At present, Kazakhstan's oil processing capacity is 18.5 million tons a year (Atyrau, Pavlodar and Shymkent oil processing plants). Kazakhstan is dependent on Russia in the processing of more than 50 per cent oil. For instance, Shymkent and Pavlodar oil processing plants process western Siberian oil through Omsk and Chardjou (Turkmenistan) pipelines. Pavlodar oil processing plant is 100 per cent dependent on western Siberian oil. Usually Shymkent oil processing plant processes 75 per cent western Siberian and 25 per cent Kumkol oil. Atyrau oil processing plant processes 100 per cent Kazakhstani oil from Manghishlak, Tengiz, Martyshi. Built in 1978, Pavlador oil processing plant is the youngest plant among Kazakhstan's processing plants. The capacity of the plant is 7.5 million tons of oil in a year. The problem of Pavlodar oil processing plant is its technological dependence on western Siberian oil. It can process only western Siberian oil where sulfur and paraffin level is low. This makes it vulnerable to pressure and leverage from Russia, which can easily hamper work of Pavlodar oil processing plant by simply closing western Siberian oil supply.

Atyrau oil processing plant is one of the oldest plants in Kazakhstan. It was built in 1945. Unlike Shymkent and Pavlodar plants, Atyrau plant is oriented for local heavy oil. However, old equipment of the plant is not able to process oil to fit modern standards. The government is now renovating the plant. The renovation costs 1.2 billion US dollars. Since internal transportation is under developed and foreign companies are reluctant to invest in local oil processing plants, the local processing of oil still remains at low level.

Being a landlocked country, up to the year 2006 all energy transit routes led north to Russian territory. Thus, Kazakh oil flowed into Black Sea terminals through pipelines whence it was shipped to European destinations. Central Asian gas pipelines also headed north, supplying Russia and freeing up Russian gas for sale in Europe. However, the three new pipelines – CPC, BTC and the China pipeline have helped

Kazakhstan move away from Russian transit control to some extent. Developed by the joint efforts of the governments of Russia and Kazakhstan with the help of a consortium of international companies 1,500 kms CPC (Caspian Pipeline Consortium) connects Kazakhstan's Caspian Sea area oil deposits with Russia's Black Sea port of Novorossiysk. The pipeline has been functional since 2001 and its capacity is currently at 560,000 barrels a day. One third of Kazakhstan's oil exports – mainly from the Tengiz field – flow through this pipeline. The project costs two billion dollars. Chevron, BP-Amoco, Lukoil and Russian government (24% of share) along with Kazakh government (19%) are playing major role in this project.

As part of its efforts attempt to diversify routes in the northern dimension, Kazakhstan's Company "KazMunayGas" (KMG) took part in the bid for Lithuanian oil processing complex "Mazeiku nafta". It lost its bid to polish PKN Orlen. In spite of cordial relations with Russia, business remains business. Kazakhstan's ambition to enter the European market is not in Russian interest. It became evident when Russian "Transneft" refused to pump 12 million tons of Kazakh oil to Lithuania. This made KMG vulnerable in the above mentioned bid. The reason for Russian reluctance in expanding Kazakh presence in European market is that oil terminal in Buting loads 1.2 million tons of oil. KMG intended to increase it by 10 times, which would offer serious competition to Russian Baltic pipeline system and Russian oil supplies from Leningrad oblast ports.

However, Kazakhstan side is still striving to find its place in the Baltic region. It looks now for opportunities in Latvia. Even in the joint Caspian pipeline consortium, Kazakhstan could have problems. In May 2006, Russia announced that 24 per cent of Russian share could be given to "Transneft" which was in favour of increasing tariffs for Kazakhstan in order to limit Kazakhstan's access to European markets.

The BTC (Baku-Tbilisi-Ceyhan) pipeline, built at the behest of the United States by a consortium led by American oil companies is 1760 kilometer long. Kazakhstan's oil exports – mainly from the Kashaghan field would flow through this pipeline. So this provides an opportunity for the Kazakh oil to flow westwards. In 1999 Kazakhstan signed treaty to join the Baku-Tbilisi-Ceyhan project. The 50 million ton capacity of the pipeline enables Kazakhstan to export 25 million tons. The Eni-led consortium has been working on developing a transportation system at a cost of 4 billion US dollars. Thus BTC undermined "Transneft" monopoly in oil transportation and became a viable non-Russian option for Europe, which after the Ukraine experience, is cautious about excessive dependence of Europe on Russian energy supplies. For the US, whose companies have taken the initiative of unlocking the oil potential of the landlocked Caspian by building the BTC pipeline, Kazakh oil is an attractive alternative to move away from dependence on unstable Persian Gulf and lessen the Russian influence in the region. Aktau port is another way to bring Kazakh oil to BTC pipeline. The port has a capacity of transporting 8 to 9 million tons. Now Kazakhstan is constructing the second part of Aktau port which would provide for the transportation of 20 million tons. The upgrading and renovation of Aktau port cost about 242 million dollars.

Baku-Tbilisi-Ceyhan (BTC) was debatable issue for ten years. When on 5 June 2006, in Ceyhan, first 300,000 tons of Azeri oil flowed through BTC, it was the end of the debate. The pipeline, which is also called "Silk way of 21st century", links Azerbaijan, Georgia and Turkey. Today Kazakhstan is exporting 48 million tons of oil, and BTC together with CPC can transport 55 million tons of Kazakh oil. However, the oil extraction is growing and Kazakhstan needs more routes for transportation and the independence of its supply.

China has been always seen as a lucrative market for Kazakh oil. For China, whose oil consumption has grown enormously over the last few years, Kazakh oil represents a promise of supply diversification. China is considered to be the second oil consumer in the world. Its economy is booming and it desperately requires oil and gas to sustain its development. At present China is importing more than half of its oil from West Asia, which means that the U.S. navy based in West Asia can always close oil flowing to China. In this regard it is logical for China to look for opportunities to secure optional oil and gas supplies. Seizing the opportunity of its geographical location, China is investing in neighboring oil rich countries such as Kazakhstan and Russia. Taking into consideration that China was late comer in the region, China has been offering very lucrative deals in order to get access to resources of the region.

As a result, in July 2006 Kazakhstan oil began to flow to China. Atasu – Alashankou pipeline allows the export of 10 million tons of Kazakh oil to China. It is expected that western Siberian oil will increase Atasu-Alashankou pipeline capacity upto 20 million tonnes. New gas pipelines are under discussion. There are two options for the gas transportation. First it would require less investment if it is constructed on the base of Atasu-Alashankou oil pipeline infrastructure. Another option of constructing gas pipeline linking southern Kazakhstan, Uzbekistan and Turkmenistan, has been accomplished.

Another eastern pipeline to China links the onshore Kumkol oil fields in southern Kazakhstan which is also controlled by Chinese National Petroleum Corporation (CNPC) now. The first stretch of 988 kilometers has already been completed. Eventually, this pipeline will be 3000 km long and could initially deliver upto 200,000 barrels of oil daily to Xinjiang where oil will be processed and sent to other markets in China. Pipeline to China gains significance especially in "Transneft" issue. Kazakhstan exports 12 million tons through Russia. If we assume that these routes prove to be unreliable, it is possible to divert the oil to eastern direction. Now it is planned to expand the capacity of eastern pipelines to 15 million tons a year.

Southern route through Iran is capable of receiving 1.4 million tons, i.e., it is possible to export 5.9 million of tons which is 12 per cent of Kazakh oil exports. Iranian route is very interesting and lucrative option. Iran is ready to transport up to 12 million tons in the framework of swapping with Kazakhstan. The swapping arrangement implies that oil (2 to 6 million tons) would be transported from Aktau port to Iranian ports and later substituted by Iranian oil in Persian Gulf. Moreover,

Iran has been actively working on Kazakhstan-Turkmenistan-Iran pipeline project. This project would allow for Kazakh and Turkmen oil and gas to get access to Persian Gulf (Hark Island) and further to Pakistan, India and South-East Asian countries. However, this route is complex in political and security terms. The route is being opposed by the U.S. The American Congress forbids any American company to work with Iran. But it doesn't mean that it closes doors for other potential investors. Iranian project is supported by Total (France) and Japan. Turkmenistan on its part will possibly construct pipeline to Northern Iran. This will change the dimension of Iranian pipelines which are now transporting gas from Southern Iran to Northern and increase Caspian oil share in Arabian Sea.

Kazakhstan has always been in the forefront of opening up new export routes. "Kazmunaigaz" concluded an agreement with a Ukrainian company to set up a joint venture to build an extension pipeline to the Odessa-Brody-Gdansk line. The Kazakhstani oil thus be transported through sea route to Ukrainian port Yujnii and further to Yujnii –Brody (on the Polish-Ukrainian border). The oil terminal Yujnii near eastern coast of Grigorievskii coastal lake is ready to receive oil. Pipeline from Yujnii – Brody – "Drujba" pipeline is also being made. It is expected that total capacity of this route will be 40 million tons. However before this project takes off, issues such as the tanker marine have to be tackled. The Ukrainian route found support from American, Kazakhstani, Polish, and Azerbaijani and Georgian governments. Eventually, this pipeline will help Kazakhstan in taking the Caspian oil to European markets directly, a move that caused considerable concern in Moscow.[5] Another option is to link Atyrau-Samara and "Drujba" pipeline with other NIS and Baltic states.

India is the sixth largest energy consumer in the world. International Energy Agency estimates that by 2010, India will be importing 3.4 mbd of crude – 83 per cent of its consumption – if it has to maintain its current growth momentum. India's newly launched Integrated Energy Policy also estimates that India's oil demand will increase to at least 200 million tonnes by 2025. Crude imports account for around 75 per cent of India's domestic consumption. Supply disruptions, therefore, have serious implications for India. India's oil imports – as much as 68 per cent – come from the Gulf region. The proposals to build a pipeline from Iran to northern India via Pakistan, another one to bring Turkmenistan's gas via Afghanistan and Pakistan to India and a third one from Myanmar's Shwe gas fields to eastern India are still at negotiating stages. Until thorny relations with Pakistan and Bangladesh are sorted out, shipping will remain India's main energy lifeline.

For some years now, India's premier exploration and production company ONGC has been participating into overseas activities through its subsidiary ONGC Videsh Limited (OVL). The company now claims its presence in 12 countries. In Kazakhstan, OVL had submitted a bid for minority stake in Kurmangazy oil field which is being shared equally by Russia and Kazakhstan. However, this field, one of the largest offshore fields in the region, went to Total of France. Instead, OVL has been offered two other fields – Satbayev and Mukhambet – both medium sized.

Energy Pipelines Routes

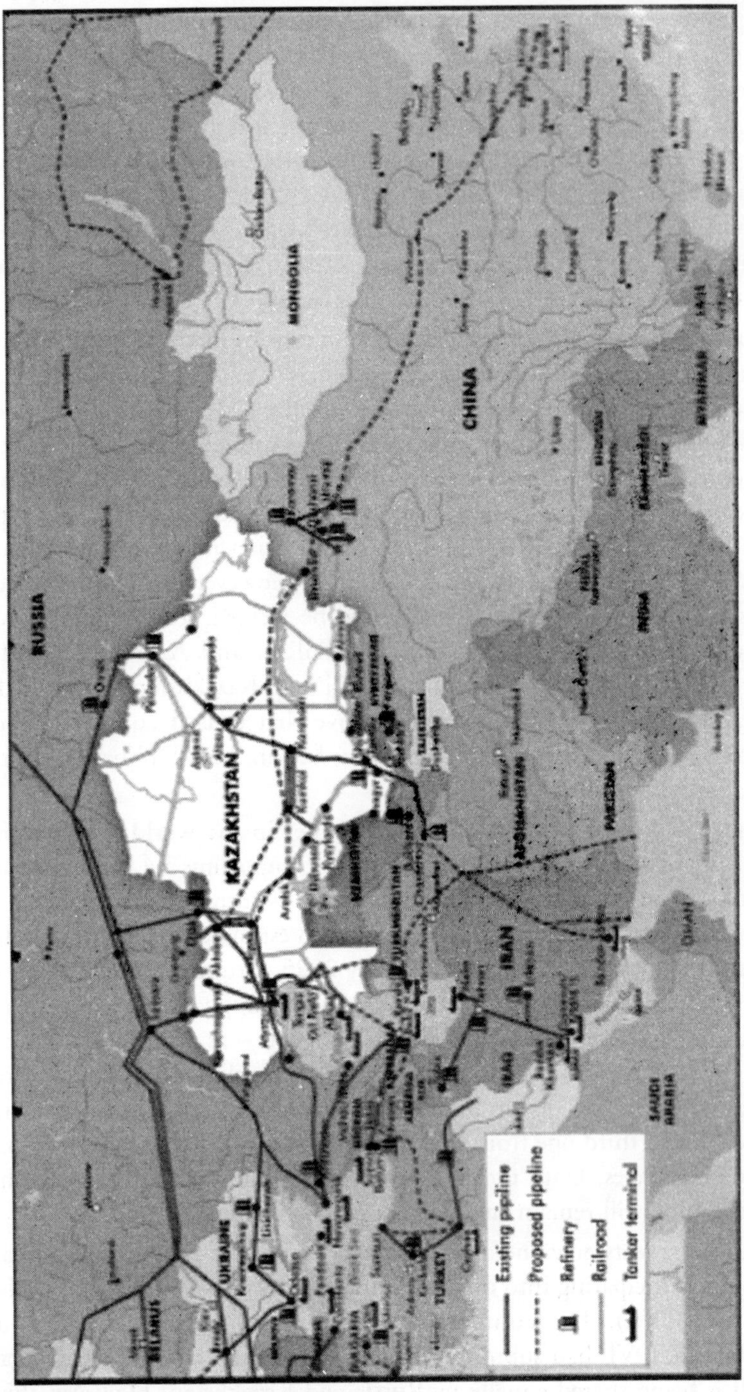

OVL had bid for another oil field owned by Petrokazakhstan in August 2005, but China's CNPC won the bid and acquired this field. Another example of successful cooperation is Mittal Group, which proved to be a flourishing company. It owns metallurgical plant and several coal mines in Karaganda oblast. The company has been interested in diversification and oil business in Kazakhstan. In December 2006, Lukoil Overseas signed an agreement with Mittal Investments (Mittal Investments is part of Mittal Group) on the sale of 50 per cent of chartered capital of Caspian Investments Resources Ltd., which owns Alibekmola, Kojasai, Severniyi Buzachi, Karakudu and Arman oilfields (in Aktobe oblast and Manghistau oblast).

Despite being located in Central Asia's extended neighbourood, India has been a late entrant into the grand oil game, owing to a variety of factors. First, the Persian Gulf is the most near and, therefore, a natural supply source for India which gets as much as two thirds of its imports from the Persian Gulf. However, in order to diversify its oil supply India needs to look beyond Persian Gulf in future. Second, the ongoing developments in the Persian Gulf made oil installations particularly vulnerable to terrorist attacks which can lead to serious supply disruptions.

India is now looking for more opportunities in the region and in Kazakhstan. It has acquired an Observer status in SCO, and has shown interest in such mega projects as "Iran-Pakistan-India" and "Turkmenistan-Afghanistan-Pakistan" pipeline. These pipeline projects are being discussed since 1995. The "Turkmenistan-Afghanistan-Pakistan" pipeline consortium comprises of Unocal-Delta, Turkmengas, Gazprom, Huyndai Co, Itochu Japan, Krefing Pakistan. The pipeline would have 1,300 km length with a capacity of 20 billion cms a year. The capacity could be increased by 60 billion cms a year after its extension to India. However, the project stands frozen because of the volatile situation in Afghanistan.

Central Asian energy resources and especially Kazakh oil could play a vital role in helping India diversify its sources of oil supply and thus enhance its energy security. In fact, thanks to the BTC pipeline, Kazakh oil has begun to flow into India as well. In 2005, India's BPCL purchased a consignment of Kazakh oil at the Mediterranean port and shipped it through the Suez Canal to Mumbai. During his tenure in the ministry, former Petroleum minister of India, Mani Shankar Aiyar had proposed a pipeline from Iran's Neka terminal all the way to Bander Abbas to be built in Iran with Indian participation. This would allow Kazakh oil to be loaded at Neka and sent through pipeline to the southern coast of Iran from where it could be shipped to refineries in western India. While international companies might be shy of investing in Iran on account of the somewhat volatile international situation, Indian companies can undertake this project in collaboration with Iranian companies and possibly Russia's Gazprom, After all, the latter is willing to participate in the Iran-Pakistan-India gas pipeline. Russia might have less objections to routing Kazakh oil to India than to the west through the BTC pipeline.[6] In this context, experts believe that it is in Russian interests to involve India in the region in order to counter balance American and Chinese influence. India could possibly collaborate with Kazakhstan in setting up refinery and processing plants. Similarly, Indian companies can also participate in downstream petrochemical and fertilizer sectors to add value to gas from Kazakhstan's offshore fields.

Kazakhstan has the third largest natural uranium deposits – as much as a fifth of global reserves. India can have access to uranium supplies from members of the Nuclear Suppliers' Group of which Kazakhstan is a member. Moreover, India could cooperate in building Kazakh atomic energy industry which is now supported mainly by Russia.

The Central Asian Republics and Caspian countries are now aware of their huge energy potential which can play a vital role in their development and independence. According to the *Statistical Review of World Energy*, Kazakhstan, Azerbaijan and Turkmenistan have 16.5 billion barrels of oil and gas and Uzbekistan has 202 billion cubic m.[7] By 2010 it is estimated that extraction will grow by 3.8 barrels of oil which is 38 per cent of what is extracted today in Northern Sea. Growing significance of Caspian region led the Assembly of Council of Europe to declare Caspian Sea as centre of European energy security. They are also putting in place investment regimes with a view to attract latest technology and financing to unlock their hydrocarbon potential. The context and timing is ripe, therefore, for India, with its acute vulnerability caused by huge and growing dependence on imported energy to turn to its extended neighbourhood in Central Asia for alternate sources of supply.

## ENDNOTES

1. *Strategy 2030*, October 1997, p. 12.
2. EIA Country Analysis Brief, Kazakhstan, July 2005. http://www.eia.doe.gov/emeu/cabs/kazak.html
3. Sudha Mahalingam, *India – Kazakhstan: Building Energy Bridges*, 2006.
4. Atasu-Alashankou Pipeline Cements Strategic Alliance between Beijing and Astana – http://jamestown.org/edm/article.php?article_id=2370620
5. Sudha Mahalingam, op. cit.
6. Integrated Energy Policy Report of the Expert Committee, Indian Planning Commission, August 2006, p. 24.
7. British Petroleum, *Statistical Review of World Energy*, 2004.

# 7

# Kazakhstan's Energy Policy and Cooperation with India

*Oxana Dolzhikova*

Energy collaboration is one of the major components of active partnership between India and newly emerged Central Asian Republics (CARs). Access to regional energy is important for India, which consumes 1.9 million barrels of oil a day, with 70 per cent of it being imported, and this is set to rise to four million barrels a day by the year 2010. However, India is not as well placed as Russia and China since it does not have a direct border with any of the Central Asian Republics. Indian Prime Minister, Dr. Manmohan Singh had warned in 2005 that "China is ahead of us in planning for its energy security – India can no longer be complacent."

During the last few years, New Delhi has been seeking access to Kazakh oil and gas and participation in mega projects like the Iran-Pakistan-India pipeline and another one linking Turkmenistan, Afghanistan, Pakistan and India. But the Indo-Pak rivalry and security concerns have made these projects more difficult to complete.

India has increased energy cooperation with its long-standing military and political ally Russia, investing in oil and gas exploration in Russia's Sakhalin Island and in the joint Russian-Kazakh Kurmangazy oilfield in the Caspian Sea. Experts argue that Russia has a vested interest in increasing its cooperation with India and China because it can keep the United States out of the Central Asian orbit.

Besides simple geographical difficulties such as the absence of boundaries and extensive distance between Kazakhstan and India, there are a number of geopolitical obstacles. However, both countries must press towards the development of energy cooperation, since it will bring benefit to both of them. India, first of all, will be able to partially satisfy its energy needs, and Kazakhstan will secure alternative access to the international energy markets.

India's intensive energy diplomacy is being observed in Kazakhstan with great interest. Kazakhstan's experts maintain that diplomacy is directed not so much towards the search for new channels of energy supply, but more towards the formation of a new energy structure in the world based on the so-called "Pan-Asian Solidarity". In essence, it implies construction of a Pan-Asian gas supply system passing through Asia and supplying energy resources from the centres of production to the consumer nations for stimulating development. The supporters of "Pan-Asian Solidarity" look at such an organization as most profitable because it can provide guaranteed markets to the producing countries and guaranteed supply to the importing countries on a long term basis. According to them, Kazakhstan – the biggest producer of energy resources in Central Asia – will derive huge benefits by participating in this process.

In general, India considers cooperation with Kazakhstan in the oil and gas sector as a major factor in bilateral relations. India intends to participate in the exploration and development of Kazakhstan's oil and gas field. The Indian side would be particularly willing to take part in exploration and estimation of the technical possibilities of new fields in the Caspian Sea, as also increasing the output of oil and gas from existing fields. India is also interested in cooperating with Kazakh companies to upgrade the existing oil refineries and also set up new ones.

While debating Kazakhstan-India relationship in the energy sector, emphasis must be given to the role of Kazakhstan in providing global energy security. The fuel and energy complex of Kazakhstan, as well as national economy as a whole, has been developing at a high rate, contributing to the total domestic product with an annual growth rate of 8 to 9 per cent for the last few years.

Meanwhile, for determining the role of Kazakhstan in providing the global energy security, it is necessary to reveal basic threats, which would be encountered in the next decades in the field of power engineering. Thus, it will be easy to show the place and role of Kazakhstan in the resistance to contemporary threats of global energy security. This threat consists of two components.

- High and growing tension in the energy market in view of the anticipating increase in global demand. This risk may lead to the appearance of the sequential (third) exponential curve of the raise in the world energy consumption. As a result of the last wave, which ended in the middle of 1990s, world energy consumption increased five-fold.
- Another danger consists in the reduction of volumes of the produced energy. At this stage, the decrease of supply on the world energy market can occur not because of the general shortage of energy resources, but as a result of the reduction of possibility of the growth of the energy production. This is caused by essential complication such as rise in price of the utilized technologies and by anticipating increase in the required infrastructure with the mastery of even more inaccessible energy resources.

In this context, the problem of attraction of large-scale investments into power engineering for guaranteeing the necessary level of production and transport of energy resources should be especially emphasized. According to the International Energy Agency (IEA) estimates, power engineering will require an investment of 17 trillion dollars up to 2030. In this case, two-third of investments is necessary for the substitution of the existing power, and one-third for creating new power.

The absence of investments directly into providing global energy security is also one of the most serious problems. As a result, reserve production capacities comprise only 2 per cent of the world oil consumption. Few years ago, this index comprised of 10 per cent. This shows that any disruption in oil supply, leads to sharp increase in prices.

Thus, the role of Kazakhstan in meeting the global energy demand is bound to increase. For example, if in recent years 33 of 48 most important oil producers (including six countries of eleven OPEC members) reduced their production of oil or at best remained at the previous level, in Kazakhstan the level of output of oil increased yearly by 15 per cent from 1999 through 2004. Kazakhstan ranks among ten leading countries in the world, ranks second after the Russian Federation among all the CIS countries for its hydrocarbon reserves and Kazakhstan ranks 15th in the world in terms of explored reserves of natural gas.

Approved by State Committee on Resources (SCR), recoverable hydrocarbon reserves of Kazakhstan include:

- Oil and gas condensate – 4.8 billion tons (35 billion barrels);
- Gas – 3.4 trillion cubic meters.

The largest explored reserves of associated gas are concentrated in Karachaganak, Tengiz and Zhanazhol.

With its low domestic consumption of the obtained hydrocarbon resources, Kazakhstan has become one of the most important producers and exporters of oil in the world. It should be noted that during last few years, Kazakhstan has catapulted to second place in the world on account of the rate of gain in the volumes of its oil exports. At present, Kazakhstan extracts 1.3 million barrels of oil per day and exports more than one million barrels. It is expected that the output will reach 3.5 million barrels of oil per day by the year 2015, out of which 3 million barrels will be exported. Thus, Kazakhstan will be among the ten most important producers of oil worldwide.

The largest oilfield (Kashagan) in the world in the last 25 years was found in Kazakhstan. Kashagan deposit in the north of Caspian Sea brings Kazakhstan close to a number of the leading countries in the world possessing hydrocarbon resources. This has attracted enormous interest from all around the world to the Caspian region, and in particular has increased investment in Kazakhstan. The share of Kazakhstan in the worldwide investigated oil stockpiles is 3.2 per cent (7th place in the world), gas – 1.5 per cent, coal – 3.1 per cent (6th place), uranium – 18.9 per cent (2nd place).

According to a Decree No. 1095 of the President of the Republic of Kazakhstan dated 16 May 2003, the State Programme for Development of Kazakhstan Sector of Caspian Sea (KSCS) was approved. The Programme is built on the principles of international mutually beneficial cooperation and respect of the interests of

Kazakhstan, mitigation of risks in awarding the contracts to use mineral resources, compliance with international standards and ensuring the environmental safety of the Caspian region. The main objectives of the Programme include stabilization of high extraction level and development of relevant infrastructure, development of domestic production and scientific-technical basis, training of highly skilled human resources and the comprehensive use of the Caspian resources in developing other sectors of the country's economy.

The first phase of the Programme (2003-05) created conditions for comprehensive development of KSCS and the second phase (2006-10) accelerated this process. The Ministry of Energy and Mineral Resources of Kazakhstan developed a Plan of Actions for development of KSCS for the second phase of the programme. In 2005, the first well on Tub-Karagan site was drilled, and preparation works for drilling on Atashski site were initiated. The competent body prepares Product Sharing Agreement with Oman Oil Company on Pearl deposit and with KazMunaiGaz and Rostneft on Kurmangazy structure. For an effective realization of large scale oil-and-gas projects in KSCS, there is need for advanced formation and development of a modern industrial and social infrastructure.

To expedite the process, a Comprehensive Development Plan for Coastal Line of KSCS determining the measures for coastal support, processing enterprises, zone of land outputs of sea pipelines and safe storage of waste products and other objects necessary for sub-soil users are being developed and authorized. The Comprehensive Plan provides the basic direction and stages of development, besides determining the list, capacities, sequence of creation and accommodation of objects of a coastal oil-and-gas infrastructure. Infrastructural objects which should be created by 2015, with forecast estimation of units cost are described, including:

- System of coastal bases support;
- Ground communications (railways, motorways, communication, electrification, water supply and others);
- Development of ports Aktau, Bautino and Kuryk for trans-shipment of large cargoes;
- Deepening of a river mouth of Ural river;
- The processing enterprises, manufactures on repair and release of special floating craft at domestic machine-building factories;
- Zones of an output(exit) on land of sea pipelines; and
- Objects on safe storage of waste products.

At present, the large part of the world's supplies of oil and gas is concentrated in the states which do not recognize market relations. According to PFC Energy, 77 per cent of the world's oil supplies is under control of the states through their national companies. The tendency of state-exporters to monopolize their energy markets of their countries has been recently observed. This circumstance negatively affects the possibility, in the first place, of an increase in production and obtaining power in view of the absence of the necessary investments, and in the second place, the introduction of innovative technologies. Furthermore, this also leads to the fact that the selection of export routes is often determined not by economic or market considerations, but by geopolitical preferences.

In this backdrop, the energy market of Kazakhstan is transparent and open for the participation of external players; favourable investment climate has been created recently. As many experts note, energy market of Kazakhstan became the most important destination for foreign investments since the large petroleum deposits were found in the North Sea. During the last 15 years, 50 billion US dollars of direct foreign investments were drawn into the country, large part (80 per cent) of which entered into the field of output and processing of hydrocarbon raw material. Today, according to the World Bank estimates, Kazakhstan is among the top twenty most attractive investment friendly countries.

Consequently, Kazakhstan emerged as a responsible and reliable supplier of energy resources contributing to the energy balance in the world economy. P. Simons, the Deputy Secretary of US Department of State, while describing the importance of international power engineering stated that Kazakhstan has all the potential for becoming the elite supplier of energy resources in the coming decades.

Another serious threat to energy security is the growth of regional energy disproportions, which is manifested in an increase of a number of countries and regions, which have not achieved development despite huge energy resources. In 1990, such countries produced 87 per cent of world GDP, which is nowadays 90 per cent. Thus, the focus is on the development of energy infrastructure, which plays an important role in providing global energy security. On the basis of this, it can be summed up that the role of Kazakhstan is not limited to the functions of the supplier of its own energy resources. Kazakhstan is an important part of the system of global energy infrastructure.

Situated between the most important energy consuming countries and the countries possessing richest energy reserves in the neighbourhood, Kazakhstan has the potential to serve as a major transit state. However, it is necessary for Kazakhstan to develop the necessary energy infrastructure as the country does not possess straight access to the deep water seaports. This hampers the access of Kazakhstan to the world market for hydrocarbons. Furthermore, one should emphasize that Kazakhstan's multi-vector policy of export development is an important contribution to the development of global energy infrastructure. This also contributes to a certain reduction of global dependence on the Middle East oil.

Putting into operation of 1,000 kilometer Atasu-Alashankou oil pipeline with a carrying capacity of 20 million tons of oil per year; joining of Kazakhstan to the project of Baku-Tbilisi-Ceyhan on which it will pass 7.5 to 10 million tons of oil per year with a further increase up to 25 million tons of oil per year; the development of north-Caspian oil pipeline and an increase of its capacity from 23 to 60 million tons are evidence of the intensive work, conducted by Kazakhstan on the development of new export routes. It is worthwhile to emphasize that the

Kazakhstan-China oil pipeline will provide Kazakhstan access to the foreign oil stockpiles. Russian oil will also be supplied along this pipeline to China.

Reduction in the oil-refining output is one of the serious threats to the global energy security. For the last ten years, the production of oil grows by higher rates than the capacity for its processing. There is not only a deficiency in the oil refineries, but it has also increased. With the retention of this tendency, the shortage of the reserve processing power will become one of the main factors contributing to an increase in the oil consumption. High prices of the oil are, to a considerable extent, caused by a deficiency in the investments into the processing fields and also by ecological pulls and pressures. Thus, a simple increase in oil production is incapable to satisfy the growing demand for energy resources. An increase in highly technological processing capacities becomes one of the most important conditions for providing global energy security.

Another serious threat to the global energy security is the absence of the progress in the diversification of power supply due to the new sources of energy and technologies. According to International Energy Agency (IEA) forecast, an increase in the world needs for the energy resources into the next 25 years will be mostly met by the mineral resources. Experts forecast that a drop in oil and gas production will begin in 2030. So, in the long-term outlook, the existing hydrocarbon raw materials will fail to satisfy an increase in the consumption of energy resources. In this connection, the only key to the global energy security is the development of low-carbon alternative and renewable kind of energy and also innovation of energy technologies.

The development of atomic and thermo-nuclear power engineering has shown a promising trend in the development of the alternative energy sources. Kazakhstan, which occupies second place in the world in the reserves of uranium, has enormous potential to enter into the league of uranium raw material suppliers in the world market, and soon will become the most important country in the atomic power engineering sector.

It is expected that the overall scarcity of uranium raw material will grow up to 16 thousand tons during next six years. Taking into account that in 2010 Kazakhstan plans to increase the output of uranium raw material up to 15 thousand tons per year, the country will make an important contribution to the world market. It is necessary to note that Kazakhstan has great advantages over other producers of uranium. First, Kazakhstan possesses all types of uranium production, and second, with the presence of the unique technologies of development via underground drilling leaching, Kazakhstan is able to obtain uranium at a very low cost.

Kazakhstan possesses the technologies of the production of fuel "tablets" for the Russian reactors at present. Therefore, at this stage, the adjustment of strategic partnership with foreign companies to produce nuclear fuel for the Western type of reactors is extremely important for Kazakhstan. The export prospects of Kazakhstan in the sphere of development of uranium fields are determined by the intention of the increasing number of countries to actively develop atomic power engineering into the next 20 years. It is possible to include India among these countries, which plans to build some 30 atomic power units.

Taking into account that the reserves of uranium are distributed throughout the world even more unevenly than oil and gas, access to the uranium reserves in the next decades will become strategically one of most important questions in providing global energy security. The strategic role of uranium raw material in the world will only grow with the passage of power engineering to the priority of ecological component. Therefore, for Kazakhstan, adherence to an independent uranium policy is an important priority.

Simultaneously, Kazakhstan works on the development of its own atomic power engineering. At present, scientists work on the creation of reactor of relatively low power (70 megawatts) conducted in the Nuclear Technology Parks in Kurchatov. This project focuses on transfer of technologies, the possession of which will allow the country not only to create its own industry, but also to contribute to the development of atomic power engineering in third countries by building nuclear power plants.

An analysis of threats to energy security makes it clear that each of the parties showing interest in energy cooperation has their particular vision of collaboration, giving preference to their national interests. It is obvious that the process of achievement of understanding in such a delicate sphere as energy politics is very complicated, especially if one considers that several countries have competing interests with their energy partners in other spheres of interaction. China, for example, is interested in the unlimited delivery of hydrocarbons into its intensively developing regions. China also feels convenient to "strive" for participation in Central Asian projects rather than taking interest in Russian petroleum and gas products. Russia has been tightening government control over the energy activities and showing big interest in Eastern markets.

Kazakhstan's attempts to appear in Asian markets diversifying its export flows have caused growing concern in Russia. However, Kazakhstan is not in a hurry to push through the routes in the direction of China. It has been making attempts to preserve the potential of establishing the economic balance with China, which is perhaps, one of the key opportunities for India. The presence of energy resources in Kazakhstan precisely determines the prospects and the parameters of economic collaboration and cooperation between India and Kazakhstan in other spheres. The parameters of energy dialogue are sufficiently complicated to be determined in view of powerful political "tying". It seems that the stumbling block in the fuel-energy collaboration between Kazakhstan and India is the absence of the harmonized principles of cooperation.

Besides China and Russia, two more countries – Iran and United States – stand between Kazakhstan-India energy cooperation. Apparently, China is the most important importer of Iranian oil and gas. In accordance with the bilateral agreement between Beijing and Tehran, in the next 25 years, China will invest 100 billion US dollars in the energy sector of Iran, and thus will ensure access to its resources. On the other hand, Iran has made a proposal to Russia to regulate the prices and flow of natural gas. In 2006 Gazprom declared its readiness to participate in the construction of Iran-India gas pipeline.

It is, therefore, imperative to solve the following problems in order to promote energy cooperation between Kazakhstan and India:

- Deviation from the principle, when the policy of interaction in the energy field is conducted exclusively within the framework of realization of particular interests of national companies and transnational corporations. The clash of their interests for energy markets frequently leads to a situation when strategic interests of countries do not obtain adequate consideration and, in practice, they are not realised. Furthermore, the policy of several national companies and transnational corporations is used for the satisfaction of a number of other purposes, i.e., it serves like a tool.
- While promoting Indo-Kazakhstan energy cooperation, one needs to stress the fact that outstanding successes in the development of the energy sector of Kazakhstan became possible in many respects because of the significant foreign capital investments. For example, United States became the first foreign partner of Kazakhstan in the sphere of power engineering. The energy partnership between two countries successfully developed from the time of Kazakhstan's independence. Until today it is one of the most important components of bilateral relations. Energy cooperation of Kazakhstan and India must cover such directions as oil production and gas, atomic power engineering, production of electricity and the development of the promising sources of the renewed energy. From that point of view, it is clear that Kazakhstan is interested in the further extension of Indian investments especially the technical know-how into the energy sector of the country.
- Earlier, Indian interests in Kazakhstan in essence were concentrated on the petroleum sector. In future, Indian investors might be interested in petrochemical and transport sectors. The interests of Indian investors in the sphere of petrochemicals and petroleum refining would be beneficial for Kazakhstan, since the development of these branches has a key value for increasing international competitive ability of the country. It is expected that production of Kazakh petrochemicals will be on high demand in the domestic market and also in the adjacent developing markets.
- But the question remains that whether the potential Indian investors can be better and competitive than investors from other countries. In this situation, it is expedient to create links in petrochemical productions, i.e., not only output, both in extraction and processing of raw material, but the development of sideline production base and infrastructure. India must count on similar possibilities, in developing concrete fields.
- Furthermore, in near future, the development of oil-producing industries

using the sea technologies will be important for Kazakhstan. Besides that, utilization of ecologically sound technologies will gradually change the situation in favour of one or another investor. India can propose to Kazakhstan for the joint creation of oil-refining industries using the latest technologies.

Generally, income from the joint Kazakhstan-India exploration of energy resources of Kazakhstan and construction of the developed energy industry and infrastructure can lead to the regional economic growth as a whole. The energy partnership of Kazakhstan and India can play an important role in this sphere. With this, Kazakhstan will become a leader in the region for the development of the infrastructure in energy sector, and also for creating the additional transit routes for energy resources.

# 8

# Indo-Kazakh Cooperation in Kazakhstan's Oil and Gas Sector

*Yelena I. Rudenko*

Current level of achievements in science and technology still keeps humankind highly dependent on usage of hydrocarbons in its multifold development. Economic performance of a country is linked to a considerable degree to the fact of either possession of hydrocarbon resources within its own territory (that is mostly considered as the best option), or its ability to have an access to such resources existing on the territory of any other country (the favorability of this option is determined by the degree of control over such "outside" resources in order to have their smooth and uninterrupted supply). Moreover, these two options increasingly influence not only economic, but also political performance of countries and their overall position at the international level. As such, countries which need hydrocarbons have been making strong efforts to get more access to it, while possessors of this valuable resource endeavor to lay down more strict terms for its provision. This interaction of contrary interests in many respects determines the actual alignment of powers in the global scale as well as international prestige of the concerned country.

Nowadays Central Asian countries and, in particular, Kazakhstan, have become one of the most important center of struggle for such prestige. A number of countries from far and near have entered this region, and even more countries are looking for the opportunity of doing the same. However, the situation is clear – the more countries try to come here, the more severe competition will develop between them, and the more struggle each one of these countries should undergo in order to prove its preemptive right over others in getting access to the hydrocarbon resources of the region.

India is one of the most active and, hence, one of the most relevant countries among these that seek their due place in Kazakhstan's oil and gas fields. India's energy requirement and its current state of virtually rising power, in many respects give this country a real opportunity of being an important strategic partner of Kazakhstan on mutually beneficial basis. In this paper, its author focuses only on the prospects of India-Kazakhstan relations in this sphere and excludes other hydrocarbons-possessing states of Central Asia.

Firstly, what is the potential of the two countries in energy cooperation, in other words, what Kazakhstan and India could offer each other. Kazakhstan's strategic hydrocarbon resource is important for Indian energy security. Kazakhstan's oil-and-gas potential is more then considerable in the overall volume of the world hydrocarbon reserves. During more than a hundred years history of Kazakhstan's oil-and-gas industry, over 250 oil and gas fields have been discovered in the country, of which more than 100 fields are under commercial development. Oil and gas bearing regions of Kazakhstan occupy an area of about 1.8 million square kilometers, the part of which lies in the waters of the Caspian Sea and Aral Sea. In Kazakhstan's continental part, there are over 160 discovered fields. Main hydrocarbon reserves are concentrated in Atyrau oblast numbering over 80 fields. Over 45 fields are at the stage of preparatory work and commercial development, and over 20 more fields are under supplementary exploration.

According to the last estimates, the proven reserves of oil only in Kazakhstan's sector of Caspian Sea have increased twice during last few years and now come to 124.3 billion barrels, or 17 billion tons on average (while overall petroleum reserves exceed 25 billion tons). The prospective hydrocarbon reserves on the newly explored sites only are estimated at over 2 billion tons of the oil equivalent. This means that in case of maintenance of current rates of petroleum production, Kazakhstan will exploit its petroleum reserves for the period of 83 years as compared to 42 years in case of Saudi Arabia. Such indicators rank Kazakhstan among the chief oil-producing countries at 13$^{th}$ position in the world.

The rate of petroleum production in Kazakhstan increases year by year (starting from 1999 Kazakhstan has strongly taken the first place according to the average annual increase of oil and gas condensate production). By the end of 2005, the overall extraction of oil and gas condensate came to 61.4 million tons (while in 2003 it was 50 million tons), including 51.2 million tons of oil and 10.2 million tons of gas condensate. During January-July 2006 production of oil and gas condensate in Kazakhstan amounted to 42,595,737 tons, of which gas condensate formed 3,686,113 tons.

Moreover, it is planned within the next few years to increase considerably the volume of petroleum production. If it came to 1.3 million barrels per day (61.4 million tons per year) in 2005, it is anticipated to increase up to 2.4 million barrels per day (118 million tons per year) by 2010 and to 3.6 million barrels per day (180 million tons per year) by 2015. Hence, during the next few years Kazakhstan is going to be among the ten leading global exporters of oil.

As regards explored reserves of natural gas, Kazakhstan holds the fifteenth place in the world and the fourth among CIS countries. Kashagan oil-gas field contains the main reserve of natural gas. Its probable geological resources amount up to 3 trillion cubic meters, including producible resources of 1 trillion cubic meters. Overall Kazakhstan's expected gas reserves considering the Caspian Sea Shelf are estimated at 8.3 trillion cubic meters, including explored reserves of about 2 trillion cubic meters. In 2005, volume of gas production was 28.7 billion cubic meters. It is planned to increase the overall gas recovery and production up to 35 billion cubic meters per year by 2010 and 40-45 billion cubic meters per year by 2015 (together with re-injected gas – up to 80 billion cubic meters). The representatives of Kazakhstan's Ministry of Energy and Mineral Resources believe such predictions to be quite realistic, being based on the volumes of established resources of hydrocarbons in Kazakhstan as well as on the rates of its gas-and-oil producing industry development.

Currently there are over 250 proven oil-and-gas fields in Kazakhstan. Among the first-rate fields there are Tengiz oil field (with over 2.26 billion tons of total oil reserves and 1 billion tons of producible reserves), Kashagan field (2.023 billion tons of producible oil), and Karachaganak (now officially Karashyganak) oil-gas condensate field (over 1.3 billion tons of gas and producible condensed fluid reserves of 700 million tons), as well as large-scale fields of Aktoty (269 million tons), Kairan (150 million tons), Kalamkas-more (159 million tons), Karazhanbas (over 53.5 million tons of producible oil), Kenbay (30.9 million tons), Uzen, Kumkol, Zhetybai, Zhanazhol, etc.

Among the leading oil-and-gas companies in Kazakhstan there are "Tengizchevroil Ltd." (with volume of crude oil production at 13.56 million tons), "Karachaganak Petroleum Operating BV" (10.32 million tons), "KazMunayGas National Joint-Stock Company" (9.39 million tons), as well as "Agip KCO", "Aktobemunaigaz", "Mangystaumunaigaz", "Karazhanbasmunaigaz" etc.

Almost all the oil and gas fields in Kazakhstan are being explored and developed with foreign experience and investments. Foreign finances participate in about 30 major projects including prospect drillings, oil and gas fields' development, modernization of refineries, hydrocarbons transportation. Nearly 224 contracts have been made in this sphere. Among the main importers of Kazakhstan's oil, gas and petroleum products are Russia, Ukraine, Great Britain, Switzerland and Italy.

Oil-and-gas industry of Kazakhstan for a long time has been represented by the "KazakhOil" National Company. The main responsibilities of the Company are: representation and protection of public interests on the side of the Republic of Kazakhstan in various agreements on exploration, production and refining of hydrocarbon resources, formation of the oil and gas fields management system, development and implementation of conversion and privatization programmes in oil-and-gas industry etc. Since the year 2002, all these functions belong to the integrated "KazMunayGas National Closed Joint-Stock Company" – the third large producer of oil and gas and the main public mega-enterprise in this sphere in Kazakhstan. It has a vertically integrated structure comprising of over 45 companies and enterprises of complementary profiles engaged in various sectors that make up the full cycle of work and services for the exploration, production, processing, transportation, and sale of hydrocarbons, as well as construction of objects for oil-and-gas industry, telecommunications and transport infrastructure. Among others, it contains such sub-units as "Razvedka Dobycha KazMunayGas JSC" ("KazMunayGas Exploration and Production"); "KazTransOil JSC" and "KazTransGaz JSC" (overall oil and gas transportation); "KazMunaiTengiz JSC" and "KazMorTransflot JSC" (maritime production and transportation of oil); "KazMunayGas Trade House", "Kazakhoil-Petrol LLC" and "Kazakholi Products LLC" (marketing and sale); "Kazakhoilkurylys LLC" (oil-and-gas infrastructure construction); "TengizService", "KazMunayGasService", "KazMunayGas-Consulting JSC", "KazMunayGas Finance BV", "Rauan Media Group", "Kazakh Contract Agency JSC", "Tenge LLC Joint Venture", "Zhambai LLC", "Kazakhoil Aktobe LLC", "Kazakhturkmunai" etc., as well as air communication lines ("Atyrau International Airport OJSC" and "Euro-Asia Air OJSC") and a network of in-house scientific-research centers in the sphere of overall hydrocarbons handling (including "Kazakh Oil and Gas Institute JSC" and "Unified Centre for Personnel Development"). The government of Kazakhstan solely owns "KazMunayGas". In February 2002, the government issued a Directive according to which the Company became the authorized public body in the Production Sharing Agreement on Karachaganak and North Caspian projects. Since that time, "KazMunayGas" coordinates operations and participates directly in the program of Karachaganak and Kalamkas-More fields' commercial development. It is also the shareholder of foreign oil-and-gas operators in Kazakhstan. For example, it holds 20 per cent stock of "Tengizchevroil Joint Venture Ltd". According to the Governmental Resolution on "KazMunayGas National Joint-Stock Company" future activity, it will share at least 50 per cent of share holding of every newly developed oil and/or gas field. Besides, "KazMunayGas" provides an active involvement of local goods producers and suppliers in the realization of offshore oil and gas operations, and makes sure that both national and international environmental, human health and safety regulations and standards are adhered to.[1]

In January 2006, the new National Holding Company "Samruk" was created in Kazakhstan. This company is expected to include the public share of "KazMunayGas" and hence the oil-and-gas sphere in Kazakhstan will shift towards even greater public control.[2] Incidentally, overall recoverable subsoil reserves of Kazakhstan included into the state balance are valued at $3.5 trillion.

In view of the strategic necessity of highly balanced completion of hydrocarbon fields in the Caspian Sea, a Government Programme of Kazakhstan's Sector of Caspian Sea Development was introduced. This Program provides for the following three stages of the Caspian region development. Stage 1 (2003-05, investments of $3.8 billion) included creation of conditions for complex development, a comprehensive environmental impact assessment of oil operations, development of infrastructure and training of Kazakhstan's personnel; at this stage it was planned to continue works at license blocks, to form information packages and hold discussions on tender blocks. Stage 2 (2006-2010, $12.9 billion) is connected with accelerated development; it seeks to increase production of hydrocarbons, to continue explorations, to retrain local staff and put the export oil pipeline into operation.

Stage 3 (2011-15, $16.8 billion) is related to the stabilization of production; it is planned to stabilize offshore production, to launch additional facilities for export transportation of hydrocarbons and to take natural recovery actions.

As a whole, first phase of the Program for the years 2003-05 has been completed and the second phase of years 2006-10, accelerated the rates of hydrocarbons development. A general plan has been developed for creating 8 to 10 petrochemical complexes in Kazakhstan until 2015.

This is what Kazakhstan has and which it is of interest to India for. And what, in its turn, India can offer to Kazakhstan?

As regards the necessity of India for Kazakhstan, India has both the opportunity and desire to pay for Kazakhstan's hydrocarbons not only in currency, as almost all other countries do, but also in its breakthroughs – technology and good experience. Indian high techs and info tech, is required by Kazakhstan. Opportunities for cooperation in this sphere are growing as Kazakhstan develops its respective infrastructure (IT parks etc.). Actually, India has already taken its worthy place in Kazakhstan's "knowledge economy" and now should only expand its presence in this sphere. There are also opportunities for India in the spheres of cotton industry, pharmaceuticals, agriculture, different kinds of training,[3] environmental tourism development etc. There is need to advertise and formulate intents for expansion of India's participation in such dimensions of Kazakhstan's developing economy and social life.

As regards India's immediate opportunities in oil-and-gas industry, one should mention prolongation of petroleum production on worked-out deposits, pipelines and refineries construction etc. (which, in fact, has already been more than once offered by India to Kazakhstan).

However, all these possibilities and perspectives in many respects stay quiescent. There are direct and indirect reasons of this situation. Among the direct reasons, firstly, India does not have direct and immediate access to Kazakhstan, including its oil and gas fields.

Though Kazakhstan's strategy of oil and gas transportation is based on the concept of multiple directions, and the South (Kazakhstan-Turkmenistan-Iran) option is considered as a priority along with West (Kazakhstan-Azerbaijan-Georgia-Turkey) and East (Kazakhstan-China's Pacific coast) options, still the first option appears to be the most uncertain and remote. And despite the statements of Kazakhstan's political scientists about the port of Gwadar in Pakistan, which offers Kazakhstan great prospects for transportation of its products, including hydrocarbons, towards South Asia as well as world markets by Indian Ocean, they do not deny the challenges of instability in Afghanistan and in India-Pakistan relations.[4]

This problem is aggravated with rather different approach to the ways of its solution. Indian scholars and decision-makers consider three main options of North-South hydrocarbons transport corridor from Kazakhstan to India. These are: (i) to let Central Asian Republics and Iran tackle this matter in real earnest and/or wait for stabilization of situation in Afghanistan and India-Pakistan relations; (ii) there is no hope about the functioning of such transport corridor even in future, so one may think of more realizable options; (iii) not to wait and not to give up, but look for other opportunities of establishing Indian presence in Kazakhstan's oil-and-gas industry by means of participation in joint exploration, production and transportation of its hydrocarbon resources and making contracts with countries, which have already established their presence in Kazakhstan's oil-and-gas sector. As the real situation has shown, the last option has proved to be the most feasible in establishment of India-China cooperation, for example, when India and China agreed about joint proposal of hydrocarbon development in Kazakhstan and purchase of energy resources from the Karazhanbas oil field.[5]

At the same time, analysts and decision-makers in Kazakhstan have only two main options. There are beliefs in either the possibility or impossibility of implementation of North-South hydrocarbon transportation project. The third stated option is not paid any real attention and this is one of the main reasons that Kazakhstan does not reply definitely on India's proposals regarding its participation in the development of oil and gas fields in Kazakhstan. One may notice that when India starts any discussion about its presence in Kazakhstan's oil-and-gas sector, Kazakhstan either keeps silent or shifts the discussion to cooperation in pharmaceuticals, cotton industry, small and medium scale enterprises etc. There are, of course, political (including influence of foreign powers) and economic (including absence of Kazakhstan-India hydrocarbons transport infrastructure) reasons. However, one more important reason is that Kazakhstan is not aware of India's real opportunities on the whole, and particularly in the sphere of hydrocarbons development.

These issues can be resolved by taking the following steps:

1. There is need to bridge the gaps in awareness of India and Kazakhstan about each other. The information gap is one of the crucial hindrances in the establishment of Indo-Kazakh overall beneficial cooperation.
2. India should more precisely study the situation in Kazakhstan, including its strategy and policies in oil-and-gas industry development and export priorities.
3. India should not perceive Kazakhstan as the country of rich hydrocarbon resources only. It is almost the same as if to take India as "tea country". In fact, Kazakhstan is proud of its human resources, its leading position among Central Asian countries, its political and economic initiatives on the world scene – to name the few. Hence, India should not see Kazakhstan as just raw materials base for its rapidly growing industries. Kazakhstan is keen to be an equal partner before other states and India needs to realize this intention.
4. One of the severe problems on the path of fruitful Indo-Kazakh cooperation lies in the fact that Kazakhstan too has not reliable information about India's

real opportunities and perspectives. India is still sometimes taken as in all respects developing and even underdeveloped country "of elephants, Maharajas and melodramatic movies", with huge poor and mostly illiterate population, which was highly dependent on close friendship with the former USSR. Only few people, who are mostly scientists, but not decision-makers, know enough about the real potential of India as the fast-growing economy and rising power, which tends to be (and in some ways already is) one of the key actors on the world scene. In this regard, India should make all possible efforts to show not only its interest in having access to Kazakhstan's hydrocarbons, but also project the benefits which Kazakhstan can accrue from cooperation with India vis-à-vis other countries. In this regard, India should work in the direction of self-advertisement for Kazakhstan, explaining its actual potential in different spheres. It should make Kazakhstan feel as an equal and beneficial partner.

5. While doing so, it is important for India to avoid excessive display of its challenges of energy security. The appeal to oil-producing countries about the extreme need in their oil-and-gas resources could lead to the perception of such a country being "permanently needy" and hence "permanently dependent" on the goodwill of oil-rich states. That is why India should not lay stress on the point that it will need oil and gas in increasing rates of this much tons/percents during that much years.[6] Quite the opposite, Indians should carefully approach this problem and make considered statements in this regard. Otherwise, Kazakhstan (and some other countries as well) may always keep the hopes for India getting access to its resources, but far from resources per se, constantly perceiving it as the reserve option which can be used in case, for example, other countries operating in Kazakhstan's oil-and-gas sector would once be discouraged to continue their work here by more tightened terms from Kazakh side. In other words, it is in the interests of India to see Kazakhstan as an equal partner and to be seen in the same way.
6. India should not pin too many hopes on full-scale and maximum presence in Kazakhstan's oil-gas-sector, at least in the near future. But, India should more loudly and emphatically publicize and advertise its achievements and opportunities in the sphere of effective and high-end exploration, production and transportation of hydrocarbons. Kazakhstan simply does not know enough about such achievements and opportunities of India, while for India there are real options for development of cooperation with Kazakhstan in its oil-and-gas sector in these very directions.

As regards the transportation of hydrocarbons from Kazakhstan's oil and gas fields, it may be stressed that Kazakhstan strongly proposes to expand its pipeline capacities – both domestic and export-oriented. Total annual capacity of export pipelines exceeds 310 million barrels, of export gas pipelines – 5 billion cubic meters and of transit gas pipelines – 110 billion cubic meters. In 2005, 382 million tons of oil was transported by "KazTransOil JSC" system and 128 billion cubic meters of gas was transported by "Intergas Central Asia" trunk gas pipelines. It is planned to increase the transmission capacity of pipelines Tengiz-Novorossiysk (Caspian Pipeline Consortium) up to 67 million tons of oil per year, Uzen-Atyrau-Samara up to 25 million tons, Atasu-Alashankou up to 20 million tons. To this may be added the prospects of Kuryk-Baku-Tbilisi-Ceyhan pipeline with transmission capacity of 5 (at the beginning) to 38 million tons of oil per year.

Besides export oil and gas pipelines, there are local pipeline projects: West Kazakhstan-Kenkiyak-Kumkol (the component part of Kazakhstan-China pipeline network, which would connect the oil fields of Atyrau and Aktobe regions with petroleum refineries in Pavlodar and Shymkent), gas pipelines Aksay-Krasniy Oktyabr-Astana, and Bakhar gas region-Almaty (the last one needs to be enlarged).

In addition, Kazakhstan proposes to increase the acceptance rate of its Caspian sea-ports (by year 2010 up to 45.8 million tons of oil per year). As a priority in this regard, there is a project on creating new capacities of transfer tank farms (including offshore oil-loading terminal and offshore operations maintenance depot) in Kuryk port. Kazakhstan has also started creating its own tanker fleet. It is also planned to create an economic zone – national industrial Petrochemical Park – in Atyrau oblast.

On the whole, Kazakhstan needs foreign investments for the further implementation of Governmental Programme of Kazakhstan's Sector of Caspian Sea Development, more precisely, for exploration and development of new oil and gas fields of Caspian Sea. In all these spheres, India has the opportunities to offer its investments, equipments and experience.

In fact, the main long term goal of Kazakhstan is to establish higher degree of public control over its oil-and-gas sector in the interest of its own population. This goal implies introduction and development of state own capacities in exploration, development and transportation of hydrocarbons. In this connection, it is important to say, that India, of course, is not a first country that wants to make its presence in Kazakhstan oil-and-gas sector. But it can be the first country, which (in case of its competently formulated policy) comes into Kazakhstan not only with need for its hydrocarbons, but also with the intention of developing Kazakhstan's petroleum infrastructure and bringing appropriate technology to achieve mutual benefit.

Generally speaking, in case India wants to establish its presence in Kazakhstan's oil-and-gas sector, it should simultaneously and even in advance establish such presence in other various spheres (as has been done, for example, by China). This includes opening of branches of Indian public and private banks, more active participation in small and medium scale enterprises (where Kazakhstan invites Indians), in various small and big projects where India has an appropriate competence and good experience. When India becomes more "familiar" and "cognate" for Kazakhstan's people and authorities, it can secure opportunities for penetrating its oil-and-gas sector as well.

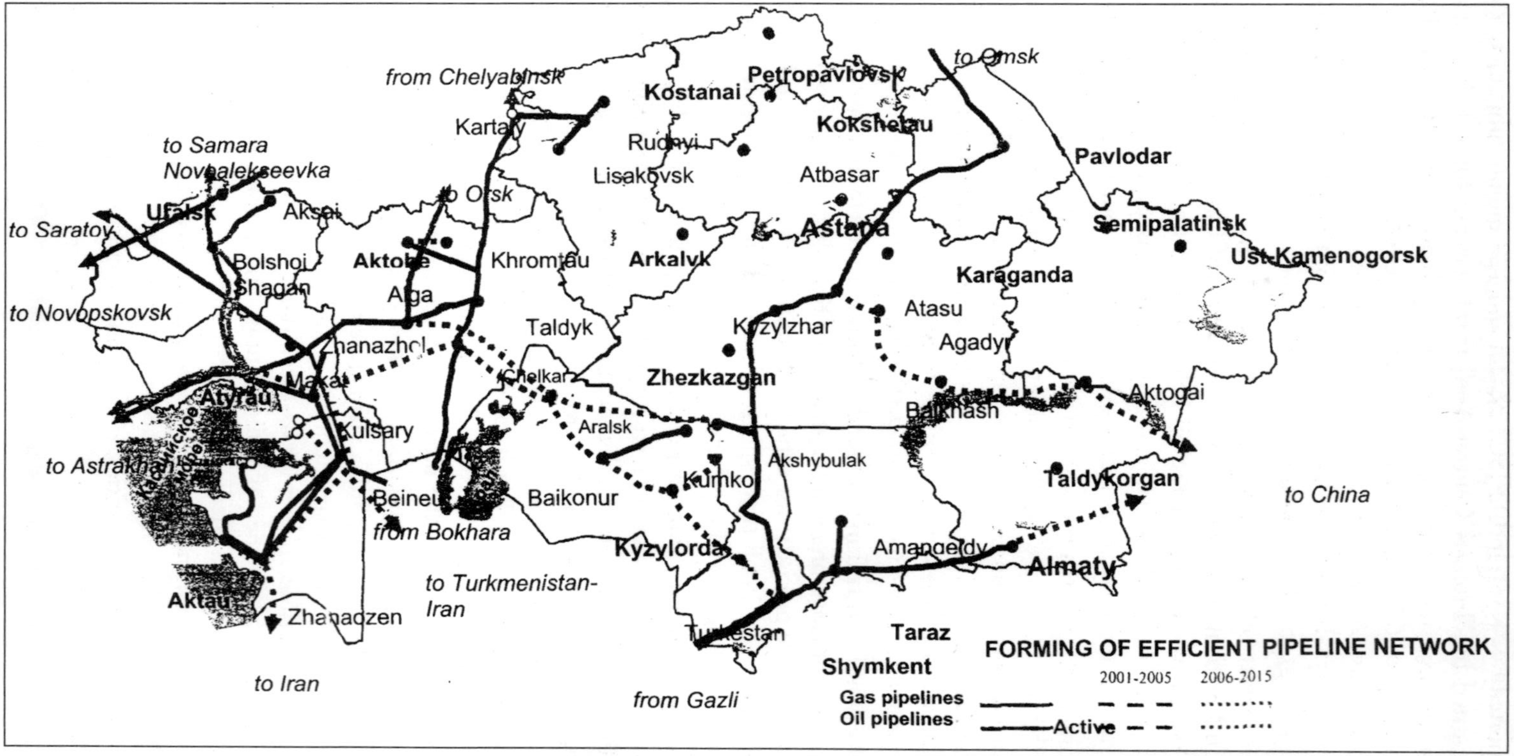


**Source:** Strategy of Territorial Development of the Republic of Kazakhstan until 2015, approved by the Decree of President of the Republic of Kazakhstan, 28 August 2006, p. 167.

To conclude, both India and Kazakhstan should develop more definite and comprehensive approach towards overall future cooperation, particularly in the sphere of hydrocarbons.

## ENDNOTES

1. Presidential Decree No. 811 of 20 February 2002 on Creation of "KazMunayGas National Closed Joint-Stock Company" (by Merging Kazakhoil CJSC and Oil & Gas Transport CJSC).
2. Pod krylom mificheskoy pticy budet otnyne neftegazovaya otrasl' (The Oil-and-Gas Industry from now on under the Wings of the Mythical Bird) – Oil & Gas of Kazakhstan, No. 2, 2006, pp. 10-12.
3. Indiya yavlyaetsya odnoy iz prioritetnyh stran-partnerov Kazakhstana (India is One of the Priority Partner-Countries for Kazakhstan) – Kazinform news agency, 26 February 2006.
4. R. Shulembayeva. Okeanskiy prospekt Kazahstana (Kazakhstan's Ocean Avenue-and-Prospectus)//*Kazahstanskaya Pravda*, 12 August 2006.
5. Sdelka nedeli (Deal of the Week), *Business Guide*, No. 21, 12 June 2006.
6. As it is stated, for instance, in *India Hydrocarbon Vision: 2025*, and in almost all relevant articles of Indian authors.

# 9

# China's Energy Cooperation with Central Asia

*Xu Qinhua*

Central Asia is a core area in which China conducts its international energy cooperation. Through more than ten years of exploration, experimentation and practice, the gas and oil cooperation between China and Central Asian countries has already formed a pattern: investing primarily in Kazakhstan; devoting great effort to building gas and oil pipelines between China and Kazakhstan; actively taking part in the gas and oil exploration of other countries such as Turkmenistan and Uzbekistan, etc. With China's increasing dependence on importing energy, realization of the 'diversification' of gas and oil sources and the 'security' of energy transportation has become an imperative demand for ensuring state energy security. Under such circumstances, Central Asia's importance in China's energy strategy deployment has further increased.

Amidst international energy competition, China's entry into Central Asian region undoubtedly creates both opportunities as well as challenges. As an area of unstable political situation, ethnic and religious conflicts, intervention by big powers and various political forces, Central Asia has had an intricate political environment. Moreover, abundant gas and oil resources enable it to become a complex stage for international interaction. Since the collapse of Soviet Union, many international actors have joined the contest in this area. Different from the geopolitical contest between Russia and Britain in this area in the 19$^{th}$ century, in the post-Cold War period, forces joining the 'New Great Game' not only include state actors (US, Russia, China, EU, Iran, Turkey), but also international organizations, transnational corporations, Islamic religious groups, secessionist forces, international terrorist organizations and transnational crime gangs engaged in smuggling and drug trafficking etc. To have energy cooperation with Central Asia in such a background, China needs to evaluate complex factors and variables in making its strategic decision.

As a big power in South Asia, India is a driving force of South Asian economic development. Both China and India are developing countries with large population;

their bilateral relationship is improving, which is presently the focus of international attention. High-speed growth of economy make these two countries not only compete but also cooperate in energy. What is India's new strategy of seeking overseas energy? What is China's energy diplomacy towards India? What are the possibilities of China's energy cooperation with Central Asia vis-à-vis India?

## Role and Position of Central Asia in China's Energy Strategy

Owing to China's rapid economic growth, along with its increasing demand for energy, China's crude oil consumption has multiplied. In 2010, the consumption of oil would reach 350-380 million tons; the consumption of natural gas would increase from 24.5 billion cubic meters to 100-120 billion cubic meters. However, in 2010, domestic supply would have a limited growth, reaching the amount of 170 to 190 million tons. Thus, the increasing demand for oil will mainly be met by imports. Domestic production of natural gas would increase drastically, reaching 80 to 100 billion cubic meters in 2010, while partial import is still needed to meet the growing demand.[1]

To guarantee the import of oil, to seek a safe channel without passing the overcrowded Malacca Strait, it becomes urgent to import certain amount of gas and oil resources from Russia and Central Asia. By doing so, China can obtain a long-term and stable energy supply from these two areas, accelerate the "Going West" campaign in its "Stabilizing East, Going West" strategy and protect its oil resources.

Participating in the gas and oil development in Central Asia is an important measure by China to maintain its oil security. Firstly, it compensates for China's gas and oil shortage; secondly, considering the aspects of secure supply and resource diversification of gas and oil, Central Asia should be listed as the first priority to China. Secondly, Caspian oil is the only oil supply resource that can be ensured without ocean transportation, this area has greater safety and potential than Middle East. Meanwhile, it can reduce China's dependence on Middle East oil; Thirdly, Central Asia is the hub connecting Russia and Middle East. Therefore, participation in the oil development of Central Asia enables China to promote good relationship with Russia and Middle East. Therefore, China could obtain long-term and stable energy supply after the energy producing areas such as Central Asia, Russia and Middle East connect with each other. Moreover, as a burgeoning world energy centre, Central Asia has strategic importance for China's "West Development Programme". China could take advantage of its geographic situation, instilling vigour to its "West Development" through oil import. The concept of "Asia-European Continental Bridge" is one result of this advantage. This concept focuses on the gas and oil development in Xinjiang and the energy imports from Caspian and Central Asia through pipelines; facilitating infrastructure development in the Asia-European continent by building railways, highways, airline network and optical fibre cable, etc; promoting energy exchange along the pipeline area; developing cities and restoring the ecosystem. On the one hand, China could use the oil pipeline from Central Asia as a route for transporting western oil to the east, and saving the cost for "West Development". On the other hand, while using the chance of pipeline installation, China could develop the setting up of infrastructure along the pipeline area, expand transportation and drive economic development. Last but not the least, it is beneficial to protect China's oil resources. This has greater strategic value than large-scale exploration in the west. It accords with both comparative cost theory and sustainable development strategy.

**China's Oil Demands, Net Imports and Degree of Dependence on Imports (2000-20)**
**(in million tons)**

| | 2000 | 2010 | 2020 |
|---|---|---|---|
| Demand Volume (Mt) | 224 | | |
| Energy Research Institute of NDRC, IEA, EIA | | 335-357<br>377<br>340 | 430-475<br>552<br>525 |
| Import volume (Mt) | 69.9 | | |
| Energy Research Institute of NDRC, IEA, EIA | | 552<br>230<br>185 | 240-295<br>425<br>380 |
| Degree of Dependence on Imports (%) | 31.0 | | |
| Energy Research Institute of NDRC, IEA, EIA | | 46-52<br>61<br>54 | 59-62<br>77<br>72 |

**Source:** *China Energy Outlook 2002*, and *DOE/EIA International Energy Outlook 2002.*

Large scale energy cooperation between China and Central Asia began in 1997. In 1997, Chinese and Kazakh governments signed gas and oil cooperation agreement. According to this agreement, China contracted to develop Aktyubinsk and Wujin oil fields, and build a pipeline of 3,000 kilometers from Wujin to Ala mountain pass. Developing Wujin oil field and laying oil pipeline combined with each other. At that time, considering various aspects, China first took the contract to develop Aktyubinsk oil field, but did not build the pipeline at once. In June 1997, Chinese company and its Kazakhstan partner signed an agreement for purchasing 60.3 per cent stake from Aktyubinsk gas and oil Company. In September 1997, these two parties signed a contract and completed the stake transfer. According to this contract, China would invest US $580 million in five years for the production and development of oil field. Five years later, the Chinese investment in Aktyubinsk oil field amounted to US $685 million, fulfilling the obligation it had promised.[2]

When Chinese company took over, Aktyubinsk Company was having losses, with a deficit of US $70 million. Through several years of effort, it has secured the profit of US $270 million. In 2002, China carried back one million tons of oil as per the share distribution. Chinese company also completed the construction and reconstruction of some large projects in Aktyubinsk oil field. For instance, it built the railway line from Zhanaruer to Remu, completed the second and third period reconstruction of Zhanaruer natural gas processing factory, built natural gas pipeline for Aktyubinsk city. China's Aktyubinsk gas and oil company has mainly operated in Zhanaruer and Kenjiyake gas and oil fields. The oil and natural gas storage of these two fields are 600 billion tons and 146 billion cubic meters respectively. At the end of 2002, the exploration of Zhanaruer field added up to more than 40 million tons and that of Kenjiyake field added up to 12.3 million tons. At present, these two fields have a capacity to produce more than 5 million tons oil and 2.2 billion cubic meters natural gas annually. According to its developing plan, the exploration quantity of oil and natural gas reached seven million tons and 5.5 billion cubic meters respectively.

China's Aktyubinsk gas and oil company has 7,949 employees, including 101 Chinese experts. Besides, this company employs 3,000 to 5,000 Kazakhstan citizens for various labour services each year. In June 2003, China and Kazakhstan signed another agreement for purchasing 25 per cent stake from Aktyubinsk oil field. From then onwards, China has controlled 85.6 per cent stake in Aktyubinsk oil field.

In 2003, China National Petroleum Corporation purchased 35 per cent and 65 per cent stake in Beibuzhaqi oil field from a Saudi Arabian company and an American company respectively. Thus Chinese company has controlled Beibuzhaqi oil field completely. Beibuzhaqi oil field is located in Mangghystau state of western Kazakhstan. The oil storage of this field is around 300 to 500 million barrels. Besides, China also seeks oil in Liman area of Atyrau state.

In August 2005, CNPC successfully purchased PetroKazakhstan Inc. at a cost of US $4.18 billion. PetroKazakhstan Inc. whose headquarter is in central Canada has an eight-year history. All its oil resource is located in Tuergai basin of central south area of Kazakhstan. Up to 2005, the total assets of PetroKazakhstan Inc were valued at US $1.269 billion, becoming the second largest foreign producer, the largest oil company and the largest product oil provider in this area. It has trade relations with Canada, US, Britain and the European continent. At present, its approvable crude oil storage amounts to 550 million barrels and it produces 152.5 thousand barrels per day. Its crude oil annual output capacity has exceeded seven million tons. Besides, it possesses an oil pipeline and a power plant.

Moreover, the construction of China-Kazakhstan oil pipeline has taken effect. The sector of Atasu to Ala mountain pass starts from the railway station and ends at Ala mountain pass, the railway port at the border of China and Kazakhstan, with a length of 1,300 kilometers. It formally started transporting oil on 26 May 2006. It transported 12 million tons crude oil annually and plans to increase the same to 20 million tons gradually.

In the near future, it is unlikely for Central Asian oil to enter Asia-Pacific market on a large scale. However, it could play an increasingly important role in China's oil market. China's energy consumption in future will increase at the rate of 4.5 per cent per year (two per cent lower than the growth rate of GDP at the same period).

The annual growth rate of oil demand will be more than 8 per cent. Although coal will still retain a primary status in China's energy consumption, its demand for gas and oil will soar owing to the development of the automobile industry and China's large scale industrialization. China's domestic oil production began to drop drastically since early 1990s and it became a completely import dependent country at the end of 1993. Although South China Sea and Talimu basin have large reserves, their exploitation requires substantive capital and advanced technology. China considers Middle East as its most important oil supply area, but Chinese government is diversifying the source of oil import. To achieve this purpose, China has accorded the oil import as well as the participation of Chinese companies in this sector a strategic importance.

**China-Central Asia Oil Balance (in million tons)**

| Countries | 1990 | 1993 | 1995 | 2000 | 2010 |
|---|---|---|---|---|---|
| **Kazakhstan** | | | | | |
| Production | 26 | 23 | 21 | 24-30 | 35-55 |
| Export | 22 | 13 | 9 | 15-8 | 25-21 |
| Import | 14 | 11 | 7 | 6 | 6 |
| Consumption | 18 | 12 | 19 | 16-28 | 16-40 |
| **Turkmenistan** | | | | | |
| Production | 6 | 5 | 5 | 4-5 | 8-11 |
| Export | 0 | 0 | 1 | 0 | 1-3 |
| Import | 0 | 1 | 0 | 0 | 0 |
| Consumption | 6 | 6 | 4 | 4-5 | 7-8 |
| **Uzbekistan** | | | | | |
| Production | 3 | 4 | 8 | 8-9 | 12-15 |
| Export | 0 | 0 | 1 | 1 | 3-5 |
| Import | 5 | 4 | 0 | 0 | 0 |
| Consumption | 6 | 7 | 7 | 7-8 | 9-10 |

Source: *World Oil Industry*, Information Research Institute of CNPC, 1997.

Turkmenistan and Kazakhstan regard exporting their natural gas to China as a feasible and long term choice. Although China's natural gas market is not big at present, it is expanding. In 1995, China's natural gas consumption was about 16.7 billion cubic meters. According to the forecast of IEA, in 2010, China's natural gas consumption will increase at 34-52 billion cubic meters per year.[3] That is to say, if the demand for fuel shifts slightly from coal to natural gas, natural gas supply will become a problem. In addition, environmental pollution caused by coal burning in enterprises, industries and families has become prominent in China and will further deteriorate. Therefore, Chinese leadership is adopting steps to substitute coal by obtaining gas.[4]

Up till now, China neither exports nor imports natural gas. From 1985 to 1995, natural gas production increased at 3.9 per cent per year, being more than its anticipated consumption growth rate. China's proven natural gas reserves are 2,060 billion cubic meters and can be exploited for 120 years. But most of the unexplored reserves are far away from China's consumption centre. China has to depend upon both domestic production and foreign imports to cater to its energy demand. For instance, in 1994, Chinese government declared that the restoration and production of Sichuan gas field required US $1 billion, which occupied 55 per cent of China's total output. Thus, Chinese government needed to consider foreign gas resources. Now, it plans to establish three liquid gas terminals to provide for Zhujiang delta, Changjiang delta and Fujian area. It also plans to import natural gas from Turkmenistan and Kazakhstan through Russia's Yakutsk, Irkutsk and Sakhalin Island.

Exporting natural gas from Central Asia to China is viable in economic terms, as has been testified by the World Bank survey. Every year, transporting 27 to 28 billion cubic meters natural gas through 6,000 kms long pipeline to China's east consumption centre costs natural gas US $106 per cubic meter. However, China's energy producers' coal cost about US $120 per cubic meter natural gas. The cost of transporting Middle East natural gas to China through India and Malaya may be higher than transporting Central Asia gas in the same destination. The cost of transporting natural gas of India, Malaya and other South Asia countries is almost the same. The most competitive choice is to transport natural gas of Irkutsk area in East Siberia to east China through pipeline. According to initial estimates, the price of about 57 US dollars per cubic meter can strike the bargain.

**China-Central Asia Natural Gas Balance (billion cubic meter)**

| Countries | 1990 | 1993 | 1995 | 2000 | 2010 |
|---|---|---|---|---|---|
| **Kazakhstan** | | | | | |
| Production | 7 | 7 | 5 | 6-18 | 17-31 |
| Export | 3 | 3 | 3 | 6-8 | 13-17 |
| Import | 9 | 10 | 7 | 7 | 9-11 |
| Consumption | 15 | 14 | 9 | 7-13 | 13-26 |
| **Turkmenistan** | | | | | |
| Production | 88 | 65 | 30 | 57-80 | 92-130 |
| Export | 72 | 52 | 20 | 45-65 | 80-110 |
| Import | 0 | 0 | 0 | 0 | 0 |
| Consumption | 16 | 13 | 10 | 12-15 | 12-20 |
| **Uzbekistan** | | | | | |
| Production | 41 | 45 | 49 | 50-51 | 52-55 |
| Export | 3 | 4 | 6 | 6-7 | 8-9 |
| Import | 0 | 2 | 2 | 2 | 2 |
| Consumption | | | | | |

**Source:** *World Oil Industry*, Information Research Institute of CNPC, 1997.

## Sino-Central Asia Energy Cooperation

Based on the geographical contiguity between China and Central Asian countries, the theory and method of new geopolitics contribute to establish a proper framework for this study. To be more specific, we need to analyze not only traditional geopolitical factors, such as geographical situation and power politics, but also geo-economic factors, and both the state and non-state actors; not only neighbouring geographic factors, but also global links in new situation; not only structural factors in international system, but also effects of internal factors.

Among the factors affecting energy cooperation between China and Central Asian countries, what the traditional geopolitics emphasizes are the unchanging macro-environment and background. After the disintegration of Soviet Union, "New Great Game" by international actors started in Central Asia due to its specific geopolitical conditions: Crossing Asian and European continents, bordering upon many countries, in the confluence of different civilizations, a dwelling place of various nations and with a rich storage of gas and oil. The energy cooperation between China and Central Asian countries is based precisely on such a geopolitical background. Geographical links and historical communication of both sides provide advantageous conditions for energy cooperation.

Cooperation between China and Central Asian countries is primarily of an economic nature, economic interest being the decisive variable for promoting development. As a result of rational choice, both sides consider that such cooperation is in accordance with their basic interests. As energy producers, Central Asian countries need a stable market; as consumer, China demands a stable supply. Such an interplay of mutual interests constitutes the driving force for their cooperation, while geographical contiguity provides a favourable condition for this cooperation. In future, Central Asian countries can transport around 50 million tons of crude oil to China through China-Kazakhstan oil pipeline annually; 30 billion cubic meter gas to China through China-Turkmenistan, China-Kazakhstan pipelines annually. Transportation through land pipelines is more favourable to provide China's energy security.

One of the factors affecting energy cooperation between China and Central Asian Republics, is the relation between big powers in Central Asia, that is, the bilateral, trilateral and multi-lateral relations of US, Japan, Russia and China. Questions arise whether the relationship is balanced and stable. Whether US will reduce its military and security presence in Central Asia is the key factor that affects great power relations in Central Asia and the foreign policies of Central Asian countries. US Department of Energy openly declared that, at least two factors decide US interests in Central Asia and Trans Caucasus region: First, ample energy resources in Caspian area; second, its important geo-strategic position in the heartland of Eurasia. US strives to realize its strategic aims through political means such as by promoting "Colour Revolution" and economic means such as by "controlling the exploitation and development of energy." Confronted with such a situation, Russia endeavours to maintain its traditional influence in this area. In the Russia-US contest, whether Central Asian countries are "pro-US" or "pro-Russia", has great bearing on their energy policies. If they are "pro-Russia", they would take a relatively active attitude in energy cooperation with China; if they are "pro-US", they would take a relatively negative or even non-cooperative attitude.

The energy cooperation between China and Central Asian countries is, of course, influenced by domestic politics besides international relations. To these countries, the developing trend of party politics, corruption, stability, and the ethnic-religious relations are all-important factors. The instability brought about by "Colour Revolutions" in Central Asian countries is a negative factor affecting energy cooperation between China and Central Asian countries. Moreover, problems in internal institutions of these countries, such as imperfect judicial system, are obstacles preventing Chinese gas and oil companies from further cooperation with these countries. However, no matter what influence "Colour Revolutions" will bring about, Central Asian countries will never give up the benefit produced through energy cooperation with China.

In the cooperation between China and Central Asian Countries, non-state actors is another important factor. Since the breakdown of former Soviet Union, various non-state actors have mushroomed, forming an important characteristic in the development of international relations of contemporary Central Asia. The non-state actors include government organizations, non-government organizations (NGOs), transnational corporations, Islamic religious and political groups, transnational criminal gangs engaging in smuggling and drug trafficking. Among these, Shanghai Cooperation Organization is an important platform where China and Central Asian countries interact. Some Western transnational companies, criminal gangs and increasingly active religious forces are likely to be negative factors affecting this cooperation. Certainly, the degree and methods of these non-state actors to influence energy cooperation between China and Central Asian countries are different. In terms of inter-state political relations, Shanghai Cooperation Organization is an important institution, which plays a vital role in preventing drug trafficking and international terrorism and creates good conditions for such energy cooperation.

## Sino-Central Asia Energy Cooperation and Possibilities for India

India has developed its economy rapidly in recent years. This has resulted in a dramatically increasing energy demand. It has been predicted that India will import 250 million tons of petroleum in the year 2020, and will surpass Korea and become the fourth biggest energy consuming country following America, China and Japan. After it came into power in May 2005, the UPA government has emphasized that if India couldn't find new oil fields in due time, the currently proven oil deposit will be dug up by 2016. So, India has adopted protective gas-exploration measures, and made a comprehensive supply plan in overseas energy expansion. As part of its energy diplomacy and strategy, India has been trying to obtain the exploration rights of Russian oil-fields to its north, to build secure oil transportation channel from Iran to India to its west, and to gain a share in Burma's oil exports to its east. In addition, India has also extended its reach to Africa and Latin America, forming an energy diplomatic arrangement at the global scale.

China and India have started entering into the petroleum exploration project of Sudan. In future, China and India should work hand in hand, taking part in international energy exploration and distribution, diversifying risks, so as to gain more energy supply than now. In June 2005, the ministers of Foreign Affairs from China, Russia and India held an informal meeting in Fuladiwosituoke. The Joint Communiqué of the meeting stressed that these three countries would develop cooperation in the fields of agriculture, energy and high technologies, and will take it as an opportunity to build a strategic energy triangle. India's presence in the Shanghai Cooperation Organization can help in exploring opportunities in the cooperation of oil and gas exploration in Central Asia.

As regards China, firstly it should avoid escalating and increasing the competition level in energy field. Within this framework, India and China can truly realize their cooperation in energy exploration in Central Asia, even a broader triangular alliance among China, India and Russia can be formed in various fields. For example, India has gained 20 per cent right of the exploitation of Iranian largest land oil field, while China Petroleum Corporation is exploiting this oil field and holding 50 per cent of its shares. This shows that there is not only competition between the two countries, but also chances for their cooperation exist. Secondly, China and India can together with Japan, Korea, and the East Asian countries, build a common Asian energy alliance, and enhance their influence in the global energy market to maintain energy security. Thirdly, China and India should establish a dialogue mechanism in energy issues between them. China and India can supplement each other in developing energy technology. China has developed well and fast in conventional energy exploration, e.g., China is much faster than India in electric power development. As India has more advantages than China in renewable energy, especially in wind power and other kinds of energy, there is a potential for the two sides to cooperate with each other in the above-mentioned fields.

## ENDNOTES

1. *China Industry Annual Report*, China Economic Information net, http://www.ceiceo.cn/Exweb/2005Report/www/AdInfo.asp?Id=6
2. Presently, China's adoption of overseas oil resource, except for the trading of futures and those on hand dealt by the entrepreneurs appointed by Chinese government in the international market, also includes other cooperation with foreigners in the field of exploration and extraction. The data comes from http://www.oilnews.com.cn/gb/zhuanti/2005-12/16/content_645965.htm
3. This anticipation is based on China's GNP and the maximum of energy consumption, while not treating natural gas as the primary fuel.
4. For instance, 80,000 coal gas users in Beijing started using natural gas by the end of March 2006. This project enables Beijing to become the first large city completely using natural gas, being the clean energy in China. The natural gas consumption will double in five years, increasing from current three billion cubic meters to more than six billion cubic-meters. This is the changing trend of China's energy consumption structure in future.

# 10

# India-China Competition and Cooperation in Energy Resources

*Nawal K. Paswan*

## Introduction

India and China together have largest pools of skilled human resources in the world and are expected to emerge as not only Asia's but also the world's super-economic powers by 2020 in terms of purchasing power parity (PPP) of national income.[1] There is also a general consensus that these two countries will be the engines of global economic growth in 21st Century. India's strong economic growth in recent years has begun to gain the world's attention.[2] Henry Kissinger predicted that in the twenty-first century the international system will be dominated by six major powers: the US, Europe, China, Japan, Russia and India. Similarly, Samuel Huntington foresees that during the coming decades, "India could move into rapid economic development and emerge as contender for influence in world affairs".[3] Even Indian Prime Minister Dr. Manmohan Singh made a statement on the occasion of Chinese Premier Wen Jiabao visit to New Delhi on 11th April 2005 that "India and China can together reshape the world order." The likely emergence of China and India as new major global players – similar to the rise of Germany in the 19th century and the United States in the early 20th century and the 21st century may be seen as the time when Asia, led by China and India, comes into its own.

Both these countries currently have a population of more than one billion each accounting for close to 40 per cent of the world's population.[4] China has already acquired the status of the most dynamic economy among the developing countries with a trend growth rate of over 8 per cent per annum during last two decades and is today among the top ten trading countries of the world since China joined the World Trade Organization (WTO) in 2001. The main reason for China's growing share in the global markets lies in its lower production costs due to an abundant labour force.[5] However, labour cost is not the whole story as China has higher labour costs than India. For example, in 2002, the typical monthly wage of a manufacturing worker in China was US$110.80 while it was only US$23.80 in India.[6] Thus, other forces must be at work, including better infrastructure, flexible labour markets, and a favourable investment climate.[7] Like China, India enjoys the advantage of a large labour force and relatively low production costs. It possesses immense potential to increase its global market share.[8] Both countries are expected to become the driving force in global trade, with their exports rising from a combined 12 per cent of world exports to 20 per cent by 2010 and 30 per cent by 2030.[9]

Over the last decade both the Asian giants have witnessed an unprecedented growth in their domestic economies. India maintained a growth rate of 7 to 8 per cent annually, while China has managed to maintain a 8-10 per cent annual growth. It is further estimated that India and China will likely maintain this growth rate for sometime at least.[10] Both countries differ vastly in their political systems (one strongly ruled by the Communist Party and the other a vibrant democracy). Both countries have gained global attention due to their market oriented economic reforms although India today clearly lags behind China in this respect.[11] China has the advantage of early start for its economic reforms (1978) as compared to India (1991).[12] China also has the advantage of more effective implementation of its economic reforms due to its political regime. Despite the dynamism of their economies, especially in the last two decades, the bilateral economic relationship between India and China remains far below of their existing potential.

Due to high economic growth based on rapid industrialization the energy consumption of India and China is rising fast and they are among the world's biggest importers of oil and gas. Both these countries are also heavily dependent on oil and gas for their economies to grow without disruption. Unfortunately, India and China are net importers of oil and gas at present and it is only likely that their import needs would increase over the coming years.[13] China relies on its state energy companies to access new resources at home and abroad. India's energy sector is mainly privatized. However, India's government plays an important role in politically supporting the international expansion of its energy sector.

In a reflection of the growing importance of India and China in determining global energy consumption patterns, the 2007 *World Energy Outlook Report* published by the International Energy Agency focused exclusively on these two countries India and China entitled *Global Energy Prospects: Impact of Developments in India and China.*[14] Already, India and China together account for 45 per cent of incremental oil demand. IEA predicts global oil demand, which stands at 4,233 million tonnes per year today, will rise to about 5,780 million tonnes per year by 2030, primarily fuelled by China and India growing at a moderate pace – one which IEA calls the '*reference scenario*' (IEA 2007.).

India obtains its energy from a number of sources such as coal, oil, gas, hydropower and nuclear power. Much of the energy produced domestically and India's energy policies are made by the ministry responsible for each energy sources.[15] In India, there is no single ministry of energy (one existed before 1992). Indian government's policy for each energy source is developed by a ministry and department, such as the Ministry of Petroleum and Natural Gas, the Ministry of Coal, the Ministry of Non-Conventional Energy Sources, the Department of Atomic Energy and the Ministry of Power. Attempts at integrating energy policies have been hindered by separate entities overseeing a particular type of energy source. Lack of a centralized energy policymaking authority and inefficient state of India's energy bureaucracies have deterred much needed foreign investment into India's energy sector and prevented the formation of a coherent energy policy. Indian Prime Minister Manmohan Singh has described energy security as being second only to food security.

In China, It has a high-level energy entity which is in charge of formulating and adjusting its overall energy development strategy. In 2005, China established the Energy Leading Group (ELG), a supra-ministerial coordination body headed by Premier Wen Jiabao, and in March 2008, China established the National Energy Administration (NEA), a national-level energy institution. This reflected China's recognition of the need to strengthen energy sector management by improving coordination across industries and ministries, and promoting the formation, implementation and enforcement of energy policies and strategies.

All economic systems depend critically on energy resources for sustainability and continuous evolution and growth. Furthermore we see that there is a direct relationship between energy use and economic development.[16] In most economies, we observe that there are inter-relationships and dependencies between the various sectors such as: agricultural, industrial, transportation, finance, distribution and advertising. And these sectors are very energy intensive depending as they do on the water, energy, transportation and telecommunication infrastructure. In both countries India and China, the level of infrastructural development varies in quality from poor to satisfactory. As one can see from Table 1 that in both countries, percentage share of GDP in agriculture is declining while in case of industry and services sectors, the share of GDP has been increasing between 2000 and 2008. Hence these indicators indicate that economic growth causes total energy consumption because energy needs in both countries have been increasing. It can also be also observed from this Table 1 that India is lagging far behind of China in all the major key and energy indicators.

How and in what areas these needs materialize will depend on five major factors. First, these energy needs will be driven by India's quest to maintain the high levels of economic growth (around 6 to 7 per cent annually) that it has enjoyed since 1994. Second, much will depend on India's ability (or lack thereof) to locate and use existing domestic gas and petroleum reserves. The third factor will be the ability of the Indian political system to address certain structural inefficiencies which contribute to significant loss and wastage. Fourth, it will also depend on its ability to adopt new and more energy efficient technologies. And fifth, much depends on India's ability to secure external sources of energy.[17] Securing external sources of energy provides avenues for extending cooperation between India and China in energy resources.

**Table 1: Comparative Economic and Energy Indicators of India and China**

| Key Indicators (Economic & Energy) | India | | | | China | | | |
|---|---|---|---|---|---|---|---|---|
| | 2000 | 2005 | 2007 | 2008 | 2000 | 2005 | 2007 | 2008 |
| **I. Economic Indicators** | | | | | | | | |
| a. Population, (billion) | 1.01 | 1.09 | 1.12 | 1.13 | 1.26 | 1.30 | 1.31 | 1.32 |
| b. Population growth (annual per cent) | 1.7 | 1.4 | 1.3 | 1.3 | 0.7 | 0.6 | 0.6 | 0.6 |
| c. Surface area (Lakh sq. km) | 3.28 | 3.28 | 3.28 | 3.28 | 9.59 | 9.59 | 9.59 | 9.59 |
| d. GDP (current US$) (trillion) | 0.46 | 0.81 | 1.17 | 1.21 | 1.19 | 2.23 | 3.38 | 4.32 |
| e. GDP growth (annual per cent) | 4.0 | 9.4 | 9.1 | 7.1 | 8.4 | 10.4 | 13.0 | 9.0 |
| f. Inflation, GDP deflator (annual per cent) | 3.5 | 4.1 | 4.9 | 7.3 | 2.1 | 3.8 | 7.4 | 7.2 |
| g. Agriculture, value added (per cent of GDP) | 23 | 19 | 18 | 18 | 15 | 13 | 11 | 11 |
| h. Industry, value added (per cent of GDP) | 26 | 29 | 30 | 29 | 46 | 48 | 49 | 49 |
| i. Services, etc., value added (per cent of GDP) | 50 | 52 | 52 | 53 | 39 | 40 | 40 | 40 |
| j. Exports of goods and services (per cent of GDP) | 13 | 20 | 21 | 24 | 23 | 37 | 43 | 35 |
| k. Imports of goods and services (per cent of GDP) | 14 | 23 | 25 | 30 | 21 | 32 | 33 | 28 |
| l. Gross capital formation (per cent of GDP) | 24 | 35 | 39 | 39 | 35 | 44 | 43 | 43 |
| m. Merchandise trade (per cent of GDP) | 20.4 | 29.9 | 30.9 | 38.7 | 39.6 | 63.6 | 64.3 | 59.2 |
| **II. Energy Indicators** | | | | | | | | |
| | 1980 | 1990 | 2000 | 2005 | 1980 | 1990 | 2000 | 2005 |
| a. Total primary energy demand (Mtoe) | 209 | 320 | 459 | 537 | 604 | 874 | 1121 | 1742 |
| b. Oil demand (mb/d) | 0.7 | 1.2 | 2.3 | 2.6 | 1.9 | 2.4 | 4.7 | 6.7 |
| c. Coal demand (Mtce) | 75 | 152 | 235 | 297 | 447 | 763 | 899 | 899 |
| d. Gas demand (bcm) | 1.4 | 11.9 | 25.4 | 34.8 | 14.3 | 15.3 | 27.7 | 27.7 |
| e. Biomass and waste demand (Mtoe) | 116 | 133 | 149 | 158 | 180 | 201 | 214 | 214 |
| f. Electricity output (TWh) | 119 | 289 | 562 | 699 | 313 | 650 | 1387 | 1387 |
| g. Primary energy demand/GDP (index, 2005=100) | 163 | 142 | 120 | 100 | 342 | 207 | 101 | 100 |
| h. Primary energy demand per capita (toe per person) | 0.30 | 0.38 | 0.45 | 0.49 | 0.60 | 0.80 | 0.90 | 1.30 |
| i. Energy-related CO2 emissions (Gt) | 0.43 | 0.69 | 0.95 | 1.05 | 1.40 | 2.20 | 3.10 | 5.10 |
| j. Oil imports (mb/d)* | 0.5 | 0.6 | 1.6 | 1.8 | -0.2 | -0.4 | 1.4 | 3.1 |
| k. Electricity demand per capita (kWh) | 174 | 341 | 553 | 639 | 318 | 570 | 1093 | 1940 |

Sources: For Economic Indicators – *World Development Indicators database* (World Bank) September 2009 and for Energy Indicators – *World Energy Outlook 2007* (IEA).

In view of the similarities in the nature of energy problems in both the economies, cooperation is possible in several areas (i.e., joint investment in oil equity abroad, joint coordination in strategic petroleum reserves system, technology transfer in energy efficiency, joint bidding in overseas and bilateral trade generating joint-ventures etc.) which would help optimize the utilization of the existing resources. The demand of oil is higher in China as compared to India. India's oil demand was 0.7 million barrels per day in 1980 which significantly increased to 2.6 million barrel per day in 2005 while in the case of China, its oil demand was 1.9 million barrel per day in 1980 which significantly increased to 6.7 million barrel per day in 2005.[18]

Despite unresolved territorial disputes, mutual suspicions over each other's military buildup and strategic intent, potential economic competition, and the changing balance of power and realignments, China and India have enjoyed over 10 years of mostly uninterrupted progress in their political, economic, and security relationship.[19] President Hu Jintao's November 2006 visit to India, the first such visit by a Chinese head of state in a decade, marked an important milestone in the bilateral relationship. During Hu's visit, the two governments issued a joint statement highlighting a 10-point strategy to elevate the relationship and signed more than a dozen agreements to strengthen cooperation in trade, investment, energy, and cultural and educational exchanges.[20]

The objective of this paper is to explore: (a) the prospects of cooperation in energy sector between India and China at bilateral level with the help of some trade indices, (b) acquisitions of equity in overseas oil reserves and investment by Indian and Chinese national oil companies at global level, (c) how the quest for energy security has transformed their aggressive competitive attitude towards each other to cooperative and partnership arrangements in energy resources especially in oil and gas sectors, and (d) to coordinate and cooperate in creation of strategic reserve of crude oil and petroleum products at domestic and international levels which is necessary to improve oil security in both countries especially during disruption of energy supply.

The paper is based on primary as well as secondary literature available and online energy data. The major sources of data and information are collected from country reports and statistics provided by the International Energy Agency (IEA) statistics, forecasts, US Energy Information Administration (EIA), BP Statistical Review of World Energy, books and articles by Indian and Chinese researchers, and reports by several European, American analysts and media. An attempt has also been made to compute some trade indices to identify the potential products where both countries can enhance their trade and investment cooperation in energy products and minimize the competition and maximize the gains bilaterally as well as globally especially in overseas investment.

This paper is organized under following four major sections besides introduction. First, it examines the trends in energy in India and China and changing pattern of production and consumption of energy resources. It also attempts to examine the future demand and supply of energy resources in both countries. Second, it examines the cooperation with the help of changing nature and composition of bilateral trade in energy resources between India and China with the help of some trade indices. It also discusses the level of India's FDI inflows in energy sector and scope for joint-ventures between India and China in energy sector. Third, it discusses the level of energy competition and how these two countries can maximize the gain and minimize the loss from cooperation in energy resources in overseas investment and projects. Finally, last section is devoted to examine the overall assessment of India-China cooperation and future prospects for mutual cooperation in energy resources and also draw some conclusions for policy implications.

## Energy Resources in India and China

China and India are the second and third largest economies in Asia, respectively. Rapid economic development, industrialization, urbanization and improved lifestyles are driving the two countries' energy demand higher and making them increasingly reliant on world energy markets. In less than a generation, China has moved from being a minor and largely self-sufficient energy consumer to become the world's fastest-growing energy consumer and a major player on the global energy market.[21] Till 1993, China was able to meet its rapidly growing energy needs entirely from domestic resources, so its impact on global markets was minimal.[22] The Indian energy sector has been characterised by low per capita commercial energy consumption, skewed distribution of primary commercial energy sources, ballooning demand supply gap, inadequate energy infrastructure, and high import dependence mainly in the form of crude oil.[23]

Table 1 clearly indicates that India has lagged behind China in almost all key energy indicators. In comparison, the energy situation of China is better than that of India in terms of energy consumption structures, international reserve status, and quest for energy supply abroad. Both countries currently rely on international markets for over half of the oil they consume. But India's dependence on foreign oil has a longer history than that of China.[24] China today imports roughly half of its oil. Consumption rose by 15 per cent last year and is forecast to jump by an additional 9 per cent in 2010. By 2025, according to projections made by the US Energy Department, China will be requiring 14.2 million barrels a day. India's oil imports are expected to rise to some 5 million barrels a day by 2020, up from around 1.4 million barrels now.

Table 2 presents the total primary energy supply, net oil imports and net oil exports in major countries of world. As can be seen from this Table, China ranks fourth major consumer of oil and gas (313 Mtoe) and followed by India as fourth largest consumer with 145 Mtoe after USA, Russia and Japan. But in terms of per capita TPES, India's position is lowest (0.52) followed by China with second lowest (1.09) in the world. India and China are also net oil importers while Saudi Arabia, Russia, Norway and Iran are major exporting countries of oil in the world.

Energy is the most important input for economic development and has causal relationship between GDP and different types of energy consumption. Therefore, energy has direct and indirect impact on the overall economic development and in turn is affected by it. Energy consumption is both a necessary condition for growth and a consequence of it.[25] The growth of economy in India and China has led to an increase in an energy-dependent lifestyle resulting in a high demand for energy sources. In 2007, China produced only 186.7 million tonnes of crude oil while its consumption was 368.0 million tonnes making it the world's second largest oil importer after the United States of America.[26]

**Table 2: Total Primary Energy Supply (TPES), Net Oil Imports and Net Oil Exports (2005) of Selected Countries**

| Country | TPES (Mtoe)* | TPES per Capita | Oil & Gas/ TPES (%) | Oil & Gas Consumption (Mtoe) | Net Oil Imports (Mtoe) | Net Oil Exports (Mtoe)* |
|---|---|---|---|---|---|---|
| Iran | 136 | 2.06 | 98.0 | 134 | — | 129 |
| Norway | 23 | 5.11 | 51.0 | 12 | — | 144 |
| Russia | 640 | 4.46 | 73.4 | 470 | — | 289 |
| Saudi Arabia | 131 | 5.81 | 100.0 | 131 | — | 392 |
| Taiwan | 99 | 4.36 | 52.8 | 52 | 45 | — |
| India | 55.3 | 0.52 | 26.2 | 145 | 84 | — |
| China | 1409 | 1.09 | 22.2 | 313 | 105 | — |
| Japan | 517 | 4.05 | 62.2 | 322 | 254 | — |
| USA | 2281 | 7.84 | 62.8 | 1432 | 571 | — |

**Notes:** * Total Primary Energy Supply (TPES) is made up of indigenous production + imports-exports-international marine bunkers+ – stock changes.

* Mtoe= million tons of oil equivalent.

**Sources:** *Key World Statistics 2005*, International Energy Agency (IEA) and IEA Energy Statistics online.

Table 3 presents primary energy demand in world, India and China in the reference scenario (Mtoe) during the period between 1980 and 2030 (also Figure 1). World primary energy demand[27] in the Reference Scenario, in which government policies are assumed to remain unchanged from mid-2007, is projected to grow by 55 per cent between 2005 and 2030, at an average annual rate of 1.8 per cent. Demand reaches 17.7 billion tonnes of oil equivalent, compared with 11.4 billion toe in 2005. The pace of demand growth slackens progressively over the projection period, from 2.3 per cent per year in 2005-15 to 1.4 per cent per year in 2015-2030. Demand grew by 1.8 per cent per year in 1980-2005. Table 3 also presents the energy demand in the reference scenario of India and China (together) during the period between 1980 and 2030. It is quite clear from this table that in both India and China together primary energy demand increased from 16.52 per cent in 1980 to 28.88 per cent in 2030.

**Table 3: Primary Energy Demand in World, India and China in the Reference Scenario (Mtoe)**

| | 1980 | 2000 | 2005 | 2015 | 2030 | 2005-30* |
|---|---|---|---|---|---|---|
| World | 7227 | 10023 | 11512 | 14362 | 17720 | |
| a. Coal | 1786 | 2292 | 2892 | 3988 | 4994 | 2.2 |
| b. Oil | 3106 | 3647 | 4000 | 4720 | 5585 | 1.3 |
| c. Gas | 1237 | 2089 | 2354 | 3044 | 3948 | 2.1 |
| d. Nuclear | 186 | 675 | 721 | 804 | 854 | 0.7 |
| e. Hydro | 147 | 226 | 251 | 327 | 416 | 2.0 |
| f. Biomass and Waste | 753 | 1041 | 1149 | 1334 | 1615 | 1.4 |
| g. Other Renewables | 12 | 53 | 145 | 145 | 308 | 6.7 |

Table 3 (*Contd.*)

| | 1980 | 2000 | 2005 | 2015 | 2030 | 2005-30* |
|---|---|---|---|---|---|---|
| China | 874 | 1121 | 1742 | 2851 | 3819 | 3.2 |
| Share of World (per cent) | (12.09) | (11.18) | (15.13) | (19.85) | (21.55) | |
| a. Coal | 534 | 629 | 1094 | 1869 | 2399 | 3.2 |
| b. Oil | 116 | 230 | 327 | 543 | 808 | 3.7 |
| c. Gas | 13 | 23 | 42 | 109 | 199 | 6.4 |
| d. Nuclear | 0 | 4 | 14 | 32 | 67 | 6.5 |
| e. Hydro | 11 | 19 | 34 | 62 | 86 | 3.8 |
| f. Biomass and Waste | 200 | 214 | 227 | 225 | 227 | 0.0 |
| g. Other Renewables | 0 | 0 | 3 | 12 | 33 | 9.9 |
| India | 320 | 459 | 537 | 770 | 1299 | 3.6 |
| Share of World (per cent) | (4.43) | (4.58) | (4.66) | (5.36) | (7.33) | |
| a. Coal | 106 | 164 | 208 | 330 | 620 | 4.5 |
| b. Oil | 63 | 114 | 129 | 188 | 328 | 3.8 |
| c. Gas | 10 | 21 | 29 | 48 | 93 | 4.8 |
| d. Nuclear | 2 | 4 | 5 | 16 | 33 | 8.3 |
| e. Hydro | 6 | 6 | 9 | 13 | 22 | 3.9 |
| f. Biomass and Waste | 133 | 149 | 158 | 171 | 194 | 0.8 |
| g. Other Renewables | 0 | 0 | 1 | 4 | 9 | 11.7 |
| Total (China+India) | 1194 | 1580 | 2279 | 3621 | 5118 | 3.3 |
| Share of World (per cent) | (16.52) | (15.76) | (19.80) | (25.21) | (28.88) | |
| a. Coal | 640 | 793 | 1302 | 2199 | 3019 | 3.4 |
| b. Oil | 179 | 344 | 456 | 731 | 1136 | 3.7 |
| c. Gas | 23 | 44 | 71 | 157 | 292 | 5.8 |
| d. Nuclear | 2 | 8 | 19 | 48 | 100 | 7.0 |
| e. Hydro | 17 | 25 | 43 | 75 | 108 | 3.8 |
| f. Biomass and Waste | 333 | 363 | 385 | 396 | 421 | 0.4 |
| g. Other Renewables | 0 | 0 | 4 | 16 | 42 | 10.2 |

**Note:** *Average annual percentage rate of growth and figures in parenthesis is percentage share of world.
**Source:** International Enegy Agency (IEA), *World Energy Outlook 2007*, p. 74 and 119, Paris, France.

**Fig. 1: Primary Energy Demand in World, India and China in the Reference Scenario (Mtoe)**

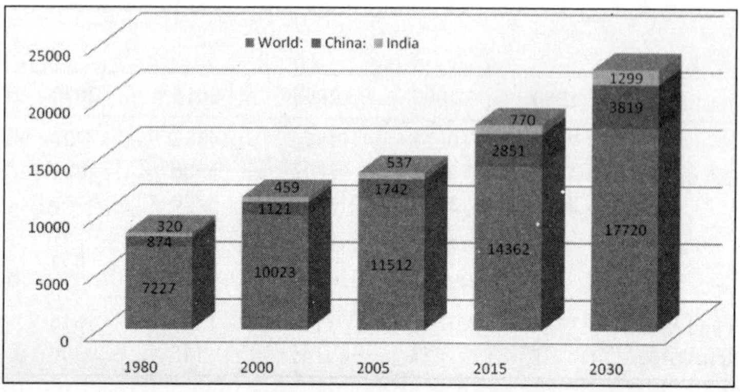


**Source:** International Enegy Agency (IEA), *World Energy Outlook 2007*, France.

A summary of comparative scenario of proved reserves, production and consumption of energy resources (crude oil, natural gas and coal) of India and China is presented in Table 4. This Table is self-explanatory to understand the status of energy in both countries. As can be seen from this Table that India's production was 37.3 million tonnes of crude oil in 2007 but consumption was 128.5 million tonnes. India is already importing about 75 per cent of its crude oil needs. Even if its domestic production increases to 50 million tonnes in two decades from the existing 37.3 million tonnes, its import dependence will rise to 87 per cent due to its high economic growth rate. India's dependence on imports stands already at 75 per cent of domestic consumption and hence is even more acute than that of China, although, in absolute quantities, India's oil demand is much smaller. Despite the burgeoning demand for oil, coal still claims primacy in China's energy mix, accounting for as much as 67 per cent in 2007. In 2006, China burned 2,392 million tons of coal, accounting for 39 per cent of the world total. A substantial portion of this went into the production of electricity.

**Table 4: Crude Oil, Natural Gas and Coal Scenario of India and China (2007-08)**

| | Proved Reserves | Production | Consumption |
|---|---|---|---|
| **a. Crude Oil** | | | |
| India | 5.5 thousand million barrels | 37.3 million tones/day | 128.5 million tones/day |
| China | 15.5 thousand million barrels | 186.7 million tones/day | 368.0 million tones/day |
| **b. Natural Gas** | | | |
| India | 1.09 Trillion cubic metres | 27.2 million tonnes oil equivalent | 36.2 million tonnes oil equivalent |
| China | 2.46 Trillion cubic metres | 62.4 million tonnes oil equivalent | 60.6 million tonnes oil equivalent |
| **c. Coal** | | | |
| India | 56498 million tonnes | 181.0 million tonnes oil equivalent | 208.0 million tonnes oil equivalent |
| China | 114500 million tonnes | 1289.6 million tones oil equivalent | 1311.4 million tones oil equivalent |

**Source:** *BP Statistical Review of World Energy, 2008.*

On the contrary, China is consuming about three hundred per cent more oil than India and it is predicted that its consumption will double in the next 25 years.[28] While China needs to import 60 per cent of its needs in 2020, India will require importing 87 per cent of its total needs.[29] Hence, the level of dependence of both India and China is going to increase and competition for scarce oil assets will continue. Table 5 presents the detailed information of reserves, production and consumption of oil, gas and coal in India and China during the period between 1980 and 2008.

Though China has ample coal reserves, its consumption is more than its production. While China produces about 41.1 per cent of the total world coal

Table 5: Reserve, Production and Consumption of Oil, Gas and Coal in India and China (1980 to 2008)

| Energy | 1980 | 1985 | 1990 | 1995 | 2000 | 2001 | 2002 | 2003 | 2004 | 2005 | 2006 | 2007 | 2008 | Change 2008 over 2007 (%) | 2008 share of total (%) |
|---|---|---|---|---|---|---|---|---|---|---|---|---|---|---|---|
| I.A. Oil: Proved reserves in Thousand million barrels | | | | | | | | | | | | | | | |
| India | 2.8 | 3.8 | 5.6 | 5.5 | 5.3 | 5.5 | 5.6 | 5.7 | 5.6 | 5.9 | 5.7 | 5.5 | 5.8 | 6.20 | 0.50 |
| China | 13.3 | 17.1 | 16 | 16.3 | 17.9 | 18.3 | 15.5 | 15.5 | 15.5 | 15.6 | 16.3 | 16.1 | 15.5 | -4.20 | 1.20 |
| I.B. Oil: Production[1] in Thousand barrels daily | | | | | | | | | | | | | | | |
| India | 193 | 627 | 715 | 774 | 726 | 727 | 753 | 756 | 773 | 738 | 762 | 770 | 766 | -0.50 | 0.90 |
| China | 2119 | 2505 | 2774 | 2989 | 3252 | 3306 | 3346 | 3401 | 3481 | 3627 | 3684 | 3743 | 3795 | 1.40 | 4.80 |
| I.C. Oil: Consumption[2] Thousand barrels daily | | | | | | | | | | | | | | | |
| India | 643 | 895 | 1211 | 1580 | 2254 | 2284 | 2374 | 2420 | 2573 | 2569 | 2580 | 2748 | 2882 | 4.80 | 3.40 |
| China | 1694 | 1825 | 2323 | 3395 | 4772 | 4872 | 5288 | 5803 | 6772 | 6984 | 7382 | 7742 | 7999 | 3.30 | 9.60 |
| II.A. Natural Gas: Proved reserves in Trillion cubic metres | | | | | | | | | | | | | | | |
| India | 0.34 | 0.48 | 0.7 | 0.68 | 0.76 | 0.76 | 0.75 | 0.85 | 0.92 | 1.1 | 1.08 | 1.06 | 1.09 | 3.30 | 0.60 |
| China | 0.7 | 0.87 | 1 | 1.67 | 1.37 | 1.37 | 1.27 | 1.34 | 1.45 | 1.53 | 1.68 | 2.26 | 2.46 | 8.90 | 1.30 |
| II.B. Natural Gas: Production[3] in Billion cubic metres | | | | | | | | | | | | | | | |
| India | 1.2 | 4.5 | 12 | 18.8 | 26.4 | 26.4 | 27.6 | 29.5 | 29.2 | 29.6 | 29.3 | 30.1 | 30.6 | 1.40 | 1.00 |
| China | 14.3 | 12.9 | 15.3 | 17.9 | 27.2 | 30.3 | 32.7 | 35 | 41.5 | 49.3 | 58.6 | 69.2 | 76.1 | 9.60 | 2.50 |
| II.C. Natural Gas: Consumption in Billion cubic metres | | | | | | | | | | | | | | | |
| India | 1.2 | 4.5 | 12 | 18.8 | 26.4 | 26.4 | 27.6 | 29.5 | 31.9 | 35.7 | 37.3 | 40.1 | 41.4 | 3.00 | 1.40 |
| China | 14.3 | 12.9 | 15.3 | 17.7 | 24.5 | 27.4 | 29.2 | 33.9 | 39.7 | 46.8 | 56.1 | 69.5 | 80.7 | 15.80 | 2.70 |
| III.A. Coal: Production[4] in Million tonnes | | | | | | | | | | | | | | | |
| India | 130.1 | 157.5 | 223.3 | 289.0 | 334.8 | 341.9 | 358.1 | 375.4 | 407.7 | 428.4 | 449.2 | 478.4 | 512.3 | 7.0 | 5.8 |
| China | 616.5 | 872.3 | 1079.9 | 1360.7 | 1299.2 | 1381.5 | 1454.6 | 1722.0 | 1992.3 | 2205.7 | 2373.0 | 2526.0 | 2782.0 | 10.0 | 42.5 |

**III.B. Coal: Consumption[5] in Million tonnes oil equivalent**

| | | | | | | | | | | | | | | |
|---|---|---|---|---|---|---|---|---|---|---|---|---|---|---|
| India | 63.2 | 72.5 | 95.5 | 125.0 | 144.2 | 145.2 | 151.8 | 156.8 | 172.3 | 184.4 | 195.4 | 212.9 | 231.4 | 8.4 | 7.0 |
| China | 304.0 | 410.7 | 529.9 | 694.6 | 667.4 | 681.3 | 713.8 | 853.1 | 983.0 | 1100.5 | 1215.0 | 1313.6 | 1406.3 | 6.8 | 42.6 |

**Note:** 1980 figure is not available in this sources that's why 1981 is presented in this Table for Coal. [1] Includes crude oil, shale oil, oil sands and NGLs (the liquid content of natural gas where this is recovered separately). [2] Inland demand plus international aviation and marine bunkers and refinery fuel and loss. Consumption of fuel ethanol and biodiesel is also included. [3] Excluding gas flared or recycled. [4] Excluding gas flared or recycled. [5] Excluding gas flared or recycled.

**Source:** Compiled from *British Petroleum (BP) Statistical Review of World Energy 2009* ( http://www.bp.com/statisticalreview).

production, it consumes about 41.3 per cent of total world output. More than 90 per cent of Chinese coal resources are located in inland provinces, but the biggest increase in demand is expected to occur in the coastal regions. This adds to the pressure on internal coal transport and makes imports into coastal provinces more competitive. China became a net coal importer in the first half of 2007. As far as India is concerned, it produces only 5.8 per cent of total world output and consumes about 6.3 per cent of total world demand. Thus both India and China are net coal importers.

While China seems comfortable with respect to natural gas, India is a net importer. China produced about 2.4 per cent of the total world production of natural gas and consumed about 2.3 per cent of total consumption. India's share of the world's natural gas production is only 1.0 per cent at the same time it accounts for about 1.4 per cent of total natural gas consumption. But due to increasing use of the environmentally friendly fuel it is expected that the demand for natural gas will rise in both the countries making China, too, a net importer.

China and India are at a stage in their economic development in which oil consumption has just taken off and is not likely to decelerate in the foreseeable future. According to ADB's (Asian Development Bank) calculation, the income elasticity of oil consumption has historically been about 0.5; 1 per cent economic growth therefore translates into 0.5 per cent growth in oil consumption.[30] China currently consumes 7.9 million barrels of oil per day (2007), which accounts for 9.3 per cent of the world's total consumption; India consumes 2.8 million barrels of oil per day, accounting for 3.3 per cent of the world's total consumption.[31] Figure 2 presents India's oil production and consumption between 1965 and 2008 and Figure 3 presents China's oil production and consumption between 1965 and 2008. It can be observed from these Figures that India was the net importer throughout the

**Fig. 2: India's Oil Production and Consumption (1965 to 2008)**

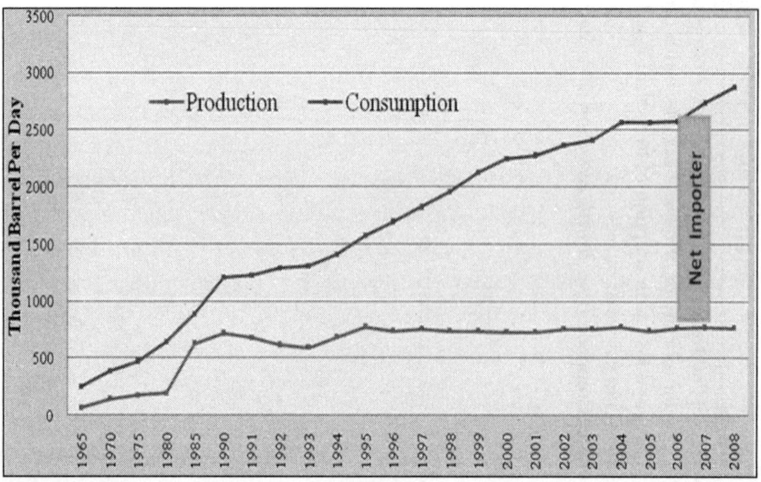


**Source:** *BP Statistical Review of World Energy*, June 2009.

**Fig. 3: China's Oil Production and Consumption (1965 to 2008)**

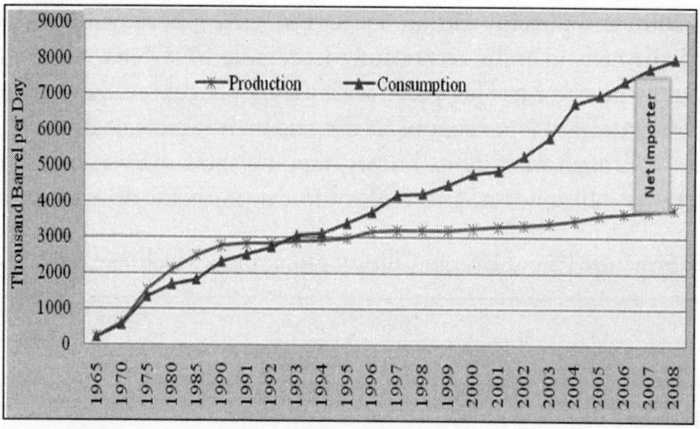


**Source:** *BP Statistical Review of World Energy*, June 2009.

reference period while China became net importer of oil from 1993, before that China was net exporter of oil. That's why Chinese and Indian firms have been competing fiercely for energy assets on offer around the world as their governments drive them to secure supplies for their growing economies.

India is a net oil importer facing an increasing gap between its domestic production and consumption trends (see Figure 2). The Indian government mandates its NOCs to source equity oil overseas to meet this demand. At present, oil and gas account for around 40 per cent of India's commercial energy consumption. Imports of crude oil and natural gas (in the form of LNG) account for about 72 per cent and 15 per cent of this consumption respectively. While consumption is only just over one third of China's, India's population is growing faster than China's. According to the influential government-commissioned report, *India's Hydrocarbon Vision 2025,*[32] the country's hydrocarbon requirements will almost triple (from 2.5mb/d in 2005 to about 7.4mb/d by 2025) while indigenous production of crude is likely to be only 1.6mb/d.[33]

According to World Bank's prediction, in spite of the current global financial crisis, India's GDP growth in 2008 was 6.3 per cent, and hovering at 5.8 per cent in 2009 and 7.7 per cent in 2010; China's GDP growth was 9.4 per cent in 2008, and remained at 7.5 per cent in 2009 and 8.5 in 2010.[34] Thus according to the calculation of ADB, as the economies keep growing at this rate, the average annual oil demand growth of China from 2007-2015 will be 0.41 million barrels per day, and that of India will be 0.125 million barrels per day.[35] Both countries' rapid growth and structural transformation will continuously fuel rapid growth of oil consumption for some time to come.

### *Energy Demand and Supply*

Compared with India, the composition of China's energy demand is more diversified. Although both economies rely heavily on domestic coal resources, especially for power generation, the share of coal in primary energy use was much higher in China at 73 per cent in 2005 and possibly hitting 55 per cent in 2030, as compared with 55 per cent and 45 per cent in India respectively (see Table 6). China relies more on coal because it has so much of it. Compared with only 1 per cent of the world's proven oil and gas reserves, nearly 13 per cent of all the known mineable coal still in the ground is in China.[36] Through most of its history, tapping these reserves has allowed China to remain energy independent, and is likely to continues for decades ahead.

**Table 6: Structure (%) of Energy Consumption: India vs China (2005 and 2030)**

| | India | | China | |
|---|---|---|---|---|
| | **2005** | **2030** | **2005** | **2030** |
| Hydro | 2 | 2 | 2 | 3 |
| Oil | 34 | 35 | 21 | 24 |
| Natural Gas | 8 | 13 | 3 | 11 |
| Nuclear | 1 | 5 | 1 | 3 |
| Coal | 55 | 45 | 73 | 55 |

**Source:** The Institute of Energy Economics, Japan (IEEJ).

Currently the world's second largest consumer of oil, only thirteen years ago China did not import any oil at all. In 2004, oil imports to China increased by 37 per cent, which contributed to soaring oil prices around the world.[37] In 2005, China consumed an average of 6.9 million barrels per day (mb/d) of oil.[38] By 2025, that amount is projected to increase to approximately 13.2 mb/d.[39] That same year China's production level is expected to be approximately 4.0 mbd, which will require the country to have a net import of at least 9.2 mb/d.[40]

China had managed to be self-sufficient until 1993, meeting all its internal consumer oil needs for the previous five decades due to the discovery of massive oil reserves at the Daqing oil fields in the far north of the country during the 1950's. With the increase in oil consumption, the Daqing oil fields can no longer be relied upon to fully sustain the country in the years to come. With economic growth running at a rate of about nine per cent per year, China is now engaged in a massive effort to reach beyond its borders and grab as much oil as possible to ensure its future economic growth. To this end China is directing much of its attention to Russia, Canada, South America, the Middle East and Africa.

## Trade and Investment Cooperation in Energy Resources

India and China in the recent past have experienced robust growth in bilateral trade especially since the mid-1990s. After more than 44 years, India and China opened the Himalayan pass through Nathu La[41] in July 2006, an ancient trading route that once connected both the countries. India and China, the two fastest growing economies in the world, are set to achieve a bilateral trade target of 60 billion dollars by 2010 despite the Indian industry becoming wary of signing a free trade agreement with the neighbouring economic giant.[42]

India's trade with China was merely US$1.8 billion in 1999-2000, which significantly increased to the level of US$41.8 billion in 2008-09 with average annual growth rate of more than 40 per cent (DGCIS). But trade in energy sector between both countries is abysmal as compared to other sectors.[43] Table 7 presents India-China trade in energy sector (Mineral fuels, oils & product as percentage share of total trade from 1999 to 2008. India holds more than 1 per cent share in major petroleum products import markets, such as Singapore, Japan, United Kingdom, Belgium and Korea. It is quite clear from this table that India's export to China in energy is negligible or merely little over 1 per cent but its import from China is quite high and has registered fluctuating trends. But if we include ores and minerals in energy sector, India's exports to China in energy is 51 per cent as can be seen in Chart 1. It is also important to note that even trade in oil within Asia remains marginal.

**Table 7: India-China Trade in Energy Sector (HS 27) as Percentage Share of Total Trade (1999 to 2008)**

**Value in US Million Dollar and Percentage Share**

| Year | Total Merchandise Trade (US$ Million) | | Mineral fuels, oils & product (HS 27) (US$ Million) | | % Share of Energy Trade in Total Trade | |
|---|---|---|---|---|---|---|
| | Exports | Imports | Exports | Imports | Exports | Imports |
| 1999 | 542.01 | 1294.88 | 0.04 | 160.31 | 0.01 | 12.38 |
| 2000 | 844.15 | 1527.51 | 0.86 | 267.71 | 0.10 | 17.53 |
| 2001 | 962.36 | 2057.85 | 1.92 | 265.39 | 0.20 | 12.90 |
| 2002 | 1966.17 | 2779.14 | 9.92 | 174.35 | 0.50 | 6.27 |
| 2003 | 2918.77 | 4004.51 | 73.39 | 218.60 | 2.51 | 5.46 |
| 2004 | 5300.80 | 6711.65 | 16.12 | 803.53 | 0.30 | 11.97 |
| 2005 | 6785.07 | 10911.18 | 18.82 | 723.81 | 0.28 | 6.63 |
| 2006 | 8278.97 | 17427.95 | 108.98 | 1255.87 | 1.32 | 7.21 |
| 2007 | 9491.98 | 24575.77 | 99.63 | 1231.20 | 1.05 | 5.01 |
| 2008 | 10093.93 | 31586.02 | 154.29 | 1498.50 | 1.53 | 4.74 |

**Source:** Author's calculations based on the MAcMAp online database, 2009.

**Chart 1: India's Exports to China by Broad Commodity Group (2006-07)**

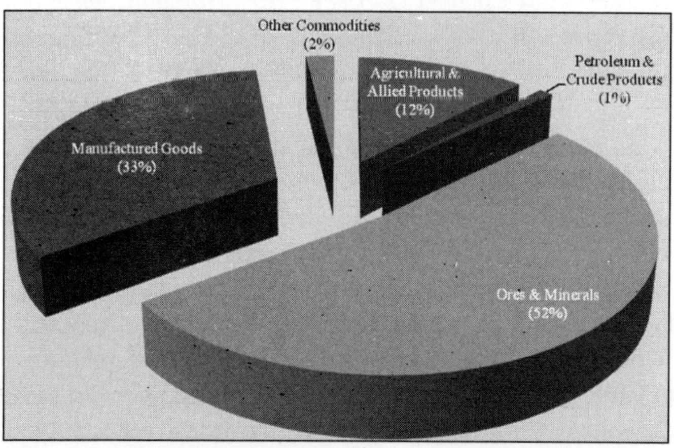


**Source:** Directorate General of Commercial Intelligence Statistics (DGCIS), Ministry of Commerce and Industry, Government of India.

Major destinations of India's exports of petroleum products include Singapore (25.5 per cent), Iran (9.8 per cent), UAE (7.4 per cent), The Netherlands (5.1 per cent), Sri Lanka (4.5 per cent), Indonesia (4.4 per cent), Brazil (4.3 per cent), Nepal (3.1 per cent), South Africa (3.1 per cent), and Togo (3 per cent). These 10 countries together account for over 70 per cent of India's total petroleum products exports. High-speed diesel (39.4 per cent), light oils and preparations (19.5 per cent), aviation turbine oil (13.8 per cent) and fuel oil (8 per cent) are the major petroleum products being exported from India.[44] India needs to take advantage of its strategic leadership in refining and increase its refining capacity, as demand for petroleum products is high in Asia. India's close neighbours themselves are energy deficient countries and there is a huge potential for exports of petroleum products to Pakistan, Myanmar and China. Besides, the huge demand that exists in Japan could also be captured.

Composition of India's exports to China is dominated by ores and minerals which accounted for more than 50 per cent of the total exports of the country, followed by manufactured goods, accounting for 33 per cent of total exports. In terms of commodities, India's export basket to China primarily comprises of iron ore and other ores & minerals, raw cotton, non-ferrous metals, plastic & linoleum products and processed minerals together accounting for 73.5 per cent of total exports to China during 2006-07. Exports of iron ore alone constitute 40 per cent of total exports. Major import items from China include: electronic goods, nonelectrical machinery, iron & steel, organic chemicals, coal, coke & briquettes together, accounting for 61.5 per cent of total exports to India.

An attempt has been made here to examine the level of India-China trade energy at HS-6 digit classification. Table 8 presents India's Trade with China in Energy Resources at 6-digit HS Classification during the period between 1999 to 2008. India's exports to China in energy sectors include: (i) Petroleum coke – Calcined (271312); (ii) Paraffin wax containing by weight (271220); (iii) Petroleum jelly (271210); (iv) Petroleum oils and oils obtained (270900); and (v) Petroleum oils and oils obtained (271000). India's imports from China in energy products include: (i) Petroleum coke – not calcined (271311); (ii) Petroleum oils and oils obtained (271000); (iii) Petroleum coke – calcined (271312); (iv) Paraffin wax containing by weight (271220); (v) Petroleum oils and oils obtained (270900); and (vi) others (271290).

Trade flow in energy products between India and China is not regular as is evident in Table 8. During the period 1999 to 2008, these selected products sometime appear in the trade basket and suddenly next year disappear, which indicates that the trade in energy products between India and China is determined by the nature of bilateral relations. It is important for both the countries to regularize the exchange of the energy products in their trade basket. It can also be observed from this Table 8 that there are few products which are common in the basket of India's exports to and imports from China. That means, both countries are trading with each other in the same products category, which is known as Intra-Industry Trade (IIT). Therefore, an attempt has been made here to identify those products which are common in

**Table 8: India's Trade with China in Energy Resources at 6-digit HS Classification (1999 to 2008) (Value in US Thousand Dollar**

| HS-6 | Product Description (brief) | 1999 | 2000 | 2001 | 2002 | 2003 | 2004 | 2005 | 2006 | 2007 | 2008 |
|---|---|---|---|---|---|---|---|---|---|---|---|
| **India's Exports to China (at 6-digit HS Classification)** | | | | | | | | | | | |
| 270900 | Petroleum oils and oils obtained fr | | | | | | | | | 31.041 | 15.119 |
| 271000 | Petroleum oils and oils obtained fr | | | 18.725 | 9566.185 | 67639.633 | 5639.081 | 16423.198 | 108845.272 | 97879.287 | 148863.827 |
| 271114 | Liquefied: Ethylene, propylene, | | | | | | | 2345.164 | | | |
| 271121 | In gaseous state: Natural gas | | | | | 21.508 | | | | | |
| 271210 | Petroleum jelly | | | | 21.69 | | | | | | 36.167 |
| 271220 | Paraffin wax containing by weight l | 36.948 | 25.881 | 454.647 | 4.24 | | 19.043 | 48.155 | 127.148 | 61.948 | 307.092 |
| 271290 | Other | | | 4.37 | 40.673 | 3.832 | | | | | 2.584 |
| 271311 | Petroleum coke: Not calcined | | | 973.892 | | | | | | | |
| 271312 | Petroleum coke: Calcined | | | | | 5706.51 | | | | 1489.483 | 5061.369 |
| | All Products | 36.948 | 25.881 | 1451.634 | 9632.788 | 73371.483 | 5658.124 | 18816.517 | 108972.42 | 99461.759 | 154286.158 |
| **India's Imports from China (at 6-digit HS Classification)** | | | | | | | | | | | |
| Product | Product Name | 1999 | 2000 | 2001 | 2002 | 2003 | 2004 | 2005 | 2006 | 2007 | 2008 |
| 270900 | Petroleum oils and oils obtained fr | | | | | | | | | | 10604.287 |
| 271000 | Petroleum oils and oils obtained fr | 12247.047 | | | | | | | 35315.845 | 18213.103 | 46309.915 |
| 271112 | Liquefied: Propane | | | | | | | | | | 12.33 |
| 271113 | Liquefied: Butanes | | | | | | | | 33.027 | 35.62 | |
| 271119 | Liquefied: Other | 25.189 | | | | | | | | | 3070.561 |
| 271129 | In gaseous state: Other | | | | | | 3.419 | | | | 0.84 |
| 271210 | Petroleum jelly | | | | | | | | 70.972 | 120.703 | 353.716 |
| 271220 | Paraffin wax containing by weight l | | | | | | | | 23300.866 | 24254.22 | 23781.483 |
| 271290 | Other | | | | | | | | 2858.231 | 2663.937 | 3867.229 |
| 271311 | Petroleum coke: Not calcined | | | | | | | | 53358.585 | 22892.756 | 74495.424 |
| 271312 | Petroleum coke: Calcined | | | | | | | | 20390.916 | 16510.729 | 33004.313 |
| 271390 | Other residues of petroleum oils or | | | | | | | | 5.048 | | |
| 271410 | Bituminous or oil shale and tar san | | | | | | 0.119 | | 0.056 | 0.057 | |
| 271490 | Other | | | | | 0.835 | 1.657 | 19.663 | 1.959 | 4.505 | 40.204 |
| 271500 | Bituminous mixtures based on natura | | 8.537 | | | | | 3.135 | 0.334 | 0.434 | 2.407 |
| | All Products | 12272.236 | 8.537 | 0 | 0 | 0.835 | 5.195 | 22.798 | 135335.839 | 84696.064 | 195542.709 |

**Source:** Extracted from Market Access Map (MAcMAp) online Database 2009.

trade basket of India and China. The next section is devoted to estimating of IIT index in energy sector between India and China at both levels, bilateral as well as global. One would urge corporations in both India and China to explore two-way FDI flows for investments in trade generating ventures with buy-back arrangements. Intra-industry trade constitutes yet another unexplored area in energy sector for business-to-business cooperation between India and China at bilateral and global levels.

### *Intra-Industry Trade (IIT) between India and China in Energy Sector*

Another important tool to measure energy cooperation between India and China is Intra-Industry Trade (IIT) index. The IIT index reflects the extent of both export orientation (EO) and import penetration (IP) within the given sector (or products). A high value indicates that there is both export and import trade within the sector (or products). A low level indicates that trade is mainly one way, i.e. the industry sector is either export oriented or mainly import focused. A value for IIT is indicative of the growing tendency of firms, or branches of multinational firms, to specialize in particular products within an industrial sector, possibly due to economies of scale, product differentiation or geographic product specialization. This results in growth in trade which can occur even when factors of production are similar between the countries, i.e. when conditions would normally result in low levels of trade.

The intra-industry trade index is defined as the proportion of total trade remaining after subtracting the absolute value of net exports or net imports. If exports and imports are equal then the IIT index is 100, i.e. whatever the level of trade it flows in both directions in about equal amounts. The index gets smaller if the net difference between imports and exports makes up a larger proportion of total trade, i.e. either as the net difference between imports and exports increases indicating a larger trade in one direction, or this net difference makes up a larger proportion of the total trade indicating that trade is only in one direction. In either case the trade is increasingly one-directional.

Table 9 presents the Intra-Industry index value between India's exports to the world and China's imports from the world in 2007 at the 6-digit HS Classification in energy products and Table 10 presents the IIT in energy product at bilateral between India and China at the 6-digit HS classification. This exercise will identify the industries where potential for investment exists. It may be observed that the firms involved in these industries, may benefit from joint ventures with firms in that are major importer (China) of the particular products. Further it can be extended to foreign direct investment promotion between India and China.

The nature of India's IIT with China at global level in 6-digit HS classification in energy sector points the possibility of India's setting up joint ventures in China in those products or sectors having higher IIT index value and China's setting up joint ventures in India in those products or sectors having lower IIT index value. This Table is self-explanatory and hence the products can be easily identified (from the listed products in this Table) for setting up joint ventures in energy products

**Table 9: Intra-Industry Trade (IIT) between India and China in Energy Sector (2007) at Global Level**
**Value in US Thousand Dollar**

| HS-6 Digit | Product Description (brief) | India's Exports | China's Imports | IIT Index Value |
|---|---|---|---|---|
| 271000 | Petroleum oils & oils obtained from bituminous miner | 11439920 | 10425543 | 95.361 |
| 271114 | Ethylene, propylene, butylene and butadiene, lique | 13747 | 18746 | 84.615 |
| 270740 | Naphthalene | 30106 | 56027 | 69.906 |
| 271220 | Paraffin wax containing by weight less than 0.75% | 8389 | 15907 | 69.057 |
| 271312 | Petroleum coke, calcined | 66675 | 31872 | 64.684 |
| 271119 | Petroleum gases and other gaseous hydrocarbons nes | 38413 | 17489 | 62.570 |
| 270600 | Tar distilled from coal, lignite or peat & other m | 2240 | 984 | 61.042 |
| 270799 | Oils&oth products of the distillation of high temp | 97909 | 34465 | 52.072 |
| 270791 | Creosote oils | 2 | 6 | 50.000 |
| 271390 | Residues of petroleum oils/of oils obtaind from bi | 315 | 1318 | 38.579 |
| 270119 | Coal nes, whether or not pulverised but not agglom | 60356 | 11361 | 31.683 |
| 271210 | Petroleum jelly | 22784 | 3162 | 24.374 |
| 270810 | Pitch | 155 | 1261 | 21.893 |
| 271121 | Natural gas in gaseous state | 74 | 8 | 19.512 |
| 270120 | Coal briquettes, ovoids and similar manufactured s | 70 | 3 | 8.219 |
| 271290 | Mineral waxes nes and similar products obtained by | 619 | 20702 | 5.806 |
| 270400 | Coke&semi-coke of coal,lignite o peat,agglomeratd | 17916 | 375 | 4.100 |
| 271500 | Bituminous mixtures based on natural asphalt etc | 145 | 7100 | 4.003 |
| 270750 | Aromatic hydrocarbon mixtures etc nes | 2592 | 205719 | 2.489 |
| 270300 | Peat (including peat litter), whether or not agglo | 18 | 1639 | 2.173 |
| 271410 | Bituminous or oil shale and tar sands | 1 | 109 | 1.818 |
| 271490 | Bitumen and asphalt; asphaltites and asphaltic roc | 1155 | 141786 | 1.616 |
| 271129 | Petroleum gases and other gaseous hydrocarbons nes | 3140 | 24 | 1.517 |
| 271311 | Petroleum coke, not calcined | 262 | 36919 | 1.409 |
| 270730 | Xylole | 1397 | 201500 | 1.377 |
| 271111 | Natural gas, liquefied | 58233 | 182 | 0.623 |
| 271320 | Petroleum bitumen | 1254 | 644642 | 0.388 |
| 270710 | Benzole | 2 | 2191 | 0.182 |
| 270820 | Pitch coke | 17 | 22585 | 0.150 |
| 270900 | Petroleum oils and oils obtained from bituminous m | 30118 | 47722764 | 0.126 |
| 270500 | Coal gas,water gas,etc,o/than petroleum gases & ga | 13567 | 6 | 0.088 |
| 271112 | Propane, liquefied | 352 | 1345997 | 0.052 |
| 270111 | Anthracite, whether or not pulverised but not aggl | 85 | 475264 | 0.036 |
| 271113 | Butanes, liquefied | 72 | 1454988 | 0.010 |
| 270112 | Bituminous coal, whether or not pulverised but not | 34 | 896826 | 0.008 |

**Source:** Author's calculations based on the MAcMAp online database, 2009.

between India and China and vice-versa.These products include: (i) Petroleum oils & oils obtained from bituminous miner (271000); (ii) Ethylene, propylene, butylene and butadiene, lique (271114); (iii) Naphthalene (270740); (iv) Paraffin wax containing by weight less than 0.75% (271220); (v) Petroleum coke, calcined (271312); (vi) Petroleum gases and other gaseous hydrocarbons nes (271119); (vii) Tar distilled from coal, lignite or peat & other m (270600); (viii) Oils and other products of the distillation of high temp (270799); and (viii) Creosote oils (270791).

We have also computed IIT at bilateral level in energy products between India and China during the period from 1999 to 2008 and estimated results of index are presented in Table 10. It can be observed from this Table that there are few products having high IIT index value in energy products. Though the numbers of products in which IIT exists are 10 in energy sector, but the overall trade has very high number of products where IIT exists. Bilateral trade between India and China is taking place in 4754 products at HS-6 digit and there are 4092 matched products in India's exports basket and China's import basket. Out of 4092 products, 2098 products are having IIT index value between 0.001 to 100.0. Only 283 products have more than 50.0 IIT index value and 1265 products are in the range of 1 to less than 0.50 IIT index value.

Table 10 presents the bilateral IIT index value in energy products between India and China at 6-digit HS classification which points the possibility of India's setting up joint ventures in China in those products or sectors having higher IIT index value. These products include: (i) Coal, whether or not pulverised, bu (270119); (ii) Coke and semi-coke of coal, of lign (270400); (iii) Petroleum oils and oils obtained fr (271000); (iv) Petroleum jelly (271210); (v) Paraffin wax containing by weight (271220); and (vi) Petroleum coke – Calcined (271312).

Therefore, India has potential to establish trade generating joint ventures in all these identified products (having high IIT Index Values more than unity) with China and scope for IIT specialization in all these products. Thus, India and China (vice-versa) could set up a joint marketing strategy in those matched products which have the potential of joint ventures which in turn, would enhance the India-China trade in energy sector. The products negotiated for fast track liberalization and concessions under preferential trade should relate to high potential/intra-industry trade in energy sector. There is a small number of products in energy sector where potential for investment exists between both countries. Therefore, it will be viable to suggest that the firms involved in these products or industries, may benefit from joint ventures with firms which are the major importers of these particular products. Further it can be extended to foreign direct investment promotion between both countries.

Indian and Chinese industry should look beyond mere exports, and need to look at possibilities of joint ventures (JV's) and investments in each other's markets. Such investments and JV's will help Indian and Chinese industries to specialize in their core competencies, cut costs and access markets not only in India and China, but also in third countries. In the context of continuously rising global economic status of both China and India and the existing and potential complementarities (as well

Table 10: Intra-Industry Trade (IIT) between India and China in Energy sector (2007) at Bilateral Level

| HS-2 | Product Description (brief) | 1999 | 2000 | 2001 | 2002 | 2003 | 2004 | 2005 | 2006 | 2007 | 2008 |
|---|---|---|---|---|---|---|---|---|---|---|---|
| 270119 | Coal, whether or not pulverised, bu | 0.000 | 0.875 | 0.003 | 0.709 | 0.000 | 0.000 | 0.000 | 0.000 | 0.000 | 0.000 |
| 270400 | Coke and semi-coke of coal, of lign | 0.000 | 0.526 | 0.000 | 0.000 | 0.000 | 0.000 | 0.000 | 0.000 | 0.001 | 0.000 |
| 270760 | Phenols | 0.000 | 0.000 | 0.000 | n/a | n/a | n/a | n/a | 0.000 | n/a | n/a |
| 270799 | Other | n/a | 0.000 | n/a | n/a | 0.000 | 0.000 | 0.000 | 72.979 | 10.659 | n/a |
| 270900 | Petroleum oils and oils | n/a | n/a | n/a | n/a | n/a | n/a | n/a | n/a | 0.000 | 0.285 |
| 271000 | Petroleum oils and oils | 0.000 | n/a | 0.000 | 0.000 | 0.000 | 0.000 | 0.000 | 48.995 | 31.377 | 47.455 |
| 271210 | Petroleum jelly | n/a | n/a | n/a | 0.000 | n/a | n/a | n/a | 0.000 | 0.000 | 18.553 |
| 271220 | Paraffin wax containing by weight l | 0.000 | 0.000 | 0.000 | 0.000 | n/a | 0.000 | 0.000 | 1.085 | 0.510 | 2.550 |
| 271290 | Other | n/a | n/a | 0.000 | 0.000 | 0.000 | n/a | n/a | 0.000 | 0.000 | 0.134 |
| 271312 | Petroleum coke: Calcined | n/a | n/a | n/a | n/a | 0.000 | n/a | n/a | 0.000 | 16.550 | 26.593 |

**Note:** n/a denotes not available.

**Source:** Author's calculations based on the MAcMAp online database, 2009.

as competition) in the Asian and the global markets, it would be ideal for India and China to forge mutually beneficial and mutually rewarding strategic partnership at business-to-business level in both countries. After computing IIT (global and bilateral) between India and China in energy products, it would be necessary to examine the existing complementarity between both countries with the help of Cosine measure, popularly known as 'trade complementarity index'.

*Trade Complementarity in Energy Resources between India and China*

In this section, India's trade complementarities with China, with India as a supplier (exporter) and China as a market (importer) and *vice-versa* for the period between 2000 and 2007 taking all products at 2-digit classification under the harmonized system (HS) have been examined. The results of computation are summarized in Table 11. This result shows that the number of matched products between India as a supplier and China as a market are higher as compared to China as supplier and India as a market.

The degree of trade complementarities (index value)[45] is moderate in India as a supplier and China as a market and poor in China as supplier and India as a market. The index value of trade complementarities in India as a supplier and China as a market was 0.261 in 2000 which increased to 0.442 in 2007 indicating poor complementarity. Reversing the trade complementarities between China as supplier and India as a market, the degree of trade complementarities was high with value of 0.831 in 2000 and 0.837 in 2007.

**Table 11: Trade Complementarity between India and China in Overall Products and Energy Sector**

| Year | Merchandise Trade | | Energy Sector Trade | |
|---|---|---|---|---|
| | India Exports & China Imports | India Imports & China Exports | India Exports & China Imports | India Imports & China Exports |
| 2000 | 0.261 | 0.831 | 0.006 | 0.625 |
| 2003 | 0.310 | 0.739 | 0.025 | 0.470 |
| 2005 | 0.323 | 0.678 | 0.285 | 0.533 |
| 2007 | 0.442 | 0.837 | 0.290 | 0.468 |

**Source:** Author's calculations based on the PCTAS CDROM database, 2002, 2005 and 2007.

Similarly, when we measure the degree of trade complementarities in energy products, we observe that there is poor complementarity in India as a supplier and China as a market and moderate in China as supplier and India as a market. The index value of trade complementarities in India as a supplier and China as a market was 0.006 in 2000 which increased to 0.290 in 2007 indicating poor complementarity. Reversing the trade complementarities between China as supplier and India as a market, the degree of trade complementarities was high with value of 0.625 in 2000 and 0.468 in 2007. Therefore, the computation results revealed that there is poor trade complementarity in India as a supplier and China as a market and moderate in China as supplier and India as a market in total merchandise trade as well as trade in energy products (HS-27).

Though the overall trade complementarity is high between India's imports and China's exports while low trade complementarities exist between India's exports and China's imports, but there are large number of products demonstrating high or moderate trade complementarity at 2-digit HS sectoral/products level between both countries. Despite the challenges posed by China and India to each other in energy sector, we find moderate complementarity in their export-import structures in energy products. This indicates a potential for trade expansion between the two countries. Moderate to high complementarity also exists between the India's exports to China and China's imports from India in overall merchandise trade. Hence both countries are expected to benefit each other if the complementarity in the trade structures can be enhanced and if they are able to further diversify their export bases.

Despite the fact that India's share in world merchandise exports is merely 1.2 per cent and in absolute terms, India is way behind China with its exports constituting 12.4 per cent of China's in 2008. The major development in the direction of India's trade is that USA which was in the first position in 2007-08 has been relegated to the third position in 2008-09, with UAE becoming India's largest trading partner, followed by China.[46] Though the existing trade level in energy sector is low but there is huge potential to enhance trade in energy sector between India and China. Expansion of trade in energy resources between both countries could be further promoted by undertaking bilateral cooperation (through the frequent interaction between government, business and industry on an institutional basis) in the broadest possible areas because there exists complementarities and opportunities for cooperation between the two countries in many areas. There is an urgent need to establish a joint promotion mechanism to promote trade in energy sectors between both countries.

## Foreign Direct Investment Inflows in Energy Sector in India

The Government of India has put in place a liberal, transparent investment regime and an investor-friendly FDI policy wherein FDI up to 100 per cent is allowed under automatic route for most of the sectors including Petroleum and Natural Gas (P&NG).[47] In refining and marketing, India has already introduced liberal policies. Investments in the refining sector are open and companies investing over Rs 20 billion (US $450 million) in the domestic oil and gas sector are also given rights to market petroleum products in India.[48] Petroleum and Natural Gas Industry accounts for 35 per cent share in the entire energy requirements in India.

Government has taken several initiatives to drive FDI inflows to Petroleum and Natural Gas (P&NG) in India.[49] The New Exploration Licensing Policy (NELP) has been introduced to enable private sector participation in oil and gas exploration which will bring in more investments to the sector and a Coal Bed Methane (CBM) Policy has been introduced to ensure attractive financial and contract terms in order to explore CBM blocks. Downstream industries like petrochemicals, fertilizers and energy play a vital role in the OIL industry in India (Table 12).

**Table 12: Summary of NELP* Exploration Blocs Awarded in India**

| Parameter | NELP-I | NELP-II | NELP-III | NELP-IV | NELP-V | NELP-VI |
|---|---|---|---|---|---|---|
| (a) No. of Blocs Offered | 48 | 25 | 27 | 24 | 20 | 55 |
| (b) No. of Blocs Bid for | 28 | 23 | 24 | 21 | 20 | 52 |
| (c) No. of Bids Received | 45 | 44 | 52 | 44 | 69 | 165 |
| (d) No. of Blocs Awarded | 25 | 23 | 23 | 21 | 20 | 52 |
| (e) No. of PSC Signed | 24 | 23 | 23 | 20 | 20 | 52 |
| (f) Area Awarded (sq km) | 194735 | 263050 | 204588 | 192810 | 115180 | 306200 |

**Note:** * New Exploration Licensing Policy (NELP) VII will be launched soon.
**Source:** Government of India, Ministry of Petroleum & Natural Gas Background Material for Economic Editors' Conference, 13 November 2007 (Economic Division).

Table 13 presents the trends in FDI inflows in petroleum and natural gas sector. FDI in petroleum and natural gas shows increasing trends during the period between 2004-05 to 2008-09. The percentage share of FDI in P&NG and annual growth rates registered fluctuating trends during the reference period and constituted around 3 per cent of the total India's FDI. It is quite clear from this table that in 2004-05, the share of FDI in petroleum and natural gas was 3.53 per cent which significantly declined in next year 2005-06 and reached merely 0.26 per cent but suddenly in 2007-08 its share climbed up and recorded highest ever 5.80 per cent.

**Table 13: Trends in Overall Inflows under Petroleum & Natural Gas (P&NG) Sector (in million rupees)**

| Year | FDI Inflows | | % of FDI in P&NG to Total FDI | Annual Growth (%) | |
|---|---|---|---|---|---|
| | Total (All sectors) | P&NG Sector | | P&NG Sector | All Sectors |
| 2004-05 | 3219 | 113 | 3.53 | | |
| 2005-06 | 5546 | 14 | 0.26 | –87.53 | 72.29 |
| 2006-07 | 15730 | 89 | 0.57 | 531.59 | 183.63 |
| 2007-08 | 24579 | 1427 | 5.80 | 1496.25 | 56.26 |
| 2008-09* | 27309 | 588 | 2.15 | –58.78 | 11.11 |
| Total | 76309 | 2232 | 2.92 | | |

**Note:** * April to December 2008.
**Source:** Foreign Direct Cell, Department of Industrial Policy & Promotion, Government of India taken from Basic Statistics on Indian Petroleum & Natural Gas 2008-09, Ministry of Petroleum & Natural Gas, Government of India, New Delhi, (Economic Division), p. 40.

It can be observed from the Table 14 that the major item in FDI inflows is oil and refinery which attracted maximum amount of inflows. Among the major foreign investors in oil and natural gas in India, Singapore ranks first with 18.37 per cent followed by Mauritius (18.37 per cent), United Kingdom (4.48 per cent), Cyprus (4.17 per cent), and United States (3.75 per cent. The total number of FDI is 202 in petroleum and natural gas sector and USA has invested in 26 projects followed by United Kingdom (21), Mauritius (21) and Cyprus (17). During the period April 2000 to January 2009, FDI inflows in petroleum and natural gas attracted US$ 2244.17 million.

**Table 14: India: Country-wise FDI Inflows Under Petroleum & Natural Gas Sector**

| Sl. No. | Country | No. of FDI | Items | Amount Inflows (Million US$) | % Share of Country Total |
|---|---|---|---|---|---|
| 1. | Australia | 2 | Oil Refinery | 0.00 | 0.00 |
| 2. | Bahamas | 1 | Others (Fuel) | 5.00 | 0.22 |
| 3. | British Virginia | 5 | Oil Refinery, & Others (Fuel) | 2.72 | 0.12 |
| 4. | Cayman Island | 3 | Others (Fuel) ;Oil Refinery, Oil Exploration | 14.48 | 0.65 |
| 5. | Cyprus | 17 | Others (Fuel) | 91.88 | 4.12 |
| 6. | France | 8 | Oil Refinery & Others (Fuel) | 30.75 | 1.38 |
| 7. | Germany | 12 | Transportation (Oil Refinery) | 3.87 | 0.17 |
| 8. | Ireland | 1 | Others; Oil Refinery & Transportation | 1.09 | 0.05 |
| 9. | Japan | 4 | Oil Refinery | 2.42 | 0.11 |
| 10. | Korea | 5 | Oil Refinery | 1.19 | 0.05 |
| 11. | Kuwait | 2 | Oil Refinery | 0.11 | 0.00 |
| 12. | Mauritius | 21 | Oil Refinery & Others (Fuel) | 360.55 | 16.16 |
| 13. | Malaysia | 3 | Oil Refinery | 0.42 | 0.02 |
| 14. | Netherland | 11 | Oil Refinery & Others (Fuel) | 40.45 | 1.81 |
| 15. | New Zealand | 1 | Oil Refinery | 0.04 | 0.00 |
| 16. | Norway | 1 | Oil Refinery | 0.11 | 0.00 |
| 17. | Spain | 1 | Oil Refinery & Transportation | 0.15 | 0.01 |
| 18. | Singapore | 13 | Oil Refinery | 1288.72 | 57.75 |
| 19. | South Africa | 1 | Transportation (Oil Refinery) | 0.04 | 0.00 |
| 20. | UAE | 4 | Oil Refinery, Oil Exploration & | 1.56 | 0.07 |
| 21. | UK | 21 | Others (Fuel) | 97.52 | 4.37 |
| 22. | USA | 26 | Oil Refinery & Others (Fuel) Transportation | 82.57 | 3.70 |
| 23. | Acquisition of Shares | 35 | Oil Refinery, Oil Exploration | 189.79 | 8.51 |
| 24. | NRI | 4 | Oil Refinery | 16.00 | 0.72 |
| | Total | 202 | | 2231.43 | 100.00 |

**Source:** Foreign Direct Cell, Department of Industrial Policy & Promotion, Government of India taken from Basic Statistics on Indian Petroleum & Natural Gas 2008-09, Ministry of Petroleum & Natural Gas, Government of India, New Delhi, (Economic Division), p.41.

It is quite clear that the bilateral investment between India and China is almost negligible but there is a huge potential for expansion of investment in energy sector between both countries. The challenge is not only to exploit the existing potential in energy sector but also to make investment more broad based and diversified in favour of energy sector. Bilateral investment flows in energy resources between the two countries can also be promoted fruitfully by both business chambers and government agencies through organized institutional promotion campaign, viz., successful business missions between India and China to explore the potential of business collaboration and investments, and organizing investment seminars and expositions focusing on products and technologies. Both countries can also enhance trade and investment cooperation in energy sector with the support and assistance of India-China Business Development Forum (ICBDF) through the exchange of technical information, rules and regulations about business activities and marketing strategies, market survey (research) and others.

Table 15 presents the structural characteristics (ownership pattern) of India's energy sector. It can be observed from this Table that in transmission of electricity sector, 100 per cent ownership lies with government but in oil & gas and coal sector the range of ownership varies between 74 to 93 per cent. It shows that prospect of Chinese investment and joint venture in energy sector between India and China is very limited and hence unless or until these sectors are not opened up for foreign investment, competition will remain there.

**Table 15: Structural Characteristics of India's Energy Sector**

| | Energy Sectors | Ownership Pattern |
|---|---|---|
| a. | Electricity Sector (2005-06) | |
| | Generation | Public (87 per cent), Private (13 per cent) |
| | Transmission | Public (100 per cent) |
| | Distribution & End-user supply | Public (87 per cent), Private (13 per cent) |
| | Trading | Public (93 per cent), Private (07 per cent) |
| b. | Oil & Gas sector (2005-06) | |
| | Crude Oil Exploration & Production | Public (86 per cent), Private (14 per cent) |
| | Natural Gas Production | Public (77 per cent), Private (23 per cent) |
| | Oil Refining | Public (74 per cent), Private (26 per cent) |
| | Marketing | Public (86 per cent), Private (14 per cent) |
| c. | Coal Sector (2005-06) | |
| | Exploration, Production & Marketing | Public (93 per cent), Private/Captive (07 per cent) |

**Sources:** CEA General Review 2006 (published by Ministry of Power, Government of India, March 2006), Petroleum Planning and Analysis Cell (PPAC) 2006 (www.ppac.org)and Basic Statistics, Ministry of Petroleum and Natural Gas (MoPNG); Provisional Coal Statistics, Coal Controller's Organization, Government of India, Ministry of Coal as Reported in S.K. Sarkar (2007), Competition in India's Energy Sector (Electricity, Oil & Gas and Coal).

There is urgent need for greater interaction between the representatives of business and industry of the two countries. To increase mutual contact, institutional mechanism between the Chambers of Commerce of India and China should be strengthened. Both countries can together formulate some outward investment strategies and investment mechanism. Each other's market must be supported by a joint investment promotion mechanism as the key institutional arrangement for investment promotion, promotion of greater flow of investments, dissemination of information on investment opportunities, identification of new areas of collaboration and facilitation of investment implementation.

***Overseas Investment by Indian and Chinese National Oil Companies (NOCs)***

It is widely accepted that a country's energy security could be more ensured with more diversified sources of energy supply. As two emerging economies, both China and India are facing increasing energy shortages. Production overseas is an effective way to hedge against high oil prices and ensure energy security. Thus acquisitions of equity oil overseas by state companies have formed the core of energy-security policy, as both governments believe that equity oil abroad will "ensure cheap and reliable oil supply."[50] The overseas acquisitions, which started off on a small scale, have reached to globally visible levels with big ticket acquisitions being announced by large corporates regularly. A report of the Boston Consulting Group (BCG) on the emerging multinationals in the world puts 21 Indian companies among the top 100 such multinationals. Only China with 44 companies is ahead of India.

Thus both these countries are and will continue to depend heavily on oil imports to fuel their economic growth. Hence, it is important to identify the major countries or regions from which both China and India import the bulk of their crude oil requirement. More than 65 per cent of India's crude oil requirement comes from the Middle East. India imports heavily from Saudi Arabia and has long-term contracts with Iran and Syria as well. Besides the Middle East, the Caspian Sea basin is another important area for India.

India has provided Azerbaijan and Kazakhstan with aid to further try and strengthen their position in the Caspian Sea region. Africa is another important area for India. India has long-term contracts with Nigeria for 4.4 million barrels of crude oil purchase annually. It has also invested more than $1 billion in Sudan and runs a pipeline and refinery in that region. Russia is another important traditional ally from which India imports bulk of its crude oil. Table 16 presents the regional distribution of Indian National Oil Corporations (NOCs) overseas projects to understand how widely Indian NOCs has been investing in different parts of the world. The total number of investment project is 43 with 15 operators (Table 16). In the list of NOCs, ONGCVL is dominating with more than 50 per cent in overseas investment project with 25 and 11 operators. Map 1 provides detailed information about overseas initiatives of India's augmenting hydrocarbon with the help of producing assets, development and exploration in overseas.[51]

In case of China, more than 70 per cent of its crude oil requirement comes from the Middle East. It signed one of the biggest contracts with Iran in 2004 and is also heavy importer from Saudi Arabia. Africa is another important area for China. More than 7 per cent of all of China's energy demands comes from Africa. It has heavy investments ($8 billion) in Sudan, Nigeria and Chad. China is also heavily banking on the South China region for reserves where it has disputes and conflict with Malaysia and Philippines. Table 17 presents the distribution of overseas investment by Chinese oil companies in different region of the world. It is quite clear from this Table that China is dominating as compared to India in terms of number of overseas investment projects. China's total overseas investment is 139 with highest number of projects in Africa and Southeast Asia and more than fifty per cent of overseas investment done by CNPC with total 74 projects out of 139.

**Table 16: Regional Distribution of Indian NOCs Foreign Upstream Projects (up to February 2007)**

| Indian NOC | Africa | America | Asia & Australasia | MENA | RCA | Operator | Total No. of Projects |
|---|---|---|---|---|---|---|---|
| **ONGC VL** | Nigeria (2)<br>Sudan (3)*<br>Congo (Bazzaville) (1) | Brazil (1)<br>Colombia (1)<br>Cuba (2)<br>Venezuela (1) | Myanmar (2)<br>Vietnam (3) | Egypt (1)<br>Iraq (1)<br>Iran (1)<br>Libya (2)<br>Qatar (1)<br>Syria (2) | Russia (1) | 11* | 25 |
| **IOCL** | | | | Iran (1)<br>Libya (2)<br>Yemen (1) | | 0 | 3 |
| **OIL**** | Gabon (1) | | | Iran (1)<br>Libya (2)<br>Yemen (1) | | 3 | 4 |
| **GAIL** | | | | Oman (1) | | 0 | 3 |
| **GSPC** | | | | Yemen (1) | | 1 | 3 |
| **HPCL** | | | | Oman (1) | | 0 | 2 |
| **BPCL** | | | | Oman (1) | | 0 | 3 |
| Total | | | | | | 15 | 43 |

**Note:** Italics indicates a project shared with one or more of the other Indian NOCs. * including 2 joint operatorship. ** It is worth noting that OIL & OVL have a joint venture pipeline project in Sudan which is not mentioned here.

**Source:** Chattam House Research (2006).

As can be seen from Table 17, simply from the perspective of the number of overseas energy projects, CNPC is the leading Chinese player in the international market. It owns over one half of Chinese foreign energy projects. Other than the three oil giants, other Chinese state-owned enterprises such as Sinochem and CICIT and private firms have also embarked on foreign oil-related investments, albeit still very small in terms of both number of projects and investment magnitude, in recent years when international oil prices kept surging. In terms of continents, Chinese foreign investments spread from Africa, Southeast Asia, Middle East, Europe and Latin America, in that order. Major countries where Chinese oil companies are investing include Sudan, Angola, Russia, Kazakhstan, Saudi Arabia, Indonesia, and so on.[52]

Map 1: India's Overseas Initiatives for Augmenting Hydrocarbon Production

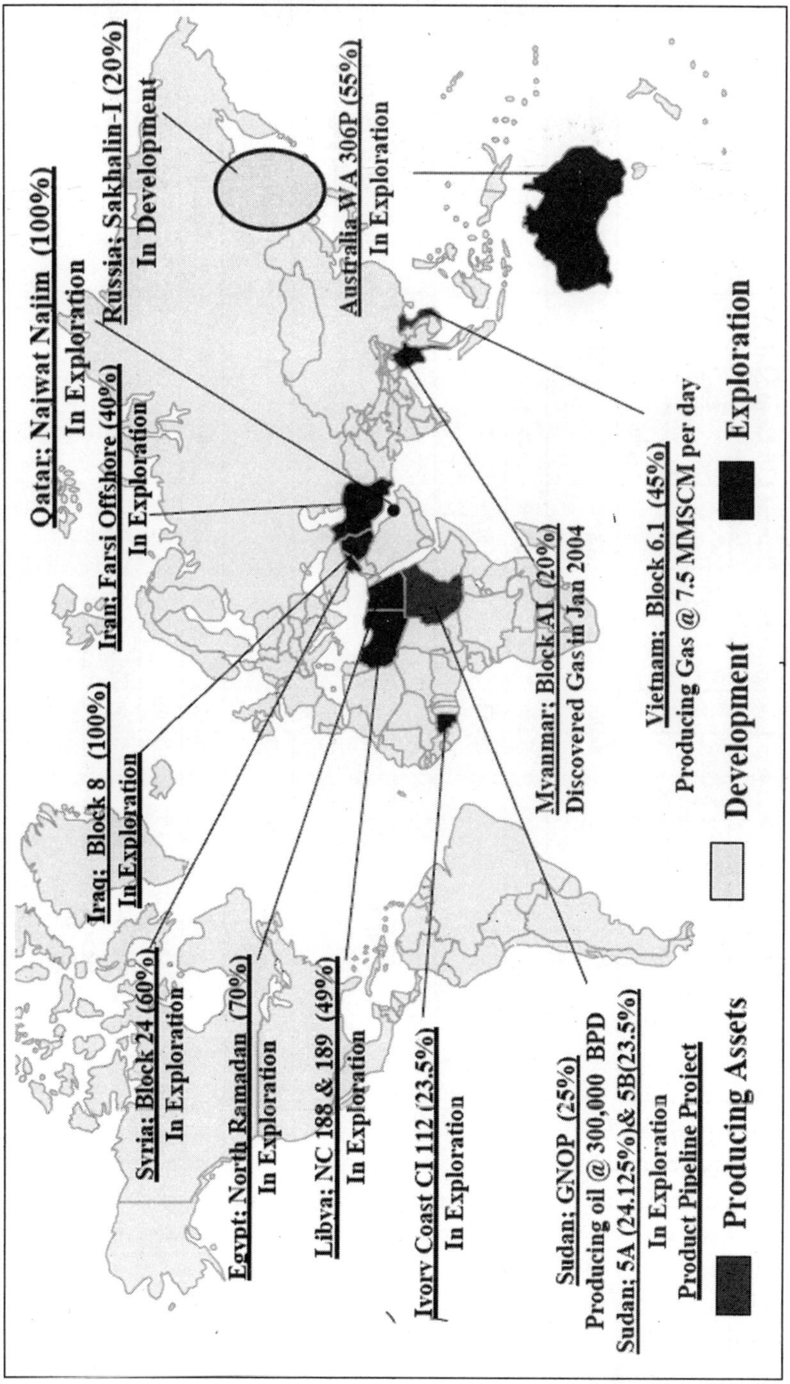

**Table 17: Distribution of Overseas Investment by Chinese Oil Companies**

| Region | CNPC | | Sinopec | | CNOOC | | Others* | | Total | | Major Countries |
|---|---|---|---|---|---|---|---|---|---|---|---|
| | Projects No. | (%) | Projects No. | (%) | Projects No. | (%) | Projects No. | (%) | Projects No. | (%) | |
| Russia and Central Asia | 16 | 21.62 | 3 | 9.38 | 0 | 0.00 | 2 | 12.50 | 21 | 15.11 | Russia, Kazakhstan, Uzbekistan |
| Middle East | 8 | 10.81 | 11 | 34.38 | 0 | 0.00 | 6 | 37.50 | 25 | 17.99 | Saudi Arabia, Yemen, Iran |
| Africa | 19 | 25.68 | 11 | 34.38 | 4 | 23.53 | 3 | 18.75 | 37 | 26.62 | Sudan, Angola, Algeria, Nigerai |
| Northeast Asia | 1 | 1.35 | 0 | 0.00 | 1 | 5.88 | 1 | 6.25 | 3 | 2.16 | Mongolia |
| Southeast Asia | 15 | 20.27 | 3 | 9.38 | 11 | 64.71 | 2 | 12.50 | 31 | 22.30 | Indonesia, Australia, Malaysia, Papua New Guinea |
| Latin America | 11 | 14.86 | 3 | 9.38 | 0 | 0.00 | 2 | 12.50 | 16 | 11.51 | Venezuela, Brazil, Ecuador, Peru |
| North America | 4 | 5.41 | 1 | 3.13 | 1 | 5.88 | 0 | 0.00 | 6 | 4.32 | Canada |
| Total | 74 | 100.00 | 32 | 100.00 | 17 | 100.00 | 16 | 100.00 | 139 | 100.00 | |

**Note:** * The other companies primarily include Sinochem, Zhuhai Zhenrong, China Aviation Oil, China National Oil & Gas Exploration and Development Corp., China National Power Equipment Corp., China Oilfield Services Ltd.

**Source:** *Zhongguo Hangye Yujing Wang* (China Industry Warning Net) (2006).

If we compare Tables 16 and 17, we find that the total number of investment projects by Chinese NOCs is 139 and by Indian NOCs only 43 which indicates that the Chinese investment in number of projects is more than three times as compared to Indian investment. CNPC of China and ONGC VL are dominating in overseas upstream projects.

The number of Chinese investment in upstream projects is higher as compared to India because Chinese NOCs get more financial support from the government and soft loans from banks. China has to rely more on foreign markets in order to meet its soaring demand for hydrocarbon resources. Securing more fossil fuels from abroad has thus become one of the priorities of China's foreign relations and an important part of its foreign strategies. The government expects the NOCs to play this role, a reason why the NOCs have the state support in their foreign energy quest.[53] For example, while crisis-hit international oil companies have been reining in their overseas expansion, China's top oil giant CNPC recently inked a US$5 billion financing deal with Kazakhstan's state oil company KazMunaiGas with the support from cash-rich state-owned banks. China's generous funding to support its oil ventures overseas has taken other forms as well. China's banks have been making headlines for showering tens of billions of loans and funds on emerging markets in Africa, Latin America and Central Asia. Beijing recently provided six resource-rich countries, including Argentina and Indonesia, with access to more than 640 billion yuan (S$141.2 billion).[54] It also announced a US$10 billion fund for ASEAN countries to support resources, among other things.

But in India, its NOCs do not receive government financial support for their overseas investment. Although Indian NOCs overseas upstream development forms a part of the government's energy security policy, they evaluate investment areas and specific deals independently and use their own funds. In this sense, their overseas upstream development is apparently more rational and sustainable than those pursued by their Chinese counterparts.[55] The detail of Chinese overseas equity in crude, geographical distribution of Chinese NOCs investment and total Chinese NOCs investment flows is presented in Table 18. Chinese overseas equity and investment is dominated in Africa and Russia and Central Asia by CNPC and SINOPEC.

Based on distribution by investment, again CNPC is the heavyweight with foreign investments of 57 per cent during 1995-2006 (see Table 18). All the three NOCs have substantial investments in Africa, indicating the growing importance of this "lost continent" to China's energy security and these corporations' takeoff. Both CNPC and Sinopec invest heavily in Russia and Central Asia. Among Chinese oil companies' overseas investments, Russia and Central Asia account for 49 per cent, and Africa attracts 29 per cent, showing the importance of the two continents to China. In terms of the percentage of the first three countries in total equity oil, foreign equity oil production by Chinese NOCs came up to 0.68mb/d in 2006, 78 per cent of which was produced in Kazakhstan, Sudan and Ecuador, whereas equity oil supplies from other countries only had a share of 22 per cent. This implies that China's equity sources are highly concentrated.

**Table 18: China Overseas Equity in Crude, Geographic Distribution of Chinese NOCs Investment and Total Chinese NOCs Investment Flows**

**I. China Overseas Equity in Crude (Barrel per Day): 2013-2015***

| NOCs | Total b/d | Africa | Middle East & North Africa | Russia & Central Asia | Asia | South & North America |
|---|---|---|---|---|---|---|
| CNPC | 733819 | 244000 | 33675 | 247683 | 60774 | 147688 |
| SINOPEC | 230590 | 105000 | 28125 | 52515 | 0 | 44950 |
| CNOOC | 142562 | 78750 | 0 | 0 | 59640 | 4173 |
| Sinochem | 7980 | 0 | 0 | 0 | 0 | 7980 |
| Total | 1114951 | 427750 | 61800 | 300198 | 120414 | 204791 |

**II. Geographic Distribution of Chinese NOCs Investment (1993-2006)**

| NOCs | Total Projects | Africa | Middle East & North Africa | Russia & Central Asia | Asia | South & North America |
|---|---|---|---|---|---|---|
| CNPC | 74 | 17 | 14 | 20 | 10 | 13 |
| SINOPEC | 29 | 14 | 6 | 6 | 1 | 2 |
| CNOOC | 13 | 4 | 2 | 0 | 6 | 1 |
| Sinochem | 4 | 0 | 3 | 0 | 0 | 1 |
| Total | 120 | 35 | 25 | 26 | 17 | 17 |

**III. Total Chinese NOCs Investment Flows by Years (US $ Million)**

| Year | Total | Africa | Middle East & North Africa | Russia & Central Asia | Asia | South & North America |
|---|---|---|---|---|---|---|
| 1993-1995 | 160 | 0 | 0 | 0 | 160 | 0 |
| 1996-1998 | 5171 | 441 | 0 | 4371 | 0 | 359 |
| 1999-2000 | 0 | 0 | 0 | 0 | 0 | 0 |
| 2001-2002 | 1869 | 0 | 444 | 81 | 1329 | 15 |
| 2003-2004 | 3506 | 1144 | 444 | 1497 | 221 | 200 |
| 2005-2006 | 16472 | 6404 | 371 | 7430 | 93 | 2175 |
| Total | 27178 | 7989 | 1259 | 13379 | 1803 | 2749 |

**Note:** * Include both current and potential future production.
**Source:** Chattam House Research (2007).

China's energy diplomacy plays a more effective role in its energy quest abroad. With China's extraordinary economic expansion and its corresponding need for energy and natural resources since the late 1990s, China's diplomacy has become more pragmatic and is mainly motivated by energy security and economic growth.[56] China has already started to channelize its diplomatic efforts into cultivating relations with oil and gas-exporting countries, and successfully using its political capital to influence pariah regions to make policy-decisions tilt to China's favour. While in India, its energy diplomacy has been restricted by its conflicting interests that may indeed clash with its energy expansion efforts. While it is engaging in more aggressive oil diplomacy with a few countries, considering more acquisitions of oil and gas assets abroad, and planning to participate in the construction of pipelines, these attempts are hindered or affected by some other strategic factors, including the US factor (see Map 1). India is also likely to run into conflict of interests with the US when considering potential energy suppliers like Myanmar, Sudan and Venezuela.

High level of urgency for oil in China and India also promotes energy competition between each other in overseas investment and acquisition. As can be seen from Figure 4 that Level of urgency for oil is one of the basic reason of competition in energy resources between India and China. Therefore, It would be appropriate here to assess the level of urgency for oil in India and China to understand the competition in energy resources.[57] There is a difference in the level of urgency for oil purchase and asset acquisition abroad between India and China in year 2007. However, this level of urgency is bound to narrow from 2010 onwards, hence competition between the two Asian giants is bound to grow from year to year. Though India's oil requirement is less than that of China and is projected to remain that way, but India's indigenous oil production will not change significantly (projected to increase from 0.85 mblpd to 1.3 mblpd in 2006 to 2030 respectively). Its dependence of oil from abroad will be more than that of China, therefore India's level of urgency is more supply oriented than consumption (which is projected to increase by 70 per cent in 25 years).

On the contrary, China's quantity of oil consumption is nearly three hundred per cent more than India and is projected to remain the same way in next 25 years with its indigenous production level increasing marginally from the current level of 3.9 mblpd to 4.9 mblpd (25 per cent increase in 25 years); during the same period its consumption will more than double. Therefore, the desperation level of both India and China is going to increase and peak from 2010, tussles for scarce oil assets acquisition will continue as both will try to get hold of scarce oil resources from abroad despite the fact that some positive measures have already taken by the governments of both India and China.

**Fig. 4: Urgency Index for Oil of India and China**

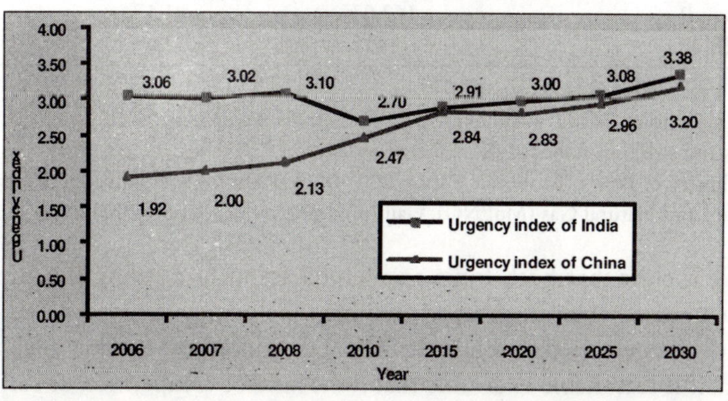


**Source:** Neeladri Chatterjee (2008), A Political Perspective on Energy Security Cooperation between India and China, *SGIA* (*School of Government and International Affairs*) *Research Working Papers Series* (SGIARWP), No. 3, April, Durham University.

In order to minimize risks by diversifying the oil import portfolio, the government of India has decided to acquire acreage in other countries. ONGC Videsh Limited, the overseas venture arm of ONGC, has entered into a production-sharing contract with British Petroleum in Vietnam. Other ongoing negotiations for oil exploration with ONGC, which are under various stages of development, include countries like Iraq, Russia, Kazakhstan, Azerbaijan, Sudan etc. Recently, Reliance Industries discovered oil in an onshore block in Yemen, which is expected to be equivalent to about half of Reliance's share of crude oil from the Panna-Mukta-Tapti offshore fields in Bombay High. However, these efforts are inadequate when compared to the current holdings of countries like China and Malaysia, whose National Oil Companies have more than 30 joint ventures with 22 of them in the upstream sector. In the Middle East, because of the presence of international oil majors, it would be difficult for Indian Companies to get any contacts. Under such circumstances, India should aggressively explore avenues on more difficult areas that are less attractive to the oil majors for reserve accretion

The primary energy requirement was expected to be 556.2 million metric ton of oil equivalent (MMTOE) and 722.3 MMTOE in the terminal years of the Tenth (2006-07) and Eleventh (2011-12) Five Year Plans respectively. However, due to an anticipated decline of energy intensity, the actual demand may be 5-10 per cent below the estimated figures. There is an urgent need for India to minimize the existing gap or shortages in energy resources as presented in Table 19. Therefore, India should promote cooperation with China and invest (or bid) jointly in third countries to maximize the benefit and reduce the demand-supply gap.

**Table 19: India: Need to Bridge the Demand-Supply Gap – The Competition Imperatives**

| Energy Source | Demand | Supply | Gap/Shortage |
|---|---|---|---|
| a. Electricity (Million KWh)# | 521872 | 480242 | 41630 |
| b. Oil (MMT) | 128 | 33* | 95 |
| c. Gas (Mscmd) | 162.03 | 81.17 | 80.86 |
| d. Coal (MMT) | 415 | 378.8 | 36.2 |

* Domestic Production, # January 2006.

KWh – Kilowatt hours, MMT – Million Metric Tonnes, MCM – Million Cubic Meter, MT – Million Tonnes; Mscmd -Million standard cubic meter per day.

**Source:** Ministry of Power; Economic Survey 2005-06 & Planning Commission, Ministry of Petroleum and Natural Gas (MoPNG), Gail Infraline, Annual Report 2004-05, Ministry of Coal.

Thus it is clear that both India and China are in fact eyeing the same regions, the same countries when it comes to securing their energy demands. And since both countries desperately need to secure their energy requirement to allow their economies to flourish, it is reasonable to assume that some kind of competition or conflict might happen.

## Competition to Cooperation in Energy Resources

Energy has been a source of both cooperation and competition between India and China in recent years.[58] Both states have competed for oil assets in Kazakhstan, Ecuador, Angola and Myanmar, and in every case China has prevailed, not only by offering a higher bid than India but also by adopting a more strategic and holistic approach that integrates financial incentives with aid, infrastructure projects, diplomatic incentives and arms packages.[59] While there have been intermittent instances of cooperation between both states in the energy sphere, cooperation by and large has been the exception rather than the rule in Sino-Indian energy interactions.

Chinese companies have often found more utility in forming joint ventures with major Western companies where they can get access to Western expertise and technology, rather than in aligning themselves with their Indian peers.[60] China and India's joint bids and development of energy assets have been limited to states that face high levels of political risk such as Iran and Sudan, or are marginal players in terms of oil and gas resources such as Columbia. In these cases, Western oil companies are either unwilling (due to lack of commercial viability or high political risk) or unable (due to government sanctions) to access the resources, leaving India as the only viable partner for China.

Soon after the Congress-led government took office in 2004, it proposed Beijing to make joint bids in order to avoid being played off oil producing countries.[61] During his visit to China in January 2006 former Petroleum Minister, Mani Shankar Aiyer advocated that the "unbridled rivalry between Indian and Chinese companies for the acquisition of overseas hydrocarbon assets is to the advantage only of the seller of the assets" and this proposal was accepted by Beijing and consolidated in five MoUs on energy cooperation. Even before that, Ministry of Mines and the Ministry of Land & Resources of the People's Republic of China signed a Memorandum of Understanding (MoU) with India for cooperation in the mining sector on 15 September 2005.[62]

Most of the MoUs dealt with information-sharing and enhancing cooperation between companies in the field of oil and natural gas. Additionally, a joint bilateral working group would be set up to monitor progress of cooperation with the focus on four main regions: the Caspian Sea region, Central Asia, Africa and Latin America.[63] CNPC Vice-President Zhou Jiping agreed to India's proposal for going together in Africa, Central Asia and Latin America. Even he went a step ahead and announced two nodal officers for identifying the areas of cooperation. Sinopec Vice-President Zhang Yaocang suggested two-tier cooperation. In January 2006, ONGC and CNPC signed an initial deal covering exploration and production, while state-run gas company GAIL concluded a pact with Sinopec, CNOOC and Beijing Gas.[64]

Country-wise proved oil reserves include Saudi Arabia (21.3 per cent), UAE (7.9 per cent), Kuwait (8.2 per cent), Iran (11.2 per cent), Iraq (9.3 per cent), FSU (10.4 per cent), China (1.3 per cent), Indonesia (0.04 per cent), Asia Pacific (1.6 per cent),

West Europe (1.9 per cent), Africa (9.5 per cent), Canada (2.2 per cent), USA (2.4 per cent), Mexico and Other Latin America (3.0 per cent). The proven oil and gas reserves in the Caspian region are estimated at about 29 billion barrels and 9.3 tcm respectively, which would certainly affect the energy policies of the countries in the Asian region in the years to come. A snapshot of country-wise major sources of India's oil and gas imports are presented in Chart 2. India's major sources of oil imports include Saudi Arabia (23 per cent), Iran (17 per cent), Nigeria (11 per cent), Iraq (10 per cent), Kuwait (9 per cent), UAE (9 per cent), Malaysia (4 per cent) and Yemen (3 per cent).

**Chart 2: India's Crude Oil Imports by Sources (2007)**

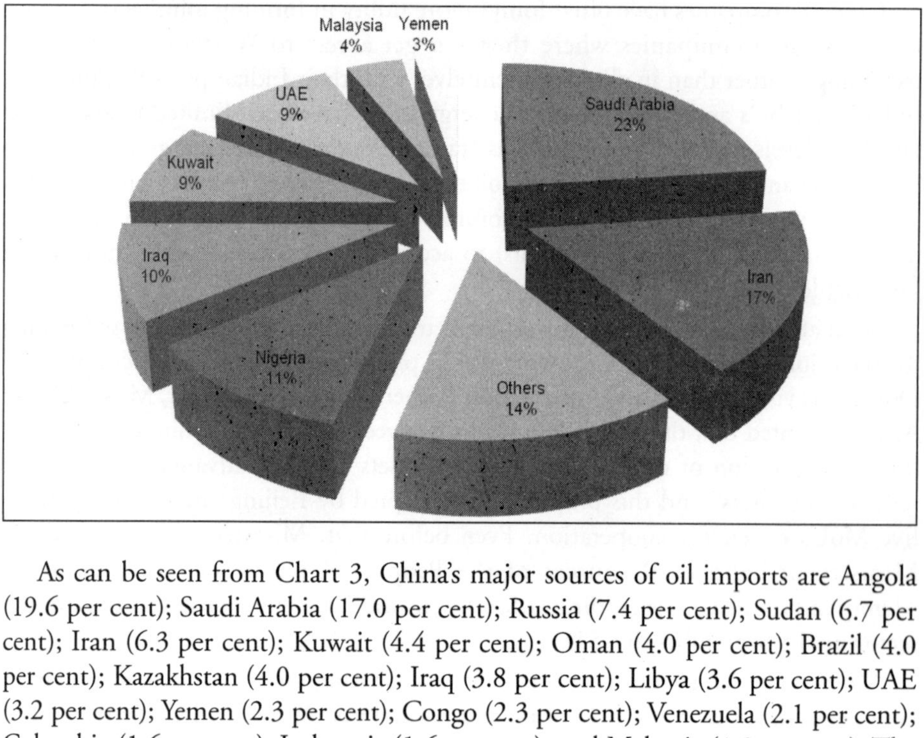


As can be seen from Chart 3, China's major sources of oil imports are Angola (19.6 per cent); Saudi Arabia (17.0 per cent); Russia (7.4 per cent); Sudan (6.7 per cent); Iran (6.3 per cent); Kuwait (4.4 per cent); Oman (4.0 per cent); Brazil (4.0 per cent); Kazakhstan (4.0 per cent); Iraq (3.8 per cent); Libya (3.6 per cent); UAE (3.2 per cent); Yemen (2.3 per cent); Congo (2.3 per cent); Venezuela (2.1 per cent); Colombia (1.6 per cent); Indonesia (1.6 per cent); and Malaysia (1.2 per cent). The other countries constituting less than 1 per cent each in China's sources of oil imports include Brunei; Equal Guinea; Qatar; Gabon; Australia; Cuba; Vietnam; Ecuador; Thailand; Mongolia and USA. China is the world's second largest net importer of oil behind the US, having surpassed Japan in 2008. Within the energy sector, in contrast to a decade ago, China today is importing massive quantities of oil and, following the modification and augmentation of its refining capacity, to be able to absorb increasing amounts of Saudi (heavy) oil.

This has catapulted Saudi Arabia into the position of China's leading foreign source of oil, while at the same time making China Saudi Arabia's leading crude oil customer. Historically, Chinese imports have been skewed toward countries capable

**Chart 3: China's Crude Oil Imports by Sources (January 2010)**

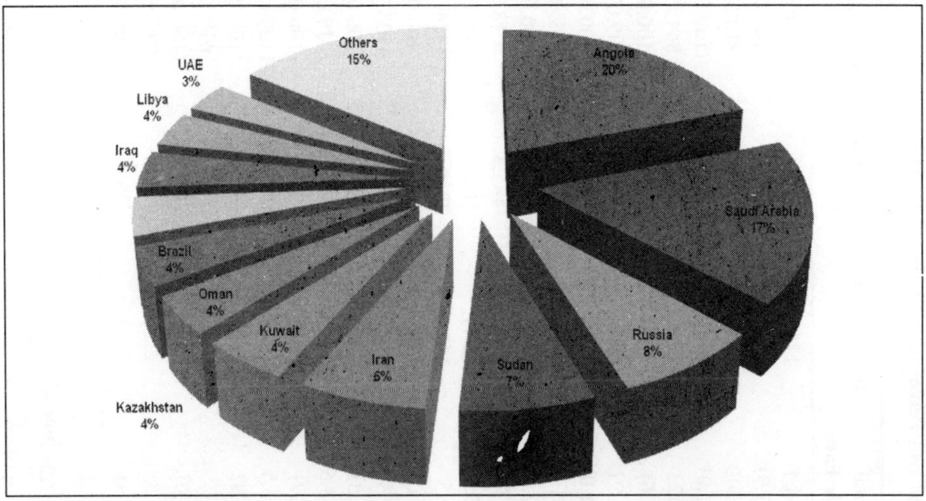


of producing very light, low-sulfur grades of crude oil, such as Oman and some West African countries. This is due to the scarcity of refining capacity in China for processing heavy and high-sulfur grades. As new refineries are built, this constraint will lessen. Over time China will likely be able to diversify supplies to some degree due to its equity investments in upstream production projects.

A comparison of Chart 2 and Chart 3, indicates that the Chinese sources of energy imports are more diversified than India. India's major source of import is Middle East (around 74 per cent) while China's major sources of energy imports are more diverse which include North America, South & Central America, Eurasia (Russia and Central Asia), Middle East and Africa. Therefore, China's is trying hard to maintain the uninterrupted flows of energy imports and investing massively in overseas to acquire energy reserves. India's cooperation with China in energy resources will make task easier to its diversification process and maintaining regular flows of energy imports as well as acquiring overseas energy.

Both countries are in the process of diversifying their sources of oil imports in addition to the Middle East region and the scope of diversification in sources of oil imports in Central Asia, Africa and Latin America is immense. We can observe from Table 20 that how much oil and gas reserves are available in North America, South & Central America, Europe & Eurasia (including Central Asia), Middle East, Africa and Asia Pacific region. Among these regions, Central Asia, Africa and Latin America are the target of the joint bilateral group to monitor progress of cooperation. It is quite clear that among the oil regions, Middle East is dominating in oil reserves (754 tmb) with 60 per cent and natural gas reserves (75.91 tcm) with 41 per cent share in the world in 2008. The consumption of oil and gas in Middle East is roughly 8 to 10 per cent of their total reserves. Proved oil reserves of world at the end of 2008 was 1258 tmb of which Middle East donates in oil reserves and ranks first

Table 20: Regional Distribution of Energy Resources in World (Values in Units and Percentage Share of World) – 2008

| | | Total North America | Total South & Central America | Total Europe & Eurasia | Total Middle East | Total Africa | Total Asia Pacific | Total World |
|---|---|---|---|---|---|---|---|---|
| a. | Oil: Proved Reserves | 70.9 | 123.2 | 142.2 | 754.1 | 125.6 | 42.0 | 1258.0 |
| | (Thousand million barrels) | (5.6) | (9.8) | (11.3) | (59.9) | (10.0) | (3.3) | (100.0) |
| b. | Oil: Production | 13131 | 6685 | 17591 | 26200 | 10285 | 7928 | 81820 |
| | (Thousand barrels daily) | (16.0) | (8.2) | (21.5) | (32.0) | (12.6) | (9.7) | (100.0) |
| c. | Oil: Consumption | 23753 | 5901 | 20158 | 6423 | 2881 | 25339 | 84455 |
| | (Thousand barrels daily) | (28.1) | (7.0) | (23.9) | (7.6) | (3.4) | (30.0) | (100.0) |
| d. | Natural Gas: Proved Reserves | 8.87 | 7.31 | 62.89 | 75.91 | 14.65 | 15.39 | 185.02 |
| | (Trillion cubic metres) | (4.8) | (4.0) | (34.0) | (41.0) | (7.9) | (8.3) | (100.0) |
| e. | Natural Gas: Production | 812.3 | 158.9 | 1087.3 | 381.1 | 214.8 | 411.2 | 3065.6 |
| | (Billion cubic metres) | (26.5) | (5.2) | (35.5) | (12.4) | (7.0) | (13.4) | (100.0) |
| f. | Natural Gas: Consumption | 824.4 | 143.0 | 1143.9 | 327.1 | 94.9 | 485.3 | 3018.7 |
| | (Billion cubic metres) | (27.3) | (4.7) | (37.9) | (10.8) | (3.1) | (16.1) | (100.0) |
| g. | Coal: Production | 638.4 | 55.5 | 456.4 | 0.5 | 143.4 | 2030.7 | 3324.9 |
| | (Million tonnes oil equivalent) | (19.2) | (1.7) | (13.7) | (0.0) | (4.3) | (61.1) | (100.0) |
| h. | Coal: Consumption | 606.9 | 23.3 | 522.7 | 9.4 | 110.3 | 2031.2 | 3303.7 |
| | (Million tonnes oil equivalent) | (18.4) | (0.7) | (15.8) | (0.3) | (3.3) | (61.5) | (100.0) |
| i. | Electricity Generation | 5171.7 | 1049.7 | 5353.5 | 738.6 | 638.4 | 7249.8 | 20201.8 |
| | (Terawatt-hours) | (25.6) | (5.2) | (26.5) | (3.7) | (3.2) | (35.9) | (100.0) |
| j. | Primary Energy: Consumption | 2799.1 | 579.6 | 2964.6 | 613.5 | 356.0 | 3981.9 | 11294.9 |
| | (Million tonnes oil equivalent) | (24.8) | (5.1) | (26.2) | (5.4) | (3.2) | (35.3) | (100.0) |
| k. | Nuclear: Consumption | 215.4 | 4.8 | 276.7 | - | 3.0 | 119.8 | 619.7 |
| | (Million tonnes oil equivalent) | (34.8) | (0.8) | (44.7) | (0.0) | (0.5) | (19.3) | (100.0) |
| l. | Hydroelectricity: Consumption | 148.9 | 152.5 | 180.2 | 2.8 | 22.2 | 210.8 | 717.5 |
| | (Million tonnes oil equivalent) | (20.8) | (21.3) | (25.1) | (0.4) | (3.1) | (29.4) | (100.0) |

**Note:** Figures in parenthesis denote percentage share of total world.
**Source:** Data extracted and computed from British Petroleum (BP) Statistical Review of World Energy, June 2009.

with around 60 per cent of total world energy, followed by Eurasia and Europe (11.3 per cent) and Africa (10 per cent).

It was former Petroleum Minister Aiyar who took the lead and presented a plan for a gas pipeline from Iran through India to China (see Map 2). He also expressed that 'We need to shed the confrontationist approach [...] and leverage the power of offshore and onshore gas for the benefit of our continent, for which India can dip into its vast reserves of foreign exchange for investment in pipelines'.[65] China's oil transport routes are by Railway from (a) Russia (Zabaikalsk-Manzhouli) and (b) Kazakhstan (Kazakhstan-Alashankou) and by sea (a) The Middle East Persian Gulf (Strait of Hormuz-Malacca Strait-Taiwan Strait- China), (b) West Africa North Africa (Mediterranean-Strait of Gibraltar-Cape of Good Hope-Malacca Strait-Taiwan Strait-China), (c) Southeast Asia Malacca Strait (Taiwan Strait-China), and (d) Venezuela (Panama Canal-Pacific Ocean).

Inter-country gas pipeline is the most cost-effective way of transporting gas from the source to the demand centers. Being environmentally clean and less volatile than oil price, share of gas in India's future energy mix would be substantial and much of this future gas demand would be met by import through pipelines. Inter-country pipeline requires good political relationship with not only source countries but also with transit countries. Though pipeline could be a future source of risks, it could also be seen as an incentive to build good political relations with transit countries because of win-win situations. There are some possible inter-country gas pipelines to India on which techno-economic feasibility is already underway which include (i) Qatar-Pakistan-India Pipeline; (ii) Turkmenistan-Afghanistan-Pakistan-India Pipeline; (iii) Iran-Pakistan-India Pipeline; (iv) Myanmar- Bangladesh-India Pipeline; (v) Uzbekistan-Turkmenistan-Kazakhstan-Russia-China-India Pipeline; and (v) Trans-ASEAN gas pipeline[66] (TAGP).

Mani Shankar Aiyer, in his public appearances while in China (January 2006), repeatedly argued that China and India, both of which have a burgeoning need for oil and natural gas imports, have a common interest in seeking to lessen competition for energy supplies and in working together to discover and develop new energy supplies. He also observed that China and India are in a similar position in the energy sector-both have substantial coal resources but are highly dependent on imported oil and gas. He urged co-operation between them in bidding for oil resources in third countries. India is currently pursuing energy production and exploration projects in more than 50 countries, often in competition with Beijing.[67]

India and China, both have declared their intentions of cooperation in oil and gas biddings, Mani Shankar Aiyer also embraced the idea of Asian regional cooperation in energy and initiated a dialogue between principal Asian suppliers (Saudi Arabia, UAE, Kuwait, Iran, Qatar, Oman) with principal Asian buyers (India, China, Japan, Korea). These efforts showed some results when China's National Petroleum Corporation (CNPC) and India's Oil and Natural Gas Corporation (ONGC) mounted a successful US$573 million joint bid to acquire Petro-Canada's

Map 2: China-India Existing and Proposed Gas Lines (IEA)

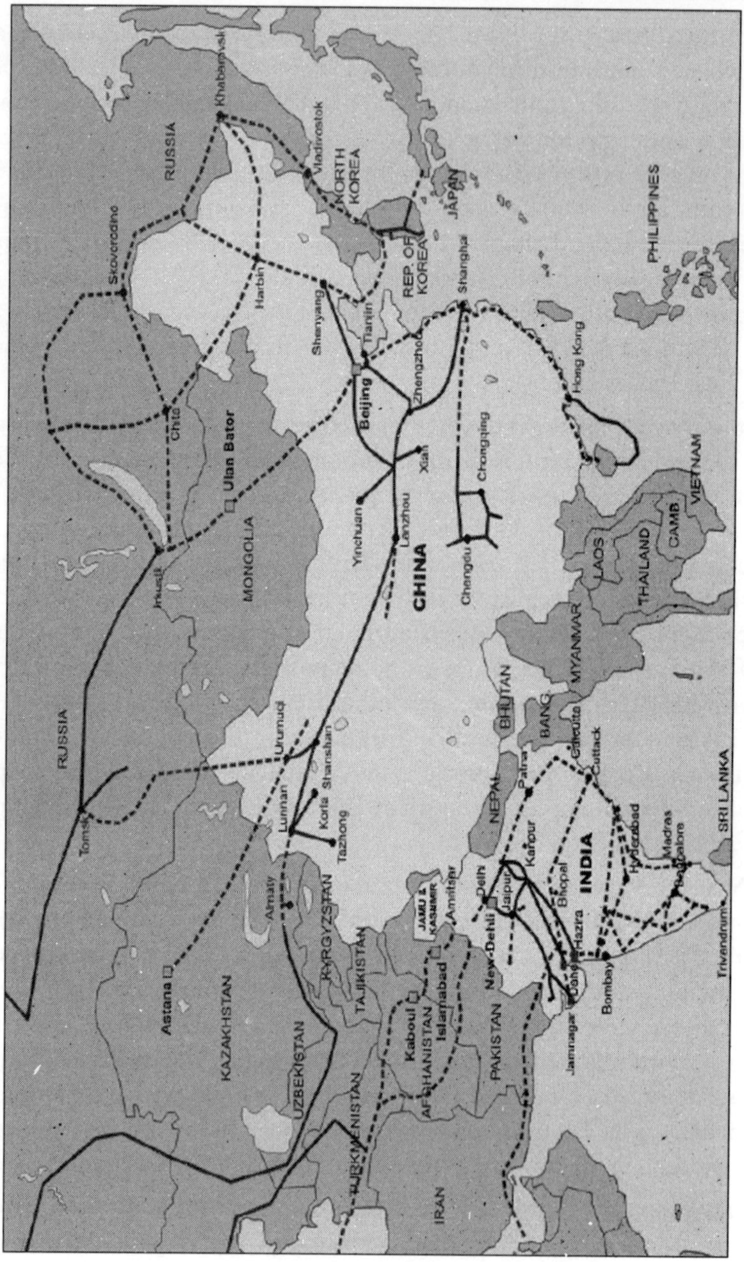

37 per cent stake in the al-Furat oil and gas fields in Syria. Earlier they worked as joint operators in Sudan. India and China may be cooperating in other areas, but when it comes to Central Asian energy, competition is fierce. This was clearly illustrated in late 2005 when China outbid India to acquire PetroKazakhstan, Kazakhstan's third-largest oil producer with CNPC raising its bid to US$4.18-billion.[68]

### *Economic Cost of Non-Cooperation in Energy Sector*

Ever since the late 1990s, China has been encouraging domestic companies to "go out" and invest abroad. The NOCs are the major players, though a few Chinese private firms, which are much smaller in scale and have much smaller production capacities, have also started to "go abroad". The NOCs, including CNPC, Sinopec and CNOOC, are tasked to acquire more equity oil/gas, diversify oil/gas imports and secure pipelines or long-term supply contract with foreign oil/gas producers. 'Equity oil' is a practice by petroleum firms to participate in foreign oil or gas projects in the form of share of stocks or investments; in return, they can annually obtain a certain portion of oil and gas produced from those projects. This is a form preferred by the NOCs.

After the 15th Party Congress, the strategy ('go out') figured more prominently and became an official strategy in 2000. As part of the 'go out' strategy, China's four NOCs-CNPC, CNOOC, Sinopec, and Sinochem-have been investing overseas aggressively, partly to push forward their dream to become an international oil company (IOC) and partly to secure the country's oil imports at the very source. The first acquisition of a production asset outside of Chinese territory was the March 1993 purchase of operating rights for the Banya block in Thailand. Acquisitions of exploration acreage in Canada and Peru followed in the same year. These were all minor assets, though, of very limited significance. The China National Offshore Oil Company (CNOOC) made an investment in its first offshore production assets in Indonesia in 1993. For the first few years the amount of equity oil generated by these projects was relatively insignificant. There are only two Chinese-invested oil development projects that currently generate more than 100,000 bpd in equity oil for the Chinese oil companies. Both of these were acquired in 1997. The first acquisition of significant existing oil production assets was of a 60.3 per cent stake in Aktobemunaigas in Kazakhstan, which took place in October 1997. It gave China National Petroleum Corporation (CNPC) control of existing production assets in Kazakhstan. The company now owns a 92 per cent stake, with current production of about 116,000 bpd, yielding equity oil of about 107,000 bpd.

In 1998, China reorganized its oil and gas industry to create three major oil companies – two of them vertically integrated, CNPC and Sinopec, and one that specialized primarily in offshore oil production, CNOOC. Prior to the reorganization, CNPC had managed state-owned upstream assets, production of oil and natural gas. Sinopec had managed downstream assets, refining and retail distribution. Among the goals of the reorganization was to create vertically-integrated Chinese major oil companies that would eventually compete with the global majors.

Freed from prior limitations on refining and distribution, Sinopec began investing in overseas exploration and production assets shortly thereafter.

Since then, the pace of Chinese acquisitions of exploration acreage has accelerated greatly, but no other projects that currently produce more than 100,000 bpd in equity oil have been developed yet. Among the largest projects currently under development is the Greater Plutonio project offshore from Angola, which will eventually produce roughly 200,000 bpd, with Sinopec's 50 per cent equity stake getting it half that amount. BP is the operator, and the project is scheduled to come on line before the end of 2007. Sinopec has also signed a preliminary memorandum of understanding with Iran's National Iranian Oil Company (NIOC) for the development of the Yadavaran oilfield, which will eventually produce around 300,000 bpd, roughly half of which would go to Sinopec, depending on the terms the two companies ultimately agree to. Strictly speaking this would probably not be "equity oil" due to Iran's use of buyback contracts rather than production sharing agreements (PSAs), but the agreement would give Sinopec effective control over the distribution of that oil.

China has consistently outbid India in the competition for energy sources, and these bidding wars have inflated prices for energy assets, prompting the two countries to agree to joint bidding on some contracts. To reduce dependence on imports and ensure reliable supply, Chinese NOCs have tried, with limited success, to acquire international reserves and to create joint ventures with resource holders. Acquisition efforts have fallen short of expectations, and China is overpaying for overseas reserves.[69] Some recent efforts to acquire E&P rights have been unsuccessful (see Table 21). They include the following:[70]

(a) *The Attempted Acquisition of Unocal:* In 2005 Chinese National Offshore Oil Corporation (CNOOC) made an $18.5 billion bid for Unocal but was forced to withdraw under political pressure from the United States, which feared that such a deal was a threat to US national security.

(b) *The Loss of Talisman's Oil stake in Sudan:* In 2003 China National Petroleum Corporation (CNPC) waived its stakeholder preemption right. India's Oil and Natural Gas Corporation (ONGC) acquired Talisman Energy's 25 per cent stake in Greater Nile Petroleum Oil Company for $720 million.

(c) *The loss of a Stake in the Kashagan Oil Field:* In 2003 CNOOC and China Petroleum and Chemical Corporation (Sinopec) attempted to buy an 8.3 per cent stake in the Kashagan oil field from BG, but BG partners preempted the deal and exercised their rights to buy stake.

Recent deals in which China overpaid for reserves include the following:

(a) *The PetroKazakhstan Acquisition:* In 2005 CNPC won the PK deal with a bid of $4.18 billion ($55 per share). That price was about 20 per cent higher than the PK market value of $3.4 billion.

(b) *The Shell Angola Stake:* In 2004 CNPC won Shell's 50 per cent stake in Block 18 Angola over ONGC's bid of $620 million coupled with a $2 billion aid offer.

(c) *The Sudan Acquisition:* In 2003, CNPC acquired Block 3 in Sudan with a price 17 per cent higher than ONGC's offer.

**Table 21: India-China Competition in Energy Sector**

| Asset | India's bid | China's bid | Winner | Date |
|---|---|---|---|---|
| Sonangol – 50% stake, offshore block 18 **(Angola)** | ONGC – $310 million | Sinopec – $725 million | China | November 2004 |
| PetroKazakhstan **(Kazakhstan)** | ONGC-Mittal – $3.9 billion | CNPC – $4.18 billion (Initial bid – $3.6 billion) | China | August 2005 |
| EnCana Corp **(Ecuador)** | ONGC –$1.4 billion (Bid Withdrawn) | Andes Petroleum (CNPC, CNOOC) – $1.42 billion | China | September 2005 |
| South Atlantic Petroleum – 45% stake **(Nigeria)** | OVL –$2 billion (Bid withdrawn) | CNOOC – $2.3 billion | China | January 2006 |

**Note:** CNPC-China National Petroleum Corporation (China); ONGC-Oil and Natural Gas Corporation (India); CNOOC-China National Offshore Oil Corporation (China); and OVL-ONGC Videsh Limited (India).

It is no surprise that rivalry in the oil sector between these two developing giants is aggressive, since India is just as hungry for supplies as China. The two are battling each other in the search for oil from Sudan to Siberia as they try to secure the resources to fuel their vast economies. The board of PetroKazakhstan, a Canadian-owned company with oil fields in Central Asia, accepted a $4.2 billion takeover bid by state-owned China National Petroleum Corporation (CNPC) on 22 August 2005. The CNPC had surpassed a $3.6 billion offer from India's own state-owned giant, Oil and Natural Gas Corporation (ONGC), and in 2006, the Chinese National Offshore Oil Corporation again beat India's ONGC to buy a 45 per cent stake in a Nigerian oil and gas field for $2.3 billion.[71] Table 21 provides the project-wise detail of competition in biding in third countries and Table 22 provides the project-wise detail of cooperation between India and China in joint bidding in overseas investment in energy resources. India and China have expressed their willingness to bid jointly for some assets and compete when they consider strategic interests more important. Next section is devoted to examine how these two countries will maximize the gain of joint bidding and joint investment in third countries.

## Economic Gains of Cooperation in Energy Sector

India and China are already showing they can work together. Recent proposals for collaboration include (a) technical collaboration on domestic resources, (b) proposals for gas pipeline network, (c) joint development of overseas oil and gas resources, (d) cooperation on unconventional oil and gas (e.g., tar sands and coal-bed methane), and (e) equity investment in petrochemicals. Both of Asia's largest rising powers desperately need energy, especially oil. China today imports roughly half of its oil. Consumption rose by 15 per cent in 2007 and is forecast to jump by an additional 9 per cent 2008. By 2025, according to projections made by the US Energy Department, China will be requiring 14.2 million barrels a day, double of year 2008 level. India's oil imports are expected to rise to some 5 million barrels a day by 2020, up from around 1.4 million barrels in 2007.

Both China and India display high deficit in meeting their fast growing energy requirements from their respective domestic energy resources. It makes business sense for both countries not to bid for acquisition of foreign energy resources without coordinating their positions. Joint bidding in such cases where national interests permit coordinated action will benefit both countries. There are several examples of successes and failures of global bidding by China and India in this regard. The case in point is a collaborative joint venture between China and India for this purpose. India's Oil and Natural Gas Commission (ONGC) and China's China Natural Petroleum Corporation (CNPC) had set up the first 50:50 equity partnership venture named as Himalaya Energy. This joint venture has successfully acquired Al–Furat of Syria in the face of tough international competition from Petro-Canada. ONGC has also formed partnership with the Chinese CNOPC to jointly operate the Greater Nile oil project in Sudan. On the other hand, India lost to China in direct competition in their recent bids for energy resources in Kazakhstan and also elsewhere. Both China and India can learn from these experiences. Consistent with and in accordance with the priority to their own national interests, both countries can further cooperate in this area wherever feasible. One such feasible area of cooperation in energy imports is negotiating mutually profitable swap deals in oil procured globally to save transport costs.[72]

**Table 22: India-China Cooperation in Energy Sector**

| Asset | Sino-Indian bid | Date |
|---|---|---|
| **Greater Nile Oil Project** (Sudan) | OVL – 25% ($750 million), CNPC – 40% ($441 million) | OVL – March 2003, CNPC – 1996 |
| **Petro-Canada** – 37% (Syria) | $573 million (OVL-CNPC – Himalaya Energy) | December 2005 |
| **Omimex de Colombia** Ltd – 50% (Columbia) | $850 million (OVL-Sinopec – Mansorovar Energy Columbia Ltd) | August 2006 |
| **Yadavaran oil field** (Iran) | OVL – 29%, Sinopec – 51% | September 2006 |

**Note:** CNPC-China National Petroleum Corporation (China); ONGC-Oil and Natural Gas Corporation (India); CNOOC-China National Offshore Oil Corporation (China); and OVL-ONGC Videsh Limited (India).

Scope for cooperation in this cut-throat competition for oil has thus been demonstrated. A good example of the broadening spirit of cooperation between India and China is in the Sudan's Greater Nile project, in which Indian ONGC Videsh Limited (OVL) and CNPC are working in a cooperative partnership together: While

China built a refinery in Khartoum, India was responsible for building a product pipeline from the refinery to the port of Sudan.

To quote India's former Petroleum Minister Mani Shankar Aiyar, "there are enormous prospects for India and China to work together. Our interests are complementary."[73] During his visit to China (12-13 January 2006), he signed not only a government-level Memorandum of Understanding (MoU), but also several MoUs between Indian and Chinese oil companies. Memorandum on Cooperation in the field of Oil and Natural Gas signed in Beijing which encourages collaboration between Chinese and Indian enterprises, including joint exploration and development of hydrocarbon resources in third countries. Also in December 2005, China and India successfully launched their first ever joint venture, Himalayan Energy, that has already won its first bid of about $700 million, buying a 38 per cent stake in a Canadian company's operations in Al Furat, Syria's largest gas and oil fields. With the current success of the Greater Nile cooperation, Aiyar's continued optimism seems warranted.

The dialogue on energy cooperation was further strengthened during Chinese Premier Wen Jiabao's visit to India in April 2005. The prime ministers of the two countries then issued a joint statement agreeing to cooperate in the field of energy security and conservation, including, among others, encouraging relevant departments and units of the two countries to engage in the survey and exploration of petroleum and natural gas in third countries. Several bilateral discussions on the agreed energy cooperation took place between India and China. In July 2005 researchers met to discuss 'Sino-Indian Energy Cooperation' in Chengdu. In August 2005 China hosted a week-long visit by a delegation of Indian officials and representatives of oil companies, for the purpose of exploring possible cooperation with their Chinese counterparts.

In January 2006 Indian Petroleum Minister Mani Shankar Aiyar and China's National Development and Reform Commission (NDRC) Chairman Ma Kai signed a bilateral hydrocarbon cooperation deal under which they agreed to create a framework for joint bids for the acquisition of oilfields in third countries. According to a statement issued by the Chinese embassy five memoranda were signed, covering a full scope of areas, including strengthening the exchange of information when bidding for oil resources in a third country, upstream exploration and production, refining and marketing of petroleum products and petrochemicals, the laying of national and trans-national oil and gas pipelines, frontier and cutting-edge research and development, and promotion of environment-friendly fuels.[74] The agreement paved the way for five state-owned oil companies in the two countries to 'begin the process of operational cooperation'.[75]

The main result of the cooperation initiatives was that Indian and Chinese oil companies have started to cooperate in purchasing shares in oil exploration in third countries. In February 2006 a 50:50 joint venture company (Himalaya Energy, Syria) covering 36 production fields in Syria was set up by subsidiaries of OVL and China's CNPC International, purchasing the entire production shares of Canadian oil company Petro-Canada. OVL and CNPC have also previously worked together on the Greater Nile Oil Project in Sudan, but the Syrian purchase was the first time that the two companies joined forces to acquire an oil asset. The remaining recoverable reserve potential of the asset is estimated to be more than 300 million barrels of oil.[76]

According to one Indian analyst, the stage is set for the two countries to make more joint oil bids.[77] Citing a report in the *Economic Times*, Indian oil companies, including downstream marketing companies like the Indian Oil Corporation, BPCL, OVL and Prize Petroleum, are set to ink agreements with China's Sinopec, CNOOC and CNPC, for collaboration in the exploration, petroleum and gas sectors. Other observers have been more sceptical. According to the *Financial Times*,[78] Beijing based energy consultant James Brock stated that the deal to exchange information before bidding for fields in third countries 'may be possible, but it is highly improbable and even less practical'. Another consultant responded that: 'It is one of these agreements that governments sign. But when it comes to the hard practice they don't help each other'.

A complete lack of cooperation between China and India was evidenced when PetroChina signed a deal with Burma in late 2005 on building a gas pipeline to China, interrupting a long-negotiated Burma-Bangladesh-India pipeline project. Burma represents one country where the India–China energy competition is playing out. In the fall of 2007, attempts of the Gas Authority of India Limited (GAIL) and other Indian companies to tap Burmese oil and gas were thwarted by Chinese pressure on Burmese authorities.[79] This was a major setback for Indian policymakers as well as oil and gas companies. It was also evidently noticed in Beijing that many commentators saw the March 2006 US-Indian agreement on nuclear power cooperation as a 'strategic alliance' aiming to contain China.[80] India was a strong proponent of the democracy movement in Burma throughout the 1980s and gave sanctuary to thousands of Burmese refugees following the military junta's assumption of power in 1988. India changed its position, however, to one of "constructive engagement" when it sought Burmese cooperation against insurgents across their porous frontier in the mid-1990s and has more recently sought oil and gas deals there to fulfill its growing energy requirements.[81]

Whether the two countries will do more to 'help each other' in the future is perhaps less of a question than who will take the lead in the cooperation. This was already evident with the signing of the mid-February 2006 joint energy deal with Iran on the Yadavaran oil field, under which Sinopec acquired a 51 per cent stake in the field, and ONGC only 29 per cent. According to the agreement Sinopec will develop the field, and China will purchase ten million tons of LNG from Iran per year, for 25 years beginning in 2009.[82] This will probably not be the last agreement where India is forced to take a 'back seat' position vis-à-vis China. It is also important to discuss as to how these two growing economies will improve their oil security and avoid any supply disruptions in future. Therefore, the next section is devoted to focus on coordination and cooperation between India and China in the creation of strategic reserves of crude oil and petroleum products (domestically as well globally) to avoid any risk during the period of energy supply disruptions.

## Cooperation and Coordination in Strategic Petroleum Reserves (SPRs) System

Availability of oil is vital for all countries to maintain their sustainable growth while an emergency stockpile is integral to energy security in oil-importing nations. India and China thus need to improve their oil security and avoid any supply disruptions. Creation of strategic reserve of crude oil and petroleum products is necessary to improve oil security in both countries. Both China and India are currently excluded from the global emergency oil sharing system managed by the IEA but are associated as enhanced engagement countries.[83] IEA has invited both these two countries to join IEA's collective emergency response system. The details of oil participation have not yet been worked out. But without the inclusion of two Asian majors, the IEA can be only partially successful in stabilizing oil markets.[84] Both China and India have decided to set up their respective stockpiles – of 90 days eventually in the case of China and 15 days, initially, in the case of India. Among the developed countries, their reserve will be able to last 158 days in the case of USA, 161 days of Japan, 117 of Germany and for 96 days of France.

In 2004, China identified four sites for its national petroleum reserves tanks and began building its strategic petroleum reserve (SPR) in three phases, to be completed by 2020. The first phase will hold 100 million barrels (13.6 million tonnes) – equivalent to 25 days of China's net oil imports. The second phase is planned to add 200 million barrels, covering 42 days of net oil imports. The completion of the third phase would increase the net storage capacity to 500 million barrels after 2010.[85] The high oil prices of recent years prompted China to delay oil purchases to fill its strategic reserve. Only one of the four sites in Phase I, consisting of 52 storage tanks – a total capacity of 33 million barrels (4.5 million tonnes) – has been filled. In addition to the national SPR, the government will reportedly require major state-owned oil companies to hold government-mandated oil stocks. China's SPR regulations are part of a comprehensive Energy Law.[86]

China has also started to formulate plans for the strategic oil reserves and construction of some oil reserve facilities. This is one of the most important strategic measures for guarding against energy supply disruptions, ensuring sustainable energy supply, and stabilizing the oil market. China's strategic oil reserve system will build from the experiences of developed countries. Accordingly, China has decided to establish a four-tier oil reserve system. The first tier is the national strategic oil reserve system, whose objective is to ensure energy security when oil supply is disrupted by unexpected events and political turbulence in oil producing areas of the world. The other three tiers are commercial reserves of the three petroleum corporations, reserves of big oil consumers, and other reserves in the society.

China's current strategic oil reserve is far from satisfactory, with planned reserves of 15 million tons. However, according to a statistical report on China's oil consumption in 2002, 15 million tons of oil reserve is only sufficient for about 20 days of domestic oil consumption. As for the scale of China's oil reserve, opinions vary whether it should be equivalent to 90 days of oil consumption or perhaps as much as 120 days. To meet this challenge, China's national strategic oil reserve base construction is in full swing. The bases of such oil reserve will be located in China's east coastal areas, including Guangdong, Zhejiang, Shandong, and Liaoning provinces. Additionally, the Xinjiang, Shaanxi-Gansu-Ningxia, Sichuan-Chongqing, and Qinghai oil fields will become China's top four reserve oil fields. Zhenhai base in Zhejiang's Ningbo City has built up 16 storage tanks in 2005, while the other three bases in Zhoushan, Dalian, and Huangdao have entered the stage of infrastructure construction and are expected to be completed soon.

Creation of strategic reserve of crude oil and petroleum products is necessary to improve oil security in India. Taking into account the oil security concerns of India, the Government has decided to set up a Strategic Crude Oil Storage of 5 million metric tons (MMT) at three locations in the country viz., Visakhapatnam (1.0 MMT), Mangalore (1.5 MMT) and Padur (2.5 MMT). The capacity of Visakhapatnam site has been enhanced to 1.33 MMT. The proposed Strategic Crude Oil Storage would be in underground rock cavern/concrete structures. A Special purpose vehicle, namely Indian Strategic Petroleum Reserve Limited (ISPRL), as a subsidiary of OIDB has been created for implementation and management of strategic storage of crude oil. Engineers India Limited (EIL) has been engaged as the Project Management Consultant. Crude oil from the Reserves will be released by a Government-appointed High Powered Committee, in the event of any short-term disruptions in supplies, a natural calamity or any unforeseen global event, leading to an abnormal increase in prices. The project involves a capital cost of approximately US$ 55 billion and crude oil cost of approximately US$ 205 billion as per estimated cost in September 2005. The project is likely to be completed by the end of 2012. This strategic storage would be in addition to the existing storage of crude oil and petroleum products with the oil companies and would provide an emergency response mechanism in case of short-term supply disruptions. The proposed facility would be managed by ISPRL a Special Purpose Vehicle, owned by IOC.

Oil Security is of particular concern for the countries like India with high oil import dependency, at present over 70 per cent. The gap between domestic crude availability and demand for crude indicates the vulnerability of the Indian economy to oil imports. At present, about 67 per cent of India's crude oil imports come from the Middle East region. The general political instability in this region is a further cause of anxiety from the oil supply security perspective. India and China can cooperate in the construction and joint management of crude stockpiles. Joint bidding for construction could bring down the costs. India has also identified the sites for its strategic stockpile and has set up a company which would oversee its establishment and management.

On regular basis, an annual dialogue on energy between India and China will strengthen bilateral cooperation in coming future. Energy companies from both countries have also nailed down five memoranda of understanding to share information and strengthen cooperation in exploration, development, and production of oil and natural gas. Both sides agreed to seek partnerships in investments and in the construction of liquid natural gas pipelines and terminals. The Ministry of Foreign Affairs of China hailed the agreement, saying that cooperation with India would not only benefit peoples in both countries, but also be conducive to peace and stability in South Asia and to the strengthening of South-South cooperation. The new alliance, aimed at preventing the two nations' competition for oil assets from pushing up energy prices, symbolizes their increasingly assertive role in global energy politics. China is currently the world's second largest energy consumer, while India is the sixth.[87]

There are numerous opportunities for both countries to collaborate with the wider international community at (a) bilateral activities, (b) APEC, and (c) International Energy Forum and Joint Oil Data Initiative. The International Energy Forum (IEF)[88] is the world's largest gathering of Energy Ministers – unique in that participants include not only IEA and OPEC countries, but also key players Brazil, China, India, Mexico, Russia and South Africa. The IEF countries account for more than 90 per cent of global oil and gas supply and demand. Through the Forum and its associated events, IEF Ministers and Energy Industry Executives participate in a dialogue which is of increasing importance to global energy security. The IEF and the global energy dialogue are promoted by a permanent Secretariat based in the Diplomatic Quarter of Riyadh, Saudi Arabia.

The IEF capitalizes on the combined efforts of six diverse international organizations to improve transparency in oil markets through its ambitious Joint Oil Data Initiative (JODI).[89] JODI, originally named as the Joint Oil Data Exercise (JODE) was launched in 2001 to address the apparent lack of transparency in oil market data perceived to be a causal factor in excessive price fluctuations. The exercise was the product of co-operation between six pioneer organizations, the Asia Pacific Economic Co-operation (APEC), the Statistical Office of the European Communities (Eurostat), the International Energy Agency (IEA), the Latin-American Energy Organization (OLADE), the Organization of Petroleum Exporting Countries (OPEC) and the United Nations (through the UN Statistics Division). Established as a permanent mechanism in 2003 and renamed as the Joint Oil Data Initiative (JODI), is now an IEF flagship activity. The JODI partner organizations submit monthly data to the IEF Secretariat on production, refining, trade, demand and stocks of seven product categories: crude oil, LPG, gasoline, kerosene, diesel oil, fuel oil and total oil.

The JODI World Database is a visible and very valuable element of the initiative, but there is much more to JODI than collecting and releasing monthly oil statistics. The initiative has played an important role in raising political awareness of the difficulties encountered in improving data reliability and timeliness. The IEF

Secretariat and its JODI partners are active in building, under-pinning, and improving the statistical infrastructure necessary to meet the evolving demands of the data transparency challenge. The initiative has come a long way in a short time, but by necessity and design it remains a dynamic work-in-progress.

The solution for India and China's energy problems lies overseas and can only be tackled through energy diplomacy. Both India and China are the members of International Energy Forum (IEF), which provides a biennial meeting of the Ministers from the energy producing and consuming nations. India being a big consumer of oil will have to ensure its oil security by strengthening the dialogue process in such meetings. Further, such forums do provide opportunities to forge ahead with individual oil-surplus countries.

The strategic reserves of crude oil/petroleum products, held by developed countries serve as a global common good. Draw down of such reserves during a crisis has an impact on the world oil market, which is integrated to a fair extent. Thus, poorer countries can reap the benefits of strategic reserves without holding it. Otherwise also, it seems practical to have regional strategic reserves that would not only entail lower costs but will also expand the possible benefits among many countries.[90] India and China can expand the possible benefit if China takes the lead and initiate the process to establish regional strategic reserves (RSRs) at Shanghai Cooperation Organization (SCO) and India at South Asian Association for Regional Cooperation (SAARC), while both can promote business and joint-ventures in energy sector at Asia Pacific Trade Agreement (APTA).[91]

## Conclusions and Policy Recommendations

We have described in detail the present and projected futuristic status of demand and supply in India and China. Section two, discussed the India-China trade cooperation in energy sector in both value-wise and product-wise at HS 6-digit level of disaggregation on the basis of some trade indices (intra-industry trade and trade complementarities index). It also highlighted the overseas investments (projects) of India and Chinese national oil companies. Section three provides in-depth analysis of cooperation to competition in overseas investment in energy resources between India and China. This concluding section provides some tentative ideas for policy recommendations based on available data and information related to India and China cooperation in energy resources.

It is observed that the low level of bilateral trade and negligible investment by China in energy sector is due to the low level of trade and investment intensity between India and China, which demonstrates that both countries are under-represented in bilateral trade and investment in energy sector.

Despite having so much potential and prioritized sector or focus industries in countries, trade and investment cooperation in energy resources between India and China is not up to the mark. Though trade in energy sector between India and China is increasing but it is below the existing potential. There is large number of products/ sectors having high potential to establish trade generating joint ventures (TGJVs) between India and China. Hence there is need to enhance cooperation at production level and establish joint marketing strategy and network to boost trade and investment cooperation in energy sector There is also a desirability to synergize partnership especially at the level of business enterprises for forging trade and investment linkages in energy sector to realize existing potential between both countries.

India has potential to establish trade generating joint ventures in some energy products (having high IIT Index Values) with China. There is scope for IIT specialization in some products at bilateral level and also China is having quite good number of energy products at global level where IIT index value is quite high. Thus, India and China (vice-versa) could set up a joint production and marketing strategy in those matched products which have the potential of joint ventures which in turn, enhance the level of India-China trade and investment in energy sector. There is need to enhance cooperation at production level and establish joint marketing strategy and network to boost trade and investment cooperation in energy resources. There is also a desirability to synergize partnership especially at the level of business enterprises for forging trade and investment linkages to realize existing potential between both countries.

The degree of trade complementarities (index value) is moderate in India as a supplier and China as a market and poor in China as supplier and India as a market in overall trade but in energy sector, estimation results are reverse. The index value of trade complementarities in India as a supplier and China as a market was 0.006 in 2000 which increased to 0.290 in 2007 indicating poor complementarity. Reversing the trade complementarities between China as supplier and India as a market, the degree of trade complementarities was high with value of 0.625 in 2000 and 0.468 in 2007. Therefore, the computation results revealed that there is poor trade complementarity in India as a supplier and China as a market and moderate in China as supplier and India as a market in total merchandise trade as well as trade in energy products (HS-27). In this context, it will be useful to identify those products that have good or moderate trade complementarities at the product level. These products can play major role in promoting and enhancing bilateral trade and investment between both the countries.

Since last few years, Indian companies witnessed competition from their Chinese counterparts in acquiring overseas petroleum resources. In an attempt to avoid competition with each other the two governments have taken various measures, which finally led to the two countries signing a Memorandum of Understanding for energy cooperation especially for joint overseas bidding for exploration and production. Although the Indian side perceives the cooperation effort as a major breakthrough in avoiding Chinese competition in the overseas energy arena, it appears to be of limited prospects to India in terms of acquiring overseas petroleum assets or exploration and production contracts. A combined India-China market will have tremendous strategic impact on any energy access and control mechanism.

India and China should evolve a joint strategy to access Oil and Natural gas in Central Asia, Iran, Bangladesh and Southeast Asia. Joint Ventures between Indian PSU's and their Chinese counterparts should be seriously explored. The most important aspect should be to evolve Joint Ventures on transportation, pipeline from Central Asia across Xinjiang and into India through Ladakh is considered feasible, and safer than any route across Afghanistan and Pakistan. Similarly India can provide China with safe transit and refining facilities for Iranian gas and oil coming from Chah Bahar in south Iran to India's western coast. Proactive strategies to tap into South-East Asian oil and gas in Bangladesh, Myanmar (Kunming Initiative can play a role in this process) and Indonesia should also be discussed.

Joint exploration and exploitation of oil and gas resources in North Africa (India has already moved into Sudan with ONGC Videsh) and Russian Siberia (both India and China are working with Russia in this area) should be considered. A joint India-China bid in Russian, North African and Central Asian oil and gas fields will make such bids globally powerful and will go a long way in ensuring energy security, not only for India and China, but whole of Asia.

There could be areas of conflict and competition which foreclose possibilities for a cooperative approach, but there are enough synergetic areas where cooperation is mutually beneficial. However, effective cooperation will require both countries to initiate a whole host of measures in sequence. A top level meeting between leaders of both countries is important to agree upon broad areas of cooperation in the energy sector. Joint working groups of policy makers and academics could then identify specific areas where cooperation would be mutually beneficial and examine the policy and legislative changes needed to proceed further. Consultations with scientists and industry representatives from both countries would then help to take specific proposals further and demarcate the framework for cooperation. In order to sustain cooperation (especially between countries such as China and India that have a history of competition and conflict), identifying specifics and ensuring follow-up are as vital as formulating ideas and articulating a vision. Moving from the general to the specific is key to transforming rhetoric into reality.

As "new comers" in the world oil markets, both India and China need to learn from each other's strengths. China has advantages in its government-driven energy strategy and energy diplomacy, whereas India has advantages in enterprise governance and management. They can combine these advantages and collaborate to expand their energy venture overseas. Thus it is important for these two big oil importing countries to strengthen cooperation in dealing with energy issues. Over-competition will result in unnecessary loss to both sides. When these two countries compete in an unhealthy manner to acquire oil fields in third countries, both countries only end up driving costs for each other.

China and India can also cooperate in areas of energy diplomacy. Today, more than 50 per cent of China's oil imports come from the Middle East, and IEA estimates that China's oil imports from this region will rise to at least 70 per cent by 2015. At present, two-thirds of India's imported oil comes from the Middle East. It goes without saying that the two countries share a large long-term interest in ensuring a steady supply of energy resources from the Middle East to meet the demand of Asian countries. To ensure this, India and China need to use their clout as large and growing consumers of energy to push for increased influence in this region.

Moreover, for historic reasons, Indian enterprises are more acquainted with Western law systems and regulations, cultures and language than their Chinese counterparts. They are more acknowledged and accepted by the western world, and have more means to merge or buy foreign companies. Once these advantages are introduced into its NOCs, India's competitiveness in this regard will be enhanced greatly. China's energy diplomacy plays a more effective role in its energy quest abroad. With China's extraordinary economic expansion and its corresponding need for energy and natural resources since the late 1990s, China's diplomacy has become more pragmatic and is mainly motivated by energy security and economic growth. These years saw China channeling diplomatic efforts into cultivating relations with oil and gas-exporting countries, and successfully using its political capital to influence pariah regions to make policy-decisions tilt to China's favour.

While considering more acquisitions of oil and gas assets abroad, and planning to participate in the construction of pipelines, these attempts are hindered or affected by some other strategic factors, including the US factor. India is also likely to run into conflict of interests with the US when considering potential energy suppliers like Myanmar, Sudan and Venezuela.

Availability of oil is vital for all countries to maintain their sustainable growth while an emergency stockpile is integral to energy security in oil-importing nations. Both China and India are currently excluded from the global emergency oil sharing system managed by the IEA but are associated as enhanced engagement countries. Though IEA has invited both India and China to join IEA's collective emergency response system, the details of oil participation have not yet been worked out. But without the inclusion of two Asian majors, the IEA can be only partially successful in stabilizing oil markets. It is also important that Chinese and Indian Strategic Petroleum Reserves (SPRs) be coordinated with IEA and western reserves to maximize their effectiveness during any supply crisis. An obvious solution to this problem would be to have China and India accepted as additional members of IEA. Hence there is a need of joint effort to chalk out some strategy and formulate some mechanism and contact other member countries of IEA who can nominate and promote the candidature of India and China in the IEA. India and China can expand the possible benefit if China takes the lead and initiate the process to establish Regional Strategic Reserves (RSRs) at Shanghai Cooperation Organization (SCO) and India at South Asian Association for Regional Cooperation (SAARC) and thereafter gradually integrate at global level.

## ENDNOTES

1. Today, China's economy is the fourth-largest and India's the fourteenth-largest in the world. But in terms of purchasing power parity, they occupy second and fourth position respectively.
2. Massive investment is required to deliver sustained GDP growth of 8.0 per cent till 2031-32. Its requisites are: (a) growth in primary energy supply by 3-4 times over current consumption; (b) electricity installed capacity should increase by 6-7 times and (c) annual coal requirement: nearly 3 times over current demand (*Draft Integrated Energy Policy*, Planning Commission of India).
3. Henry Kissinger, *Diplomacy*, New York: Simon & Schuster, 1994, pp. 23-24; and Samuel Huntington, *The Clash of Civilizations and the Remaking of World Order*, New York: Simon & Schuster, 1996, p.121.
4. Indian and Chinese population curves will cross in 2030 and it has been predicted that India will take a demographic advantage over China by 10 per cent. In 2008, India's population was 1.13 billion and China's population 1.32 billion. India and China together account for more than a third of the world population.
5. Blazquez-Lidoy et al. (2004) report that the average wage in China is between three and four times lower than in Latin America.
6. Kalish, I., 'China and India: The Reality beyond Hype', research report prepared by Deloitte Services LP, 2006.
7. Ahya, C., A. Xie, A. Agarwal, D. Yam, S. Lam and M. Sheth, *India and China: A Special Economic Analysis,* Shanghai: Morgan Stanley, 2004.
8. China and India account for 23 per cent and 17 per cent, respectively, of the global working age population. By 2010, China and India would add a further 56 and 83 million to the global labour supply. The contribution of the US and Europe would be only 13 million and 0.1 million, respectively, whereas the working population of Japan would decrease by about 3 million. See, Ahya et al., 2004).
9. Ahya, C., A. Xie, A. Agarwal, D. Yam, S. Lam and M. Sheth, *India and China: A Special Economic Analysis,* Shanghai: Morgan Stanley, 2004.
10. After recording a sustained growth of over 9 per cent for the last 3 consecutive years (growth rates were estimated at 9.5, 9.7 and 9 per cent respectively over the last 3 fiscal years), the Indian economy is expected to continue to demonstrate robust growth going forward; the growth rate is approximately 6.6 percent in 2008-09. India's annual economic growth averaged 6 per cent during 1992-2001 and 8 per cent during 2002-07.
11. India had followed a socialistic pattern of society and an import substitution model of planned economic development from 1951 until 1990 with a resultant sustained low rate of growth.
12. Chairman Mao Zedong founded the People's Republic of China (PRC) in 1949, establishing the Communist Party of China (CPC) as the sole authority. Approximately around the same time, India opted for a democratic regime under the leadership of Prime Minister Jawaharlal Nehru. While most Indians have a good idea of what democracy delivered to them between 1950 and 1980, they perhaps know far less about China. Today, it is commonplace to argue that the Chinese economy is performing better because authoritarianism allows its government to be more effective. But few observers record the gigantic failures of the same authoritarianism in the early decades (Arvind Pangariya, A Tale of two Trajectories, *Times of India,* 6 February 2010, p.16).
13. The year 1993 marked a watershed in China's energy frontier when, after three decades of self-sufficiency and several years of oil exports, the economy became a net oil importer.
14. International Energy Agency (IEA), *World Energy Outlook 2007: Global Energy Prospects: Impact of Developments in India and China,* Paris, 2007.

15. Dinshaw Mistry, "Domestic and International Influences on India's Energy Policy, 1947-2008" in *India's Foreign Policy: Retrospect and Prospect* edited by Sumit Ganguli, Oxford University Press, New Delhi, 2010, p. 323.
16. Development involves a number of other steps besides those associated with energy, notably including the evolution of education and labor markets, financial institutions to support capital investment, modernization of agriculture, and provision of infrastructure for water, sanitation, and communications.
17. Sumit Ganguli, *Energy Trends in China and India: Implications for the USA* http://www.usindiafriendship.net/viewpoints1/ganguly.htm
18. China's oil demand has been forecast by International Energy Agency (IEA) to rise from 6.5 million barrels per day to over 14 million barrels per day by 2025.
19. Sino-Indian relations have gone through three distinct phases in the past 60 years: the friendly vibes of the 1950s; the bitter fallout of the 1962 border conflict: and, finally, the guarded friendship that has grown slowly but steadily since the landmark visit to China by Prime Minister Rajiv Gandhi in 1988. See Sankhya Krishnan, "India's Security Dilemma vis-à-vis China:A Case of Optimum or Sub-Optimum Restraint?" *RCSS Policy Studies 47*, Regional Centre for Strategic Studies, Colombo, Sri Lanka, 2008.
20. Jing-dong Yuan, "The Dragon and the Elephant: Chinese-Indian Relations in 21st Century", The *Washington Quarterly*, summer, Vol. 3, Issue 30, 2007, pp. 131-144.
21. IEA, *World Energy Outlook 2007*, p. 262.
22. China managed to be self-sufficient until 1993, meeting all its internal consumer oil needs for the previous five decades due to the discovery of massive oil reserves at the Daqing oil fields in the far north of the country during the 1950's.
23. Sajal Ghosh, "Investment opportunities in Indian energy sector" *International Journal of Indian Culture and Business Management*, Vol. 1, Nos. 1-2, 2007, pp. 64-82.
24. Zhao Hong, "China and India: The Energy Policies", *EAI Background Brief No. 4622*, July 2009.
25. *World Energy Council Report*, 1993.
26. Tanaka, *India, China hold key to Energy Security:* Tanaka, 2007, http:/www.rediff.com/cms/print.jsp?docpath=//money/jan/05energy.htm
27. World total primary energy demand, which is equivalent to total primary energy supply, includes international marine bunkers, which are excluded from the regional totals. Primary energy refers to energy in its initial form, after production or importation. Some energy is transformed, mainly in refineries, power stations and heat plants. Final consumption refers to consumption in end-use sectors, net of losses in transformation and distribution. In all regions, total primary and final demand includes traditional biomass and waste, such as fuelwood, charcoal, dung and crop residues, some of which are not traded commercially. Details of statistical conventions and conversion factors is available on www.iea.org.
28. According to Petrol World, at present, China imports over 30 per cent of its oil supplies, consuming 5.46 million barrels a day (mbd); that's 7 per cent of world demand. India imports a frightening 75 per cent of its oil, using 2 mbd. Figures from the International Energy Agency place world oil demand in 2030 at 121.3 mbd, with China and India accounting for 12 per cent and 5.6 per cent, respectively. By then, it predicts, India's oil import dependency will climb to 94 per cent.
29. *World Energy Outlook*, 2007.
30. Asian Development Bank *Outlook 2009* Update, www.adb.org/Documents/Book/ADB/2008/update/default.asp
31. *International Energy Outlook*, 2008, Energy Information Administration, Washington,
32. The report was presented to the Indian Prime Minister on 27 March 2000.
33. Ram Naik (former Indian Minister of Petroleum and Natural Gas), "Oil and Gas in India",

Key Note address delivered at "The World Petroleum Congress: Asia Regional Meeting", Shanghai, China, 19 September 2001.

34. World Bank, *Global Economic Prospects 2009.*
35. *Asian Development Bank Outlook 2008* Update.
36. Daniel H. Rosen, "China Energy: A Guide for the Perplexed", Peterson Institute for International Economics, May 2007.
37. "IEA Raises 2005 China Oil Demand to 6.8 Mln bpd," *AFX News Limited,* 11 March 2005, <http://www.rigzone.com> .
38. "Table 2.4 World Petroleum (Oil) Demand, 2002-2006," *Energy Information Administration,* <http://www.eia.doe.gov/emeu/ipsr/t24.xls>
39. "Table A4. World Oil Consumption by Region, Reference Case, 1990-2030," *Energy Information Administration,* <http://www.eia.doe.gov/oiaf/ieo/pdf/ieoreftab_4.pdf>
40. "International Energy Outlook 2006," *Energy Information Administration,* Appendix E, pg 160. <http://www.eia.doe.gov/oiaf/ieo/pdf/ieooil.pdf>
41. The Nathu La pass was closed in 1962 after war broke out between China and India. Three months after the road was reopened, Chinese exports through the pass totaled approximately $12,500 per week. Indian exports have been slightly higher. The Nathu La Study Group, which was commissioned by the Sikkim government, predicted that trade flows would reach $4.57 million by 2007. "China-India Cross-Border Trade at Nathu La Pass 'Not Ideal': Chinese Official," *People's Daily* (Beijing), August 11, 2006.
42. While the two governments have set the 60 billion dollars trade target in the next three years, a study by the Federation of Indian Micro and Small and Medium Enterprises (FISME) indicated that it would surpass it and reach the 100 billion dollars mark by 2010. see, "Indo-China trade to touch $60 billion by 2010", *Financial Express,* 25 March 2008. But another source indicates that trade between India and China will likely cross the US$100 billion mark in the next five years, even as trade imbalance remains in favour of China (http://www.indiaenews.com/pdf/150067.pdf).
43. Trade in energy goods is, in principle, subject to the rules of the World Trade Organization. In practice, however, WTO does not deal with this area very well and energy goods are not covered by a separate agreement. This is partly because, when WTO was founded in 1995, most oil-exporting countries were not members, but the situation is changing rapidly. Saudi Arabia has recently acceded to WTO, and Iraq and the Islamic Republic of Iran have started the accession process. Another reason is that the WTO agreements deal largely with imports while the trade in energy goods also raises a number of issues concerned with exports.
44. Exim Bank of India, *Indian Petroleum Products Industry: Opportunities and Challenges,* Exim Bank: Research Brief, No. 24, March 2006.
45. Thus, for identifying the different levels of trade potential on the basis of computed EIS and IES measures, we have applied three cut-off points which lie between zero to one. (a) *Low Potential* (LP) falls under the range of more than 0.001 but less than 0.250; (b) *Moderate Potential* (MP) falls under the range of more than 0.250 but less than 0.550; and (c) *High Potential* (HP) falls under the range between 0.550 to 1.000. Low Potential indicates Poor Complementarity; Moderate Potential indicates Partial Complementarity; and High Potential indicates Perfect Trade Complementarity. Since not much of difference was noticed in these cut-off points in 2000, the same were retained for 2003, 2005 and 2007.
46. For details, see *Economic Survey, 2009-10,* Government of India. In terms of economic and trade cooperation, in 2008 China became India's largest trade partner and India the 10th largest trade partner of China.
47. FDI is prohibited for retail trade, atomic energy, lottery business, gambling and betting, housing and real-estate business except construction development projects and

development of integrated townships, and agriculture plantations. Caps on foreign equity remain in a few sectors such as domestic airlines, broadcasting, telecommunication, defence production, etc.

48. A Speech Delivered on "India's Quest for Energy Security: The Oil and Gas Perspective" by Murli Deora, Minister of Petroleum and Natural Gas, Government of India, Presented in the Shell Distinguished Lecture Series, James A. Baker III Institute for Public Policy, Rice University, 31 March 2006.
49. India's FDI Policy related to energy resources are (a) Under Exploration Policy: up to 100 per cent FDI permitted; (b) Refining: Up to 100 per cent FDI as Private Indian Company under automatic route, up to 26 per cent FDI along with Public Sector Companies; (c) Marketing & Trading: (i) 100 per cent wholly owned subsidiary, of a foreign company, for market study, investment & financing, and (ii) FDI up to 100 per cent permitted in petroleum product marketing, subject to introducing 26 per cent minimum Indian equity over 5 years, (d) Pipelines: up to 100 per cent FDI: Under automatic route for product pipelines, and (e) Natural Gas/LNG Pipelines: up to 100 per cent FDI: With prior Government approval.
50. Equity oil refers to standard industry production sharing agreements where the foreign oil company is given the right to sell a specified share of the oil produced.
51. A.M. Uplenchwar, "Energy security policy and resource diplomacy in India" presentation on "Regional cooperation in Asia for stabilising energy demand and supply" On Behalf of Indian Oil Corporation Limited, Government of India, 25 November 2005, IEEJ,Tokyo, Japan.
52. Shaofeng Chen, "Assessing the Impact of China's Foreign Energy Quest on its Energy Security", *EAI Working Paper No. 145,* 3 March 2009.
53. Shaofeng Chen, "Motivations behind China's Foreign Oil Quest – A Perspective from the Chinese Government and the Oil Companies," *Journal of Chinese Political Science,* Vol. 13, No. 1, Spring 2008, pp. 79-103.
54. NG Grace, "China dangles loans to get key resources", *The Strait Times*, 23 April 2009.
55. Zhao Hong, "China and India: The Energy Policies", *EAI Background Brief No. 4622*, July 2009.
56. Stephanie Kleine, "China's New Dictatorship Diplomacy", *Foreign Affairs*, February 2008.
57. See detail in Neeladri Chatterjee, A Political Perspective on Energy Security Cooperation between India and China, *SGIA (School of Government and International Affairs) Research Working Papers Series* (SGIARWP), No. 3, April 2008.
58. India and China are unlikely to become cooperative partners, except in a limited opportunistic sense, any time in the foreseeable future. They have historically been commercial and cultural competitors in Asia; Today, they not only champion radically different systems of governance, they have too many points of friction between them in the region. For details, see Gautam Adhikari, "A Tale of Two Nations", *Times of India*, 24 February 2010.
59. For instance, in 2004, China's Export-Import Bank extended $2 billion in soft loans to Angola, which led Sonangol to support CNPC's bid over that of ONGC for a stake in an offshore block. See, "China, India fight for African oil," *AFP*, 15 October 2004. Similarly, in 2005 CNPC's successful bid for PetroKazakhstan over the initially higher price offered by ONGC Mittal was supported by China's diplomatic initiatives, both bilaterally and through the aegis of the Shanghai Cooperation Organization (SCO) as well as the fact that India's acquisition of Kazakh energy assets would likely increase Kazakhstan's dependence on Russia, which would be the likely route for transporting oil to India, which has no direct overland route to the region. See, "India loses PetroKaz bid to China," *The Times of India*, 23 August 2005.

60. Chietigj Bajpaee, "The Panda and the Peacock", *China Security*, World Security Institute, Vol. 3 No. 4, Autumn 2007, p. 108.
61. "India, China plans for oil sector cooperation at early stage", *India Daily*, 26 April 2005.
62. This MoU is expected to set-up a framework to promote cooperation on the basis of applied research in the field of metallic and non-metallic minerals, formulation of mining regulations and policies, technical assistance and training programmes and also undertaking joint ventures in other countries. To enhance cooperation between the two countries, the Geological Survey of India (GSI) and the Chinese Academy of Geological Sciences (CAGS) discussed and finalised various proposals for co-operation.
63. China, India sign five memoranda on energy cooperation, *People's Daily*, 13 January 2006.
64. Jonathan Holslag, Fuelling Competition? China and India's Need for Natural Resources and the Options for Cooperation, *ICCS Asia Paper*, Vol. 3, No. 3, 9 January 2008.
65. Balaji Reddy, "India calls for Asian Gas grid connecting India, China, Japan to Gas producing areas of Asia", *India Daily*, 15 February 2005.
66. The master plan study for the Trans-ASEAN Gas Pipeline identified seven new possible gas interconnections covering a length of 4,500 kilometers, with total investment requirements of US $7 billion. The TAGP project would optimize the utilization of natural gas by linking gas demand and utilization centers with a pipeline infrastructure tapping the gas fields of the Andaman Sea, the Gulf of Thailand, the South China Sea, and Kalimantan and Sumatra in Indonesia. The major gas demand centers are Bangkok, Kuala Lumpur, Singapore, Batam, Jakarta, Surabaya and Manila. The infrastructure could be further extended to link the East Asian markets.
67. Parwini Zora and Niall Green, "China and India manoeuvre to secure energy supplies, 31 January 2006, *http://www.wsws.org/articles/2006/jan2006/indi-j31.shtml*
68. "India Loses Kazakh Oil firm to China," *The Tribune*, 23 August 2005. <www.tribuneindia.com/2005/20050823/biz.htm#2> (July 5 2006).
69. On several occasions in the past few years India has lost significant bids to China, including in Angola, Kazakhstan, Ecuador and Burma. Chinese oil firms, meanwhile, are reported to have made several deals in which they overpaid for energy assets. In August 2006, CNPC paid $4.18 billion to acquire Canadian oil company PetroKazakhstan. India's Oil and Natural Gas Corporation (ONGC) had bid $3.9 billion. See, Parwini Zora and Niall Green, "China and India manoeuvre to Secure Energy Supplies", 31 January 2006.
70. Brad Van Tassel and others, "Unlocking China's Energy Potential", *Report of The Boston Consulting Group*, September 2006.
71. Sino-Indian competition over energy resources is not restricted to oil and is taking place in various parts of the world, for example in Myanmar, where both countries are vying for natural gas pipelines to be built. China signed an agreement in November 2005 for consideration of a pipeline from Myanmar's Shwe field to Yunnan Province. On 11 March 2006, Indian President Abdul Kalam made a similar proposal for India and Myanmar.
72. Charan D Wadhva, "Management of Rising Power by China and India in the 21st Century: Scope for Strategic Partnership", *Vikalpa*, Volume 31, No. 3, July-September 2006.
73. *Business Standard*, New Delhi, 24 March 2005 at <http://www.businessstandard.com/bsonline/storypage.php?&autono=184297>
74. "China, India agree on Energy Cooperation", Embassy of the People's Republic of China in the United States of America, 13 January 2006.
75. 'India, China move to energy cooperation', *United Press International*, 13 January 2006.
76. 'ONGC acquires shares of Petro-Canada in Syria', New Delhi, 21 December 2005, and 'ONGC completes transaction of acquisition of producing asset in Syria' New Delhi, 1 February 2006, online at: http://www.ongcvidesh.com.

77. Indrajit Basu, "India, China pin down $573m Syria deal", *Asia Times Online*, 22 December 2005.
78. "Cynicism greets Sino-Indian deal to end rivalry over oil supplies", *Financial Times*, 15 January 2005.
79. June Teufel Dreyer, "A New Era in Sino–Indian Relations or Deja-vu All Over Again?" January 18, 2008, at *http://www.strategycenter.net/research/pubID.178/pub_detail.asp*
80. Stein Tønnesson, "Regionale stormakters globale rolle: Kina, India, Brasil og Sør-Afrika." *Internasjonal politick*, Vol. 64, No.1, 2006, pp. 75-94 & 92-93.
81. Surjit Mansingh, "Rising China and Emergent India in the 21st Century: Friends or Rivals?" *The Korean Journal of Defense Analysis*, Vol. XIX, No. 4, Winter 2007, p. 140.
82. Michael Piskur, 'Iran's nuclear plans complicate China's Energy Security', *Power and Interest News Report*, 13 March 2006.
83. These are the details of IEA member countries. (a) *Founding Member (1974)*: (i) Austria; (ii) Belgium; (iii) Canada; (iv) Denmark; (v) Germany; (vi) Ireland; (vii) Italy; (viii) Japan; (ix) Sweden; (x) Switzerland; (xi) Turkey; (xii) United Kingdom; (xiii) United States; (xiv) Luxembourg; (xv) The Netherlands; and (xvi) Spain. (b) *Member* (i) Australia (1979); (ii) Czech Republic (2001); (iii) Finland (1992); (iv) France (1992); (v) Greece (1977); (vi) Hungary (1997); (vii) Republic of Korea (2002); (viii) Portugal (1981); (ix) Slovak Republic (2007); (x) New Zealand (1977); (xi) Poland (2008); and Norway (*participates in the Agency under a special Agreement since 1974).* These countries (founding member and member) are also all member countries of the Organisation for Economic Co-operation and Development (OECD), as the IEA is an autonomous agency linked with the OECD. (c) *The Commission of the European Community* takes part in the work of the OECD (d) *Accession candidate countries*: (i) Chile; (ii) Estonia; (iii) Israel; (iv) Russia and (v) Slovenia (e) *Enhanced engagement countries*: (i) Brazil, (ii) India, (iii) China, (iv) Indonesia and (v) South Africa. For details, see IEA webpage at http://www.iea.org
84. Sudha Mahalingam, "India-China Energy Cooperation: Commonalities, Synergies and Complementarity", in Lingia Noronha and Anant Sudarshan (eds), *India's Energy Security*, Routledge, UK, 2009.
85. Harbert, K.A., *China's Energy Consumption and Opportunities for US-China Cooperation to address the effects of China's Energy Use*. Presentation to the US-China Economic and Security Review Commission, June 2007.
86. Ibid.
87. *Financial Times*, 12 January 2006.
88. The International Energy Forum (IEF), *News Letter*, May 2009, No. 13. (http://www.ief.org/Pages/IEFSNewsletters.aspx)
89. Joint Oil Data Initiative (JODI), *News Letter*, August 2009, No. 16 (http://www.ief.org/Pages/JODINewsletters.aspx)
90. Government of India, *Integrated Energy Policy: Report of the Expert Committee*, Planning Commission, New Delhi, 2006.
91. SCO member countries are China, Kazakhstan, Kyrgyzstan, Russia, Tajikistan and Uzbekistan; SAARC member countries are Afghanistan, Bangladesh, Bhutan, India, Maldives, Nepal, Pakistan and Sri Lanka; and APTA member countries are Bangladesh, China, India, Republic of Korea, Lao and Sri Lanka.

# 11

## The Iran-Pakistan-India Pipeline

*Savita Pande*

The trilateral Iran-Pakistan-India gas pipeline, or IPI as it is popularly called, has almost become a bilateral pipeline, between Iran and Pakistan, as the two signed an agreement in March 2010, leaving options open, the questionable economic viability of the project notwithstanding. The much debated and negotiated IPI pipeline was proposed to be 2,775 kms (1,724 miles) in length and if and when successfully completed, is expected to deliver natural gas from Iran to Pakistan and India.

When the idea was first mooted, India was in favour of the project of a pipeline through Pakistan, but Pakistan was not interested. Later on, both sides changed their positions: Pakistan became willing to allow the pipeline to pass through its territory but India refused to buy gas through any pipeline project in which Pakistan was involved. As the deadlock continued, Iran made moves to push the project, largely guided by its own motives – political, economic and strategic. As negotiations reached a dead-end, with India and Iran failing to settle matters and India's vague stance on its participation in the project, Iran even floated the China bogey in April 2008, proclaiming Chinese willingness to join the project. Pakistan was more than happy, elated even, and suggested that this would be a very good idea as it would provide a stable partner to the project and also resolve the issue of continued Indian wavering.

### Energy Scenario

#### *India*

From being the fifth-largest consumer in the world, India is poised to rise to third-largest consumer by 2030, surpassing even Japan. The International Energy Agency predicts the potential rise of primary energy demand in India to 3.6 percent per year, doubling from 537 million ton oil equivalents (mtoe) in 2005 to 1,299 mtoe in 2030.[1] Presently, India's energy mix is dominated by coal, the quality and cleanliness of which is generally not rated very high. Coal constitutes more than half of India's total energy consumption followed by oil, which forms 31 percent of the total energy consumption followed by natural gas and hydroelectric power accounting for 8 and 6 percent of consumption, respectively; 30 percent of India's total energy needs are met through imports. Of late, there have been gas finds, but these remain far behind meeting India's domestic energy needs.

India had 5.6 billion barrels of proven oil reserves as of January 2009, the second-largest amount in the Asia-Pacific region after China. This notwithstanding, demand exceeds the domestic production (880 thousand bbl/d of total oil in 2008), and is expected to rise.[2] In 2007, India consumed approximately 2.8 million barrels per day (bpd), making it the fifth-largest consumer of oil in the world. In 2008, the demand grew to nearly 3 million bpd. As of January 2009, India had 38 trillion cubic feet (tcf) of proven natural gas reserves.[3] It produced approximately 1.1 tcf of natural gas and consumed roughly 1.5 tcf in 2007. India's net imports reached an estimated 353 billion cubic feet (bcf) in 2007. India imports natural gas via liquefied natural gas (LNG).[4] It is more than clear that India faces an acute shortage of domestic energy resources and hence must import them. It is pursuing domestic oil and gas exploration besides production, along with stepping up its natural gas imports, currently as LNG.

### *Pakistan*

Natural gas accounts for the largest share in Pakistan's energy use, Pakistan consumes all the domestic natural gas that it produces amounting to nearly 968 bcf. The share of gas in the energy supply mix of Pakistan declined from 50.4 percent in 2006 to 48.5 percent in 2007 and stood at 29.3 mtoe. A surge in the oil supply led to an increase in oil's share in the energy mix from 28.4 percent in 2006 to 30.0 percent in 2007 at 18.1 mtoe. Nuclear electricity and LPG contribute the least to the overall energy supply at 0.9 percent and 0.5 percent respectively.[5]

As per Pakistani sources, oil and gas production witnessed an increase by 4 percent and 2.9 percent respectively during 2008 as compared to the corresponding year 2007.[6] The oil production in the fiscal year 2008 was recorded at 71,120 bpd as compared to 68,374 bpd 2007. According to EIA sources, it was producing around 61,870 bpd oil in 2008.[7] Pakistan's gas reserves in 2007 stood at 28,000 bcf.[8] While gas production of the country stood at 4,039 million cubic feet per day (mcfd) in 2008 as against 3,927 mcfd in 2007, LPG production fell by 1.7pc per year to 1,517 tons per day (tpd).[9] The power sector is the largest consumer of gas (33.5 percent share), followed by the industrial sector (23.8 percent), household (18.1 percent), fertilizer (15.6 percent), transport (5.4 percent) and cement (0.9 percent).[10]

Hydroelectric power is the third most important element in Pakistan's energy mix. The Water and Power Development Authority has control over the major hydroelectric plants, with the Tarbela plant being the largest at 3,046 megawatts (MW) installed capacity. Other operational plants include Mangla (1,000 MW), Warsak (240 MW), and Chashma (184 MW).[11] Hydel energy accounts for 33.1 percent of total power generation in the country. Pakistan's hydel generation potential is estimated to be 46,000 MW, out of which only 14 percent has been exploited till now.[12]

### *Iran*

Despite having the second-largest gas reserves after Russia, Iran has yet to emerge as a large exporter because of Western sanctions, and periodic political upheavals. Iran's interests in gas supply to the subcontinent are stated to lie in the geographical location of Iranian gas resources, especially South Pars field in the center of the Persian Gulf. The latter makes India the best market for country's gas export in the coming years. Iranian policy makers have also studied the Pakistani and Indian markets for export of gas in the form of LNG and via pipeline for some time."[13] Iran plans to increase its gas exports through pipelines to 303.6 million cubic meters per day (mcm/d) by 2025 from some 13 mcm/d in 2006. Iran's LNG exports are also expected to grow to 18 mcm/d by 2025. Therefore, Iran's total natural gas export can reach around 18 billion cubic meters (bcm) in 2025, assuming all goes well.[14]

## The Project

The pipeline idea dates as far back as 1989, when the then head of the Tata Energy Research Institute (TERI), R.K. Pachauri, invited Iran's former Deputy Foreign Minister Ali Shams Ardekani to New Delhi to deliver a paper on the subject. Pachauri recalls, "At that time, policy-makers and others thought of it as nothing more than a pipedream."[15] However, Abbas Maleki says the first serious proposal on natural gas export to India on land was presented to the Asian Energy Institute in 1989. The "Asian Gas Pipeline" was presented as a scheme to construct a pipeline with the capacity of 36 billion cubic meters per year from Bandar Abbas in Iran to Calcutta. It was envisaged *that 10 percent of this gas would be consumed in the Iranian provinces en route, 20 percent were to be used in Pakistan and the balance would be left in India's field.*[16] (emphasis added)

Sometimes in 1990, former Iranian President Ali Akbar Hashemi Rafsanjani put forward the proposal for the IPI pipeline. Three years later India and Iran signed an MoU for the project and the focus was initially on laying an offshore pipeline outside the territorial waters of Pakistan.[17] Pipeline Engineering GMB of Germany and Sazeh consultant of Iran were given the job of feasibility study by the Joint Working Committee of the National Iranian Gas Company (NIGC) and Gas Authority of India Limited (GAIL). As Pakistan did not allow work in its territorial waters, the study remained incomplete.[18]

Many analysts, however, trace the origin of the idea to 1993, when Iran and Pakistan declared their intention to construct a natural gas pipeline, which the former, subsequently, proposed extending into India and popularly came to be known as the IPI or the so called "peace pipeline", covering over 2,775 kms from Assalouyeh in Iran, south Pars fields, and stretch over 1,100 kms through Khuzdhar in Pakistan, from where it would branch into two: one to Karachi and another via Multan to India.[19]

**Map 1**

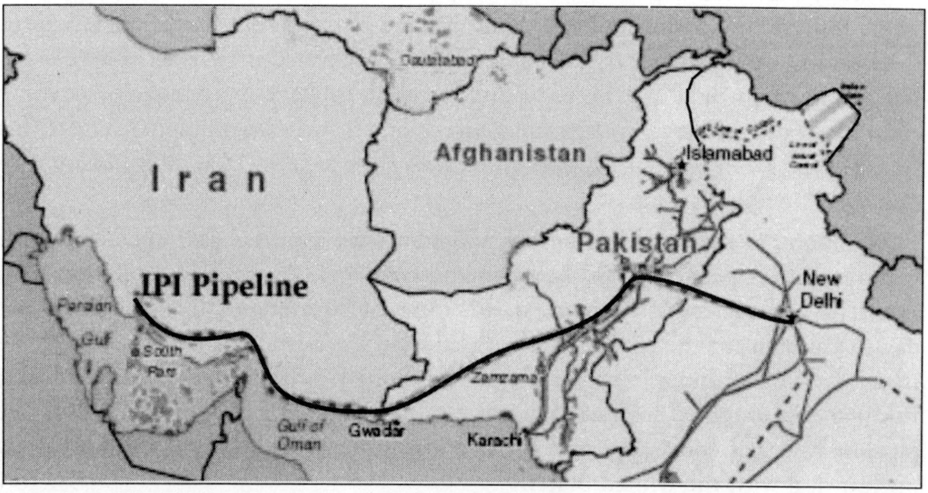


**Source:** Modified from image at www.eia.doe.gov/cabs/Iran/NaturalGas.html. Map not to scale.

Initially, a total of 60 million cubic meters of gas would be transported daily from Iran to Pakistan and India, (half for each), later it would be raised to 150 million cubic meters.[20] Another estimate says, the proposed pipeline is expected to transport 90 million standard cubic meters of gas every day from Iran's South Pars fields to India while Pakistan would receive 60 million standard cubic meters.[21] The construction of the pipeline is expected to cost $ 7.5 bn.[22] That notwithstanding, despite the above stated MoU, progress remained very slow, if not dead. The pipeline talks remained deadlocked from 1999 to 2003 largely because of the state of Indo-Pakistani tensions, and gained momentum only after the dialogue started between them in 2004. In July 2005, Indian and Pakistani officials after a meeting stated that they planned to appoint separate legal and financial consultants to begin work on the project to build the 2,600-kilometer pipeline. The two-day talks in New Delhi also discussed issues such as financing and security of the pipeline, pricing and sharing of the gas.[23] A meeting to approve the tripartite agreement scheduled for December 31, 2005 was postponed because of delays in Iran-Pakistan talks and the impact of the October 8, 2005 earthquake in Pak-occupied Kashmir that year.[24] Iranian first Vice President Pervez Dawoodi in May 2006 gave optimistic indication of resolution of all issues, stating that the project would become "operational within two months, with experts working only on the pricing formula."[25]

Initial hurdle came in July 2006 when Iran demanded a price of $7.20 per million British thermal unit of gas against India's price of $4.20 per million British thermal unit. To India, the Iranian offer was 50 percent above the prevailing market price in India.[26] India and Pakistan finally agreed in February 2007 to pay Iran US$ 4.93 per million British thermal units, but some details still needed to be resolved.[27] Since mid-2007, India has been boycotting trilateral meetings on the IPI pipeline, as it first wanted to resolve the issues of transit fees and transportation tariffs with Pakistan.

Differences between parties over issues of pricing, transit fee and security have practically paralysed negotiations on the pipeline for quite some time now. India wants Iran to take responsibility for safe passage of gas through pipeline length in Pakistan and would pay for the fuel only when it is delivered at Pakistan-India border. Iran, on its part would like this to be done through trilateral mechanism by devising contractual provisions to ensure safe delivery of gas to India, implying, under this system, *New Delhi pays for its share of gas even if the supplies were to be disrupted in Pakistan.*[28] (emphasis added)

It is another matter that Pakistan and Iran have signed a gas pipeline accord, without India's participation, between the Iranian National Oil Company and Interstate Gas System of Pakistan. Iran is to give 750 million cubic feet of gas per day to Pakistan for the next 25 years.[29] Pakistan has been permitted to charge the transit fee in case India joins the pipeline, although earlier, in its usual gimmicks, Pakistan had proposed to Iran to buy the Indian share of gas from a proposed IPI pipeline as it felt India appeared to have lost interest in the project following its nuclear deal with the United States.[30]

### *Stakeholders*

As far as the stakeholders in the project are concerned, apart from the three governments, there is a wide network of oil companies and their subsidiaries in the three countries. In Iran it is being done by owner of gas fields, the National Iranian Oil Company (NIOC), through its subsidiary, National Iranian Gas Export Company (NIGEC), while the pipeline segment will be owned and operated by another NIOC subsidiary, National Iranian Gas Company (NIGC).

In Pakistan, negotiations are being dealt with by the Inter-State Gas System (ISGS) for natural gas imports. It is a subsidiary of Sui Southern Gas Company (SSGC) and Sui Northern Gas Pipelines Limited (SNGPL), having 51 and 41 percent control respectively. In India, Gas Authority India Limited (GAIL), would own and operate, negotiate and be the beneficiary of the project.[31] Experts believe financing the Iran-India gas pipeline project is very complex because of high investment costs, high degree of inflexibility and high dependence on the economics of scale.

### *Benefits*

Some benefits are too commonly well known to elaborate. It begins with the fuel itself, the natural gas, the main advantages of which, apart from fuel efficiency and cost, are that it is the only biological fuel that can be transported to customers without energy transformation and costly processing; its transmissions are unaffected by climatic changes, it is environment friendly, non-toxic, etc.[32]

Then there are benefits of the pipeline to all, traversing social, political, multilateral and economic factors. These include *employment creation* stretching close to a thousand miles, as the pipeline will generate substantial employment along its route; *improved political cooperation* in view of need to safeguard the investment interests and other economic advantages spilled over from investment; *promotion of multilateralism*, as an offshoot of dependence on energy and the involvement of multiple participants in the project, and lastly, but certainly not the least *Energy Security* – India and Pakistan are increasingly import-dependent for their energy needs.[33]

Interestingly, many optimists have dubbed it as the "peace pipeline" as it would create economic bondings between India and Pakistan which in turn would promote stable relations between the traditional rivals who have gone to war on four occasions since 1947. In a joint statement issued in New York on the sidelines of the United Nations General Assembly in September 2004, the Indian Prime Minister Dr. Manmohan Singh and the then Pakistan President General Pervez Musharraf reiterated the crucial role that this pipeline could play in contributing to the welfare and prosperity of both countries. The former Pakistani Prime Minister Shaukat Aziz of Pakistan, said, "If we do this pipeline and it does take off, I sincerely believe India-Pakistan relations will move forward in the right direction."[34] In January 2005, Pakistan's Prime Minister Shaukat Aziz described the pipeline proposal as a "win-win situation for all, as we believe that creating interdependence between different countries will help promote peace…".[35]

A utopian extent is presented in the view that the pipeline "could also serve as the mother of all confidence-building measures. For the passage of natural gas through Pakistan to India, its price set at a fair level by Tehran and its uninterrupted flow guaranteed by Islamabad, will change the geopolitical landscape of the Subcontinent. In one stroke, the joint stakeholding of an economic resource will defuse the five and a half decade long India-Pakistan hostility. Many tightly-wound bilateral problems, including the matter of Kashmir, will suddenly become manageable."[36]

There is no doubt that the project benefits both Pakistan and Iran enormously. For Pakistan, the benefits are manifold: securing supply of two-thirds of gas would be delivered to India, the remainder would go to Pakistan; transit fees, and a control button over India's energy supply as well as a place in Indo-Iran relations between Tehran and Delhi. Islamabad fears that closer cooperation between the two governments could leave it isolated. Although Pakistan has tried to maintain good relations with Iran, there are tensions.[37] Pakistan itself had hoped to earn about $14 billion in 30 years from the project, including $8 billion in transit fees, $1 billion in taxes and $5 billion in savings.[38] Another estimate says Pakistan will earn $500 million per year as transportation charges from India other than about $200 million transit fee.[39]

Similarly for Iran, pipeline benefits include: (1) a major boost for job creation and economic prosperity of the provinces on the pipeline route; (2) the enhancement of Iran's strategic positioning and standing both regionally and on a global level; and (3) regional economic integration.[40] While on the one hand the project would help it battle American quest to isolate it economically and diplomatically, on the other it is an economic boosting venture. Besides, while the pipeline may improve its relations with India, it can consolidate its ties with Pakistan".[41]

## Problems and Challenges

Depending upon time and negotiations, problems have ranged from massive financial implications, geo-political, environmental considerations, unsure confirmation of natural gas resources, pricing of supplied gas.[42]

### *Fear of Blackmail*

Given the fragile nature of relationship between India and Pakistan, India has legitimate fears that Islamabad could threaten to cut off the supply during adverse times. The situation is more so after the 2008 Mumbai attacks by Pakistani terrorists. Leading Pakistani analysts like Ayesha Siddiqa Agha say that the proposed onshore pipeline passing through Pakistan could be a far greater guarantee against an Indian attack than even nuclear weapons ... "no matter how much India spends on acquiring an anti-ballistic missile technology or for becoming a member of the US sponsored NMD club, New Delhi would have to think twice before launching a military offensive against Pakistan if a strategic pipeline passes through the latter's territory."[43]

### *Security of the Pipeline*

Security of the pipeline is one of the major hurdles concerned for the simple reason that the pipeline crosses the disturbed area of Balochistan. The insurgents in Balochistan oppose any energy projects in their area. Thus in January 2003, sabotage of a gas pipeline from Sui cut off gas supply to the Punjab. Later, in June, a wave of attacks against gas installations caused the government to send troops to protect the installations.[44] The Balochistan Assembly in June 2006 unanimously passed a resolution, seeking royalty on the proposed IPI gas pipeline.[45] This is one major reason behind India's insistence for the gas to be delivered at the India-Pakistan border and not at the Pakistan-Iran border.

The Pakistani Province of Balochistan, which apart from the ongoing insurgency particularly since 2005 also borders the Iranian Sunni Sistan Balochistan province of the Shia-dominant country Iran. Balochi separatists have been crossing the border and clashing repeatedly with Iranian paramilitaries in an attempt to unite the Iranian part of Balochistan with its Pakistani counterpart.[46] Iran openly accused Pakistan of supporting *Jundollah*, the terrorist organizations in the region. Apart from attacks on the pipelines in the Sui gas fields by the Baluch insurgents, the area also harbours Taliban in Quetta Shura.

Even after the buyers had agreed on the price formula proposed by Iran, [$4.93 per million British thermal unit (mbtu)] and the formula to be reviewed as per the international practices, Iran wanted the formula to be reviewed every three years.[47] Besides, between India and Pakistan, an agreement was reached on the principle of calculating the transportation tariff, to be paid by India to Pakistan for transmission of gas through its territory but transit fee payable to Pakistan for passage of the pipeline remained unresolved.

## US Opposition

The U.S. stand on the issue is a subset of its Iran policy, considerations being largely strategic underlined by a host of considerations, beginning with Iran's nuclear ambitions. In August 2006, the US Congress unanimously passed the "Iran, Libya Sanctions Act" (ILSA), which provides for imposition of US sanctions on companies, irrespective of their "corporate nationality" that invest more than $20 million annually in the Iranian oil and gas sector. In 2006, US Advisor on Caspian Energy Stephen Mann is reported to have said that although the US has been supporting pipelines in the Caspian region, but it "remains absolutely opposed to pipelines involving Iran."[48]

In April 2010, Robert Blake, Assistant Secretary of State for South and Central Asia said that the American concerns were known, in view of the Iranian attitude and global concerns over its nuclear programme. He stated, "we don't think that this is the time for such transactions to be taking place with Iran."[49] In 2010, during the US-Pakistan strategic dialogue, Pakistan put energy as one of its critical concern, seeking a nuclear civil technology deal, notwithstanding its proliferation record a la A.Q. Khan. The US did not concede Pakistan's request but announced its offer to provide $125 million for energy, including repair of thermal plants.

### *Iran's Concerns*

Domestically the deal faces its own challenges, a former Iranian deputy oil minister, Hadi Nejad Hosseinian, reportedly questioned the deal on the ground that it gives a huge discount to India and is some 30 percent below the value of gas being sold to Turkey. Another Iranian politician, Akbar Mohtashemipour, from Iran's reformist side, also publicly questioned the wisdom of exporting Iran's gas at a time when the cold regions of Iran face gas shortages. Besides, Iran's negotiating team itself has been changed several times, as the project moved to Ministry of External Affairs.

## China

In February 2010, Iranian Foreign Minister Manucher Mottaki reportedly urged Pakistan not to yield to American pressure, as it (Iran) was prepared to launch the pipeline at any time – even without India – *as China could soon replace India.*[50] China is an expanding energy market, and it has signed important contracts with Iran. Pakistan anyway has a comfortable relationship with China. It has all win-win situations, it gets energy, transit fee, consolidation of ties, if it actually replaces India, or the latter can serve as accelerator to India, if it does not. India on its part, doesn't think China is seriously contemplating joining the pipeline. During Mahmoud Ahmadinejad's stopover in April 2008, the then Indian Foreign Secretary said it (China replacing India) was only an idea.[51]

Iran has political problems with India. Notwithstanding the Balochistan problem, Pakistan-Iran relations have enjoyed bonhomie of times, including support for its Kashmir policy. Pakistan served as a window for China to Iran, whereas with India things have not been smooth, certainly over its nuclear programme. It voted against

Iran at the International Atomic Energy Agency in 2006. Besides, Iran would also be wary of upswing in India-Israel relations, including in the defence sector. However, as far as China's joining the pipeline is concerned, the logistical challenges are immense, including traversing and connecting troubled provinces of Gilgit in Pak-occupied Kashmir and Xinjiang in Pakistan and China respectively. India is also one of the biggest markets for its petroleum and gas products. While much has been said about Chinese linking to Gwadar and expanding energy hub, the Chinese motive could be as modest as seeking a better deal with Russia on Siberia-China gas pipelines.[52]

Conjectures have also been made about the Russian company Gazprom's interest in the deal expressing willingness to join the project. The Russian limited objectives are easy to discern: by preventing Iran from competing with it in Europe, the pipeline would keep Iranian gas in South Asian markets.[53] Russia maintains supremacy in Europe, taking care of over one quarter of the continent's gas needs. However the EU has now tried to reduce this dependence by constructing Nabucco pipeline which would pump Caspian Sea gas to Europe, bypassing Russia.

## Conclusions

Nothing is clear as far as the pipeline is concerned. But it seems for all practical purposes that India is out of the India-Pakistan-Iran pipeline. At a meeting in Cancun, the Indian Petroleum Secretary said that two outstanding issues remained, i.e., the price formula and India's insistence for the gas to be delivered at the India-Pakistan border and not at the Pakistan-Iran border. Much has been made about the statement coming close on the heels of the March 2010 Pakistan-Iran agreement on the pipeline.

Without undermining the importance of energy security for India, as far as IPI is concerned, stakes are greater for Pakistan and Iran than India. Surprisingly, these are the two countries which are posing hard bargains. Besides, irrespective of the fact that the two enjoy good relations, there are problems between them – Balochistan and Afghanistan, to mention just two. And yet the two have colluded in playing the China card to push India into the deal.

In any case, the Indians know, the Pakistanis know and the Iranians know that the deal is not an economically viable proposition unless India joins the pipeline. To quote Nadeem Iqbal, "The project is only viable if it is extended up to Pakistan's arch-rival India, as Iran stands to make US$ 3.06 per MMBTU (million British thermal units) of gas sold to India, but would get only $1.48 if the commodity does not go beyond Pakistan.... Pakistan itself had hoped to earn about $14 billion in 30 years from the project, including $8 billion in transit fees, $1 billion in taxes and $5 billion in savings".[54] This point is also conceded by Musarrat Jabeen.[55]

As for the cost of pipelines, Pakistan abandoned off shore route for onshore to bring the pipeline from Iran to Pakistan under sea, as the cost of the offshore route had been estimated at $4.460 billion, which is almost twice the cost of on-shore route $2.538 billion, a cost differential that would have risen to $10.2 billion over the 25 years.[56] Even in the Pakistan-Iran venture it has been argued that choice of overland pipeline was exercised because it would be four times cheaper than the deep-sea route, even after including transit fee payments to Pakistan.

There is much talk of the US backed $3.3 bn Turkmenistan-Afghanistan-Pakistan-India (TAPI) pipeline, to bring natural gas from Turkmenistan to India. TAPI is expected to transport 100 mm cmpd of gas, of which India's share is 60 mm cmpd. The latter was initially reluctant to join the project for security reasons, as half of it would traverse restive parts of Afghanistan and Pakistan. In May 2006 it decided to become part of the project, also supported by the ADB.[57] The project, however, confronts the problems, ranging from availability of Turkmen gas (after fulfilling its commitment to Russia), security situation in Afghanistan and Pakistan, to name a few.

Is bypassing Pakistan option? Comparing the various options, Maleki says the cost of transmitting 30 bcm per year of gas from Iran to Indian sub-continent would be in the onshore of $3 billion considering the land route ... each part of the pipeline in each country needs $1 billion but the operating cost is lower comparing with the offshore pipeline. If the option of a combination of land and sea from Iran to shallow waters of Pakistan and then Indian land is taken into consideration, it would be about $4 billion. More importantly, the pipeline which bypasses Pakistan through deep sea needs $4.4 billion. It covers $3.6 billion for pipe and $800 million for compressors. Only two countries, Iran and India might share it by equal. Operating cost in this option is higher. Hence, the land gas pipeline would have the highest value added for the economy of the region, as over fifty percent of the total costs would be in local currencies and engineering and construction firms in Iran, Pakistan and India could build the gas pipeline within two to three years.[58]

However, India disagrees saying: "we feel that even though laying a submarine pipeline is more expensive, in the long run, it will benefit us."[59] Assured supply is a serious issue with India, after all even if on high scale of optimism, international guarantees are sought and got, what if penalties do not ensure compliance and make Pakistan to fulfill its contractual obligations, such as refusal to grant India the Most Favoured Nation (MFN) despite getting it from India.[60]

In any case India is a coal based energy basket. As high as 50 percent of the energy mix and 70 percent of power generation is through coal. LNG is another powerful option; apart from its contacts with Qatar, it has two LNG terminals. Two additional terminals have also been on the pipeline. This is not to deny importance of gas or undermine India's growing needs. However, its case is very different from that of Pakistan where demand for gas by 2014 is projected to reach 8 billion cubic feet per day, whereas, production as of April 2010 is less than 4 billion cubic feet per day. Thus even if one takes into account gas from Iran, and from the one LNG plant that is in the offing, "there will still be an estimated shortfall of 2-3 billion cubic feet of gas per day by 2013-14."[61]

Although India has not participated in the trilateral talks since mid-2007, it has not made any statement on withdrawal from the project. Partly because it doesn't want to be seen as buckling under the US pressure, both domestically, regionally as well as globally, and partly because of its interests in Iran, including energy interests, which have already seen a downturn after its vote at the IAEA against Iran's nuclear programme. Over and above India knows, as also Iran and Pakistan, that the economic viability of the project is there only if India joins the project. That being the case, India may not be seeing the utility of saying "it is over". Since nothing is certain in international relations generally, and in the subcontinent particularly, India may not be wanting to close the option. However, as things stand currently, notwithstanding the security assurances for the pipeline given by Pakistan to India recently, law and order scenario in Pakistan generally and Balochistan in particular, warrant alternative options. A pipeline bypassing Pakistan or an LNG deal with Iran are two good options. After all cost calculations run beyond pure economics and certainly projects of this nature are based on long term calculations.

## ENDNOTES

1. International Energy Agency, *World Energy Outlook 2007*, pp. 7, 465.
2. US Energy Information Administration, *India:Oil*,http://www.eia.doe.gov/emeu/cabs/India/Oil.html
3. US Energy Information Administration, *India: Natural Gas* http://www.eia.doe.gov/emeu/cabs/India/NaturalGas.html; http://tonto.eia.doe.gov/country/country_energy_data.cfm?fips=IN
4. http://www.eia.doe.gov/emeu/cabs/India/NaturalGas.html
5. Government of Pakistan, "Energy Year Book FY-07: Growing Reliance on Oil", at http://202.83.164.26/wps/connect/34d92780497ba5a896fb9eab4ed50e43/enryearbook.pdf?MOD=AJPERES
6. "Oil, gas production witnesses increase", *The Nation*, November 26, 2008, at http://www.nation.com.pk/pakistan-news-newspaper-daily-english-online/Business/26-Nov-2008/Oil-gas-production-witnesses-increase/1
7. Country Analysis Briefs, EIA, 2006, p. 2.
8. US Energy International Agency, "Pakistan's Energy Profile", at http://tonto.eia.doe.gov/country/country_energy_data.cfm?fips=PK
9. "Oil, gas production witnesses increase", *The Nation* November 26, 2008, at http://www.nation.com.pk/pakistan-news-newspaper-daily-english-online/Business/26-Nov-2008/Oil-gas-production-witnesses-increase/1
10. *Economic Survey of Pakistan 2007-2008*, Government of Pakistan, Finance Division, Economic Advisers Wing, Islamabad, Pakistan, at http://www.finance.gov.pk/admin/images/survey/chapters/15-Energy 08.pdf, p. 248.
11. Energy Information Administration, *Country Analysis Briefs, Pakistan*, December 2006, at http://www.eia.doe.gov/emeu/cabs/Pakistan/pdf.pdf.
12. *Economic Survey of Pakistan 2007-2008*, Government of Pakistan, Finance Division, Economic Advisers Wing, Islamabad, Pakistan, at http://www.finance.gov.pk/admin/images/survey/chapters/15-Energy 08.pdf, p. 257.
13. Abbas Maleki, "Gas Pipelines: A bridge among Iran, Pakistan, and India", International Institute for Caspian Studies, http://www.caspianstudies.com/article/Gas-Pipline.htm

14. Kaveh L Afrasiabi, "A blockage in the peace pipeline", *Asia Times*, July 10, 2007, at http://www.atimes.com/atimes/South_Asia/IG10Df01.html
15. Kanak Mani Dixit, "Within Grasp: Persian Gas for the South Asian Engine", *Himal Southasia, Reintroductory Issue*,http://www.himalmag.com/2005/july/cover_1.html
16. Abbas Maleki, "Gas Pipelines: A bridge among Iran, Pakistan, and India", International Institute for Caspian Studies, http://www.caspianstudies.com/article/Gas-Pipline.htm
17. Neha Misra, "Pipelines in the Pipeline", *Regulateri: Quarterly Review of Regulatory Developments*, Issue 25, June 2005 (The Energy and Resources Institute, New Delhi), p. 9; Shishir Gupta, "Peace Pipeline", *India Today*, 26 June-2 July 2001, Vol. 26, No. 27, p.36.
18. The preliminary data also showed a major technical obstacle when the pipeline reaches the area where Indus river pours into the Arabian Sea. See Abbas Maleki, "Gas Pipelines: A bridge among Iran, Pakistan, and India", International Institute for Caspian Studies, http://www.caspianstudies.com/article/Gas-Pipline.htm
19. Ali Mostashari, "The Political Economy of the Iran–Pakistan–India Gas Pipeline," *Iran Analysis Quarterly*, Vol. 4, No. 1 (January–March 2007), p. 28, at http://isg-mit.org/IAQ-storage/IAQ.Vol.4.No.1.2007.pdf
20. Bappa Majumdar Nidhi Verma, "Iranian president Tries to seal India Pipeline", *Reuters*, April 29, 2008, at http://www.reuters.com/article/idUSISL26015020080429
21. Paranjoy Guha Thakurta, "Iran-Pakistan-India Gas Pipeline in Trouble", *IPS News*, February 14, 2006, at http://ipsnews.net/news.asp?idnews=3215
22. "Alexander's Gas and Oil connections", *News and Trends*, Middle East, Vol. 14, Issue 17, December 18, 2009.
23. Anjana Pasricha, "India, Pakistan Commit to Building Gas Pipeline", July 21, 2005, http://petrochemical.ihs.com/news-05Q3/india-pakistan-pipeline.jsp
24. Sony Fatah, Will opposition from Washington block a 1,600-mile gas pipeline connecting Iran, Pakistan, and India?, The International Institute for Strategic Studies, December 26, 2005, at http://www.iiss.org/whats-new/iiss-in-the-press/press-coverage-2005/december-2005/pipeline-or-a-pipe-dream
25. Gasline project to start in two months: Dawoodi", *The Nation*, May 27, 2006, at http://www.nation.com.pk/daily/may-2006/27/index1.php
26. "Iran rejects Indian price for tripartite gas pipeline", *The Hindustan Times*, July 16, 2006, at http://www.hindustantimes.com/StoryPage/StoryPage.aspx?id=9fd6c349-c4f6-48e6-825d-fd1782638ef8&ParentID=9c222620-7c82-40e6-a6bd-5a965f6d5807
27. "Peace Pipeline Contract Soon, Gas Flow by 2011", *Iran Daily*, July 01, 2007, at http://iran-daily.com/1386/2880/html/economy.htm#s238905
28. PTI, "India proposes dialogue with Iran on IPI pipeline", March 31, 2010, at http://www.hindustantimes.com/News-Feed/americas/India-proposes-dialogue-with Iran on IPI pipeline/526115/Article1-525360.aspx
29. Zeeshan Haider, "Pakistan Iran sign a deal on natural gas pipeline", *Reuters*, March 17, 2010, at http://uk.reuters.com/article/idUSTRE62G12C20100317?sp=true; also see, Syed Fazl-e-Haider, "Pakistan, Iran Sign Gas Pipeline Deal", *Asia Times*, May 27, 2009, at http://www.atimes.com/atimes/South_Asia/KE27Df03.html
30. Sher Baz Khan, "Pakistan offers to buy India's share of IPI gas: Team leaves for Tehran on 29th, *The Dawn* December 25, 2008, at http://www.dawn.com/2008/12/25/top3.htm
31. "The Iran-Pakistan-India Pipeline Project: Cross-border Gas Pipeline Challenges", http://www.igu.org/knowledge/publications/mag/apr-09/igu_april_2009_pages_234-back.pdf
32. "The Advantages of Natural Gas" at http://www.pseg.com/customer/business/industrial/convert/advantages.jsp; also see R.K. Pachauri, "Not All Hot Air Indo-Pak Peace in the Pipeline" *The Times of India*, February 5, 2004, at http://www.teriin.org/pub/articles/art36.pdf

33. "Iran-India Gas Pipeline: Prospects Brighten for a 21st Century Silk Route", September 30, 2004, at http://www.teriin.org/press_inside.php?id=10480; Paranjoy Guha Thakurta, "Iran-Pakistan-India Gas Pipeline in Trouble", *IPS News,* February 14, 2006, at http://ipsnews.net/news.asp?idnews=3215
34. George Perkovich, Revati Prasad, "A Pipeline to Peace," *New York Times*, April 18, 2005, reprinted in http://www.carnegieendowment.org/publications/index.cfm?fa=view&id=16789
35. Shaukat Aziz's press conference at the World Economic Forum in Davos, *Washington Times/UPI*, January 30, 2005, at http://www.washtimes.com/upi-breaking/20050128-011154-8034r.htm.
36. Kanak Mani Dixit, "Within Grasp: Persian Gas for the Southasian Engine", *Himal Southasiuan, Reintroductory Issue,* http://www.himalmag.com/2005/july/cover_1.html
37. Owen Bennett Jones and Farzana Shaikh, "Pakistan's foreign policy under Musharraf: between a rock and a hard place", *Briefing Paper*, Chatham House, March 2006, at http://www.chathamhouse.org.uk/pdf/research/asia/BPpakistan.pdf
38. Nadeem Iqbal, "New era in Pakistan, Iran ties", *Asia Times Online*, December 13, 2001, http://www.atimes.com/ind-pak/CL13Df04.html
39. "Pakistan May Start laying its part of the Pipeline", *The News*, April 28, 2006, at http://www.thenews.com.pk/print3.asp?id=519
40. N. Ghorban, "Op-Ed: Monetizing Iran's Gas Resources and the Debate Over Gas Export and Gas-Based Industries Options", *Middle East Economic Survey*, vol. 49, no. 28, (July 2006), pp. 25-29 cited in "The Iran-Pakistan-Iran Pipeline Project: Cross Border Linkages", at http://www.igu.org/knowledge/publications/mag/apr-09/igu_april_2009_ pages_234-back.pdf
41. S. Pandian, "The Political Economy of Trans-Pakistan Gas Pipeline Project: Assessing the Political and Economic Risks for India", *Energy Policy*, Vol.33, no. 5, p. 667.
42. For details, see, Asma Shakir Khawaja, "Iran-Pakistan-India Gas Pipeline Project: Paving Way for Regional Cooperation", *IPRI Journal*, p. 120.
43. Ayesha Siddiqa-Agha, "The Politics of the Gas pipeline", *Dawn*, June 30, 2001.
44. Institute for the Analysis of Global Security, "Iran-Pakistan-India Pipeline: The Baloch Wildcard Energy Security" January 12, 2005, at http://www.iags.org/n0115042.htm
45. "Balochistan PA demands royalty on IPI pipeline", *The News*, June 10, 2006, at http://www.thenews.com.pk/daily_detail.asp?id=10233
46. In October 2009, *Jundollah*, a militant Iranian Balochi organisation, *Jundollah*, claimed killing several prominent members of Iran's Islamic Revolutionary Guard Corps in an explosion. Among the killed were, reportedly, the lieutenant commander of ground forces, Brig. Gen. Nourali Shoushtari, and commanders of Sistan-Baluchistan province, the Iranshahr Corps, the Sarbaz Corps and the Amiralmoemenin Brigade. Michael Slackman, "Iran Guard Commanders Are Killed in Bombings", *New York Times*, October 18, 2009, at http://www.nytimes.com/2009/10/19/world/middleeast/19iran.html. In March 2009, Iranian ambassador to Pakistan, Mashallah Shakeri, had publicly accused Islamabad of allowing Balochistan to be a *Jundallah* base for the destabilization of Iran; Iran in May 2009 had hanged three Pakistanis for their role in blast in Mosque earlier that month. Pepe Escobar, "The shadow war in Balochistan", *Asia Times online*, June 09, 2009.
47. Kamal Narang, "Gas pipeline hitch: Iran wants 3-year review of price formula", *Business Line*, June 30, 2007, http://www.blonnet.com/2007/06/30/stories/2007063051220100.htm
48. Abbas Maleki, "Iran-Pakistan-India Pipeline: Is It a Peace Pipeline?", Massachusetts Institute of Technology, Center for International Studies, September 2007, at *http://web.mit.edu/cis/editorspick_maleki07_audit.html*

49. "US warns India, Pak against Iran pipeline project", *The News*, April 03, 2010, at http://www.thenews.com.pk/updates.asp?id=102078US
50. Stephen Blank, "China hangs fire on Iran-Pakistan pipeline", *Asia Times*, March 09, 2010, http://www.atimes.com/atimes/China_Business/LC09Cb01.html
51. Bappa Majumdar Nidhi Verma, "Iranian president Tries to seal India Pipeline", *Reuters*, April 29, 2008, at http://www.reuters.com/article/idUSISL26015020080429
52. Zachary Fillingham, "India, China & the IPI Pipeline", www.geopoliicalmonitor.com, November 5, 2009.
53. "Gazprom eyes role in Iran-Pakistan gas pipeline", *The News*, May 29, 2009, at http://www.thenews.com.pk/daily_detail.asp?id=179821
54. Nadeem Iqbal, "New era in Pakistan, Iran ties", *Asia Times Online*, December 13, 2001, at http://www.atimes.com/ind-pak/CL13Df04.html
55. Musarrat Jabeen, "South Asia and Management of Energy Security", *Regional Studies*, Vol. xxiv, no. 3, Summer 2006, p. 18.
56. Khalid Mustafa, "Pakistan, Iran hold talks on gas pipeline project today", *The News*, August 31, 2009, at http://www.thenews.com.pk/top_story_detail.asp?Id=24217,
57. "Work on TAPI gas pipeline to be accelerated", *Alexander's Gas and Oil connections, News and Trends: Central Asia*, Vol. 11, Issue 24, December 21, 2006, at http://www.gasandoil.com/goc/news/ntc65139.htm
58. Abbas Maleki, "Gas Pipelines: A bridge among Iran, Pakistan, and India", International Institute for Caspian Studies, at http://www.caspianstudies.com/article/Gas-Pipline.htm
59. A.K. Diwanji, "Geo-political Issues set to Dominate Proposed Gas Pipeline from Iran to India", April 13, 2000, *Rediff*, at http://www.rediff.com/business/2000/apr/13gas.htm
60. S. Pandian, "The Political Economy of Trans-Pakistan Gas Pipeline Project: Assessing the Political and Economic Risks for India", *Energy Policy*, Vol. 33, no. 5, p. 667.
61. Zafar Hilaly, "Pipeline or pipedream?", *The News*, April 10, 2010, at http://www.thenews.com.pk/daily_detail.asp?id=233539

# 12

# Turkmenistan-Afghanistan-Pakistan-India (TAPI): Pipeline or Pipedream?

*Mahesh Ranjan Debata*

## Introduction

The Turkmenistan-Afghanistan-Pakistan-India Natural Gas Pipeline Project (TAPI), which is a pioneering effort to link the gas-rich Central Asian economies with the energy-deficient economies of South Asia, is a 1,680 kms (1,040 miles) long gas pipeline that can transport up to 33 billion cubic meters of natural gas annually from the Dauletabad field[1] in southeast Turkmenistan to Afghanistan, Pakistan and India. Following the ancient trading route from Central Asia to South Asia, about 735 kms of the pipeline will pass through the south Afghan cities of Herat, Helmand and Kandahar, before entering Pakistan at Quetta (Balochistan) and proceeding 800 kms through Multan and Pakpattan in Pakistan towards the Indian border town of Fazilka.[2] The 56 inch (1,420 mm) gas pipeline with the normal pressure of 100 atmospheres will have six compressor stations along the pipeline route.[3] The pipeline is estimated to cost 7.6 billion US dollars and according to original projections, work should have started in 2010 and end after five years, possibly by 2015. However, since the construction process has not yet started even after two months of the year 2011 have passed, as per some estimates, the pipeline can not be completed earlier than 2018.[4] It is in this context that this paper discusses the TAPI pipeline in detail, with the stakes of the involving parties (Turkmenistan, Afghanistan, Pakistan and India) and significance of the pipeline for them, particularly for India, besides examining the challenges and constraints. The paper argues that despite the relentless endeavours by the stakeholders and even the intervention of the USA, the pipeline has not achieved any success as over one and a half decade have passed since the proposal was put forward in the 1990s.

**Basic Facts about TAPI Natural Gas Pipeline**

| | |
|---|---|
| **Length** | 1,680 kms (1,040 miles) |
| **Source of the Pipeline** | Dauletabad Natural Gas Field, Turkmenistan |
| **Final Destination** | Fazilka, Punjab (India) |
| **Countries involved** | Turkmenistan, Afghanistan Pakistan, India |
| **Direction** | North-South |
| **Passes through** | Herat, Helmand, Kandahar (Afghanistan)<br>Quetta, Multan (Pakistan) |
| **Estimated Cost of Construction** | 7.6 billion US dollars |
| **Time Period of Construction** | Five years |
| **Estimated Gas Supply per annum** | 33 billion cubic meters |
| **Lead Development Partner** | Asian Development Bank (ADB) |

**Map of the proposed TAPI Pipeline**

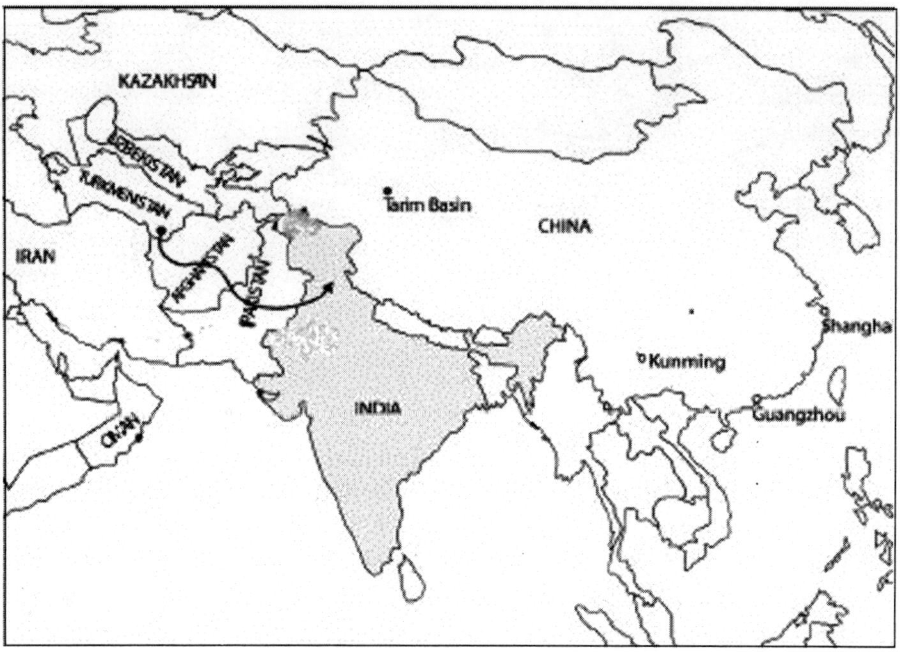

**Map of the Proposed IPI Pipeline**

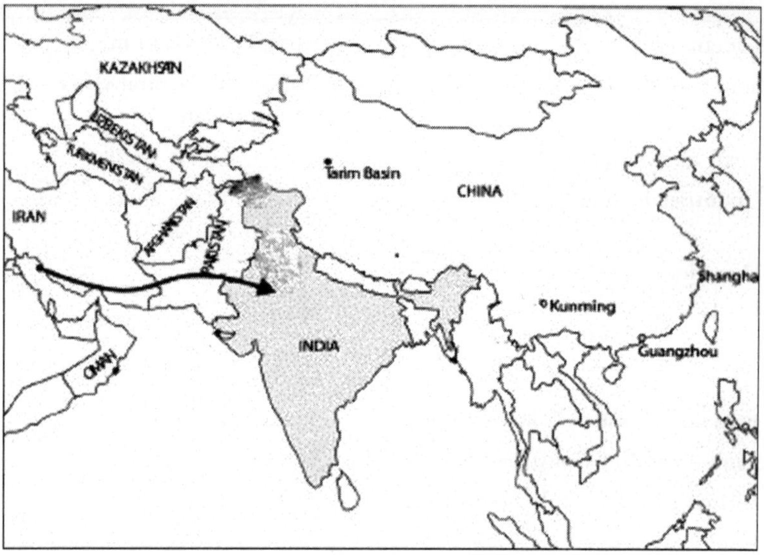


**Map of the proposed TAPI and IPI Pipelines**

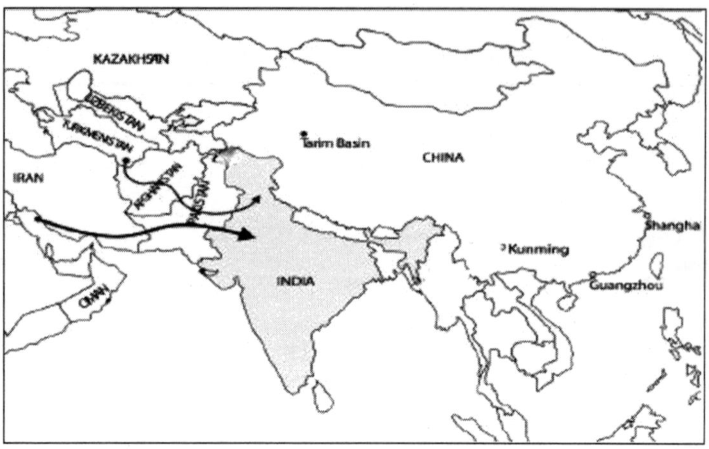


The original pipeline project, known as Turkmenistan-Afghanistan-Pakistan (TAP) pipeline started in March 1995 when a Memorandum of Understanding (MoU) between Turkmenistan and Pakistan was signed. As a follow up action, the Central Asia Gas Pipeline Ltd. (CentGas) Consortium was formed in August 1996, which was incorporated in a formal ceremony in the Turkmen capital of Ashgabat on 27 October 1997, by some international oil companies along with the government of Turkmenistan.[5] In January 1998, the Taliban, which was in power in Afghanistan, favoured CentGas over Argentinian oil major Bridas Corporation, and signed an agreement in order to expedite the project. In March 1998, Unocal announced a delay in finalizing project details due to Afghanistan's continuing civil war. However, the pipeline project received a jolt in June 1998, when Russia's Gazprom relinquished its 10 per cent stake in the project. As of June 1998, Unocal and Saudi Arabia's Delta Oil held a combined 85 per cent stake in Centgas, while Turkmenrusgas owned five per cent. On 8 December 1998, Unocal announced that it was withdrawing from the Centgas consortium, citing low oil prices and turmoil in Afghanistan as making the pipeline project uneconomical and too risky. Unocal's announcement followed an earlier stand in August 1998 that the company was suspending its role in the Afghanistan gas pipeline project in the light of the recent US military action in Afghanistan, and also due to intensified fighting between the Taliban and opposition groups. Unocal had previously stressed that the Centgas pipeline project would not proceed until an internationally recognized government was in place in Afghanistan.[6]

Afghan President Hamid Karzai and Pakistan's President Pervez Musharraf agreed in Islamabad in February 2002 to cooperate on the proposed pipeline. The heads of state of Turkmenistan, Afghanistan and Pakistan, who met in Islamabad on 29-30 May 2002, agreed to cooperate on the project. As a result, a Steering Committee of Oil and Gas ministers of Turkmenistan, Afghanistan and Pakistan was established to oversee the project development. In its first meeting on 9–10 July 2002 at Ashgabat, the Steering Committee requested the Asian Development Bank (ADB) to act as a broker as well as an active development partner besides extending regional technical assistance (TA) for feasibility study of the project. ADB agreed to finance a techno-economic feasibility study about the pipeline routing, preliminary design, cost estimates, rapid environmental impact assessment and volume-price sensitivity assessment. ADB also agreed to carry out a market study on demand for natural gas in Pakistan and northern India, and a risk analysis and risk mitigation study on concerns of gas-consuming countries and of consumers in case gas supply is disrupted along the pipeline route. The ADB outlined five important issues regarding the TAPI Project: (i) confirmation of a market for the gas in Pakistan and India and commitment of potential buyers to enter into gas sale and purchase agreements; (ii) certification that the natural gas reserves at Dauletabad field can produce the envisaged quantities of gas over a period of 25-30 years; (iii) security concerns of Pakistan and India with regard to possible disruption of gas supplies through the pipeline; (iv) techno-economic feasibility of the pipeline and preparation of its basic design, considering the terrain conditions and logistical constraints; and (v) required mobilization of international oil and gas companies to take the lead role in the pipeline consortium for timely and cost-efficient construction of the pipeline, and operation and maintenance of the same in accordance with international standards.[7]

During the second meeting of the Steering Committee held in Kabul on 16 September 2002, the process of fact-finding was completed and the draft terms of reference approved.[8] However, during the period between the second Steering Committee meeting in September 2002 and the 9th Steering Committee meeting at Ashgabat on 13-15 February 2006, nothing substantial was achieved despite several meetings and agreements. However, there appeared a glimmer of hope for the construction of the pipeline when Turkmenistan, Afghanistan, Pakistan and India, vowed to accelerate the work on the pipeline project, while congregating at the two-day Regional Economic Cooperation Forum on Afghanistan being organised in New Delhi on 26-27 November 2006. A Declaration adopted at the meeting gave all the stakeholders a clarion call to expedite the project. While welcoming India's entry into this project, Afghan President stated that this would give an added impetus to move the project closer to realization.[9]

A Gas Pipeline Framework Agreement (GPFA), signed by Pakistan's Minister for Petroleum, Khawaja Muhammad Asif, Turkmenistan's Minister for Oil and Gas Industry, Baymurad Hojamuhamedov, Afghanistan's Minister for Mines, Muhammad Ibrahim Adel, and India's Petroleum Minister, Murli Deora during the 10th Steering Committee meeting in Islamabad held on 25 April 2008,[10] envisaged construction of TAPI to start in 2010, supplying gas by 2015. The ADB's feasibility study conducted in mid-2005 was updated in 2008. The ADB reported that the estimated capital cost was $7.6 billion. Plans called for the line to be built and operated by a consortium of national oil companies from the four countries. A special-purpose financial vehicle would be floated, and international companies would likely join in laying and operating the pipeline. Turkmenistan promised independent certification of the gas available for the pipeline, and in case of any problem, Turkmen officials stated that they would offer gas from the Yasrak field, instead of the planned Dauletabad field, and they provided a reserves certification for Yasrak.[11] The 11th Steering Committee meeting was scheduled for November 2008 in New Delhi.[12] However, the meeting was postponed due to the terrorist attacks in Mumbai on 26 November 2008, but later rescheduled for April 2009.[13]

## Significance of TAPI

TAPI has very long-term and widespread positive implications for the countries involved in particular, and for the region as a whole. While speaking at an energy conference in Turkmenistan in November 2010, US Deputy Assistant Secretary of State on South and Central Asian Affairs, Susan Elliot said that "TAPI route may serve as a stabilizing corridor, linking neighbors together in economic growth and prosperity."[14]

### *Political and Multilateral Cooperation*

Two major stakeholders of the TAPI – India and Pakistan – have not only been at loggerheads since their independence in 1947, but also have fought as many as four wars in the last six decades or so. Pakistan and Afghanistan have also not been pulling on well for the last few years. Amidst this situation, the stakeholders of TAPI, particularly India, Pakistan and Afghanistan need to improve as well as maintain political cooperation, so that the investment interest can be safeguarded and other economic benefits be ensured. Considering the dependence on energy and the involvement of multiple participants in the project, all stakeholders can strengthen their mutual diplomatic and other multilateral relations. In a press conference on 7 January 2011, India's External Affairs Minister, S.M. Krishna underscored the importance of TAPI stating that this pipeline could become an important confidence building measure among the four countries and enhance mutually beneficial economic linkages.[15]

### *Energy Security*

India and Pakistan, the two major energy consumers in the South Asia region, are increasingly dependent on oil and natural gas being imported from abroad for their energy needs. The TAPI pipeline project is a crucial aspect of India's energy security, since it currently imports three-fourth of its requirements of crude oil.[16] TAPI, if successful, could be a ray of hope for these two estranged neighbours, and both could improve their already strained relationship on the basis of cooperation in the energy sector. At a time of possible energy crisis, an alliance through pipeline for energy security can augur well and bring about economic benefits.[17] Besides, it will provide cheaper and cleaner energy to consumers across the region.

### *Economic Benefits*

Since the TAPI project is a concerted effort to link the gas-rich Central Asian economies with the energy-deficient economies of South Asia, it could significantly boost the economies of the four countries involved. The project, which is the first attempt to find an outlet for natural gas from Central Asia to new markets in the East, can contribute to the improvement of the peoples' standard of living in Central and South Asia. As a capital intensive project, the pipeline will generate substantial employment along its route. It can fetch substantial and sustainable revenues which can be used for ameliorating the social sectors. In 2008, Pakistan's Prime Minister described the pipeline as a vital project for the development and progress of the region.[18] While speaking at the two-day Regional Economic Cooperation Forum on Afghanistan being organised in New Delhi on 26-27 November 2006, Afghan President Hamid Karzai stated that Afghanistan's location can be exploited to the region's economic benefit.[19]

### *Peace and Stability*

This pipeline can usher in peace and stability in this region, which has so far been seriously affected by the internal situation in Afghanistan and Pakistan. To quote Turkmen President Berdimuhamedov, "the pipeline between Turkmenistan, Afghanistan, Pakistan and India will be a weighty contribution to the positive cooperation in this continent."[20] It can bring about regional security through joint project ownership. In addition, the TAPI project will bring about considerable environmental benefits. Once the TAPI gas pipeline project becomes successful, the proposal of laying the oil pipeline along the same route will become a reality.[21]

## Benefits for Countries Involved in TAPI

The pipeline is believed to accrue many benefits for each of the individual stakeholders of this project.

### *TAPI and Turkmenistan*

Turkmenistan will have significant financial gains once this pipeline is built. This would pave Turkmenistan's way to become the natural gas hub of Eurasia. Turkmenistan has the world's fourth largest reserves of natural gas, 7.94 trillion cubic meters (TCM) after Russia, Iran and Qatar. The huge South Yoloten-Osman field in western Turkmenistan has an estimated reserve of between 4 and 14 TCM of gas, making it the world's fourth or fifth largest field.[22] If it fulfills all its commitments to Russia, the European Union, China, and Iran, Turkmenistan can earn billions of dollars from gas exports, which will cater to its domestic economic needs and provide the thrust for its prosperity.

While delivering the welcome address at the Oil and Gas of Turkmenistan-2011 International Conference hosted by Singapore on 3 March 2011, Turkmen President Gurbanguly Berdimuhamedov said the Summit of Heads of States participating in the Turkmenistan-Afghanistan-Pakistan-India gas pipeline project in Ashgabat speeded up its implementation. This is illustrated by the meetings of the technical work groups of the four states conducted on a regular basis.[23]

### *Afghanistan's Gain from TAPI*

TAPI would benefit Afghanistan the most by providing steady transit fees further strengthening its economy. During the initial years of pipeline operation, Afghanistan is expected to benefit mainly from its participation in the pipeline consortium by receiving a share of the transit fees from the consortium, an approximate 8 per cent of the total revenue. According to the Ambassador of Afghanistan to Canada, transit revenue could amount to 300 million US dollars per annum. Transit fees could be used to pay salaries of employees and help building infrastructure in the region.[24] After the domestic consumption, Afghanistan can sell the surplus gas provided by the TAPI pipeline to gas consumers both within Afghanistan as well as outside the country. This would bring about investment in exploration and use of natural gas in Afghanistan. If the pipeline goes ahead successfully, it could be Afghanistan's largest development project. The Afghan delegation informed that more than 1,000 industrial units, which have already been established along the TAPI pipeline route in Afghanistan, would need gas for operation and the TAPI project's early implementation was essential to meet their requirements.[25] Under GPFA, Afghanistan is expected to tap 5 million cubic metres (mcm) per day from the pipeline during the first two years of its operation and 14 mcm per day thereafter.[26]

To ensure the construction of TAPI, the Afghan government has undertaken several measures. Firstly, all land plots located on the route of the pipeline have been redeemed from the landowners.[27] Secondly, the government proposes to deploy 5,000 to 7,000 security forces to safeguard the pipeline route, as assured by

Wahidullah Shahrani, Afghanistan's Mines and Industries Minister.[28] Since the development of energy resources has emerged as a major thrust area for Afghanistan's development, as put by Afghan Mines and Industries Minister, Wahidullay Shahrani, preparations are being made to develop the Sheberghan gas field in northern Afghanistan, which has reserves up to eight trillion cubic feet, as well as the most promising oil reserves in Kashgari oil block in the Amu Darya basin and Mazar-e-Sharif.[29] And in this process, TAPI could be of immense help.

### *TAPI and Pakistan*

For Pakistan, TAPI could provide both an energy resource and revenue in the form of transit fees. Under GPFA, 38 million standard cubic meters per day of gas would go to India and Pakistan each.[30] Like Afghanistan, Pakistan can also use the surplus capacity in the pipeline either for domestic consumption or for export. The potential for export to other countries through the Gwadar port is an added advantage. In 2008, Pakistan's Prime Minister described the pipeline as a vital project for the development and progress of the region.[31] In April 2009, a Pakistani delegation visiting Ashgabat, Turkmenistan, suggested a new TAPI route that would skirt the war-torn area and add a spur to Gwadar, a Pakistani deep-water port.[32] Besides, Pakistan is going to get a whopping million dollars as transit fees.

### *US Interests in TAPI*

The US has been promoting the TAPI pipeline since 1997. When the Taliban was ruling over Afghanistan, US oil major Unocal had led a consortium to expedite the TAPI project.[33] Further, recently in June 2008, US Assistant Secretary of State Richard Boucher advocated for the flow of energy, ideas, people, trade, goods from Central Asia and other places down to the Arabian Sea."[34] US interests in TAPI stem from the following facts:

1. TAPI, which is considered by the USA as an alternative route for Central Asian gas that will bypass the Russian pipeline's network,[35] would diminish Russia's dominance of Central Asian energy exports.
2. It is consistent with the US declared policy of linking Central and South Asia and diversifying export routes for Turkmen gas.
3. The US government is eager to block a competing pipeline [Iran-Pakistan-India (IPI) Pipeline] that would bring gas to Pakistan and India from Iran.[36]
4. For the US government, TAPI can contribute to reconstruction and peaceful development of Afghanistan.[37]

## Bottlenecks

However, TAPI faces several challenges on its way to become a reality.

### *Political Challenges*

Both India and Pakistan, and Pakistan and Afghanistan are not in the best of the terms. India considers Pakistan as its inveterate enemy and the source of many cross-border terrorist activities in its territory, particularly in the State of Jammu and Kashmir. Similarly, Afghanistan views Pakistan as being responsible for numerous internal disturbances in its territory and also being the main support system of the Taliban. If relations between the countries deteriorate, a country upstream of the pipeline system might deliberately disrupt gas supply to downstream countries, like India, causing major economic losses.

Several countries, which have deployed troops in Afghanistan under the umbrella of the Coalition Forces, such as United States, Britain, Canada, France, Germany, Italy, the Netherlands and Norway, are active members of the Asian Development Bank, the main sponsor of the TAPI project. So, financing for the project would require the prior approval of the member countries, and a project as sensitive as TAPI would require the blessings of the US and Japan, the two major donors for Afghanistan reconstruction process. As such, with such a heavy military presence, US/NATO influence on Kabul is obvious. Discussions of NATO support for TAPI pipeline security raise questions about the links between military and development decisions.[38]

India has objected to the ADB's idea of involving Chinese firms, who have experience in building such long pipelines in a short time period. Senior Petroleum Ministry officials of Government of India while expressing fear that Chinese involvement in TAPI could lead to China being perceived as an "avuncular arbiter of peace" between India and Pakistan, pointed out that this could reinforce the notion that China is capable of managing the security issues in Afghanistan. It could even be interpreted as sign of China playing a bigger role in the SAARC region, the officials added.[39]

### *Security Challenges*

Both Afghanistan and Pakistan are complex countries. Their mix of ethnic groups, long-standing tribal traditions, and problems of security and terrorism are the major challenges. The security situation in Afghanistan is the major cause of concern for the TAPI project. Taliban is still active in southwest part of the country which is close to the proposed route for the pipeline. Since 1,535 kms of the proposed TAPI pipeline will pass through Afghanistan and Pakistan, there is an irreducible fear that the pipeline could fall prey to the mad whims of the unlawful elements in Afghanistan or on the Afghanistan-Pakistan border. During the Steering Committee meeting in April 2008, the Afghan government assured that by 2010, the pipeline route would be cleared of landmines and Taliban influence. However, the planned route of TAPI remains insecure even now. Companies are unlikely to invest within a war zone. The prospect of building the pipeline under armed guard and then safeguarding it in the coming years is formidable, in terms of both manpower and cost.[40]

### *Pashtun Factor*

The other important factor is Pashtun factor. The Pashtuns, who are roughly 40 per cent of Afghanistan's total population, are a major constituent of Taliban insurgents, and the pipeline route goes through the Pashtun area in both Afghanistan and Pakistan. There are about 30 million Pashtuns on both sides of the Afghan-Pakistan border. In fact, Pashtuns in Kandahar sought to dominate Kabul, and, Pashtuns in Pakistan have been relatively independent from Islamabad.[41] So, it is feared that TAPI may fall prey to the whims and fancies of the Talibanised Pashtuns, which will affect the interests of the concerned parties, particularly India.

### *Doubts over Sufficiency of Turkmen Gas*

There is also doubt over sufficiency of gas reserves in Turkmenistan to meet all its commitments to China, Russia as well as Pakistan and India. Turkmenistan's commitments for side projects of the Caspian Sea Gas Pipeline, modernisation of the Central Asian Pipeline and also the gas pipeline with China alone will account for all of Turkmenistan's natural gas production targets of 2030. Taking into account these considerations, the resource base of TAPI appears to be at a level that is too low to initiate this project. The volumes may be enough to cover other commitments, but there is no gas for other markets.[42]

The issue of shortages came to the fore during the beginning of 2008 after the disruption of gas exports from Turkmenistan to Iran which also led to reduced supplies to Turkey and Greece. The main reason, apart from differences between Iran and Turkmenistan on prices, was the shortage of gas to meet Ashgabat's internal demands during severe winter. In 2007, Turkmenistan produced 70 billion cubic metres of gas which was short of the target in 2006 by 10 billion cubic metres. This makes it highly unlikely that Turkmenistan would be able to achieve its projected target of 250 billion cubic metres of gas and 110 million tonnes of oil by 2030.[43]

Turkmenistan can overcome the problem of guaranteeing an adequate quality of natural gas for TAPI, (i) by undertaking development of new gas field(s) and (ii) by agreeing to connect the pipeline from its Dauletabad gas field to the IPI gas pipeline. However, both seem impracticable, as in the first case, developing a new gas field would take at least 10 years and in the second instance, the future of IPI seems bleak.

Another problem surfaced during a meeting on 29 May 2008, where Turkmenistan threw a tantrum indicating that it could sell gas on its border without getting involved in the construction of the TAPI pipeline across the three nations which are not at the best of terms with each other.[44]

### *Topographic Challenge*

In terms of topography, the pipeline will have to negotiate rugged mountainous terrain in much of south Afghanistan while in the region around Quetta it will have to take into account challenges posed by frequent seismic activities. Thus, the project will have to grapple with considerable engineering challenges.[45]

### *Is TAPI Important for India?*

TAPI's importance for India stems from the fact that there has been a tremendous increase in its energy consumption after India experienced rapid and robust economic growth. TAPI is expected to transport 100 mm cmpd of gas, of which India's share will be 60 mm cmpd.[46]

While interacting with the Afghan media on 27 January 2011, India's Foreign Secretary, Nirupama Rao emphasized the importance of TAPI for India stating that "The project is important because India is a growing economy and has very large requirements in terms of energy. India would like to source energy from wherever it can. TAPI is going to bring benefits for all the countries involved. It will help our economy, it will create jobs in our countries as in other countries through which it transits. There is a consensus among all these countries to work on this project. It will help to build more stakes in ensuring that there is peace and stability in our region."[47]

India has total reserves (proven and indicated) of 1,201 million metric tonnes of crude oil and 1,437 billion cubic metres of natural gas as on 1 April 2010. Crude oil production of 33.69 million metric tonnes during 2009-10 has been 0.55 per cent higher than 33.51 million metric tonnes produced during 2008-09. In India too, the natural gas sector has gained importance, particularly over the last decade. Production of natural gas, which was almost negligible at the time of India's independence in 1947, is around 87 million standard cubic meters per day (MMSCMD). The main producers of natural gas are Oil & Natural Gas Corporation Ltd. (ONGC), Oil India Limited (OIL) and Joint Ventures of Tapti, Panna-Mukta and Ravva.[48] Gross production of natural gas in the country at 47.51 billion cubic metres during 2009-10 is 44.63% higher than the production of 32.85 billion cubic metres during 2008-09.[49] Demand for natural gas was over 1.2 trillion cubic feet (tcf) by 2010 and would be 1.6 tcf by 2015. By 2025, India is projected to have a gas deficit of over 200 MMSCMD.[50]

**Table 1: Oil and Gas Reserves in India, 2005-10**

| | 2005 | 2006 | 2007 | 2008 | 2009 | 2010 |
|---|---|---|---|---|---|---|
| **Crude Oil** (Million Metric Tonnes) | | | | | | |
| Onshore | 376 | 387 | 357 | 403 | 405 | 614 |
| Offshore | 410 | 369 | 368 | 366 | 369 | 587 |
| Total | 786 | 756 | 725 | 769 | 775 | 1201 |
| **Natural Gas** (Billion Cubic Metres) | | | | | | |
| Onshore | 340 | 330 | 270 | 264 | 287 | 829 |
| Offshore | 761 | 745 | 785 | 786 | 787 | 608 |
| Total | 1101 | 1075 | 1055 | 1050 | 1074 | 1437 |

Source: *Basic Statistics on Indian Petroleum & Natural Gas 2009-10*, Ministry of Petroleum & Natural Gas Government of India, New Delhi (Economic Division), October 2010, p. 8.

**Table 2: Energy Generation (Gross) in India, 2005-10**

| | 2005-06 | 2006-07 | 2007-08 | 2008-09 | 2009-10 |
|---|---|---|---|---|---|
| Coal (million tons) | 407.04 | 425.04 | 450.5 | 492.95 | 549.00 |
| Lignite (million tons) | 30.06 | 31.29 | 33.98 | 32.42 | 16.30 |
| Natural Gas (BCM) | 32.202 | 31.747 | 32.417 | 32.849 | 47.51 |
| Crude Oil (million tons) | 32.19 | 33.988 | 34.118 | 33.506 | 33.691 |
| Petroleum Products | 131.08 | 148.27 | 158.74 | 164.59 | 163.505 |

Source: *Basic Statistics on Indian Petroleum & Natural Gas 2009-10*, Ministry of Petroleum & Natural Gas Government of India, New Delhi (Economic Division), October 2010, p. 4.

Although India is trying hard to provide appropriate energy, increase its energy efficiency and diversify its sources of supply, it is becoming increasingly dependent on imported oil, particularly from the Middle East. Since the Middle East has been reeling in crisis, sole dependence on it without finding any other outlet will pose serious challenge to the energy security of India. At this juncture, an energy deficient country like India has the following options: (i) to boost its own energy production; (ii) to diversify its sources of energy import; (iii) to secure the transportation of oil and natural gas on vulnerable sea routes; and (iv) to secure the transportation of oil and natural gas over land through pipelines.[51]

India's efforts to enhance its energy security have intensified significantly since 2004. India increasingly sees energy security as a national priority and central aspect of its foreign policy. Several committees have been working on Indian energy policy and security issues over the last few years. The first committee was constituted in early 2004 under the Planning Commission. The latter committee issued a "draft integrated energy policy" in mid-2005. In July 2005 the Indian Prime Minister announced the establishment of an "Energy Co-ordination Committee" (ECC) to guide the country's energy policy. The ECC will enable the government to take a holistic view of India's energy needs and policy options.

The 2nd Technical Working Group Meeting and the 10th Steering Committee Meeting of the participating countries of Turkmenistan-Afghanistan-Pakistan-India (TAPI) gas pipeline project have been held on 21-22 April 2008 and 23-24 April 2008 respectively at Islamabad. India, which had been an Observer in previous meetings of the Steering Committee on TAPI, was admitted as an official member of the project during the 10th Steering Committee meeting.[52] The Minister for Petroleum and Natural Gas was representing India.[53] As per GPFA, 38 million standard cubic meters per day of gas would go to India once TAPI is completed.[54]

Turkmenistan has been pushing the project for years and even discussed the issue with the Taliban officials in the late 1990s to try to secure guarantees for the pipeline. Unocal estimated in 1997 that the Dauletabad natural gas field has 708 bcm of natural-gas reserves.[55]

A fresh round of technical level talks on Turkmenistan, Afghanistan, Pakistan, India gas pipe line was held in Islamabad in April 2008. The talks on the project were postponed twice due to domestic problems in Pakistan. India's inclusion in the project makes it more viable. Indian Vice President Hamid Ansari during his visit to Turkmenistan on 4 April 2008, declared that India had full member status of the TAPI project.[56] During an official visit to Turkmenistan on 18-19 September 2009, India's External Affairs Minister S.M. Krishna discussed the TAPI project with the President, Minister of Foreign Affairs and Deputy Prime Minister who is in charge of Oil and Gas of Turkmenistan.[57]

## Conclusion

Some 15 years have passed since the first proposal for TAPI pipeline was mooted, but due to continued instability in Afghanistan and strained ties between Pakistan and India, the project has not been carried out.[58] The challenges on the path of TAPI posed by Afghanistan and Pakistan require political, not military solutions. TAPI pipeline construction cannot begin until the Taliban stops insurgent and terrorist activities and all stakeholders, including the Pashtuns, participate and cooperate for the success of this project. The strategy of national reconciliation offered at the Conference on Afghanistan held in London in January 2010[59] could be a step forward in this regard. If TAPI is to take the shape of a sustainable pipeline, certain fundamental issues need to be addressed. There is an urgent need to actively encourage state and nation-building exercises that could usher in political stability and economic credibility in Afghanistan and Pakistan.[60] Though, Iranian gas appears to be a better option for India economically, because the lower project cost would lead to cheaper gas to Indian consumers, India should keep its commitments towards the TAPI and as an important power of the region can play the lead role in realizing the project. Since the Iran-Pakistan-India (IPI) pipeline's future is bleak due to several international constraints, particularly the strong US objections, the stakeholders of TAPI should make a combined endeavour for the construction of this pipeline. However, Turkmenistan, Afghanistan and Pakistan need to take into account the security concerns of India and look for ways and means to have the natural gas delivered at India's borders, with guarantees of assured and unhindered supply.

### ENDNOTES

1. Dauletabad gas field is situated in the Ahal province of the Republic of Turkmenistan. Natural gas was discovered in this onshore gas field in 1974 and gas production started in 1984. The estimated gas reserve in this gas field is about 25,000 billion cubic feet.
2. Jayanth Jacob, "TAPI Pipeline: India Opposes Chinese Role", *Hindustan Times*, 17 January 2011.
3. www.turkmenistan.ru
4. Bruce Pannier, "Central Asia: Trans-Afghan Pipeline Discussions Open in Islamabad", April 2004, http://www.rferl.org/featuresarticle/2008/04/
5. CentGas Consortium was led by US oil major Union Oil Company of California (UNOCAL) and Delta Oil Company of Saudi Arabia. The other members of the Consortium were Gazprom (Russia), Turkmenrusgas (Turkmenistan), Indonesia Petroleum Limited (INPEX), ITOCHU Oil Exploration Company Limited (Japan), Hyundai Engineering and Constructions (South Korea) and Crescent Group (Pakistan).

6. "Afghanistan: Natural Resources and Energy", September 2001, http://www.institute-for-afghan-studies.org/ECONOMY/natural%20resources.htm
7. "Technical Assistance For The Feasibility Study of the Turkmenistan-Afghanistan-Pakistan Natural Gas Pipeline Project (Phase II)", December 2002, Asian Development Bank, TAR: STU 36488, pp. 1-2.
8. N. Jung, "Technical Assistance For The Turkmenistan-Afghanistan-Pakistan Natural Gas Pipeline Project (Phase II)", December 2003, Asian Development Bank, TAR: OTH 37098, pp. 1-2.
9. Karzai's Statement at the Second Regional Economic Cooperation Conference on Afghanistan, in New Delhi on 19 November 2006.
10. "PITA Gas Pipeline Agreement", 25 April 2008, http://www.neftegaz.ru/en/news/view/78403
11. "EAM's Visit to Turkmenistan", 19 September 2009, http://meaindia.nic.in/mystart.php?id=550315173
12. The main agenda of this meeting was that how price negotiations were to be advanced. Afghanistan was to report on physical security along the pipeline route, including the clearing of landmines and Taliban activity. Turkmenistan was to present the gas reserves certification.
13. John Foster, "Afghanistan, the TAPI Pipeline and the Energy Geopolitics", *Journal of Energy Security*, March 2010.
14. Abdujalil Abdurasulov, "New TAPI Gas Pipeline could Boost Afghanistan, Regional Stability", *Christian Science Monitor*, 10 December 2010.
15. http://meaindia.nic.in/mystart.php?id=550317029, 7 January 2011.
16. Paranjoy Guha Thakurta, "Iran-Pakistan-India Gas Pipeline in Trouble", *IPS News, 14* February 2006 *http://ipsnews.net/news.asp?idnews=3215*
17. "Iran-India Gas Pipeline: Prospects Brighten for a 21st Century Silk Route", 30 September 2004, http://www.teriin.org/press_inside.php?id=10480 —>
18. John Foster, op. cit.
19. See Note 9.
20. John Foster, op. cit.
21. www.turkmenistan.ru
22. John Foster, op. cit.
23. http://www.turkmenistan.gov.tm/_en/?idr=4&id=110303a
24. John Foster, op. cit.
25. Ibid.
26. "Trio Sign up for Turkmen Gas", 25 April 2008, http://www.upstreamonline.com/live/article153168.ece
27. www.turkmenistan.ru
28. "Afghanistan to Deploy 7,000 troops to guard TAPI Pipeline", *Newstrack*, 13 December 2010.
29. Atul Aneja, "TAPI Gas Pipeline Project Poised for Breakthrough", *The Hindu*, 1 December 2010.
30. "India Offered Lead Role in TAPI gas Pipeline", *Deccan Chronicle*, 15 December 2010.
31. John Foster, op. cit.
32. See Note 11.
33. John Foster, op. cit.
34. Shawn Mccarthy, "Pipeline Opens New Front in Afghan War", 19 June 2008, http://v1.theglobeandmail.com/servlet/story/RTGAM.20080619.wafghanpipeline19/BNStory/Afghanistan
35. Jayanth Jacob, op. cit.
36. Shawn Mccarthy, op. cit.

37. Abdujalil Abdurasulov, op. cit.
38. John Foster, op. cit.
39. Jayanth Jacob, op. cit.
40. John Foster, op. cit.
41. Ibid.
42. Ibid.
43. Ibid.
44. Sandeep Dikshit, "TAPI Gas Pipeline Project Doubtful, Say Energy Experts", 18 October 2008, http://www.thehindu.com/2008/10/18/stories/2008101859541000.htm
45. Raghav Sharma, "Will TAPI Remain a Pipedream", IPCS Paper No. 2661, 27 August 2008, http://www.ipcs.org/article/terrorism/will-tapi-remain-a-pipedream-2661.html
46. "Work on TAPI Gas Pipeline to be Accelerated", *Alexander's Oil and Gas Connections*, vol. 11, no. 24, 26 November 2011.
47. "Foreign Secretary's Interaction with Visiting Afghan Journalists", 27 January 2011, http://meaindia.nic.in/mystart.php?id=550317117
48. http://petroleum.nic.in/ng.htm
49. *Basic Statistics on Indian Petroleum & Natural Gas 2009-10*, Ministry of Petroleum & Natural Gas Government of India, New Delhi (Economic Division), October 2010, p. 3.
50. For more details see 'Report of the Group on India Hydrocarbons Vision–2025', Volume-I (Government of India: New Delhi), 25 February 2011.
51. http://petroleum.nic.in/ng.htm
52. "Speech by Shri Murli Deora, hon'ble Minister of Petroleum and Natural Gas at the Meeting of the consultative Committee of Members of Parliament for the Ministry of Petroleum & Natural Gas in New Delhi on Wednesday, the 4 June 2008", http://petroleum.nic.in:80/speeches/04-06-2008.pdf
53. http://meaindia.nic.in/mystart.php?id=550314553, 18 December 2008.
54. See Note 30.
55. www.turkmenistan.ru
56. Bruce Pannier, op. cit.
57. See Note 11.
58. Bruce Pannier, op. cit.
59. John Foster, op. cit.
60. Raghav Sharma, op. cit.

# PART II
# Transport Linkages

# 13

# Pipelines as a "Means of Transport" for the Land-Locked Caspian Basin

*Martin Ira Glassner* and *Avinoam Idan*

This paper explores the question: Do pipelines fulfill the traditional strategic function of road and rail for land-locked countries which are energy producers and potential or actual energy transit States? We consider the similarities and differences between road/rail and pipelines in the strategic picture of the land-locked States. This leads us to examine whether in fact there is the necessary cooperation in pipeline planning, design, construction, maintenance, administration and financing in the seven Central Asian and Caucasian States or whether political, economic, social and technical considerations necessitate significant changes in the definition of the term "means of transport."

## Background

In the contemporary international system, forty-three States are land-locked; that is, they have no sea coast at all. Prior to the twentieth century, there were only a few land-locked States, but decolonization led to a dramatic increase in their number. Ever since the early 1990s the number of land-locked States has increased dramatically – from twenty-seven to forty-three – largely as a consequence of the breakup of the Soviet Union and Yugoslavia. Unlike the previous waves of land-locked States, a number of these new countries are oil and gas producers and/or energy transit States and many of them have assigned high priority to establishing energy transit routes over road and rail transport routes.

In recognition of the unique challenges to land-locked States and the potential for conflict in their drive for transport access, a number of international treaties have been concluded defining their rights. These agreements focused on the use by land-locked States of road and rail transport through neighboring countries. However, it seems that pipelines may fulfill the strategic function previously performed by roads and railways. Consequently, the existing treaties may not provide sufficient legal protection for the most important strategic infrastructures of the new land-locked States.

We begin our inquiry with an analysis of the major relevant treaties and continue with a discussion of the strategic infrastructure decisions of two land-locked States of the Caspian region, Azerbaijan and Kazakhstan, following their separation from the Soviet Union. The analysis focuses on these countries' prioritization of their transport infrastructure projects and the role that each of these plays for them in their overall strategic policies.

## International Concern with Transit Rights of Land-Locked States

The most important of the treaties is the Convention and Statute on Freedom of Transit, Barcelona, 20 April 1921, commonly known as the Barcelona Convention. In its first article, it defines in some detail the term "traffic in transit." Subsequent articles spell out the basic requirements and rights of shippers and (in Article 2) introduces the term "other means of transport." Perhaps the most important phrase in this document appears in Article 7: "it being understood that the principle of freedom of transit must be observed to the utmost possible extent." Although land-locked States are never mentioned explicitly in the Barcelona Convention, it is widely accepted as the foundation for subsequent agreements and practices that facilitate international trade.

The next important multilateral convention concerning transit was the United Nations Convention on Transit Trade of Land-locked States, commonly referred to as the New York Convention, of 1965. This treaty is particularly relevant to the topic under discussion since Article 1(d) includes as "means of transport": "...if agreed upon by the contracting States, other means of transport and pipelines and gas lines, when they are used for traffic in transit." Thus, for the first time a multilateral agreement concerning transit mentioned pipelines and gas lines."[1]

At the Third United Nations Conference on the Law of the Sea (UNCLOS III, 1973–82), several changes in the Barcelona and New York conventions were proposed and debated but the result was virtually no change. Article 124(2) reads: "Land-locked States and Transit States may, by agreement between them, include as means of transport pipelines and gas lines and means of transport other than those included in paragraph 1."

In the "Virginia Commentary" on UNCLOS III and the Convention that it produced, an explanation is offered for the seemingly peculiar wording of this paragraph: "Paragraph 2 has to be read in conjunction with the preceding paragraph. Paragraph 1(d) mentions those means of traffic in transit which may be used without the specific consent of the transit State. In contrast, the use of the means of transport covered by paragraph 2 requires agreement between the land-locked State and the transit State." This may be considered the most authoritative statement on the subject to date.[2]

In addition, the United Nations' Almaty Programme of Action (APA) states that: "Pipelines provide a cost-effective means of transport for both oil and natural gas. The planning and construction of pipelines require close cooperation between landlocked and transit developing countries. The substantive investments that are required for the construction of pipelines necessitate capital investment from the private sector as well....[L]andlocked and transit developing countries should cooperate and coordinate to construct pipelines along the most cost-effective and most suitable or shortest routes, taking into account the interests of the parties concerned."[3]

The Organization for Security and Co-operation in Europe held a Transit Transport Conference in Dushanbe, Tajikistan in October 2007, aimed at strengthening political cooperation with regard to transit transportation issues across the region. Regional integration and collaboration will allow the dismantling of barriers to trade, cut transaction costs and encourage economies of scale, all contributing to mutual economic growth of both land-locked and transit developing countries. In addition, regional economic groupings, transit agreements and bilateral agreements continue to play a critical role in promoting transit transport cooperation.[4]

## CASE STUDIES

The Soviet breakup led to the establishment of nine new land-locked States, most of them in Central Asia and the Caucasus. They are unique in a number of ways. They are in geographic zones that are different than the bulk of the previous waves of land-locked countries. Many are energy producers or potential energy transit States, and many of them are situated in locations that are considered strategically vital for a number of the world's global and regional powers. Following the independence of this group of States, the energy producers placed their highest policy priority on determining their energy export transit routes. They saw this designation as cardinal to determining their policies and alliances, as well as their trade options. A number of neighboring States, among them other land-locked countries, also sought to serve as transit routes for the land-locked energy producers.

### *Azerbaijan*

The Republic of Azerbaijan attained full independence in December 1991. It is a land-locked country that borders Russia, Armenia, Iran, Georgia and the land-locked Caspian Sea. The new republic was born into a conflict with neighboring Armenia over the disputed Karabagh region, further limiting its transport options. Following independence and in the midst of the battles, a number of short-lived governments were in power in Azerbaijan until June 1993, when the Soviet-era leader, Heydar Alíyev, returned to power. Government stability was restored and coherent policies on infrastructure priorities and routes were formed.

The Alíyev regime viewed developing and strengthening oil and gas pipelines as its top infrastructure priority and as a means to realize the aim of joining U.S.-led political and security structures. Alíyev viewed increasing the State's energy exports as critical to gaining resources that will allow the regime longevity and for the State to fully establish its independence. Furthermore, establishment of energy transport routes was viewed as a means to gain international support for Azerbaijan's drive to regain the territories that it lost in its war with Armenia and as a means to gain resources that would allow it to confront Armenia diplomatically, or, if necessary, militarily, from a position of strength.[5]

In this context, in September 1994, Azerbaijan signed the "Contract of the Century" with a number of Western oil companies, initiating the development of the main Azerbaijan oil and gas fields. Concurrently, Azerbaijan took steps to reinforce its existing oil pipeline through Russia to the Black Sea port of Novorossiysk. Azerbaijani oil exports commenced on this route in 1997, and a Chechnya bypass spur was completed in 2000, increasing the viability of this route.

In its first decade of independence, Baku also made major decisions on its natural gas exports. In 1997 large natural gas reserves were discovered in the Shah Deniz field, necessitating a strategic decision on the desired route for export of the gas. Baku decided in 1997 to strive to export its natural gas on an east-west route, with the aim of export to Turkey and perhaps on to markets in Europe. The final project on this route is called the South Caucasus Pipeline (SCP) and is built on the route of Baku-Tbilisi-Erzerum. The decision on gas export may have impacted the viability of the building of the Baku-Tbilisi-Ceyhan oil export route, as the east-west oil export option became commercially more feasible once the decision to build a parallel gas pipeline was made.[6]

In the early 1990s, Azerbaijan explored joining the Europe-led initiative TRACECA (Transport Corridor Europe-Caucasus-Asia – www.traceca-org.org) in establishing a road network that links Europe to Asia through the Caucasus and Central Asia. However, only in 1998 this initiative was formally established. A feasibility study was conducted for expanding the road sector in the Caucasus in December 2000. In the first part of the decade, a number of existing roads were improved and attempts were made to simplify border crossing regimes, but no new strategic roadways have yet been built from Azerbaijan within the framework of this project.

In the sphere of railways, in 2005 Azerbaijan announced its decision to establish a railway route through Georgia to East Turkey, building upon existing rail/road networks. In February 2005, representatives of Turkey, Georgia and Azerbaijan agreed to conduct a feasibility study for the proposed railway network, and in early 2007 funding was put in place by the participating sides for this project.

To summarize, following its independence in 1991, Baku gave priority to developing oil and gas export pipelines rather than its roads and railways, but railway routes have since been established along the route of the pipelines. Baku also viewed these energy transport lines as a tool in its efforts to join Euro-Atlantic political and strategic frameworks.

*Kazakhstan*

Land-locked Kazakhstan gained independence in December 1991 with the fall of the Soviet Union. It borders on Russia, China, Kyrgyzstan, Uzbekistan, Turkmenistan and the Caspian Sea. Recognizing its strategic challenge nestled in between Russia and China, Kazakhstan developed cooperation with both of these powers while developing strategic interests for the United States in Kazakhstan's independence and prosperity. It called this policy its "multi-vector" foreign policy.[7] This strategic orientation was reflected in Kazakhstan's oil export infrastructure decisions. First and foremost, it decided to build its main energy export line from Tengiz to Novorossiysk through Russia to the Black Sea, in partnership with U.S. energy companies and with the strong encouragement of the USA government. The pipeline was funded and built within the framework of the Caspian Pipeline Consortium (CPC) which was established in 1992, following Kazakhstan's independence.

As part of its multi-vector policy, Kazakhstan also decided in 1997 to build an oil export pipeline to China which was inaugurated in December 2005. The second stage of the Atasú-Alashánkou pipeline became operational toward the end of 2006. This oil pipeline between Kazakhstan and China is unique in that it does not lead to exports to world markets, but directly to China. Consistent with this same multi-vector policy, Kazakhstan in 2006 joined the BTC project and export part of its oil on this east-west route. Kazakhstan and China are also building a natural gas export pipeline to China.

In contrast to the significant investments and political effort to establish energy export pipelines, Kazakhstan has invested minimal funds and efforts in trans-state railways and roads since its independence. In fact, by 2006 no major strategic road or railway projects had become operational during the country's first decade of independence.

## Geostrategy

The question now arises: Do energy export pipelines fulfill the strategic function of roads and rails for land-locked countries that are energy exporters and energy transit States? The Baku-Tbilisi-Erzerum project, for example, cost some four billion US dollars; the Kazakhstan-China pipeline three billion dollars, and the SCP natural gas pipeline one and a half billion dollars.[8] Road and railway transport in the Caspian region, however, has attracted significantly less external and internal investment. In the framework of TRACECA, road planning and investments by 2006 amounted to 18,464,000 US dollars.[9] Furthermore, the building of the Kars-Akhalkalaki-Tbilisi-Baku railway corridor required about 350 million US dollars.[10] This sum obviously dwarfs the cost of the energy export pipelines.

In analyzing the strategic function of energy export pipelines, we make the following points: As in the case of roads and railways, land-locked energy transport States view the stability of their transit countries as part of their national interest and consequently their security policies. However, in contrast to roads and rails, the linking of energy-producing land-locked States with energy transit countries creates new political and strategic entities and they themselves have become actors in their regions and the international system. Second, the relations between energy exports and transit States linked by energy pipelines are mutually dependent. Thus these pipelines have an even more significant impact on the strategic situation of land-locked States than roads and railroads.

Third, energy export transit routes create more international interest and invite security involvement and guarantees of global powers that possess an interest in preserving the stability of the export transit routes. Consequently, global and regional powers often view these routes in important ways. In addition, international energy corporations and other major transnational companies view the stability of the energy transport routes as among their policy goals. Moreover, challenges to the stability of the energy transport routes are viewed as threats by a number of global powers and international companies. This contrasts with the function of roads and railroads that link land-locked countries and their neighbors, whose influence is generally local.

## Economic and Technical Factors

Having explored some of the legal and strategic factors involved in Caspian oil and gas transit, we turn our attention to some economic and technical factors. The World Bank and the United Nations Development Programme collaborated on a major study of international oil and gas pipelines (ESMAP) which speaks directly to some of the questions raised early in this chapter. We briefly consider three of them here, with excerpts from this study.

"In the near future, the world will need more cross-border pipelines for oil and gas. Two factors explain the reasons for this need:

> Reserves close to traditional markets are being depleted. Newer, more remote sources of oil and gas will be required. Many of these will require pipeline delivery either because they are landlocked or, in the case of gas, because liquified natural gas (LNG) projects are less attractive than pipelines, other than for distances in excess of 3,000 miles.
>
> Many gas markets have in the past been constrained by regulatory and institutional factors. In recent years these constraints have been eroded. A potential 'dash for gas' furthermore is being reinforced in many areas by a combination of gas sector reform, creating gas-to-gas competition; electricity sector reform ... and concerns about the environmental damage caused by the consumption of other hydrocarbons.[11]

The international conventions cited earlier contain some ambiguous phraseology which raise questions about their meaning and import. Why, for example, do the

United Nations Convention on the Law of the Sea and its antecedents treat gas pipelines differently from oil pipelines? A satisfactory explanation is found in the ESMAP study:

- "There is normally much greater rent associated with oil than with gas.
- Security of supply is more important for gas than for oil, because gas outages involve much greater reconnection problems.
- Gas pipeline transportation involves very different technical issues from those of oil; for example, in terms of issues such as grid balancing.
- The environmental threats from oil and gas pipelines differ significantly.
- The extent of competition, in terms of transport methods, differs."[12]

The Almaty Programme of Action urges, as we noted above, that "[L]andlocked and transit developing countries should cooperate and coordinate to construct pipelines along the most cost-effective and most suitable or shortest routes, taking into account the interests of the parties concerned."

An important example of this high-minded exhortation in practice is the Energy Charter Treaty (ECT). Brainchild of the then-prime minister of The Netherlands, Ruud Lubbers, who wanted to facilitate trade and cooperation between the energy sectors of Eastern and Western Europe and the Former Soviet Union, the plan was presented in Dublin in June 1990. Out of the Lubbers plan came the European Energy Charter, signed by 49 States and the European Union at The Hague in December 1990. The Energy Charter Treaty, the legally binding multilateral instrument, was signed at Lisbon in December 1994 and entered into force in April 2000.

It lays out a framework for the development of an international regime to deal, *inter alia,* with issues relating to investment, trade, transit, competition and environmental concerns. It includes high-pressure gas pipelines, electricity grids and lines, crude oil, pipelines, coal slurry (Hydraulic transport of solids in pipes, Washington: Slurry Transport Association.) pipelines and POL product pipelines. The ECT has been proposed as a model for an organization that would perform similar functions in Central Asia and the Caucasus. However, caution is warranted here. Experience in the developing world illustrates that elaborate plans with little solid support seldom achieve their objectives.

## Conclusion

In this chapter we have considered two very important questions. First, as noted above, Article 124(2) of the 1982 United Nations Convention on the Law of the Sea may be considered the most authoritative statement on the subject to date. It would seem to be adequate now and into the intermediate future, notwithstanding (a) the exponential growth since 1921 and even since 1982 of international trade in gas and POL products (petroleum, oils and lubricants); (b) the greatly increased number of land-locked States in the world; and (c) ever-more-sophisticated technology, including that applied to overland movement of gas and POL products.

The second question is: Do pipelines fulfill the strategic function of road and rail for land-locked countries which are energy producers and potential or actual energy transit States? A survey of all oil and gas pipelines in use, under construction, and proposed for the Caspian Basin would very likely reveal that planning for such projects is heavily influenced by the persistent efforts of Russia and Iran to route them through their territories, but economic considerations appear to be even more determinative.

"In conclusion," say two experts in the field, "building cross-border pipelines in landlocked regions depends not only on politics but also on economics. Economic realities and oil companies' strategies should not be neglected to understand the 'politics of pipelines'."[13]

## ENDNOTES

1. Uprety, Kishor, *The Transit Regime for Landlocked States; International Law and Development Perspectives*, Washington: The World Bank, 2006, p. 116.
2. Nandan, Satya N. and Shabtai Rosenne, *United Nations Convention on the Law of the Sea 1982, A Commentary,* Volume III, The Hague: Nijhoff, 1995, p. 407.
3. A/CONF.202/PC.2/1, Almaty Programme of Action: Addressing the Special Needs of Landlocked Developing Countries Within a New Global Framework for Transit Transport Cooperation for Landlocked and Transit Developing Countries, August 2003.
4. OSCE, Office of the Co-ordinator of OSCE Economic and Environmental Activities, *Road Map Leading to the Transit Transport Conference*, Dushanbe, Tajikistan, 23-24 October 2007, pp. 2-3.
5. *Rossiyskaya Gazeta*, 21 June 1997, p. 1 (FBIS-SOV-97-123).
6. Shaffer, Brenda, "From Pipedream to Pipeline: Lessons from the Baku-Tbilisi-Ceyhan Pipeline Project" *Current History*, October 2005, p. 345.
7. *Interfax* 6 July 2001, p. 2 (FBIS-SOV-2001-0706).
8. Energy Information Administration – www.eia.dov.gov/emeu/cabs/caspian/exportissues Caspian Pipeline Consortium – www.cpc.ru/portal/allias!press/lang!en-us
9. Transport Corridor Europe-Caucasus-Asia – www.mt.ro/traceca/english/projects
10. *Kavkasia-Press*, 29 December 2004 (FBIS-SOV-2004-1229).
11. Joint *UNDP/World Bank*, Energy Sector Management Assistance Programme (ESMAP). *Cross-Border Oil and Gas Pipelines: Problems and Prospects,* by Paul Stevens, June 2003, p. xiii.
12. *Ibid,* p. xiv.
13. Raballand, Gaël and Ferhat Esen, "Economics and Politics of Cross-border Pipelines – The Case of the Caspian Basin," *Asia Europe Journal*, Vol. 5, 2007, p. 146.

# 14

## The Great Silk Route: Historical Perspective

*Victor M. Mitypov*

The Great Silk Route is an important world trading communication in Eurasia in ancient and middle ages. It was the trading caravan way from China to the capital of Roman empire. It existed from the 2nd century BC till the 16th century AD, and its total length was about 7,000 kms. It got its name from the first item of transit trade – Chinese silk, later besides silk, other goods like jewellry, glass, iron etc. appeared.

Being the great material monument of the civilization's openness to external world and international economic relations, the Silk Route provided not only a trading, information and cultural exchange, but also served as the guarantor of peace on the Eurasian borders. Depending on geopolitics, inter-civilization dialogue sometimes increased, sometimes decreased. The Great Silk Route is the branched communication network, connecting civilizations.

The main route went through the territories of China, Tarim basin, over Pamir and Tien-Shan mountains, Central Asia, Afghanistan, Iran, along the eastern shore of Mediterranean and further to the main trading centers of Near East, North Africa and Europe. The Great Silk Route played an important role in the lifestyle of many nations of Eurasia.

In the 2nd century BC, people made many attempts to cross Tien-Shan mountains, some scientists suppose that this part of the Great Silk Route already functioned in 4th century BC. In any way the territory and nations of ancient Tien-Shan were located in the heart of this huge economic and cultural phenomenon. Many caravan routes on the Great Silk Route changed over time, and only the main direction from the East to the West and back remained.

Caravan traffic was very slow, in good day the caravan consisted from 100 to 10,000 camels covered 8 *farsah* (50 km), in nasty days – 4 *farsah* (25 km).[1] Along the route, one could take a rest in caravanserais. The Great Silk Route promoted the transition to settled way of life, and developing of animal breeding. There was no similar phenomenon in the history of humanity with the same economic and cultural importance. The Great Silk Route introduced order, commonwealth and peace in the general chaos of the Middle Ages.

The area along the caravan trails in Central Asia has been a hotly contested region. Already in the middle of the first millennium BC the Persian rulers levied tributes on their vassal territories in Sogdiana and Bactria. The troops of Alexander the Great were the first to open the route from Europe to Asia in the 4th century BC. Together with the warriors, there moved eastwards the merchants who transported various goods to the remote lands and brought back to their native countries many other things. From Asia Minor and Arabia to the banks of the Yangtze the vast territory was intersected by trade routes along which sprang up many kingdoms and states, which prospered and later declined or vanished under the attacks of stronger conquerors. But trade caravans kept laying new routes.

The great overland thoroughfare that put together a series of caravan trails heading from Central Asia to the West and to the South and the paths leading from China to Eastern Turkestan, originated in the mid-second century BC when the Chinese for the first time discovered the territories lying beyond the western borders – the countries of Central Asia. Retreating for a long time from the western world China itself opened its "door to the west". In 138 BC Chinese emperor Wu Di of the Han dynasty sent an emissary, experienced commander and diplomat Zhang Qian, on a secret mission to Yueh-chi tribes in quest of an alliance against the disruptive Xiongnu. Zhang Qian presented to the emperor the results of his travels in a report called "The journey that is 25 thousand li long". In this report, he suggested a thorough plan of developing the relations with the western countries, the plan that soon was put into operation. Thus there met two branches of the great trans-continental road: the trail heading east from the Mediterranean world and the one heading west from the Hun Empire.[2]

It should be noted that there was never a single, static Silk Route, but rather a network of various routes which forked and branched like a big tree. The principal branch traversing Asia from East to West originated in Changan, an ancient capital of China, skirted the Gobi desert up to the north-western borders, across the Tarim Basin and further across Eastern Turkestan. Passing through the Tien Shan some caravans continued their way via the Ferghana Valley and Tashkent oasis to Samarkand – the capital of Sogdiana, to Bukhara, Khorezm and further to the Caspian Sea. From Samarkand a number of caravans headed for Bactria and crossing the Kashka Darya valley reached Termez where they got across the Amu Darya river and headed further south to Kabul and India. Another branch of the road skirted the Taklamakan desert in the south and via Khotan and Yarkand headed to Bactria (northern Afghanistan) and Merv and then through Persia and Syria reached the Mediterranean coast where by maritime routes some goods were delivered to Rome and Greece.[3]

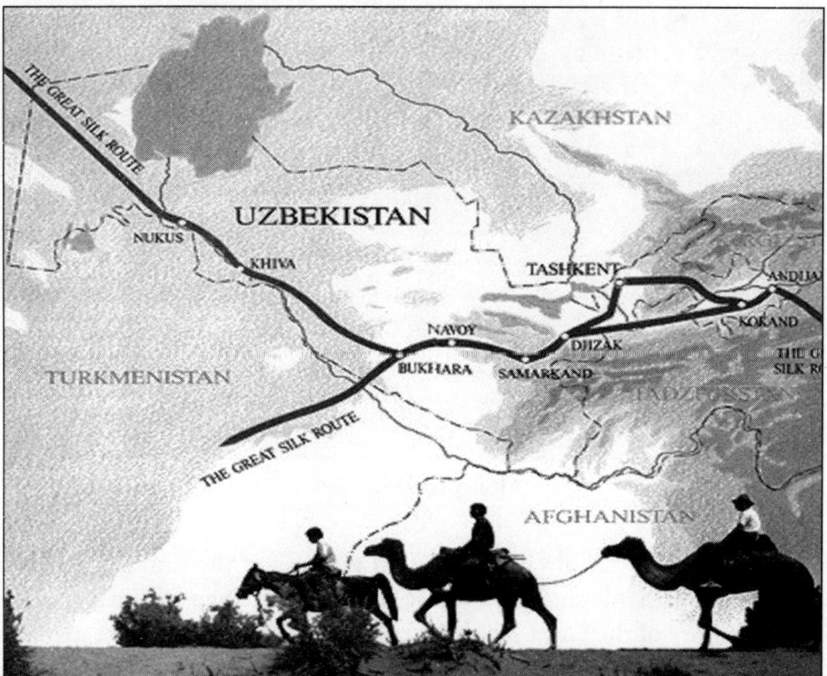

But the fabled Silk Route was not a mere channel of trade: it was the means of propagation of the cultural achievements of the peoples, spiritual wealth and religious doctrines. Ancient Zoroastrian cults prevalent in Khorezm, Sogdiana and Bactria, were replaced by Buddhism which became the main religion of the mighty Kushan empire and expanded to China. At the beginning of our era, from Asia Minor, Christianity eventually reached Central Asia and China via the Silk Route. In the 8th century the rigorous warriors of Arabia brought Islam to the eastern lands. In the later period the hordes of Genghis Khan rushed from the Mongol steppes to the European plains following the tracks treaded out by tradesmen and missionaries. From Samarkand – the city situated in the very heart of the Great Silk Route – Tamerlane, the great commander of the Middle Ages, started his military campaigns.[4]

The convertible commodity had been invented in the form of Chinese silk, which was capable to overcome economic costs of a long and dangerous way, and was equal under the price to gold and had become the international currency. Trade was conducted through intermediaries, among them were Jews. In the Middle Ages there were two general directions from China through Balkh and Samarkand to India and Byzantium (to the south and to the north of Caspian sea). It lasted until 15th century when newly-discovered sea routes to Asia opened up.

**Mongolian Warriors**

Flourishing poles were always the desired purpose of the Eurasian geopolitics. Greatest commanders Alexander the Great and Genghis Khan left their traces here. During the history of the Great Silk Route only the Mongolian empire managed to have control over this transcontinental line. By the 13th century, of all the countries on the Great Silk Route, the most extensive and powerful country was the Mongolian empire, which spread across Northern China, Eastern and Western Turkistan (Central Asia), Iran, Mesopotamia, the Caucasus and Eastern Europe.

Genghis Khan's successors continued the western campaign and finished it on the coast of Dunai and Black Sea. The trading stations created by Mongols were sold to the Venetian and Genoa merchants. In this policy the strategic thinking of the Golden Horde Khans was shown differing not only on the fields of battles, but also in housekeeping. Preservation of autonomy of the Genoa colonies promoted the prosperity of Golden Horde and effective division of international work, where foreign trade communications were carried out by skilled merchants excellently knowing the European market.

In Northern Black Sea Coast the Genoa trading stations in Ak-Kermane (Belgrad) and in the city of Kilie based by Mongols on coast of Dunai became the centers of transit trade (except Kafy), in particular. The huge communication bridge of empire started moving. Capitals of Golden Horde were based on the crossing of great trading ways from the East to the West. The Khans controlled the markets which sold jewellry, fabrics, furs, and various items of luxury. These markets attracted, firstly, Asian tradesmen, and later merchants from Western Europe.

In 1260 AD, two Venetian merchants – Nikkolo and Maffeo (the father and uncle of Marco Polo) left for the East taking the "northern way". This caravan journey lasted for a whole year, and finished at the residence of great Kublai Khan. Marco Polo recounts that his father and uncle made a successful trade agreement during this first year of travel and when returning to China after two years, the brothers decided to take seventeen year old Marco with them. They had no idea that this decision would be such a historically significant decision[5] . Marco Polo's journey with his father and uncle in China, bearing a message to the great Kublai Khan from the Head of the Catholic Church, Father Gregory X, began in 1271. Their route passed through modern Akka (Israel) to the Persian Gulf, then to the north through Iran to Amu Darya, and on to Oksus (Aral sea) through the Pamir mountains to modern Sinkiang (an Uighur area) and then finally through the Gobi Desert to Shangtu.

The Venetians were greeted with great honor and soon appeared in the presence of the great Khan. Young Marco was especially liked by Kublai Khan who gave him authority as his personal envoy. Using this authority Marco Polo traveled to the provinces of China, carrying out numerous, mainly diplomatic assignments. These trips, coupled with his natural curiosity and extraordinary memory, allowed Marco Polo to get acquainted with the lifestyle of the people of this country, and subsequently to document a unique and descriptive story about his findings and impressions. It is known that he went overland from Bukhara to China. In one of the versions of his "Book" he describes his visit to Samarkand. The Venetians stayed for 17 years in the service of Kublai Khan. Most of their return journey was done by sea around the coast of South-East Asia, Hindustan, visiting many seaports on the way. They arrived in Venice in 1295, completing the greatest journey of that time both in terms of distance and time.

Centuries have passed since the travels of Marco Polo and the creation of his remarkable "Book", but people will never forget his humanistic feat. In 1994 the World Tourist Organization, together with UNESCO, carried out an international seminar in Tashkent called "The Great Silk Road". The Samarkand Declaration was accepted where Uzbekistan was officially named the center of the project to bring the Great Silk Route back to life as a major channel for cooperation between the states through which this famous route passed. The main tourist route crosses 32 towns and cities of Central Asia. In other words, once the legendary Great Silk Route reopens, crowds of tourists will be visiting Tashkent, Samarkand, Bukhara, Khiva and the cities of Fergana Valley.

The idea of revival of the Great Silk Route was worked out by the European Commission in 1991, after the disintegration of the former Soviet Union. The main Eurasian communication bridge is proposed to connect poles of economic and technological development in Western Europe and Asia-Pacific region. The project was financed by the European Union. Annual payments reached 9-11 million euros. But since 2004 it was offered to countries-participants to pay from their general budget at a rate of 15 per cent. Azerbaijan, Armenia, Bulgaria, Georgia, Kazakhstan, Kyrgyzstan, Moldova, Romania, Tajikistan, Turkmenia, Turkey, Uzbekistan, Ukraine participate in TRACECA project.

Today uniqueness of the Eurasian situation is in the revival of Great Silk Route. There is an international project of railway Istanbul-Beijing through Central Asia (Mary, Tashkent, Almaty) with branch through Afghanistan to India. Thus there is a formation of new transport direction for the admission of powerful and steady goods traffic from Asia-Pacific region to Central Asia, Persian gulf and Western Europe, passing through the transport system of Russia, and first of all, its Trans-Siberian railway.

**The bridge on the Iran-Turkmenistan border, Sarakhs**

More than forty states are drawn to this line. Fourteen years ago in 1996 the construction of railway Mary (Turkmenistan) – Meshed (Iran) was finished. Turkey plans building of a transport tunnel under Bosporus costing 1 billion dollars. China has carried out reconstruction of a railway from coast of Pacific ocean to border with Kazakhstan and intends to create together with the Post-Soviet countries a transport corridor up to Rotterdam.

**Kazakhstan-Turkmenistan-Iran railway**

There is a median variant of a route of the Great Silk Way through the Black Sea Coast, Transcaucasia, Caspian Sea and Central Asia. In 1990, railways of China and former Soviet Union in Central Asia joined. Nowadays railway border stations Druzhba (Kazakhstan) and Alashankau (China) are the important transport link on the shortest way from China to Europe. But transit through border is not great.

But at the end of $20^{th}$ century, the Trans-Siberian main line gave up to new transport route between East and West on its volume of container transportations. The Trans-Siberian Railway annually transported only 22 million containers, that is 7 times below the reached level of 1980s.[6] The revival of the Great Silk Way started with opening of railway route Ljanjungan – Hamburg – Rotterdam. The route was named the Northern corridor of Trans-Asian railway. Cargo delivery by railway from Chinese port Ljanjungan to Hamburg (distance of 11,000 kilometers) takes 11 days, whereas by sea, it takes 20 to 30 days. The railway through Kazakhstan is shorter than Trans-Siberian railway in 1,500 to 2,000 kilometers. In Dzungaria there is sharp continental climate with big fluctuation of seasonal temperatures and hurricane winds. In summer time the temperature reaches 45 degrees centigrade, and in winter it is minus 40 degrees. Storming hurricane winds could tear off containers from railway platform and that's why it is necessary additional measures of fastening cargoes.

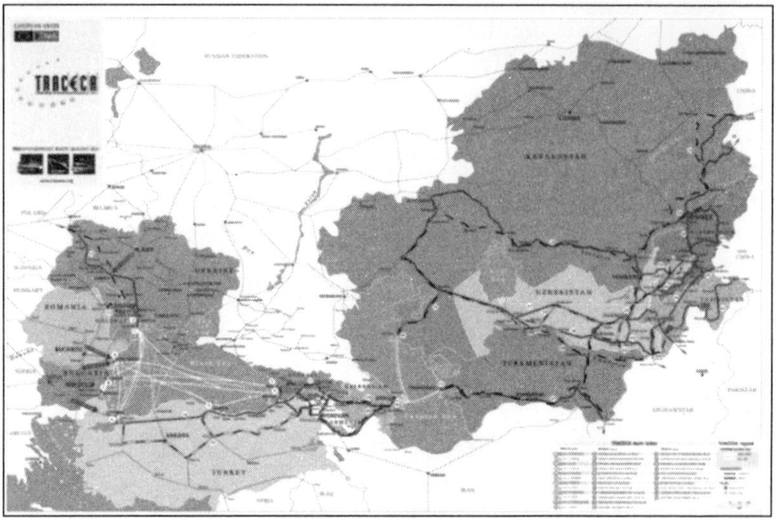

**TRACECA**

The strategy of creating latitude transport corridor bypassing Russia has been confirmed at the conferences of TRACECA[7] . In reality, TRACECA project is an alternative to the Russian transport monopoly for an exit to Europe in case of deterioration of geopolitical situation in the North Caucasus which has been caused by the Chechen conflict. At the same time, the intentions of the West to strengthen their military presence in Southern Caucasus under the pretext of protection of the international project, are obvious. Low profitability of cargo transportation on offered routes can be explained by geopolitical factor, in comparison with existing railways from Central Asia to Europe through Russia and Ukraine. Existing transportation tariffs of oil, grain and clap are much more lower, and time of delivery of cargoes are two times less than projected under the program TRACECA. Hopes of fast revival of Great Silk Route are not justified. Geopolitical situation in the Near and Middle East do not promote realization of its program. There are only a few countries capable to offer an optimal variant of the Trans-Eurasian route – Russia, Kazakhstan and China.

The modern day arms race, local conflicts, terrorism, narcotic criminal activity, natural disasters and urgent unmet social needs are the major problems requiring the resolution of these chronic problems by peaceful negotiation. The advantages offered by regional integration and cooperation are clear and as information infrastructures enable the region to access the worldwide computer networks, the power of information technology can be harnessed in support of the drive for economic stability and the development of business and civil society.

The Silk Route has always been about connectivity and communication. The United States is actively promoting Silk Route development in recognition of the strategic importance of the countries encompassed within the Silk Route and in 1999 the U.S. Senate adopted a Silk Road Strategy Act, but it never became law. Despite this legislative setback, the Silk Road Strategy became, under the Bush Administration, the de facto basis of US-NATO interventionism, largely with a view to integrating the former Soviet republics of the South Caucasus and Central Asia into the US sphere of influence.

Apart from being a major trading route the Great Silk Route was of immeasurable significance in the establishment and maintenance of diplomatic relations. Today there is a revival of the Silk Road Diplomacy as technological advances in information communication systems and networks speed up the process of globalization and increasing interdependence. The dynamic development of political, trade and economic relations needs strengthening if mutually advantageous partnerships are to develop between all States on the Silk Route. Interdependence and globalization has led to an awareness of the unarguable fact that no country, however powerful it may be in military and economic terms, can face alone the challenges that call in question the survival of the whole of mankind.

A huge tourist potential of the Great Silk Route is forcing states to pool their efforts to preserve the monuments located on the route of the famous highway. Not so long ago, member countries of the Great Silk Route, including China, Italy, Kyrgyzstan, Kazakhstan, Uzbekistan and others, decided to jointly prepare to apply to UNESCO for inclusion of the Great Silk Route in the World Heritage List. This means, possibly, the emergence in the near future on the tourist market of a new grand tour, which will pass through the territory of a dozen states. It promises to become one of the most ambitious projects of the tourist industry in recent years.

## ENDNOTES

1. http://www.krugosvet.ru/enc/istoriya/
2. V.V. Struve, *Ancient East*, Moscow: State Pedagogical Publishing House, 1951, p. 211.
3. *Encyclopedia Britannica*, 15th Ed., p. 204.
4. D. Marozzi, *Tamerlan, Conqueror of the World*. Moscow: AST, 2009, p. 54.
5. A.G. Yurchenko, *The Book of Marco Polo. Notes of Traveller or Imperial Cosmography*, St. Petersburg: Eurasia, 2007, p. 49.
6. H. Tsuji, "Perspectives on Linking the Trans-Siberian and Trans-Korean Railways", *ERINA Report*, Vol. 56, February 2004, p. 33.
7. The European Commission's TRACECA project "Strengthening of Transport Training Capacities in NIS countries", 2008; Regional symposium "Transport planning technique and tools – traffic forecasting and simulation" (March 17-19, 2009, Tbilisi, Georgia); Regional symposium "Economic and financial appraisal techniques including Cost Benefit Analysis and Environmental Impact Assessment" (April 20-24, 2009, Istanbul, Turkey); Training, study tour "Multimodal transport and interoperability" (May 11-18, 2009, Netherlands, Germany), etc.

# 15

## The Trans-Siberian Railway: Eurasian Resource

*M. Baldano*

The Great Siberian Way for the first time was named the Trans-Siberian Railway by Englishmen. They meant a single-track railway from Chelyabinsk to Vladivostok. Nowadays the Trans-Siberian Railway is the back-bone of Russia from Moscow to Vladivostok. In spite of R. Kipling's phrase that "West is West, and East is East, and they never unite", the Trans-Siberian Railway connected two continents as iron hoop, reducing distances and geographical borders between them.

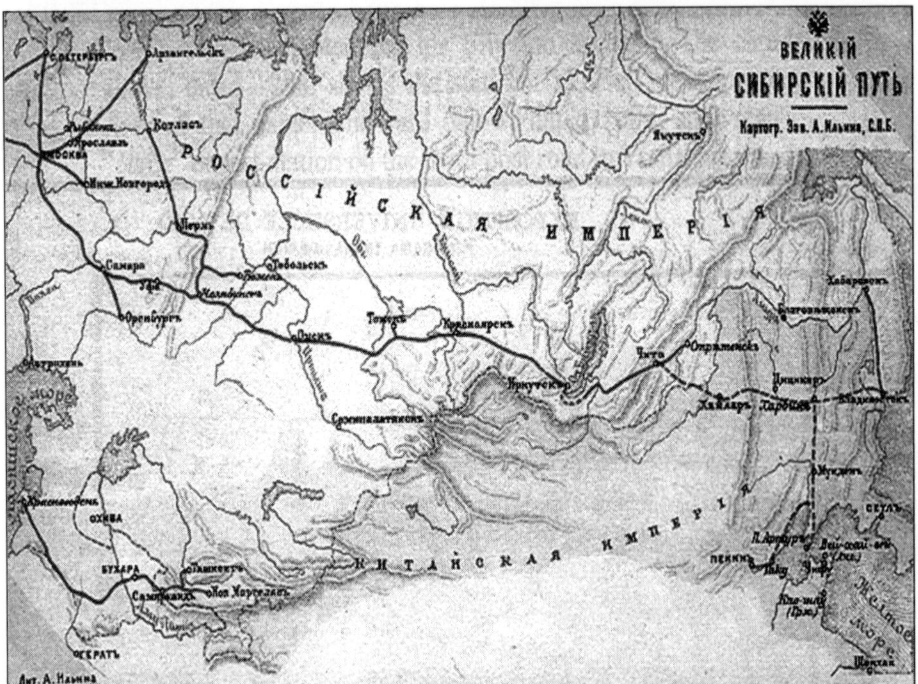


Map of the Great Siberian Way

In the second half of the 19th century, Russia underwent a period of extensive rail development that culminated in the construction of the Trans-Siberian Railway. Akin to the great railways of the Pacific in both the United States and Canada, Russia's transcontinental line was intended to supply and populate Siberia as well as deliver raw materials to the burgeoning industries west of the Urals. Working against an ambitious timetable and under severe conditions of climate and terrain, the Russian citizens effectively united the European and Asian parts of the empire by completing this Herculean project.

When Russia began constructing the Trans-Siberian Railway, it hoped to tame and exploit its eastern frontier as the Americans had done in their frontier. Czar Alexander III also realized the importance of a Trans-Siberian Railway to consolidate Russia's eastern territory, and he took action. Plans to build a railway across Siberia had circulated within the highest levels of the Russian bureaucracy for years before construction finally began in 1891. The project had strong backing from Emperor Alexander III and other notables. The heir apparent, Grand Duke Nicholas, served as chairman of the Siberian Railway Committee and performed a variety of ceremonial duties, connected with the project, including the first wheelbarrow with sand near Vladivostok to start the construction.

**The Railway was started here in Ussuri on 19 May 1891**

The real force behind the project, however, was Sergei Witte, the indomitable minister of finance to both Alexander and later Nicholas.[1] In order to begin rail operations on parts of the line as soon as possible, Witte set firm deadlines for the completion of various sections of the project. With the schedule under constant threat of slippage from the difficult working conditions and remoteness of Siberia, Witte insisted on adhering to his plans and cajoled subordinates to maintain the pace. This pressure contributed to accidents, as well as supply and equipment breakdowns. As disease and exposure took their toll on the labor force, the state turned to prisoners in great numbers to finish the job. About 100,000 persons – peasants from neighboring provinces, workers from central parts of the country, convicts and prisoners – worked only with picks, shovels and hand-carts and they accomplished a feat unprecedented in chronicles of engineering.[2] The costs of construction eventually reached over $250 million, twice the original estimate. Witte remained resolute in his goal, however, recalling in his memoirs: "I devoted myself – body and soul – to the task".[3]

**Construction of Great Siberian Way**

Workers began laying tracks from both the east and west. Like other rail lines throughout the empire, the track used on the Trans-Siberian was wider than the standard European gauge – 5 feet 3.5 inches as opposed to 4 feet 8.5 inches. The engineering plans provided for the sequential construction of six basic segments. In order of completion, these branches were the West Siberian line from Cheliabinsk to Novonikolaevsk (the future city of Novosibirsk) on the Ob River; the Ussuri line from Khabarovsk to Vladivostok; the mid-Siberian line from Novonikolaevsk to Innokentievskaia near Irkutsk, with a spur line to Tomsk; the circum-Baikal line from Irkutsk to the eastern side of Lake Baikal; and the trans-Baikal line from Lake Baikal to Sretensk. A sixth section, the Amur line, from Sretensk to Khabarovsk, was not completed until 1916. Before its completion, Russia was able to establish a link to the Pacific by negotiating an agreement with China to run track across Manchuria via the Chinese Eastern Railway.

Before construction of railway to Siberia the Moscow-Siberian road was added and on some parts replaced by a waterway. For example, on the route between Tomsk and Irkutsk about 4 million poods of cargo were carried. Sixteen thousand persons were carriers and used about 80,000 horses. The road was in a bad condition.

**The Great Siberian Way near village Taiga**

Construction of the Circum-Baikal road was the most difficult and expensive. The total volume of its works exceeds scales of the Suez Channel. In winter before construction of the Circum-Baikal road they crossed the frozen Baikal, putting rails directly on ice. When a thaw was set in, rails were taken to pieces and conveyed by ferries.

**The Circum-Baikal road**

The most talented Russian engineers of that time were working on the Trans-Siberian Railway in carrying out expeditions, road and bridge construction. In total 40 tunnels, almost 1500 bridges and viaducts were constructed. They were erected under the projects of N. Belelyubsky, L. Proskuryakov, G.Perederiy.[4] The most unique is the bridge through the Amur river with a length of 2,600 meters.

**Bridge construction through the Amur river, 1901**

On 21 December 1901 the traffic on the Trans-Siberian Railway was started. This day is considered as a last day of the railway construction stretching over 7 time zones. The Trans-Siberian Railway transformed the transportation in Russia. Before the railroad, travel time from Moscow (in the west) to Vladivostok (in the east) was nearly a year. With the advent of the Trans-Siberian Railway, that time was reduced dramatically. As expected, efficient transportation unified Western Russia with its Eastern frontier, just as the Transcontinental Railroad had unified America.[5]

Efficient transportation on the Trans-Siberian Railroad also opened the door to settlement in Russia's eastern regions. Prior to the construction of the railroad, Russia's eastern region of Siberia was virtually uninhabited. After the railway was finished, many Russian citizens migrated to this area. There was no necessity for forced settlement of the area – only within ten years the population increased by 3 times due to the Stolypin's policy. Omsk, Novosibirsk, Krasnoyarsk, Irkutsk, Khabarovsk and Vladivostok became big industrial centers. As such, the Trans-Siberian Railway resulted in the rapid settlement of frontier lands.

**Taiga Railway Station**

Russia started to turn into united economic organism. Thanks to updated farming techniques, farmers began producing grains and dairy products in southern Siberia.[6] Several coal-mining operations and iron and steel ventures were established. Siberia's rich natural resources were exploited and then shipped by railroad to western Russia or to the eastern port of Vladivostok. In fact, the Trans-Siberian Railway still contributes significantly to Russia's economy, transporting approximately one third of all of Russia's exports.

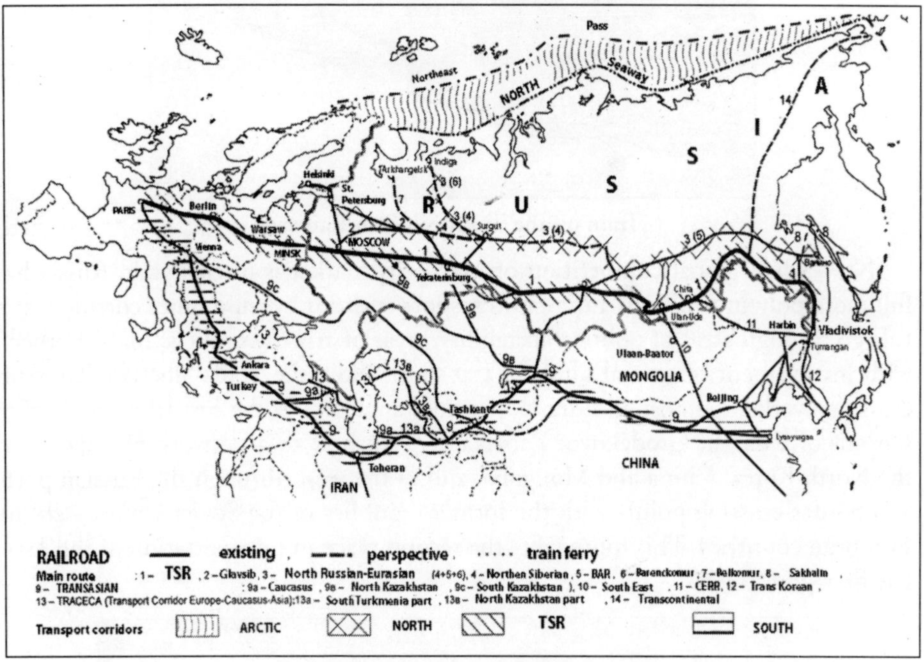


**Trans-Siberian Railroad**

Today the Trans-Siberian railway is the high-capacity high-tech transport complex. After some decades of development it became an important factor linking Russian regions and states of the Eurasian continent. The Trans-Siberian is one of the most modern railways in the world which complies with high international standards, is electrified all through its length (10,000 kms), equipped with modern automatic machinery, communications and information technologies that provide rail-safety and safety of movement of freight and passengers. As traction rolling stock on the railway the powerful locomotives for high-capacity trains and high-speed locomotives for high-speed passenger and container trains are used.[7] UN Economic and Social Commission for Asia and the Pacific included the Trans-Siberian land bridge into the common system of international transport corridors as a priority route in Eurasian communication.

**Train on the Trans-Siberian Railway**

Now, when global competition on transport market is intensifying, Russia has full monopoly in the Trans-Eurasian transport corridor because other corridors as a rule go through areas of political instability, areas of armed conflicts, many borders, with involvement of several kinds of transport. Now the Trans-Siberian Railroad, crossing overland almost all Eurasia, provides an access in the east (through border stations of Khasan, Grodekovo, Zabaikalsk, Naushki) to a network of railways of the North Korea, China and Mongolia, and in the west, through the Russian ports and border crossing points with the former republics of the Soviet Union – to the European countries. This route takes the second place in transportation of the Asia-Pacific region states.

**Vladivostok sea port and railway junction**

The Trans-Siberian corridor represents alternative to traditional sea route of delivery of containers from South East Asia round India and through Suez Channel to Europe. At present the dominant position in providing the Eurasian transportation still belongs to sea transport with the share of 98 per cent of the total volume of cargo between the countries of Europe, Asia and Pacific region. However, over the last few years there is a tendency of constant increase of freight rates by sea carriers and this, naturally, increases the transport component in final cost of the transported goods. In this connection more and more cargo owners consider the use of possibilities of the Trans-Siberian Railway as economic alternative to sea transportation. Objective advantage of transportation by the Trans-Siberian Railway is, first of all, double and triple reduction of cargo delivery time. For example, as the experience of container transportation shows, the time of coming of a container train from China to Finland by the Trans-Siberian Railway can make less than 10 days, while by sea it is a minimum of 28 days. One more key advantage of railway transportation of containers is reduction of cargo transfers to the minimum. It is well-known that the overwhelming majority of insurance events happens when cargo is transferred. Thus, the use of Trans-Siberian Railway helps in reducing the risk of casual damage of cargo to the minimum.

The most important strategic resource of the Trans-Siberian Railway consists in politically stable Russia. The history of Eurasian transcontinental routes testifies that their efficiency depends not only on reduction of boundary customs and other barriers, but also on geopolitical factors. It is obvious that in the 20$^{th}$ century there was no success in creating alternative to the Trans-Siberian Railway. Though it seemed that this problem is close to be solved, the Baghdad railway (western "shoulder" of the Great Silk Route) constructed by Germany at the beginning of 20$^{th}$ century could not be maintained effectively because of wars and regional conflicts. Soviet Union and China could not finish construction of alternative route through Kazakhstan. The project of Eurasian railway offered by the European Union bypassing Russia appeared even more utopian.

The main events of the 21$^{st}$ century are deploying between West European and Asian-Pacific poles of economic and technological development from Atlantic to Pacific Ocean where the most extended boundary for the international business was formed. Absence of modern market infrastructure and latitude communications, transport corridors through civilization boundaries in the Caucasus, Central Asia and Southeast Europe creates the threat of regional conflicts. In the 21$^{st}$ century transport systems of Eurasia and America would form a world transcontinental network.

Almost all countries of the Commonwealth of Independent States declare their intentions to create communication corridors – "personal window panes" to the West or East. These aspirations can materialize only after becoming a component of the communication frame of Eurasia. Today uniqueness of the Eurasian situation is in revival of Great Silk Route. There is an international railway project Istanbul-Beijing through Central Asia (Mary, Tashkent, Alma-Ata) with branch through Afghanistan to India. More than forty states gravitate to this line. China has carried out reconstruction of railway from Pacific Ocean to its border with Kazakhstan and intends to create transport corridor towards Rotterdam. The definitive choice of the trans-continental way will depend upon the geopolitical conditions in the regions.

The future of Trans-Siberian Railway as a land bridge between Europe and South-Eastern Asia cannot be overestimated. Fast developing APEC economies, such as China and the Republic of Korea, are able in the nearest future to increase volume of freight transportation via the Trans-Siberian land bridge several times. Regional Train Traffic Centers on the Trans-Siberian Railway together with the Main Train Traffic Center located in Moscow manage traffic on large areas. This technology gives opportunity to significantly increase train speed, especially container trains and block trains, to shorten goods delivery time by 25-30% and reach average daily going forward of container trains up to 1,200 km/day, that corresponds to international standards.

Construction of fiber-optic transmission lines, microwave lines and satellite communications system created a modern digital network and improved the management of traffic on the Trans-Siberian Railway. But absence of a flexible customs policy, social and economic shocks lowered the attractioon of the Trans-Siberian Railway. Additional measures to restore lost positions are required. Optimization of all transport chain, including introduction of modern management methods in the process of cargo transportation, creation of logistical centers, simplification of customs and boundary procedures, etc. are the key issues to be sorted out for the Trans-Siberian Railway. As a result of improvement of technical conditions high-speed container trains began to pass 10,000 kilometer's distance from Nakhodka to Brest within 9 days. Delivery of cargo by sea from Japan to Germany takes 17 days.

**Vladivostok Railway Station**

In recent years there has been a stable tendency of providing safety of cargo transported in accelerated container trains via the Trans-Siberian Railway. This became possible due to improvement of work of commercial check points on this direction, improvement of their technical capabilities by providing modern means of control of wagons condition and containers in trains. For increasing the competitiveness of the Trans-Siberian Railway, some technological steps were taken. Particularly to shorten the time trains are tied up at border stations, customs formalities have been simplified and some other measures have been taken which facilitate the procedure of border crossing.

**Container loading**

Today the Trans-Siberian Railway has not only geopolitical, but also strategic importance. The Trans-Siberian Railway takes a leading place in the state policy of Russia on forming the international transport corridors. The Trans-Siberian Railway possesses today necessary resources to become a leading transport artery of world importance. It remains the great bridge connecting Europe and Asia, and it should execute the mission to the full extent.

## ENDNOTES

1. *Economic Integration of European North-East, Ural and Siberia,* Novosibirsk, 2002, p. 58.
2. *Siberian Peasantry in the Epoch of Capitalism*, Novosibirsk, 1982, p. 116 (in Russian).
3. S. Yu Witte, *Memoirs*, St. Petersburg, 1994, p. 92 (in Russian)
4. Sergey Sigachyov. How the Trans-Siberian Railroad Was Built, 31 January1999. <http://www.geocities.com/MotorCity/Speedway/4283/dates.htm> (20 November 2003).
5. *Encyclopedia Americana* International Edition. Danbury, Connecticut, Scholastic Library Publishing Inc, 2004. s.v. "Trans-Siberian Railroad".
6. A.A. Khramkov, Rail Transportation of Bread from Siberia in Western Direction in the end of XIX - the Beginning of XX Centuries, *Businessmen and Business in Siberia*. Vol. 3. 2001. p. 28.
7. Russian Railways: <http://eng.rzd.ru/isvp/public/rzdeng?STRUCTURE_ID=87>

# 16

## North-South Corridor: Prospects and Challenges for India

*Meena Singh Roy*

Central Asia provides a transit route for the Asian and European continents. Through history, it has been the meeting point for traders, travellers and mercantile communities from India, Iran, China and Europe.[1] By the first century BC, the Silk Route was the longest network of land trade routes in ancient time, connecting cities over a dozen countries, which included China, Central Asian Republics (CARs), Afghanistan, and ancient Taxila on the Indian subcontinent, Iraq, Alexandria, and Rome. In fact Silk Route was not one but a network of many routes.[2] For centuries one saw the bazaars all along these routes filled with crowds of people speaking diverse languages. Long caravans went along these dusty roads carrying precious gems and silks, spices and dyes, gold and silver, exotic birds and animals to European countries.[3] Merchant cargoes also included salt, wool, jade and many other items.[4] This was also the route through which Buddhism travelled to other parts of the world. It was in the 19th century that the Central Asian region became the region of barriers and conflict rather than the area which used to connect the economies and people along the famous Silk Route. Now the region became an area of Great Game between the imperial powers. In current times, the 'New Silk Road strategy' is being pursued by various actors to gain greater influence in this resource rich region.

The significance of Central Asia's geographic location and its transit potential was realised by the international community immediately after its emergence in 1991. Since then the process of developing new transport networks and reviving the corridors, linking Central Asia and South Asia with Europe, has been underway. In this context, the International North-South Transport Corridor (INSTC) that connects South Asia, Central Asia and Europe is one of the important projects. This is a multi modal transportation network established on 12 September 2000 at St. Petersburg, by Iran, Russia and India for the purpose of promoting transportation cooperation among the member states.

This study is an attempt to understand various dynamisms related to the North South Corridor and other initiatives taken by India to improve the connectivity with Central Asia. It examines the importance of this corridor and analyses the challenges and prospects for India. The paper argues that INSTC is an important corridor for India. However, it has not been able to utilise the full potential of this gateway to Central Asia because of three factors: economic and geopolitical interests of the regional and extra-regional powers; security fears and political differences among the states and finally geographical and economic constraints. Before we analyse the North-South corridor it is important to understand how important Central Asia is for India and what are its interests.

## Central Asia's Importance for India

For India, importance of Central Asia lies in its historical and civilisational links. As noted by an Indian analyst, "Few regions of the World can claim such uninterrupted multifaceted ties going back to antiquity as India and Central Asia".[5] Today, the importance of Central Asia is not merely civilisational and historical, it goes much beyond this. Central Asia, which lies as a bridge between Asia and Europe, rich in natural resources and the shortest transit route to Europe, is geopolitically axial and offers lot of economic opportunities.

This region is of great strategic significance to India.[6] India's security interests in CARs emanate from its geo-strategic location. It shares borders with China, Afghanistan and is located in proximity to Pakistan occupied Kashmir (POK). In fact, CARs can play an important role in maintaining peace along Afghanistan's northern border, to battle *jihadis*, drug traffickers and to stop the flow of illegal weapons.[7] Both India and CARs share many commonalities and perceptions on different world issues. There is scope for pragmatic and profitable engagement between the two sides. The focus of relationship between the CARs and India can be defined by the importance of Central Asia for peace and stability in our region. However, India's limitation in this strategically important region is non-accessibility, as India does not share border with the CARs.

Trade and economic relations between India and CARs stay the most unsatisfactory aspect of an otherwise what can be a potentially beneficial relationship. The ground situation portrays a very low level of trade (Graph-I), limited number of joint ventures and no worthwhile investment in Central Asia by Indian business and industry. Nevertheless, potential for comparative economic advantages for the two regions is vast. Central Asia provides a sizeable consumer market for a range of goods and services, which India can provide. In future, these countries are likely to offer good economic opportunity for India. Their GDP growth has been different, yet promising (see Table 1). Both have economic complementarities in terms of resources, manpower and markets. For India economic cooperation is possible through joint ventures in banking, insurance, agriculture, information technology, and the pharmaceutical industry.

**Graph I: India-Central Asia Trade 1996-2010**
**(in US million $)**

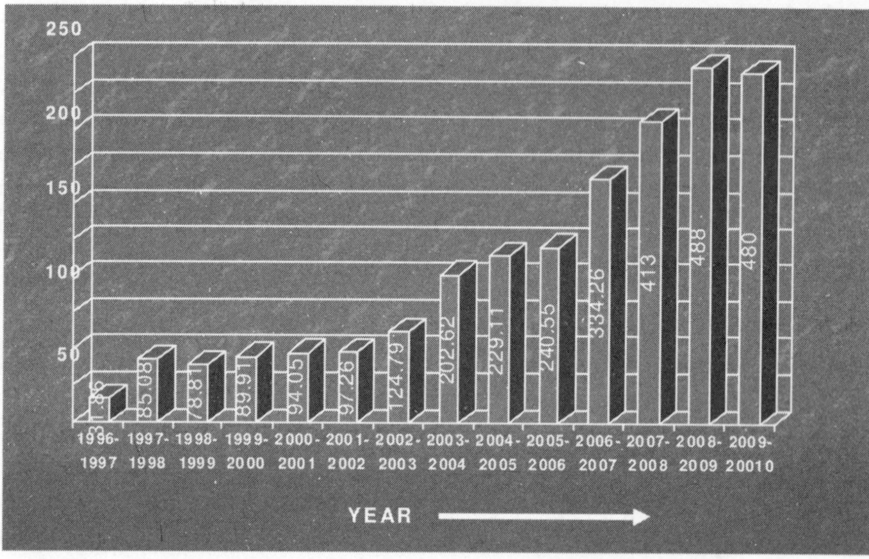


**Source:** Ministry of Commerce, India at http://commerce.nic.in/eidb/default.asp

**Table 1: GDP Growth in Central Asian Republics (Annual %)**

| Country | 2001 | 2002 | 2003 | 2004 | 2005 | 2006 | 2007 | 2008 | 2009 | 2010* | 2011* |
|---|---|---|---|---|---|---|---|---|---|---|---|
| Kazakhstan | 13.5 | 9.8 | 9.2 | 9.4 | 9.4 | 10.6 | 8.6 | 8.9 | 1.2 | 4.8 | 5.2 |
| Kyrgyzstan | 5.3 | 0.0 | 7.0 | 7.0 | 0.6 | 2.6 | 4.0 | 5.0 | 2.3 | -3.5 | 7.0 |
| Tajikistan | 10.2 | 9.5 | 10.1 | 10.6 | 6.7 | 7.0 | 7.5 | 7.1 | 3.4 | 4.5 | 5.5 |
| Turkmenistan | 20.2 | 19.8 | 23.0 | 21.0 | 10.0 | 9.0 | 8.5 | 8.5 | 6.1 | 6.5 | 11.0 |
| Uzbekistan | 4.2 | 4.2 | 4.4 | 7.7 | 7.0 | 7.3 | 7.4 | 7.1 | 8.1 | 8.5 | 9.0 |

**Projections* http://www.adb.org/Documents/Books/ADO/2010/Update/ado2010-update-subregional.pdf (Accessed on January 20, 2011)
**Source:** *Asian Development Outlook* database 2006-10.

Central Asia's importance also needs to be seen in the context of India's energy needs. Central Asian energy resources are of great significance to India. In addition to oil and gas, Central Asia also has uranium reserves. Kazakhstan, Uzbekistan and Turkmenistan have oil reserves and Turkmenistan has gas reserves. Central Asia could become important source of energy supply for India to meet its increasing energy demand for its economic growth. Currently, India is the sixth largest energy consumer in the world (with coal accounting for 52%, oil 40% and gas 7%) and is expected to emerge as the fourth largest consumer, after the US, China and Japan, by 2010. India imports 70 percent of its oil requirements and this is likely to grow up to 90 per cent by 2025. Its oil consumption is expected to rise to 245 million tons annually by 2020, the country is likely to be the World's single largest importer of oil by 2050. Similarly, India's demand for natural gas for the non-power sector alone is expected to increase from 120 million cubic meters a day (mcmd) to 391 mcmd by 2025.[8] India's gas consumption, 41.7 billion cum, is ten times higher than its production which is 31.7 billion cum.[9] (See Tables 2, 3, 4, 5)

**Table 2: World Uranium Production 2005 (Major Countries)**

| Country | Tonnes | % of total |
|---|---|---|
| Canada | 11,628 | 27.96 |
| Australia | 9,519 | 22.88 |
| Kazakhstan | 4,357 | 10.47 |
| Russia | 3,431 | 8.25 |
| Namibia | 3,147 | 7.57 |
| Niger | 3,093 | 5.53 |
| Uzbekistan | 2,300 | 5.53 |
| Total | 41,595 | 100.00 |

**Table 3: World Proven Gas Reserves – Top 10 Countries**

| | Country | Proven Gas Reserves (Trillion cubic metres) |
|---|---|---|
| 1 | Russia | 44.38 |
| 2 | Iran | 26.61 |
| 3 | Qatar | 25.37 |
| 4 | **Turkmenistan** | 8.10 |
| 5 | Saudi Arabia | 7.92 |
| 6 | US | 6.93 |
| 7 | UAE | 6.43 |
| 8 | Venezuela | 5.67 |
| 9 | Nigeria | 5.25 |
| 10 | Algeria | 4.50 |
| | **Uzbekistan*** | 1.74 |
| | **Kazakhstan*** | 1.90 |

**BP Statistical Review June 2008* in Energy Map of Russia & neighbouring countries 2009, Petroleum Economist, London at www.petroleum.economist.com. Here Kazakhstan and Uzbekistan only indicate their proven reserves and are not shown as part of Worlds top ten countries with gas reserve.

**Source:** *BP Statistical Review 2010* in World oil & Gas Map 2010/2011, Petroleum Economist, London at www.petroleum.economist.com

**Table 4: World's Proven Oil Reserves – Top 10 Countries**

| | Country | Proven oil Reserves (billion barrels) |
|---|---|---|
| 1 | Saudi Arabia | 264.6 |
| 2 | Vnezuela | 172.3 |
| 3 | Iran | 137.6 |
| 4 | Iraq | 115.0 |
| 5 | Kuwait | 101 |
| 6 | UAE | 97.8 |
| 7 | Russia | 74.2 |

*(Contd.)*

| | Country | Proven oil Reserves (billion barrels) |
|---|---|---|
| 8 | Libya | 44.3 |
| 9 | **Kazakhstan** | 39.8 |
| 10 | Nigeria | 37.2 |
| | **Turkmenistan*** | 0.6 |
| | **Uzbekistan*** | 0.6 |

* *BP Statistical Review June 2008* in Energy Map of Russia & neighbouring countries 2009, Petroleum Economist, London at www.petroleum.economist.com. Here Turkmenistan and Uzbekistan only indicate their proven reserves and are not shown as part of Worlds top ten countries with oil reserve.

**Source:** *BP Statistical Review 2010* in World Oil & Gas Map 2010/2011, Petroleum Economist, London; BP Statistical Review of World Energy 2008 in Energy Map of Russia & Neighbouring Countries 2009 at www.petroleum.economist.com

**Table 5: Share of Future Energy Supply in India (%)**

| Year | Coal | Oil | Gas | Hydro-electricity | Nuclear |
|---|---|---|---|---|---|
| 1997-98 | 55 | 35 | 7 | 2 | 1 |
| 2001-02 | 50 | 32 | 15 | 2 | 1 |
| 2006-07 | 50 | 32 | 15 | 2 | 1 |
| 2010-11 | 53 | 30 | 14 | 2 | 1 |
| 2024-25 | 50 | 25 | 20 | 2 | 3 |

**Source:** *Report of the Group on India Hydrocarbons Vision 2025.*

India's efforts to enhance its energy security have intensified significantly since 2004. India increasingly sees energy security as a national priority and central aspect of its foreign policy. Several committees have been working on Indian energy policy and security issues over the last few years. The first committee which was constituted in early 2004 under the Planning Commission, issued a "draft integrated energy policy" in mid-2005. In July 2005, Indian Prime Minister announced the establishment of an "Energy Co-ordination Committee" (ECC) to guide the country's energy policy. The ECC will enable the government to take a holistic view of India's energy needs and policy options. The Indian Strategic Petroleum Reserves Limited (ISPRL) was created in June 2004 and a general agreement was reached about the financing mechanism. The government expects to have 5 million tonnes of strategic reserves in place by 2009. Since late 2004, discussions of different pipeline options to import gas intensified. India's major limitation in this strategically important region is non-accessibility. India does not have direct access to Central Asia, as it does not share border with the CARs. To improve its connectivity India has been trying to explore routes through Iran, Russia and Afghanistan.

## New Strategic Environment and Significance of Transcontinental Corridors

The relevance of trade routes and corridors for the nation states is undisputable. While these routes have opened the opportunities and prospects for political, economic, scientific and cultural cooperation, they have also created a number of complex problems. On the one hand, they describe how transportation and communication networks have linked the communities of the globe; how it has spread religion, art, painting, peace and prosperity; how the physical features of the land influenced the location of the trade route, growth of settlements and cultural diffusion along those routes. On the other hand, it explains how empires have used these routes for wars, destruction, diplomacy, advancing their national interests and for expanding their influence.

This brings us to the question why these transcontinental corridors should be developed? Are these initiatives a part of the grand strategy adopted by the international community for the economic development of Eurasia or these initiatives are used by countries to promote their own interests and influence in this resource rich region? The current developments in the region indicate two trends: First, the struggle among the major powers to control the resources and pipelines in the region is underway. But it is also interesting to note, that development of these corridors is helping CARs improve their economies. It is also providing enormous opportunities to the neighbouring countries to enhance their trade with this region.

Jonathan Tennenbaum argues that by integrating the two poles,[10] Europe and Asia through a network of high-efficient infrastructure corridors,[11] and using these corridors as instruments to promote the rapid development of the relatively backward interior areas between them, has the potential to unleash a sustained period of real economic growth over the next 30-40 years. Such a project would have a worldwide economic impact, mainly due to the concentration of the human population (which is about three fourth of the total population on this planet) all along this corridor which connects Europe, South and East Asia.[12] Once these corridors are fully operational, they will not only promise considerable saving in transport cost, as compared to sea routes, but will promote greater regional economic development, and establish political stability in the region.

The competition among the major players (Russia, China and US) has brought about the geo-political competition for enhancing their influence and gaining foothold in the region to control the energy resources of CARs. While this power play in some ways has helped the region by bringing investment in the energy sector it has also brought about conflicting interests among these major players. This geo-political competition among major players and conflicting interests are in some ways also hampering the progress of new transport corridors and oil and gas pipelines which are being developed in this region.

To understand the unfolding situation it is important to examine the new security dynamics of Central Asia underscored by competing interests, of US, Russia and China. The end of cold war brought major consequences for the regional and international security system, hence new opportunities and challenges for various states. The security environment in Central Asia has undergone significant geopolitical shifts during the past few years. The major features of these shifts have been the increasing profile of Russia and China underscored by the 'Colour

Revolution' in Kyrgyzstan; unrest in Andijan leading to a significant change in Uzbekistan's foreign policy; closing of American military base in Uzbekistan; and the growing prominence of the Shanghai Cooperation Organisation (SCO).

China has been able to use the Silk Route to expand its political, economic and commercial engagements.[13] In the past 18 years China has used the Silk Route to increase its trade, and access the natural resources from Central Asian region. China stands to gain maximum from the corridors which are being developed in and around CARs. Central Asia is of great significance to China.[14] The SCO mirrors China's carefully calibrated approach towards Central Asia. These are mainly to integrate the Xinjiang region, address the problems of separatism, extremism, and terrorism within China's Xinjiang province,[15] and gain access to the region's energy resources.[16] In 2000, China unveiled its "go-west" policy, which represents a shift in the focus of development from coastal areas to the country's inland and western regions, including Xinjiang Uyghur Autonomous Region and Inner Mongolia Autonomous Region. This strategic shift has accelerated the increase in the trade volume between China and CARs and greater efforts on part of China to enhance the connectivity with this region. Besides its "go-west policy", China also sees Central Asia as a future source of its energy supply.[17] China imports nearly half the oil it uses, most of it from the unstable Middle East. With demand growing and domestic production unable to meet its needs, China now sees Central Asia as a vital energy source. China's Ministry of Finance estimated that by 2010, the country's annual energy needs will require the country to import 130 million tonnes of oil per year, up from the 60 million tonnes it imported in 2002.[18]

Though Central Asia may not figure as important and significant as the oil rich Gulf region but in recent years US has developed important stakes in and around Central Asia. This region is embedded with "strategic concerns" that lie at the core of the United States interests.[19] As Secretary of State, Colin L. Powell stated, "America will have a continued interest and presence in Central Asia of a kind that we could not have dreamt of before."[20] Post-9/11, officials in the U.S. felt that larger U.S. interest lied in ensuring that Central Asia does not become the next Afghanistan.[21] In addition to increasing its military profile US also enhanced its economic ties with the region. It signed a Trade and Investment Framework Agreement (TIFA) with all the five Central Asian states in June 2004. This agreement is intended to provide a forum for various trade issues and would increase and diversify trade and investment opportunities between the United States and Central Asia. The agreement also sets up a U.S.-Central Asia trade council. The United States imported $571 million in goods from Central Asia in 2003 and exported $548 million.[22]

While Washington's strategic, political and economic interests were seen growing stronger in Central Asia,[23] the ground realities suggest that its strategic position weakened considerably in 2006. Washington came out with new plans and worked towards creating a stronger Central-South Asian energy and trade links to counterbalance Russian influence. Richard A. Boucher, Assistant Secretary of State for South and Central Asian Affairs stated:

> Our goal is to revive ancient ties between South and Central Asia and to help create new links in the area of trade, transport, democracy, energy and communications. At the same time, we seek to preserve and enhance the ties of Central Asian countries to Europe, especially through organisations like NATO and its Partnership for Peace (PfP) and the Organisation for Security and Cooperation in Europe (OSCE) as well as the important interests Japan has in Central Asia.[24]

These plans were premised on the fears that China and Russia were pulling the region into their strategic fold and marginalising the US. Despite its weakening strategic position, its interests are very much intact and there are no signs of Washington's withdrawal from this region. Importantly, US role in Central Asian region will significantly impact the future political, economic and security trends.

Focused on the potential consequences of the new great power rivalry, Russia has moved to cement its Central Asian position in recent years by promoting multilateral organisations such as the Collective Security Treaty Organisation (CSTO) and the Shanghai Cooperation Organisation (SCO). In recent months Russian profile (economic, political and military) has been increasing in CARs.[25] Geographical proximity, past linkages, and politico-economic realities stamp Russia as an influential player in the region.

The increasing violence in Afghanistan and re-emergence of Taliban forces is a disturbing factor from the point of view of developing and connecting CARs through Afghanistan routes. This was pointed out by President Obama in its revised Af-Pak Strategy where he stated that "Yet huge challenges remain. Afghanistan is not lost, but for several years it has moved backwards. There's no imminent threat of the government being overthrown, but the Taliban have gained momentum. Al Qaeda has not reemerged in Afghanistan in the same numbers as before 9/11, but they retain their safe havens along the border. ... In short: The status quo is not sustainable."[26] Therefore, for developing the new transport routes to CARs, the stability in Afghanistan is an important factor.

In such a scenario, the development of transport corridors in and around Central Asia would also be conditioned by the new strategic environment and competing interests of major players in this region. The complex relations between US-Iran-Russia, US-China, US-Russia and US-Central Asia are likely to have significant implications for building these corridors and pipelines. The US wants to deny Iran any entry in the energy sector of this resource rich region. Not so openly, but US also wants to bypass Russia in this sector. Therefore, how things would unfold in future is to be seen. Such a relationship of rivalry and competition is likely to slow down any process of development of transport infrastructure in the region.

## Transport Corridor: India's Initiatives

### *International North South Transport Corridor*

India like other regional powers has been keen to increase its connectivity with the region. India wants Central Asia to be part of an extended trade network through north-south corridor. The inter-governmental agreement between India, Iran and Russia was signed in St Petersburg on 12 September 2000.[27] This agreement has been ratified by all the three signatory states and it has been in force since 16 May 2002. This corridor connects Indian Ocean and Persian Gulf to the Caspian Sea via Islamic Republic of Iran, and then it is connected to St. Petersburg and North Europe via Russia. From India's point of view this is a very significant route.

Initially India, Iran and Russia were part of this agreement but over the years, other countries have become part of this agreement. (See Graph 2 and Table 6) The INSTC has now expanded to include eleven new members, namely: Republic of Azerbaijan, Republic of Armenia, Republic of Kazakhstan, Kyrgyz Republic, Republic of Tajikistan, Republic of Turkey, Republic of Ukraine, Republic of Belarus, Oman, Syria, Bulgaria (as Observer).The corridor is much more than a link connecting just Mumbai, Tehran and Moscow. It provides Europe access to Asia and vice versa. The Russian network of roads and railroads are connected to Central and Western Europe via Eastern Europe. Iran has land links to Central Asia and its ports offer warm water sea routes to India.

The potential of this corridor will be manifold with India, Myanmar and Thailand getting linked by road. This will boost trade between Europe and South East Asia as well. As compared to the route through Suez Canal and the Mediterranean sea that is currently used, INSTC is much shorter and cost effective.[28]

**Graph 2: Accession Process in International North-South Transport Corridor**

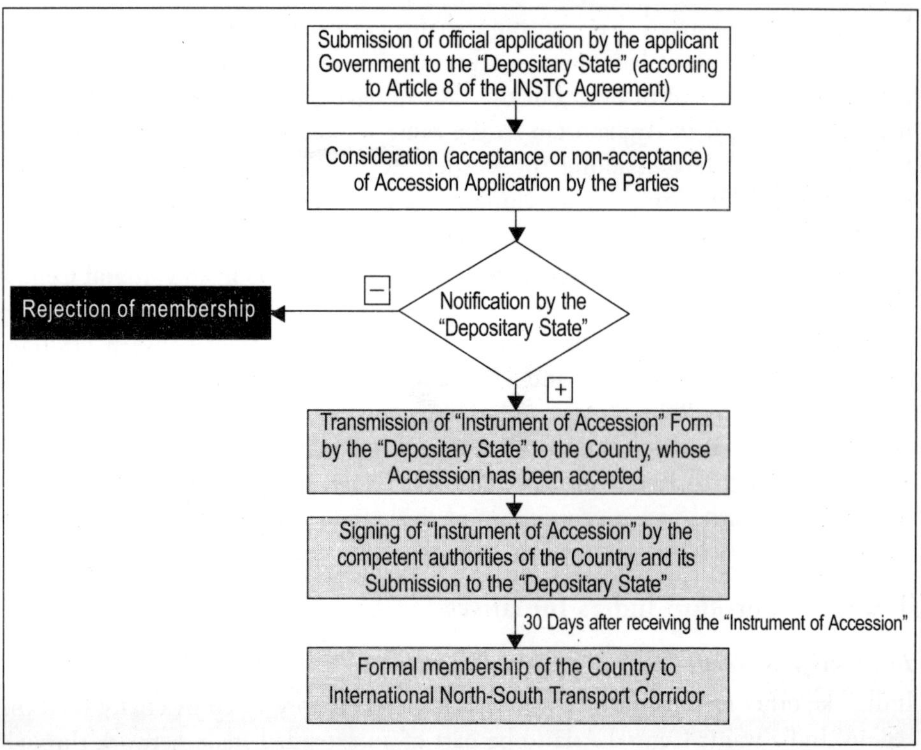

**Table 6: Member States of North South Corridor**

| Member Countries | Requested Date For Membership | Approved Date of Membership by: Iran | Russia | India | Received Date of Instrument of Accession | Date of Membership |
|---|---|---|---|---|---|---|
| Kazakhstan | 24 Oct 02 | 07 Apr 02 | 22 Feb 03 | 31 Oct 02 | 06 Aug 03 | 06 Sep 03 |
| Belarus | 19 Mar 02 | 07 Apr 02 | 22 Feb 03 | 31 Oct 02 | 14 Dec 03 | 10 Jan 04 |
| Oman | 08 Oct 02 | 01 Feb 03 | 13 May 03 | 07 Jan 03 | 08 Nov 04 | 08 Dec 04 |
| Tajikistan | 20 Jun 02 | 01Feb 03 | 13 May 03 | 07 Jan 03 | 08 Nov 05 | 08 Dec 05 |
| Bulgaria | 24 Apr 01 | 08 Jun 03 | 14 Feb 06 | 31 Oct 02 | From 11 Apr 06 Observer Member | |
| Azerbaijan | 31 Dec01 | 08 Jun 03 | 11 Nov 04 | 31 Oct 02 | 12 Dec 05 | 12 Jan 06 |
| Armenia | 05 Jun 01 | 08 Jun 03 | 11 Nov 04 | 31 Oct 02 | 20 Dec 06 | 20 Jan 06 |
| Syria | 14 Jan 04 | 05 Jul 04 | 11 Nov 04 | 11 Jun 03 | 22 Jan 06 | 22 Feb 06 |
| Ukraine | 23 Jan 03 | 08 Jun 04 | 14 Feb 06 | 20 Apr 04 | | |
| Turkey | 14 Mar 04 | 08 Jun 04 | 14 Feb06 | 19 Nov 04 | | |
| Kyrgyzstan | 27 Sep 04 | 02 Dec 04 | 14 Feb 06 | 17 Aug 05 | | |

**Source:** http://www.instc.org/MemberShip/MemberShip.asp (accessed on 14 Oct 2008).

The Suez Canal route takes 45-60 days, whereas this route would take only 25-30 days. In fact, the INSTC is 40 per cent shorter and 30 per cent cheaper. From India's point of view the North-South Corridor not only helps India bypass Pakistan and yet reach out to Central Asia but also enables it to transport goods at cheaper cost to European markets. (Maps 1-2)

To make this route more usable, governments of India, Iran and Russia have been working together. The 4th Session of Coordination Council and 5th Session

**Map 1: North-South Corridor**

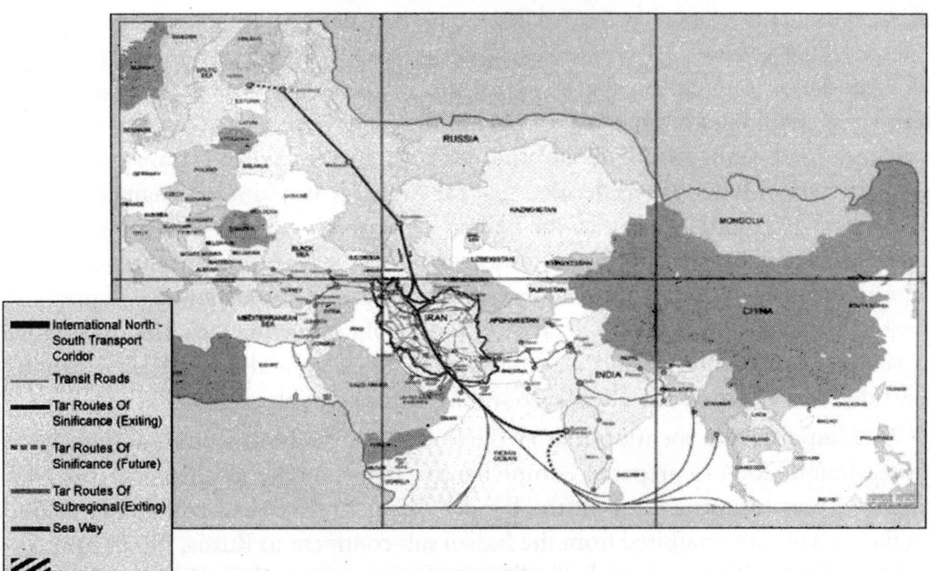


**Source:** http://www.instc.org/Map/Map.asp

**Map 2: Previous Route and New Route**

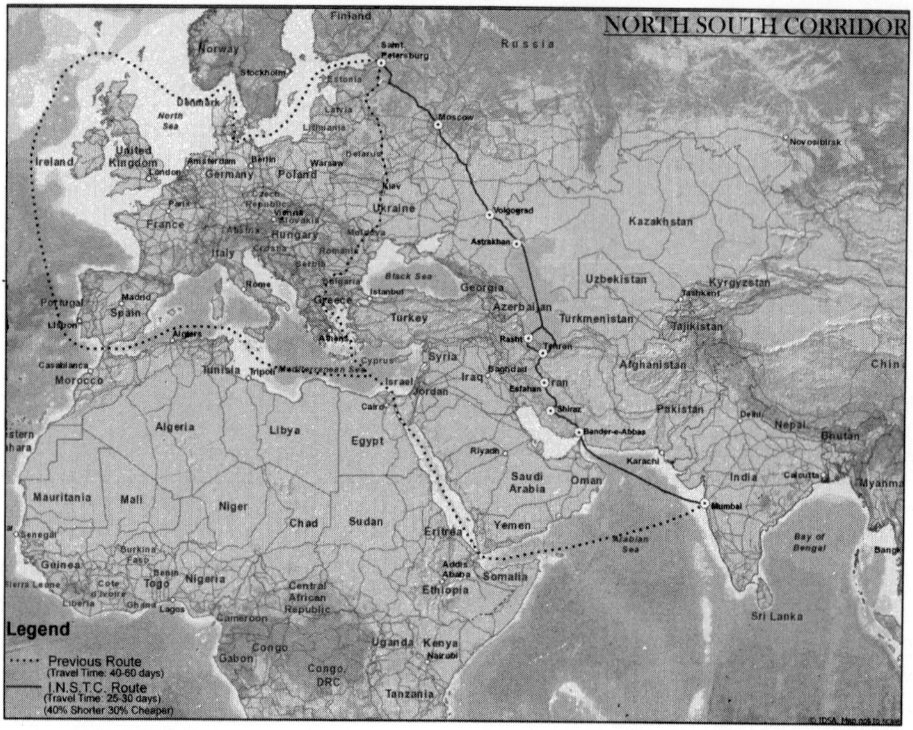


**Source:** IDSA Database.

of the Expert Group of "International North-South Transport Corridor" was held on 2-3 November 2007 in Astana, Kazakhstan. This Session considered the results of the agreements adopted at the 3rd Session of the Coordination Council of INSTC (October 2005, New Delhi) and discussed ways to develop coordinated position on extension of the transit capacity of corridor. Prior to this, the study group from Iran visited India in October 2007. During their eight day visit, they met marine, rail and road transportation companies and the ports and transportation infrastructure in India. It was decided that the NOSTRAC Planning Council would dispatch study groups from India, the Islamic Republic of Iran and Russia to member States to inspect the transportation infrastructures as well as the transportation and transit potentials of the relevant countries. Accordingly each study group will prepare a report for activation of the NOSTRAC Corridor after studying the potential transit capacities of each country and identification of obstacles and issues related to the Corridor and to provide applicable solutions to these problems.

It is important to mention that at the first stage, the Indian Study Group had visited Iran in 2004 to prepare a comprehensive report on the facilities and the rail, road and port infrastructures on the Bandar Abbas to Amirabad and Anzali route on the path of cargo transited from the Indian sub-continent to Russia, North Europe and Scandinavia. The result of the findings in the report was submitted to the Iranian transportation organizations and stakeholders to remove the obstacles and increase the facilities and the road, rail and port capacities.[29]

Despite various initiatives taken by member countries, the North-South Corridor has not been utilized by member countries to its existing potential for several reasons. Firstly, there is a need to upgrade the rail and road networks and other related infrastructure within the member states of INSTC. This demands heavy investments by member countries which could be a problem. In fact the potential of this corridor will be determined by the funds available with the member countries.

Secondly, the North-South corridor runs through the politically unstable Caucasus region. Few will be willing to send cargo through conflict-ridden Chechnya or Daghestan. Besides, some western countries are reluctant to opt for a route that runs through Iran. In addition to this for the expansion of this route stability in Afghanistan is an important factor. Finally, it will take some years for shipping companies to take the risk of putting their cargo through an unexplored passage. However, the political support seems to be slowly building not only among India, Iran and Russia but in Central Asia as well. Kazakh President Nursultan Nazarbaev supports the Turkmen-Iranian agreement to include Iran in a regional railway project. Turkmenistan, Kazakhstan and Iran have signed a trilateral agreement for linking their railways systems together. Such regional initiatives will enhance the potential of the INSTC.

## Other Initiatives

New railroads, modern pipelines and hydroelectric lines are being built in and around Central Asia. Uzbekistan is extending its rail links to Mazar-e-Sharif with the financial help from Asian Development Bank (ADB). In Tajikistan, a road across Pamir Mountains from China to new US built bridge to Afghanistan has been opened with help from Iran and China. In addition a rail line from Dushanbe to the Afghan border is also being planned. Pakistan and China are building the main north-south road across Pakistan that will link Afghanistan through the Khyber Pass to China and the Arabian Sea. The Gwadar port built with the help from China will provide Central Asia and Afghanistan important sea link to West Asia. Iran is extending its railroad and highway system to Herat in Afghanistan.[30] It is also constructing new port at Chabahar. Aforesaid initiatives can bring about immense economic prosperity in this region if all the regional countries-India-Iran-China-CARs-Pakistan can work towards cooperative regional framework to provide this network of rail, road and energy pipelines.

India has also been exploring the possibility of land route option through Iran and Turkmenistan. In this context the trilateral agreement on international transit of goods between Turkmenistan, India and Iran was signed in February 1997 at Tehran.[31] Before this, in April 1995, a trilateral Memorandum of Understanding on trade and transit to facilitate the use of Iranian and Turkmen territory for trade with other Central Asian countries was signed.[32] However, full potential of these routes is yet to be utilised for which greater initiative is needed by signing countries.

India's External Affairs Minister during his visit to Tajikistan in January 2003 said, "We wish to bring out the best, so that trade between Central Asia and India increases manifold. Not just in one direction, but in both directions"[33] India has air connectivity with the Central Asian Republics. India is also trying to open new sea and road route through Iran and Afghanistan. India has built 200 kms of road in Afghanistan linking Zaranj and Delaram. This reduces the distance from India to Central Asia by 1,500 kms.[34] There is also a possibility to extend this road to reach to Tajikistan and Uzbekistan.

Another important initiative was taken during Prime Minister Atal Behari Vajpayee's two-day visit to Tajikistan in November 2003.This visit was seen as a landmark in not only enhancing the Indo-Tajik cooperation but also in improving the links with Central Asian region. Agreements were signed on establishing direct air links between Dushanbe and New Delhi, opening up of Tajik mission in Delhi, and forming of a working group (represented by Afghanistan, India and Tajikistan) on a direct land route between two countries via Afghanistan. The Indian Prime Minister expressed his desire to extend the New Delhi-Dushanbe air route to Kabul. The main theme of this meeting was the importance of developing regional transport infrastructure to improve Tajikistan's economic outlook. On the eve of this visit Tajik parliament endorsed a resolution to join the Treaty on International Transit of Goods, a tripartite agreement between India, Iran, and Turkmenistan dating from 1997. The treaty aims to facilitate trade cooperation by eliminating various import duties and customs procedures.[35]

India has another option to build land road to reach Central Asia through Xinjiang and Tibet into Ladakh or Himachal Pradesh. China is already connected through railway link (which is 1,350 km) from Almaty to Urumchi in Xinjiang.[36] The extension of China-Kyrgyz overland route to India through road would benefit all the countries concerned.

The aforesaid initiatives indicate that after 2000 India's policy towards Central Asia has been more focused and coherent. It has been trying to improve its connectivity with the Central Asian states. Given its geographical limitations, India has three options to improve its connectivity. First, to engage China and work with it in sectors where their interests converge (e.g. IT sector) and initiate discussion with China for opening the corridor to Central Asia. India's option to reach CARs through Xinjiang and Tibet into Ladakh or Himachal Pradesh needs a serious consideration. This would be a win-win situation for not only India and China but also the CARs. This could significantly transform the geopolitics of the region.

Second, build intense cooperation with Iran, Russia, CARs and Afghanistan to make INSTC work effectively and to build new routes through Afghanistan to Central Asia. This option is the most promising one due to India's friendly relations with all the three countries. Third option is that of engaging Pakistan. The important project in the southern direction is that of Turkmenistan-Afghanistan-Pakistan route (this includes both railway as well as route to export energy from Central Asia). This is the shortest route from Central Asia to South Asia.[37] There are serious problems with this route; as far as railroad is concerned, there is competition between Turkmenistan and Uzbekistan. While Uzbekistan wants this railroad to pass through Termez, Turkmenistan wants it to start from Kushka. Moreover the situation in Afghanistan is also not conducive to carry out such a project. There are serious security concerns related to this route, both for transport corridor and pipeline in India because of tensions between India and Pakistan.

In this context, the recent dialogues between India and Pakistan had raised some hopes for this pipeline. In fact, some experts are of the view that such cooperation between India and Pakistan would be the biggest confidence building measures (CBMs) for peace between the two.[38] But possibility of such a route would depend on how India-Pakistan relations evolve in future. Of all the corridors Pakistan-Afghanistan corridor is not only economically viable, but would also serve as a confidence building measure (CBM) between the two countries. However, volatility of India-Pakistan relations has been the biggest political hurdle in developing this corridor. It is also important to note that the most powerful approach to address international and regional problems is through building strong economic ties. In case of India and Pakistan, the opening of overland routes between them to CARs, can open an era of mutually beneficial economic relations not only for these two countries but for the entire region.

## Impediments in Reviving and Developing New Corridors

There are inherent constraints limiting the progress of developing the regional transport infrastructure. In this respect some scholars believe that "it is an irony that silk route is no longer a bridge but an obstacle for cooperation"[39] The main impediments for building the new transport corridors in Central Asian region are[40]:

- Geographical Constraints
- Security fears and political differences
- Economic constraints

First and the foremost impediment in developing these new routes is geographical constraint. Central Asia inherited a network of transport routes linking the region to Moscow, but with very little alternative options for its links to the outside world. During early years after independence, CARs were unable to maintain even the Soviet time infrastructure. Various factors starting from poor economic conditions, civil war in Tajikistan, lack of funds to break down in inter-economic ties led to the decline in internal transport infrastructure. Out of five republics, Uzbekistan had a relatively developed transport network. It still has the highest density rail and road network in Central Asia.[41] It also has good international air links, though its regional air links remain limited. As compared to Uzbekistan, Kazakhstan and Turkmenistan, the transport network in Tajikistan and Kyrgyzstan is poor and needs urgent upgrading. In Kyrgyzstan, some 70 per cent of roads are believed to be in urgent need of upgrading. Over 50 per cent of bridges do not meet the existing requirements in terms of the vehicles size or axle load. In Tajikistan, the situation remains extremely limited. There is lack of direct road connections to state capitals, production centres, markets, and ports. In addition to above there are non-physical barriers as well. These include unjustified delay while crossing the border, bureaucratic trammels, frequent changes in transit regulations, arbitrary practices while weighing goods, high transit charges (especially for foreigners) as well as officials and unofficial taxes imposed by authorities controlling international shipments. With respect to the rail transport the key issues affecting the region are:

- The dislocations caused by the break up of the railways into national units have resulted in numerous cross-border operational obstacles. Among these obstacles are a lack of track-sharing agreements, lack of joint planning of infrastructure investment, frequent changes of locomotives and crews at borders, time consuming and expensive train remarshalling at borders, complicated documentation requirements, and inter-railway payment delays.
- Technology is obsolete and poor in quality, and management lacks a developed marketing orientation. This has contributed to excessive tariffs for international traffic, tariffs that do not separate movement and terminal costs, lack of convenient billing systems, and lack of consignment information for shippers.

Second, important impediment is that of security fears and political differences within Central Asian states and among the countries interested in developing these new routes. There are inherent border disputes between the Central Asian states. Despite improved security situation after the end of Taliban rule in Afghanistan, there has been very little improvement in the border regimes between these Republics. The issue of border delimitation remains unresolved, which has very often ended into border disputes. This has restricted the possible development of regional trade development. Security fears emanating from Afghanistan have further hampered the development of these new corridors. The long-term investments in developing various transport networks and pipelines have slowed due to the political differences among countries, which are interested in the region. Political differences between Iran-US and India-Pakistan are some of the examples.

Insufficient economic growth in the region and low level of investment has also hampered any meaningful progress in developing the transport infrastructure. Since economic conditions are unlikely to improve rapidly in Central Asia (with an exception of Kazakhstan and Turkmenistan due to their energy exports) in the short term, the major investment in transport infrastructures would be low. Perhaps Kazakhstan and Turkmenistan would be able to fund significant transport improvements from their own financial resources. To take the example of Kazakhstan, it needs to be mentioned that Kazakhstan's transport infrastructure, which includes railroad, motorways, air, water, and pipeline transport, is a priority sector for the country. The transport and communication complex contributes about 13 per cent of GDP in Kazakhstan.[42] According to Kazakhstan's transport ministry, it invested 319 million dollars in roads projects in 2004, which includes $72 million in borrowed funds. Financing in road sector grew to $414 million in 2005. Kazakhstan planned to invest $1.1 billion in the railroad industry in 2004-2006, including $900 million of its own money and $201 million in borrowed funds.[43]

In order to arouse the interest of foreign shippers in the current and planned transit routes, Central Asian governments will have to establish closer and more efficient cooperation in customs and tariff policy.[44] It is also important to note that the transit rates are different in different Republics causing problems. The transit rate in Uzbekistan and Turkmenistan are $460 and $740 respectively, whereas in Kazakhstan it is $66.[45] In this respect Kazakhstan has asked other countries to consider abolishing the transit permit fee for automobile transport. It has reached such agreement with Russia and Kyrgyzstan. For any effective progress in the development of the transport network, greater regional cooperation is required.

## Conclusion

To conclude, it can be said that while opportunities for developing the new routes to Central Asian region exist, greater regional and international cooperation is required. Central Asian countries involved in developing these routes need to take commensurate political and economic steps to make full use of the prospects. While elements of competition and rivalry remain the main feature of the power play in Central Asia, there lies an opportunity for these countries to advance their mutual interests in partnership to develop a cooperative mechanism and address the challenges and constraints faced by them in developing various transport networks in the region. Multilateral and regional cooperation remains the most important and effective means to manage the deficiencies of the transport sector in CARs.

## ENDNOTES

1. "A Perspective for Central Asia-India Relation: Common Ties of History" *The Times of Central Asia*, January 27, 2000. The Islamic geographer Yaqut noted in the twelfth century that "a prosperous merchant of Merv had one warehouse on the Volga river and another in Gujarat, India and he owned his prosperity to his role as a middle man in trade." Central Asia was a meeting point for traders and travellers, where mercantile communities lived in perfect harmony.
2. It was a network of roads, going East to West, with spurs into Southern Iran, the northern Eurasian steppe, and south over the Hindu Kush to the Indian Subcontinent.
3. "Great Silk Road", *http://www.orexca.com/silkroad.php*
4. Susan Whitfield, *Life Along the Silk Road*, London, John Murray Ltd., 1999, p. 2.
5. Devendra Kaushik, "India and Central Asia renewing a traditional relationship" *South Asian Survey*, Vol. 5(2), July-December 1998, p. 231.
6. See Meena Singh Roy, "India's Interests in Central Asia" *Strategic Analyses*, Vol. 24 (12), March 2001.
7. Views expressed by Jasjit Singh, former Director, IDSA in Rahul Bedi, "India dabbles in the new 'great game'" *Jane's Intelligence Review*, Vol. 13 (6), June 2002, p.19.
8. Speech by Foreign Secretary at National Maritime Foundation on "India as a Consensual Stakeholder in the Indian Ocean: Policy Contours", November 19, 2010, at http://meaindia.nic.in/mystart.php?id=530116701 (accessed on November 30, 2010); Report of the Group on India Hydrocarbon Vision 2025.
9. EIA, " India", March 2009 at www.eia.doe.gov/india, (accessed on April14,2010); CIA World Fact Book, "India", 2007 at www.cia.gov/library/publication/the-world-factbook/countrylisting.html (accessed on 14 April 2010)

10. At one pole there is Europe, having scientific-technologically advanced industrial potential. At other pole there is East and South Asia with their enormous population, vast natural resources and significant industrial capabilities.
11. By 'infrastructure development corridors' what he means is the building up a basic network of high-efficiency, high-speed transport lines reaching into the hinterland and at the same time concentrating additional investment into creating a dense network of secondary 'capillaries' in the form of transport, energy, water, communications and other basic infrastructure within the band-like region located along the main transport lines.
12. Jonathan Tennenbaum, "The Eurasian Land Bridge", *World Affairs,* Vol.8 (1), 2007, p.37.
13. John Calabrese, "China's Policy towards Central Asia: Renewal and Accommodation", *Eurasian Studies,* Vol.16, Autumn-Winter 1999, pp. 75-97; Adam Wolfe, "China takes the lead in strategic Central Asia", *http://www.atimes.com/atimes/China/fl17Ad04.html.*
14. There are three main reasons for increasing Chinese interests, oil and gas, improving trade especially in Chinese western provinces and thirdly, security, primarily the Uyghur movement in Xinjiang. Heda Bayron, "China Flexes Economic & Diplomatic Muscles in Central Asia", *http://www1.voanews.com/article.efm?objectID=CB497C79-4AE6-4BCB-90 FC85D189...*
15. China faces a host of Uyghur insurgent groups – United Revolutionary Front of Eastern Turkestan, Xinjiang Liberation Organization, Uyhgur Liberation Organization, Wolves of Lop Nor, Free Turkistan Movement, Home of East Turkistan Youth, and Organization for the Liberation of Uyghuristan. See Dewardic McNeal, "China's relations with Central Asian states and problems with terrorism", in US Department of State, Congressional Research Service Report for Congress, 17 December 2001, at http://fpc.state.gov/documents/organisation/7945.pdf; Russell Ong, n. 6.
16. Li Lifan and Ding Shiwu, "Geopolitical interests of Russia, the U.S. and China in Central Asia", *Central Asia and Caucasus,* (Sweden) Vol. 3 (27), 2004, p. 144.
17. Huasheng Zhao, "Central Asia in China's Diplomacy", Eugene Rumer, Dmitri Trenin, and Huasheng Zhao edt. *Central Asia View from Washington, Moscow and Beijing,* M.E. Sharpe, New York, 2007 pp. 137-213. Taleh Ziyadov, "Prospects of Caspian gas and its potential markets", Central Asia and the Caucasus, Vol. 5(29), 2004, pp. 52-60; *http://www.adb.org/Documents/csps/CARE/2004/appendix9.pdf*
18. International Energy Agency (IEA) estimates that by 2020, China is projected to become the second largest consumer of oil in the world, next only to the U.S.; *http://www.eia.doe.gov*
19. Meena Singh Roy, "Central Asian Republics: The US factor". Paper presented at IDSA fellow Seminar on 20 December 2003.
20. Vernon Loeb, "Footprints in Steppes of Central Asia", *Washington Post,* 9 February 2002. This is Powell's statement to the House International Relations Committee on 7 February 2002.
21. "Securing Central Asia", *The Times of Central Asia* (Bishkek), Vol. 4 (8) (155), 21 February 2002, p. 4.
22. "United States Signs Trade Frame work with Central Asia", *http://www.eurasianet.org/resource/uzbekistan/hypermail/200406/0006.shtml*
23. Heather Maher, "Central Asia: U.S. Helsinki Commission Concerned About SCO's Influence", at http://www.edi.org/russia/johnson/2006-217-40.efm, and www.rferl.org; The Overseas Basing Commission in its May 2005 Report, acknowledged that US national security might be enhanced by future Cooperative Security Locations (CSLS) in Central Asia. For details see Jim Nichol, "Central Asia: Regional Developments and Implications for U.S. Interests", *CRS Brief for Congress,* Foreign Affairs, Defense, and Trade Division, Update 12 May 2006 at http://digital.library.unt.edu/govdocs/crs/data/2006/upl-meta-crs-8922/1B93108-2006may12.pdf
24. "U.S. Policy in Central Asia: Balancing Priorities (Part II)", Richard A. Boucher, Assistant Secretary of State for South and Central Asian Affairs, Statement to the House

International Relations Committee, Subcommittee on the Middle East and Central Asia, 26 April 2006 at http://www.state.gov/p/sca/rls/rm/2006/65292.htm

25. Meena Singh Roy, "Changing Contours of Russia Central Asia relations" *World Focus*, vol. 125 (3), March 2004, p.12.
26. "Remarks by the President in Address to the Nation on the Way Forward in Afghanistan and Pakistan" at http://www.whitehouse.gov/the-press-office/remarks-president-address-nation-way-forward-afghanistan-and-pakistan (accessed on December 2,2009)
27. Amit Baruah, "India to build key roads in Afghanistan", *The Hindu*, 21 November 2002
28. National Report of Iran on the latest measures taken in line with promotion of multimodal Transport, Iran Ministry of Roads and Transportation, General Directorate of International Affairs, November 2004; A. Spector, "The North-South Transport Corridor", http://www.brook.edu/printme.wbs?page=/pagedefs/e9e50344b3c7ff3b4670f6410a14146
29. http://www.instc.org/Main.asp (Accessed on 15 November 2007)
30. S. Frederick Starr, Afghanistan Beyond the Fog of Nation Building: Giving Economic Strategy a Chance, *Silk Road Paper*, January 2011, Central Asia-Caucasus Institute Silk Road Studies Program at http://www.silkroadstudies.org/new/docs/silkroadpapers/1101Afghanistan-starr.pdf. accessed on January 20, 2011.
31. Ministry of External Affairs Reports (Government of India), 1996-97, p. 32.
32. Ibid, 1995-96, pp. 32-33.
33. External Affairs Minister's Address at the Tajik National State University, 29 January 2003 in *http://www.meadev.nic.in/speeches/eam-tajikuniv.htm*
34. Keynote Address by Yashwant Sinha, Minister of External Affairs of the Republic of India at Third India-Central Asia Regional Conference, Tashkent November 6, 2003; Voice of the Islamic Republic of Iran, Mashad, BBC Global Monitoring-Central Asia, 6 January 2003.
35. Radio Free Europe/Radio Liberty (RFE/RL), Prague, *Central Asia Report*, Vol. 3 (39), 21 November 2003.
36. *The Times of Central Asia*, 1 May 2003.
37. Igor Azovskiy, "Railroads in Central Asian Countries: Problems and Prospects", *Central Asia and the Caucasus*, (Sweden), No.1 (25) 2004 p133-135.
38. Hilal A. Raza, "Potential of Trade in oil and Gas," in Jasjit Singh (ed.) *Oil and Gas in India's Security*, New Delhi, Knowledge World, 2001, pp. 101-106.
39. P. Stobdan, "Reviving the silk route-the way Forward", Paper presented in Seminar on "Central Asia and Indian Business: Emerging trends and Opportunities" organized by Confederation of Indian Industry, Delhi, 22 May 2003.
40. David Lewis, "Transportation and Communication Corridors in the Context of Central Asia", Paper presented in "3rd India-Central Asia Regional Conference" Organized jointly by Institute for Defence Studies and Analyses and Uzbekistan's Institute for Strategic and Regional Studies at Tashkent November 6-8 2003; Igor Azovskiy, n. 37; L. Gusseva, "Transit potential of the Central Asian region's transport complex: conditions and prospects of development," *Central Asia's Affairs*, (Almaty) No. 3 (3) 2003, p. 30; *http://www.adb.org/Documents/csps/CARE/2004/appendix9.pdf*
41. This density in Uzbekistan is with over 6,700 km of railways. Over 80 per cent of road surface are paved and are of higher standard than its neighbours.
42. According to the statistics agency, pipeline transport in the first half of 2004 totaled 94.1 million tonnes, up 16 per cent from the same period last year. This includes 29.7 million tones of oil and petroleum products, up 23.6 per cent year-on-year, and 64.4million tonnes of gas, up 13.2 per cent. "Transport System in Kazakhstan," *http://www.interfax.com/com?item=Kaz&a=on&id=5747489*
43. *http://www.interfax.com/com?item=Kaz&a=on&id=5747489*
44. L. Gusseva, n. 7, p. 34.
45. *http://www.interfax.com/com?item=Kaz&a=on&id=5747489*

# 17

# Ladakh: India's Gateway to Central Asia

*K. Warikoo*

With its borders abutting Xinjiang and Tibet regions of China to its north and east, and Baltistan/Skardo in Pak-occupied Kashmir to its west, Ladakh enjoys a unique geo-strategic location. Due to its contiguity with Xinjiang and Tibet and its close proximity to Central Asia, Ladakh played an important role in the history and culture of this frontier region. Enjoying a central position in the network of overland caravan routes that were linked to the Silk Route, Ladakh acted as an important gateway in the Indo-Central Asian exchange of men, materials and ideas through the ages. However, during the nineteenth and early twentieth centuries, the extent and pattern of these exchanges was influenced on the one hand by the state of diplomatic relations between the three empires – Britain, Russia and China, and on the other hand by the level of influence exercised by the Dogra rulers of Jammu and Kashmir. Whereas 1830s witnessed the beginning of Great Game played by Britain and Russia in Central Asia, it was during this period that Ladakh came under Dogra control. It was by 1840 that the Dogra forces led by General Zorawar Singh had established their authority throughout Ladakh and Baltistan. In 1846, Ladakh became a part of the newly founded State of Jammu and Kashmir under the Dogra ruler Maharaja Gulab Singh and his successors. And after 1947, Ladakh including Kargil has been a province of Jammu and Kashmir State.

The Dogra rulers followed a pro-active policy towards Central Asia, as they despatched several secret missions to Yarkand, Kashgar etc. through Ladakh to maintain friendly contacts with the neighbouring Central Asian chiefs and also to acquire political intelligence about the rapidly changing course of events in Central Asia. Indo-Central Asian trade was developed through Ladakh, as the Srinagar-Leh-Yarkand trade route was declared a Treaty Road in 1870 through an agreement concluded between Maharaja Ranbir Singh and the British. And no duties on goods bound for Central Asia were levied on this route. Besides, two Joint Commissioners, one British and the other being the Maharaja's officer resident at Leh, were supervising the conduct of the Indo-Central Asian trade through Ladakh.

Numerous caravan routes that converged near Leh acted as the channels of communication between India and Central Asia. From the Indian side bulk of trade passed through the Srinagar-Leh route, though traders from Skardu, Kishtwar, Kullu, Lahoul, Spiti, Nurpur and Bushahr used to carry on their business with Ladakh directly through the Khapalu-Chorbat-Nobra, Kishtwar-Zanskar and Kullu-Rohtang pass-Lahoul-Key Long-Bara Lacha pass-Rupshu-Longa Lacha pass-Thung Lung La and Leh routes respectively. To the east of Ladakh a caravan trail passed through Gartok towards Lhasa-the capital of Tibet. In the north, Ladakh stood connected with the Silk Route at Yarkand by a caravan route running across the Karakoram pass. From Leh there existed three paths leading to Yarkand – the nearest big trading centre of Central Asia. Those traders and travellers who opted to travel to Yarkand in winter would cross Digar La and follow the narrow and winding valleys of Shyok river, Shyok, which was frozen during winter, was to be crossed and recrossed several times. After negotiating the Karakoram pass, traders would start their descent towards Yarkand passing through Kugiar and Karghalik. But it was usual for the Central Asian and Indian traders to bring their caravans to Ladakh in summer and start their return journey homewards in the autumn. The summer route from Leh to Yarkand passed through Khardung La, Nubra valley, Saser La, Karakoram pass and the Suget pass. Yet another route ran across the Changla pass, the Chang Chenmo valley and Lingzithang plains to join the Leh-Yarkand summer route at Shahidulla. The Chang Chenmo valley route to Eastern Turkestan was improved considerably after the conclusion of a treaty between Kashmir Durbar and the British Indian government in 1870. Under the treaty this route was also declared a free highway. Efforts were made to establish this track as the main trade route between Leh and Yarkand, as it was easier than those by the Shyok or Saser pass. But being relatively longer in distance and fuel, grass and water not being so abundantly available on this route, it did not become so popular with the traders, excepting those who used camels to transport their goods.

Notwithstanding its physical difficulties, the Srinagar-Leh-Yarkand route was the most important and long established thorough-fare between India and Central Asia. Even though the British authorities took numerous steps to improve the Kullu-Leh route with a view to encourage direct trading between British India and Central Asia, traders continued to use the Srinagar-Leh route as it was "the easiest and best supplied as to grass, provisions etc. and thoroughly open for two or three months longer than the Kullu route."[1] It was through this route that Kashmir shawl industry received its supplies of pashm wool that was imported into Ladakh from Tibet and Yarkand. This road was kept in excellent repair throughout the period of Dogra rule in Kashmir. Such was the safety of this route that in the event of unfavourable weather or death of ponies, traders would march on to the next safer stage leaving behind their goods which were fetched after the climate became favourable or substitute transport became available. As a result the Srinagar-Leh-Yarkand route became the most important thoroughfare between India and Central Asia during the Dogra rule in Kashmir.

As regards ladakh's trade with Tibet, it was regulated by the Treaty of Tingmosgang concluded in 1684, under which Ladakh got the monopoly over shawl-wool produced in Tibet, and the Tibetans acquired the exclusive right to the brick-tea trade with Ladakh.[2] The treaty also provided for the despatch of periodical missions by Ladakh to Lhasa carrying presents for the Dalai Lama.[3] Since the bearers of this religious mission were allowed to carry merchandise, it soon acquired a commercial character. The shawl wool that was imported from Tibet and Xinjiang into Ladakh was exclusively exported to Kashmir through the agency of Kashmiri merchants. Brick-tea imported from Tibet was almost entirely consumed within Ladakh and also forwarded to Kashmir. Such trade ties between Ladakh and Tibet were reinforced by the Treaty of 1842 concluded between the Dogra and Tibetan officials. This Treaty reaffirmed the established frontiers on the Tibet-Ladakh border and also accepted the Dogras as the legitimate authority in Ladakh. Under this treaty semi-official trade missions were exchanged at intervals between Leh and Lhasa.[4] The triennial mission which left Leh for Lhasa carrying presents and merchandise was known as the *Lapchak* mission. The annual Tibetan caravan coming to Leh with brick-tea and other goods was called *Chaba*. Whereas the Ladakhi traders were entitled to free transport and accommodation during their travel and stay in Tibet, traders from Tibet enjoyed similar facilities during their sojourn in Ladakh. After the acquisition of Ladakh by the Dogras in 1842, the Lapchak mission lost its religious character. It was now being managed by the professional traders mainly Kashmiri Muslims settled in Leh, who earned large profits in the transactions. A Muslim family of about one hundred members headed by Nazer Shah, was entrusted "the duty of carrying out the Lopchak mission" by the Maharaja of Kashmir and at the time of Sven Hedin's visit in 1906 they had been retaining this confidential post "for some fifty years."[5] The close involvement of Kashmiri Muslim settlers in Ladakh's trade with Tibet can be gauged from the fact that even as late as in 1959 about 129 such families having about 600 members were residing in Lhasa-Shigatse area of Tibet.[6]

On account of its geographical contiguity with Eastern Turkestan in the north and Tibet in the east and its direct linkage with the 'Silk Route' Ladakh developed into an important transit emporium of multilateral trade between India, Central Asia and Tibet. Leh was the starting point of a trade route that followed the course of the Indus upstream and passed through Demchok, Gartok and Lake Mansarowar to reach Shigatse and Lhasa. Its cultural affinity with Tibet in terms of religion, language, dress and food habits facilitated the exchange of men and material between Ladakh and Tibet. The political, economic and cultural history of Ladakh is intertwined with that of Western Tibet which was the main source for the supply of shawl-wool. Ladakhis engaged in regular trade with the adjoining areas of Guge, Rudok and Gartok in Western Tibet. It was connected with Eastern Turkestan by the Leh-Yarkand trade route that passed through the Karakoram Pass. Gartok was the main trading mart of Western Tibet, where a trade fair was held each year during the summer months. Merchants from neighbouring areas of Ladakh, Koonawar, Rampur, Kumaon, East Turkestan and even from as far as the Russian dominions, attended this fair to exchange their wares and local raw materials such as borax, salt, shawl-wool and gold.[7] This bilateral trade not only sustained the poor and backward economies of semi-closed systems in these remote and high altitude areas, it also provided the essential raw materials for the flourishing shawl and carpet industry of Kashmir.

The Ladakhi imports from Tibet comprised fine pashm wool, coarse wool, brick-tea, salt, silver, gold, turquoises, tea cups, paper and musk. Ladakh's exports to Tibet included silver *Yambus*, gold, China silk and coarse cotton goods received from Eastern Turkestan, glass-ware, coral, silver coins, cotton cloths, chintzes, brocades, goatskins and furs imported from British India, saffron and rice from Kashmir, apricots and barley of Ladakh and Baltistan. Apricots, Chinese silver, Turkestan made cotton goods and silk cloth, Kashmir saffron and grains constituted the bulk of Ladakhi exports to Tibet. Much of this trade was generated by the heavy demand for pashm wool in Kashmir which had developed into the main centre of shawl production. The assured supplies of pashm wool from Tibet not only sustained Kashmir's shawl-industry, but also provided new avenues of employment to skilled and unskilled workers in Ladakh and Kashmir.

That Kashmir maintained close economic ties with Ladakh and through it with Tibet since ancient times, is established by the very fact that the shawl industry existed in Kashmir in that period. Its looms were fed with *pashm*,[8] the fine shawl-wool procured from Tibet and Ladakh. Even today Kashmiri ladies retain the tradition of hand-spinning *pashm* on the wheel (*Charkha*). The emergence of Kashmir as the main center of shawl production in medieval times resulted in the settlement of some Kashmiris who dealt with the collection and onward transmission of shawl-wool to Kashmir, in Ladakh. They came to be known as *Tibet-baqals*. They also exchanged their raw wool for manufactured shawl-goods, which were sold in various markets of Central Asia. The nomads inhabiting Chang Thang and its adjoining highlands also engaged in barter trade of Tibetan goods like salt, *Jadwar* (medicine), gold and shawl wool for Indian cloth, sweets rice and barley.

Tibet was dependent on Ladakh and Kashmir for supplies of essential goods like food grains, saffron, shawls, coarse cotton cloth, leathr and apricots. That the cotton and silk fabrics and carpets produced in Kashgar and Khotan were also transmitted to Tibet through Ladakh, shows that there existed no direct communication between Western Tibet and Eastern Turkestan during this period. The annual turnover of Ladakh's trade with Tibet during the Dogra rule amounted to several lakh rupees. This trade suffered heavily after the incorporation of Tibet in China. It, however, continued to operate though under strains, until it came to a standstill in 1959 following disturbances in Tibet.

Bulk of Indian trade with Central Asian towns of Yarkand, Kashgar and Khotan was carried through Kashmir and Ladakh. Central Asian exports to Ladakh and Kashmir comprised gold and silver, hemp drug, shawl wool, carpets and felts, tea, Chinese tea-cups, leather-ware, coarse cotton cloths, raw silk and ponies. Out of these items bullion, cannabis (*charas*) and shawl-wool constituted the major imports.

The Yarkandi and Andijani traders used to bring these goods to Ladakh where they exchanged the same with their Indian counterparts. Occasionally the Central Asian traders would move forward to Kashmir and Punjab in the hope of realizing better profits. Similarly Indian traders would also proceed beyond Ladakh towards Yarkand to make direct purchases at relatively lower prices. Indian traders brought to Leh, Indian and British made cotton cloths, brocades, Kashmir shawls, indigo, spices, dyed goat skins, opium, preserved fruits, coral, indigenous medicines, sugar and books. Whereas most of the Indian imports were exported to Yarkand, part of it also went to Lhasa.

The extent and pattern of overland Indo-Central Asian trade carried through Ladakh fluctuated from time to time due to the changing political situation in Central Asia. In the early nineteenth century, when the relations between Omar Khan, the rular of Kokand and the Chinese authorities in Eastern Turkestan had become strained, all the Andijani traders left Yarkand for their country and abandoned their business trips to Ladakh. This resulted in a considerable decrease in Yarkandi exports to Ladakh. Such disruptions in trade did occur even afterwards when Eastern Turkestan was rife with turmoil caused due to Khoja uprisings against the Chinese rulers. The volume of trade between India and Kashqaria registered a steady increase after the Chinese were driven out of that Country by Yakub Beg in 1867. This was owing to the stoppage of all Chinese imports into Eastern Turkestan and also due to the development of harmonious relations between Yakub Beg and the British Indian authorities. The abolition of all transit duties on merchandise passing to and from Central Asia through Kashmir and Ladakh by Maharaja Ranbir Singh also encouraged this trade. During the rule of Yakub Beg in Kashgaria, export of Indian tea to that quarter increased considerably. Even the Chinese tea imported into Ladakh via Lhasa and Punjab was exported to Eastern Turkestan to meet the shortages caused there by the cessation of its trade with China. The British manufactured cotton and silk cloths now began to substitute the Indian cotton prints and silks. However, *charas*, pashm wool and ponies continued to be imported into Ladakh from Eastern Turkestan as heretofore. Indian exports to Eastern Turkestan shot up to an unprecedented figure of over 8 lakh rupees during the year 1874.

The death of Yakub Beg in 1877 and the subsequent re-occupation of Eastern Turkestan by the Chinese did not result in any adverse impact on the Indo-Central Asian trade. Several factors were responsible for the continuance of this trade even after Xinjiang had become a Chinese possession in 1878. Firstly, the Chinese authorities did not interfere in the long established trade between India and the southern oasis-towns of Xinjiang. Their restrictions on the import of Indian tea and opium also proved ineffective in the face of smuggling of these commodities in connivance with the Chinese customs officials. Secondly, Xinjiang did not possess an industrial base to cater to its demand for manufactured and other piece goods that were imported mainly from Russia through Kokand-Kashgar route and partly from India through the Srinagar-Leh-Yarkand route. Thirdly, Indian trade with Bukhara, Kokand and other parts of Russian Central Asia, which was hitherto carried through Peshawar-Kabul-Bukhara route was partly diverted to the Srinagar-Leh-Yarkand route after the Russians imposed strict restrictions on the import of British Indian goods into Russian Central Asia. Fourthly, the arrival at Leh of Central Asian pilgrims enroute their Haj Pilgrimage to Mecca via India also contributed to the increased Central Asian imports into Ladakh as they brought alongwith a large quantity of bullion, silks and ponies for sale in Leh or Srinagar. Fifthly the complete security of Srinagar-Leh-Yarkand route which was devoid of robbers and the facilities available at various stages of this route so far as the supply of ponies, transporters, food and fodder was concerned, also helped in the development of Ladakh as an important trading centre.

After the conclusion of the Russo-Chinese treaty at St. Petersburgh in 1881 the bilateral overland trade between Xinjiang and Russia scaled new heights. This in turn affected Indian trade with Xinjiang in more than one way, as it had now to face stiff competition from Russia in that quarter. Now the import of Khotanese gold dust and Chinese silver ingots into Ladakh was substituted by that of Russian gold and paper rubles. The Yarkandi felts and Khotanese carpets became dearer in Ladakh and Kashmir as their prices appreciated due to increased demand in the Russian markets. And lesser quantity of Turfani fine wool was imported into Ladakh, as the same was being supplied to Russian Turkestan in large quantities. Import of coarse wool and *pashm* from Chinese Turkestan dropped considerably in value from 1930 onwards. However, *charas* continued to be imported into Ladakh despite its heavy taxation in India. An average of 3,000 to 3,500 maunds of *charas* was annually imported into Ladakh from Chinese Turkestan during the years 1882 to 1932. Most of this *charas* was consumed in Punjab and Qudh whence it was carried by Indian traders via Leh-Kullu route.

With the establishment of Soviet power in Central Asia, the bilateral trade between Xinjiang and Russian Turkestan received a setback. It was now diverted to Ladakh and Kashmir. This resulted in an unusual increase in the Indian exports to Xinjiang through Ladakh. During the years 1917 to 1931 goods worth about 285 lakhs rupees were exported from India to Chinese Turkestan through Kashmir and Ladakh of which European cotton goods and silks, dyed skins, indigo, spices and tea constituted the main items. In the same period merchandise valued at about 330 lakh rupees was imported from Chinese Turkestan into Ladakh and Kashmir of which *charas*, Russian gold and paper rubles, gold dust, raw silk, carpets and felts were the main items. The balance of trade thus stood in Xinjiang's favour. The Indo-Central Asian trade through Kashmir and Ladakh, which had scaled an unprecedented height of more than 68 lakh rupees during the year 1920-21, began to decline in value soon after the opening of Russian overland trade with Xinjiang. From late 1930s onwards internal disorders in Xinjiang began to act as a stumbling block to this trade which finally ceased to flow since 1949 following the Communist takeover of Xinjiang and the subsequent closure of Xinjiang to outside traffic. This deprived Ladakh and Kashmir of their importance as emporiums of the Indo-Central Asian overland trade that passed through a network of caravan trails criss-crossing

Ladakh and Kashmir. As the traditional and historical trade linkages between India and Central Asia via Kashmir and Ladakh ceased to be functional after 1949, time has come to reflect upon the legacy of such a rich and productive experience and revive these linkages and trade relations on a new and dynamic footing. Chinese experience in Xinjiang shows how this remote north-western region has been brought closer to China's mainland both by air rail and road network, notwithstanding the enormous distance and inhospitable deserts intervening between the two regions.

China and the Central Asian Republics of Uzbekistan, Kazakhstan and Kyrgyzstan are extending their transportation links via Osh, Naryn, (Turgart pass/ Irkeshtam) through Kashgar and Yarkand in Xinjiang to be linked to the Karakoram Highway running through Pak–occupied Kashmir, so that these Central Asian countries secure access to the sea via Pakistan. China has also been working on projects aimed at linking CIS-Pamir mountain territories of Karategin (Komsomolabad, Garm, Tajikabad, Jirghital), Darvaz and Vahio (Tavildara) in eastern Tajikistan, to Kyrgyzstan and Kashgar region of Xinjiang by formation of a transport and economic corridor through Suhov and Kyzyl Su (in Kyrgyzstan), Sary Tash in Pamirs, and via Irkeshtam to Kashgar in China. This 750 kms. route is reported to have no high passes or inaccessible sections and could be made operational throughout the year. Besides, there already exists road on some sections of this route and the whole section from Dushanbe to Kashagar (750 to 800 kms) has asphalt or pebble stone cover. Only a few sections of this road are reported to be not metalled.

This transport network is sought to facilitate development of marginal, peripheral and developed areas of Tajikistan, Kyrgyzstan and Southern Xinjiang. It will embrace Pamir tract, Karakoram Highway and new routes to Kazakhstan and Kyrgyzstan (through Turgart pass). The Euro-Asian land-bridge/highway project has envisaged the completion of the following trans-border roads, to connect the Central Asian Republics, and the Xinjiang region of China:

(a) Khorgos (Kazakhstan) – Kuldja (Xinjiang)

(b) Bishkek – Turgart Pass (Kyrgyzstan) – Kashgar (Xinjiang)

(c) Osh – Sary Tash (Kyrgyzstan) – Kashgar (Xinjiang)

It is high time, that the following steps are initiated to revive the traditional India-Central Asia overland routes through Ladakh on a priority basis:

(a) Whereas the recent reopening of border trade point at Nathu La in Sikkim is a welcome development, the traditional India-Central Asia overland trade routes via Leh, Yarkand, Kashgar and onwards to the Central Asian Republics, and Leh-Demchok-Gartok-Lhasa need to be reopened in the same manner.

(b) The proposal of Jammu and Kashmir government to open the Leh-Demchok route to Western Tibet as a viable and easier alternative route for pilgrimage to the Kailash-Mansarovar across the LOC in Ladakh needs to be persued and got accepted by the Chinese side. This will help in reducing the journey time and provide a safer passage to pilgrims. (More than 300 pilgrims had died due to landslides at Malpa in the U.P. hills in October 1998).

(c) The possibilities of opening an oil/gas pipeline linkage across the LOC in Ladakh with the proposed Xinjiang – Kazakhstan pipeline, need to be studied.

## ENDNOTES

1. T.G. Montgomerie, Supdt. G.T. Survey of India, Dehradun to the Lt. Governor, Punjab dated 6 April 1871. See *Foreign Political A* June 1871, 560-597 (National Archives of India).
2. Sven Hedin, *Trans Himalaya*, London, 1909, Vol. 1, p. 57.
3. Ibid., p. 59.
4. Ibid., p. 58.
5. For further details see K. Warikoo, Ladakh's Trade Relations with Tibet under the Dogras. *China Report*, Vol. 26, No. 2, 1990, pp. 133-143.
6. Ibid.
7. According to a contemporary estimate about 10,000 to 12,000 people participated in this fair. See Alexander Geared, in George Lloyd (Ed.), *Account of Koonawar in the Himalaya* (London, 1841), p. 145.
8. *Pashm* is very fine, soft, short an flossy underwool of *Kel* of shawl-goat, a variety of *Caprahircus* which is found is found in Chang Thang, Budok, Gartok and the Tine Shan mountains in Turkestan.

# 18

## Transport Corridor between Central Asia-India through Pakistan

### *Possible Routes and SRMTS*

*Neeladri Chatterjee*

The littoral states around the Caspian Sea in Central Asia can play a major role in regional geopolitics as an alternative to Persian Gulf countries for ensuring energy security in Asia. Amongst all the Central Asian States, Turkmenistan, is not only the nearest Central Asian State rich in gas and oil but also a stepping stone for more inwards access to Kazakhstan and Russian energy linkages for South Asia. However, the major impediment for India is that it is cut off from access to these oil and gas rich nations by Pakistan, Afghanistan and Iran. Though India shares cordial relationship with Iran, Pakistan is a major drawback for a transport corridor through that country to Central Asia for exchange of energy and goods. The vast source of energy in the Caspian region of Central Asia can find a ready market in India. Transnational pipeline is the cheapest mode of transport of energy, from littoral nations around Caspian Sea like Turkmenistan, which has to pass through Pakistan to reach Indian industries and households. Pakistan thus has become the crucial transit corridor for overland energy transit from Central Asia to India. The two proposed pipelines, Iran-Pakistan-India (IPI) and Tukmenistan-Afganistan-Pakistan-India (TAPI) pipelines have important role in India's energy security and so will Pakistan, as intermediary country through which all the proposed pipelines will pass to India. The TAPI (Central Asian) pipeline originating from Dauletabad gas fields in Turkmenistan would run through Herat and Kandahar in Afghanistan and enter Pakistan at Quetta (Baluchistan) from where it would move to Multan and enter India at Fazilka. Apart from the pipeline transit route, it is necessary to open a transport corridor for movement of goods to and from Central Asia to South Asia. Pakistan stands to gain in opening up a transport corridor through its state from India to Afghanistan and Iran which could then run to Turkmenistan and further north. Pakistan will earn millions of dollars in the form of transit fees for the pipelines running through its territory and also stand to gain millions from trade with the whole South Asian region through India. Pakistan, therefore, has a great potential to play a crucial role in integrating the energy security vision of India and Central Asia besides opening up smoother linkages between regions and states for trade and commerce. (Fig. 1)

## Regional Transport Corridor and SRMTS

The South Asian Association for Regional Cooperation (SAARC) is playing a key role in resolving the differences between the South Asian countries and trying to establish foundation for sustainable regional and interstate transportation system in South Asia. To consolidate the commitment to energy cooperation and linkages between South Asian states a study was initiated under the aegis of SAARC Secretariat. This study was termed as the SAARC Regional Multimodal Transportation Study (SRMTS) and Asian Development Bank was assigned the task to do the study. The SRMTS project if implemented will go a long way in integrating the whole South Asian region by established set up of road and railway connections between India and Pakistan and other South Asian nations. This will bring parity in economic development in the region apart from providing a gateway to the Central Asian countries for energy and trade. However, SRMTS under SAARC has an uphill task of developing the corridor between these two countries, firstly due to Pakistan's negative policy over this issue. Secondly, even if Pakistan allows India to build a corridor to Central Asia through its territory, the existing minimal overland linkage between India and Pakistan will not be able to sustain smooth and fast transportation of goods and energy. Therefore, it is necessary for SAARC to build up a consensus on the possible roads to be built or renovated, to be able to sustain such a heavy volume of trade in minimum possible time. (Fig. 2)

The main objective of SRMTS is to develop regional understanding and trade across boundaries and establish transnational multimodal routes between and inside South Asian countries. During the 12th SAARC summit held in January 2004 in Islamabad, the heads of states of all countries agreed to build, strengthen and facilitate fast transport, links and communication between countries so as to have a balanced economic development in the region. Subsequently, Asian Development Bank was given the responsibility to render a regional technical assistance (TA) to promote regional cooperation among the member states of the SAARC. The TA has four major components amongst which SRMTS occupies the first priority for India in relation to energy and transport linkages with Pakistan. The TA includes analyzing current constraints and challenges, and potential benefits of improved regional connectivity through several transport modes, and prepare a detailed road map for enhancing regional connectivity and a time bound policy and investment action plan with possible external assistance. The 32nd Session of the Standing Committee held at Dhaka, on 31 July – 1 August 2006 emphasized the need to consider and prioritize the important recommendations of the Report of the SRMTS. The Standing Committee also agreed to establish an Inter-governmental Group on Transport at

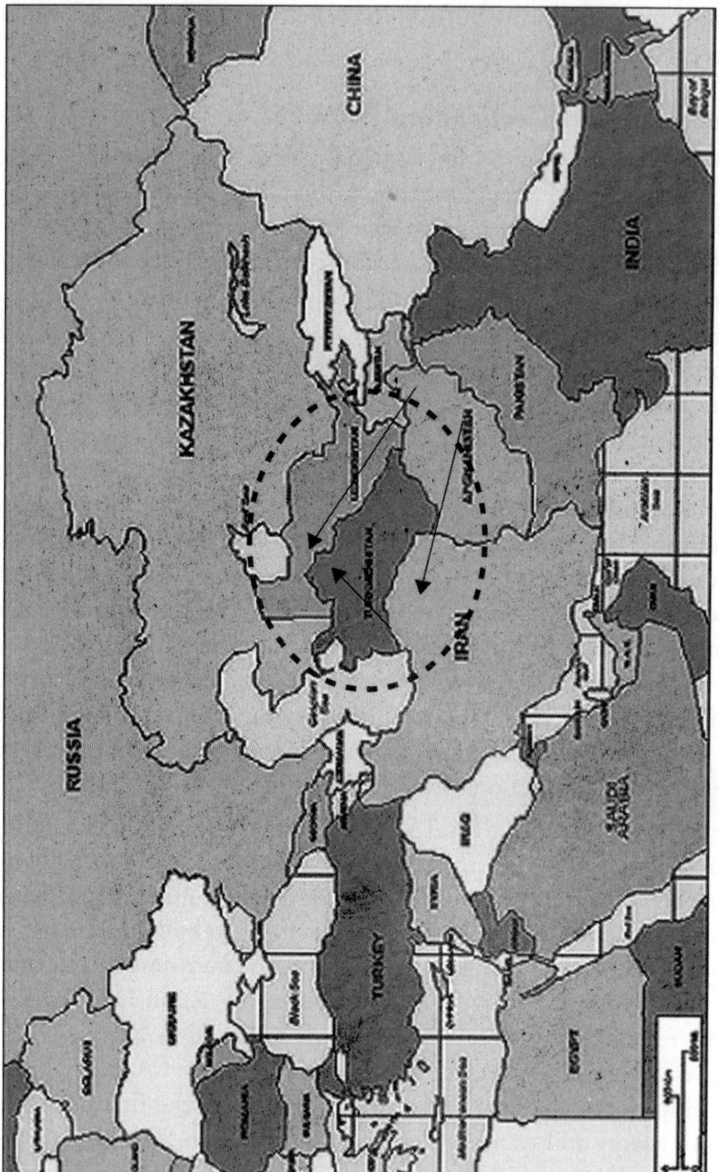


Fig. 1: Central Asia and India

**Source:** http://alabamamaps.ua.edu (edited).

Fig. 2: Two Proposed Pipelines in South Asia

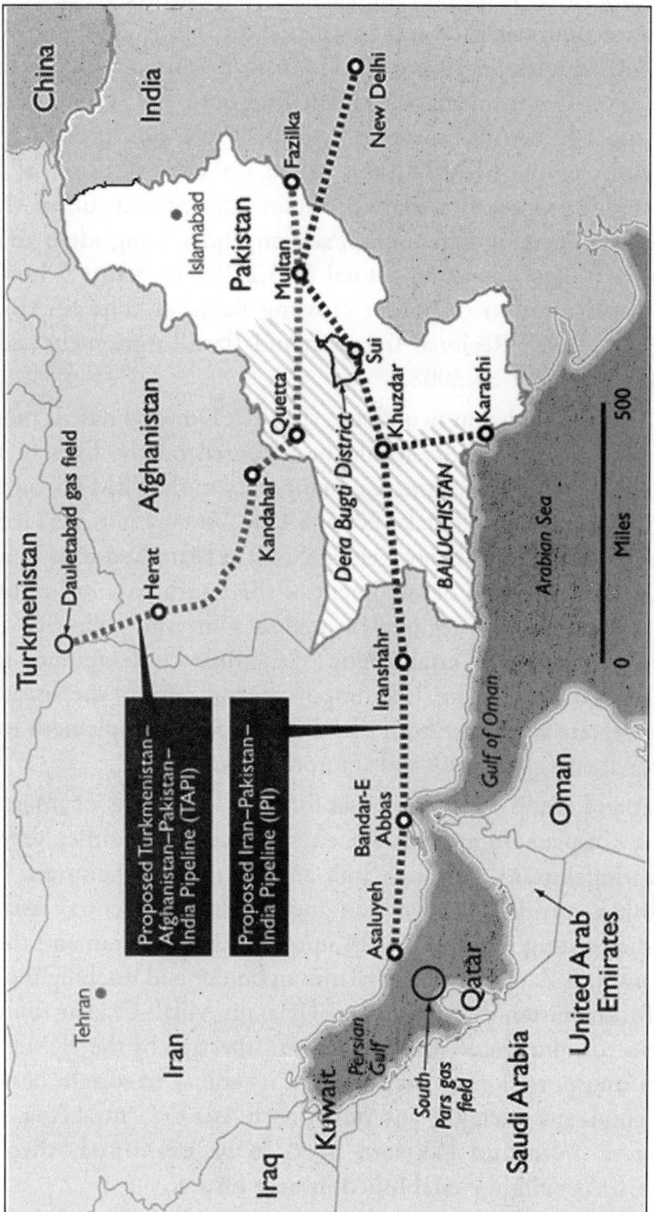


Source: http://www.heritage.org (edited).

the level of Secretaries, supported by experts in the relevant sectors. In continuity of the commitment of SAARC, it decided to have an inter-governmental Group on Transport and prioritize the project implementation schedule based on the SRMTS report. The TA recommendation was completed on 7 June 2006 and was accepted by higher SAARC bodies, including the Council of Ministers in the first meeting of the SAARC Inter-Governmental Group on Transport (IGGT) in December 2006. Subsequently the 14th SAARC meeting held in New Delhi in 2007 endrosed the recommendations of the SRMTS, and called for the extension of SRMTS to Afghanistan. It also proposed to take up certain pilot projects under the new 'Silk Route' (APIBM) connecting Afganistan, Pakistan, India, Bangladesh and Myanmar, linking Kabul to Yangon covering a total of 5,272 kms across 5 borders. It also focussed on modernization of border crossing facilities. The SAARC transport minsiters agreed to have a Regional Transport and Transit Agreement and a Regional Motor Vehicle Agreement by 2008.

The SRMTS was divided in two Phases (I & II). During Phase I, model regional transit and transport agreements would be prepared on the lines of the Greater Mekong Subregion (GMS) countries. Contemporary to the SRMTS, on the occasion of the 13th SAARC summit at Dhaka 2005, SAARC energy ministers recommended the setting up of the SAARC Energy Center (SEC) at Islamabad so as to be "a catalyst for the economic growth and development of the South Asia region by initiating, coordinating and facilitating regional as well as joint and collective activities on energy." SAARC purpose of establishing SEC while contemporary talks on the SRMTS model were progressing, is an important indicator of the vision of SAARC countries to integrate and make both SRMTS and SEC complement each other in ensuring regional energy security and transport linkages.

India's overland access to Central Asia through Pakistan is of interest to India's interest in the Caspian oil and gas for energy security. Another very important corridor to Turkmenistan is through Iran and Pakistan-Afghanistan. India would like to establish a corridor through Iran and Pakistan to Central Asia which will concur with the existing route of the IPI upto Iranshahr in Iran and then bifurcate to the North towards Zaranj, in the Afghanistan border and reaching the Dauletabad gas fields in Turkmenistan through Zaranj-Delaram-Milak-Chabar route. However, vision of such a corridor would need a good introspection by the SRMTS of existing road, railways transportation in Pakistan, and its ability to sustain heavy traffic on the transit of goods and energy to and from South Asia to Central Asia. The possible routes between India and Pakistan need to be examined, through which transportation links could be established in near future.

## Routes to Central Asia

### *(A) Through Pakistan-Afghanistan*

One of the routes to the Afghan border of Chaman from India could be from Jaisalmer (Rajasthan-India) to Sukkur-Jacobabad-Sibi-Quetta and finally reach

Chaman at the Afghan border and continue to Kandahar (Afghanistan). It converges at Delaram and runs towards the Afghan-Turkmenistan border through Herat. National Highway Authority of Pakistan has already taken up the project of linking Karachi-Quetta-Chaman route, which is the National Highway-25. SRMTS should focus on the Sukkur-Jacobabad-Sibi sector which is connected by the N-55 Indus Highway, since in the case of opening of the border for transport corridor, Sukkur will be very crucial for all travel to the Afghanistan border. Sukkur is well connected from Karachi in the south to Multan-Lahore in the north via the main artery national highway (N-5). N-5 stretches through the length of Pakistan from Karachi-Multan-Torkam-Lahore-Rawalpindi-Peshawar. The Samjhauta Express currently running from Amristar-Attari-Lahore, can be turned into the main railway connection between the two countries due to its link with N-5 highway. This will carry to Sukkur in South or carry to Kabul through the Islamabad-Peshawar-Khyber Pass route and then the route moves forward through Charikar-Baghilan-Kunduz or divert North East through Charikar to the Tajikistan border.

**Fig. 3: Existing National Highways and Motorways**

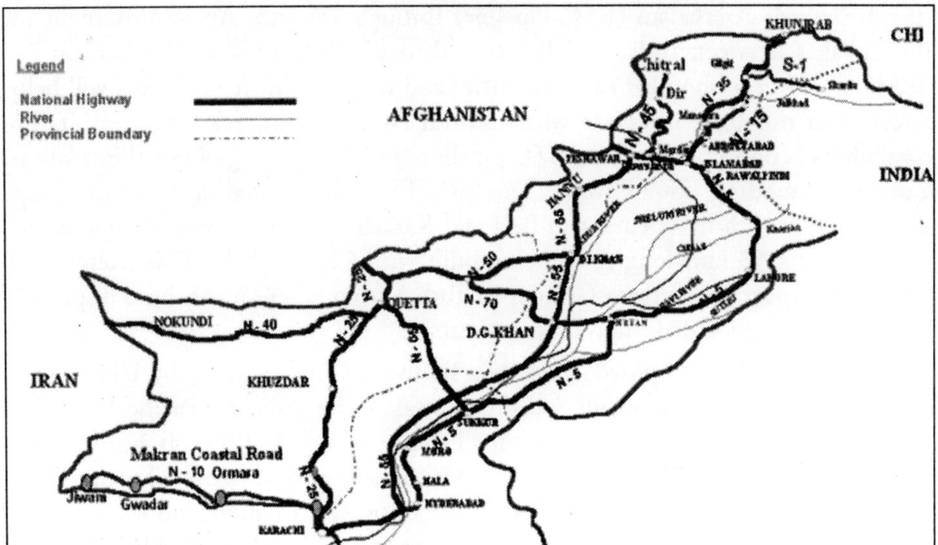


**Source:** www.findpk.com/yp/html/roads.html

SRMTS should put forward in the IGGT forum to consider reopening of Barmer (India) rail connection upto Hyderabad (Pakistan) through Mirpur Khas. Though this line is a not a broad gauge line and it used to operate upto 1965, this route could be looked into and converted into a Broad Gauge line. This line used to connect Ahmedabad with Karachi through Luni-Barmer-Lunabao-Khokhrapar-Mirpur Khas-Hyderabad. The importance of the line is because Hyderabad is an important link to North (towards Afghanistan) and South (towards Iran). On either side it is connected by road and rail. On the North the rail runs upto Sukkur and further to Sibi-Quetta-Chaman. The importance of this linkage is due to the refineries at Bhatinda and Panipat, which can use the oil and gas from the Caspian region in Central Asia and also supply petroleum byproducts to Central Asia through this route.

*(B) Through Pakistan-Iran*

The advent of the TAPI and IPI pipeline concept and efforts to implement it alongside with the development of the Gwadar Port in the south coast of Pakistan with Chinese help has shifted focus on the southern coast. Developing and increasing linkages of Gwadar and Indian ports of Mundra and Kandla will be an important aspect of transfer of goods and energy from Central Asia through Iran. Karachi is well connected by rail and road to the north, towards the west National Highway (NH-10) which runs parallel to Gwadar and connects Karachi to Turbat through Bela upto Iran border. Therein the road stretches towards Iranshahr-Zahadari-Zabol in Iran to the border town of Zaranj (Afghanistan). From Iranshahr there is another stretch towards Azerbaijan (BTC-Pipeline) through Teheran. An improvement in the linkages between India and Pakistan through this corridor, if taken up by SRMTS, will be a boon for energy security and trade of this region. This will help South Asia not only integrate with Central Asia but also take into ambit the possibility of connection with the BTC pipelines and the opening of the North South Corridor extending upto Europe. The SRMTS with external agencies can help develop the stretch from Turbat to Bela and Karachi. Turbat is being connected to Gawadar by a 53 kms long road, being built with Chinese help. This stretch will help to transport goods from Gwadar to Turbat from where it can be transported to Iran-Afganistan-Uzbekistan-Turkmenistan.

There is also the proposed Trans Asia Railways (TAR) studied by UNESCAP (United Nations Economic and Social Commission for Asia and Pacific) as a part of Asian Land Transport Infrastructure Development (ALTID). It proposes to connect New Delhi with Kazakhstan, Turkmenistan upto Moscow. This proposed route will enter Pakistan through Wagah border to Attari-Lahore and extend upto Zahedan in Iran to Bafq. From Bafq one route goes south towards the Bandar Abbas. The second route which turns towards north, may extend upto Turkmenbashi (on Caspian Sea) in Turkmenistan or extend further from Sarakhs (in Turkmenistan) towards Kazakhstan or Russia. SRMTS can take up the model of the UNESCAP studies for further implementation in the regional models for integrating the SRMTS into the ALTID action plan to bring Europe and Asia closer through Central Asia.

## Conclusion

Energy requirement has increased exponentially in South Asia, Indian economy being the main contributor to such an increase in consumption. India's indigenous production of crude oil is less than 25 per cent of its requirement; hence it is dependent on imported energy. Majority of imports to India come from the Persian Gulf region. This region being volatile and prices of crude oil being high, importing gas from the Caspian region is a viable alternative for India. However, the major drawback of Central Asian gas rich states like Turkmenistan and Kazakhstan is that these are separated from India by Pakistan, Afghanistan and Iran. In order to have any substantial oil and gas supply from Central Asian states to India, it is required to have transnational pipelines from Central Asia to India through Pakistan, Afghanistan or through Iran. Therefore, Pakistan could be a vital transit corridor for the transnational pipelines coming from Central Asia, Iran or Russia. Apart from the pipelines, it is essential to open up a transport corridor through Pakistan into Central Asia in order to consolidate a transport and energy corridor. This will not only integrate the regional energy security program of South Asia but also help trade across the border and Pakistan will stand to gain especially. The SRMTS project initiated by SAARC is being conducted by ADB to find out the possible corridor and develop regional and inter-regional multimodal transport corridor. The project is of great importance to the whole region as it envisages making communication, transport linkages between South Asian countries smooth, fast and efficient. This, if completed, will provide a base for partnership with the extended neighborhood in Central Asia. Consolidation of the existing transport system and possibility of convergence with the transport linkages of India can establish transport and energy linkages upto Central Asian states in future. Such energy and transport linkages if established by the efforts of the SAARC will dramatically change the energy security and trade paradigm of the region.

# 19

## Gwadar Port: A South Asian Gateway for Central Asia?

*Alok Bansal*

Geography links the states of Central Asia to South Asia and there have been strong trade and cultural relations between the two regions through history. However, one and a quarter century of Russian/Soviet presence in Central Asia, tied this region to the Russian heartland. During the Soviet era, the entire economic infrastructure of the region was developed to complement the economic requirements of Soviet Union and East Europe. Rail and road linkages of Central Asia with other Soviet and East European states led to the virtual isolation of the region from South Asia and these states looked to their northwest for openings to the outside world. After the disintegration of Soviet Union, the Central Asian Republics continue to be linked with the Russian economy but as they seek to break off the Russian influence, they are looking for their geographical access to the sea. However, the nearest ports in Iran and South Asia – Bandar Abbas and Karachi, are not conveniently located for the countries of Central Asia. Moreover, both these ports are congested and do not have spare capacities to cater to the growing requirements of Afghanistan and Central Asia. Gwadar and Chah Bahar on Makran coast in Pakistan and Iran are being developed exclusively as gateways to Afghanistan and Central Asia. Iran's political stand off with the West and instability in Afghanistan have raised uncertainties about the future of Chah Bahar, but Gwadar appears to be emerging as the gateway to Central Asia, as it has the added advantage of Chinese support and the option of accessing Central Asia through Xinjiang, thereby bypassing the unstable Afghanistan. This paper examines the implications of Gwadar Port Project for Central and South Asia.

In June 2006, Pakistan's former President General Pervez Musharraf, while welcoming the Emir of Kuwait to Islamabad, emphasised the significance of Gwadar Deep Sea Port Project, which could function as a commercial hub providing land link to Central Asia and Xinjiang and maritime trade links with The Gulf.[1] Similarly,

China has also realised the potential of this port and Hu Jintao stated during Musharraf's visit to Beijing that China would strive to evolve Pakistan as an energy corridor between the Gulf and Xinjiang through the Gwadar deep seaport.[2] China is showing interest "in the construction of a pipeline from Gwadar to Xinjiang, a road linking Gwadar with the Karakoram Highway and a huge oil refinery complex at Gwadar, which would partly meet the requirements of Pakistan and Xinjiang".[3] Pakistan does not visualise Gwadar as a gateway to Xinjiang only, but as an ideal point of entry for the huge merchandise bound for and originating from Central Asia. It plans to set up an export processing zone in Gwadar with a 15-year tax holiday "as an incentive for potential investors". It hopes that the deep sea port would open up "new opportunities for trade, import and export as well as transit trade facilities for Afghanistan and beyond. This can serve as the shortest route to sea for the land-locked Central Asian Republics at a time when Pakistan is considering importing gas and electricity from these countries via Afghanistan". Various warlords in Afghanistan could develop stakes in the transit trade to Central Asia and thereby facilitate normalisation of situation in Afghanistan and improve its relations with Pakistan. "Gwadar thus provides an avenue for improving relations between Pakistan and the region to its immediate northwest".[4]

Gwadar Deep Sea Port Project is an important project with tremendous economic spin offs. It has the potential to emerge as the gateway to Central Asia and change the landscape of arid and inhospitable Balochistan. Besides economic potential, its location at the entrance of the Persian Gulf has immense geostrategic significance. It could provide the ideal and most cost-effective gateway to Afghanistan and through it to the resource rich states of Central Asia. The continued unstable regional environment in the Persian Gulf and the emergence of the independent Central Asian Republics has added to its geopolitical importance.[5] The Port also eliminates Pakistan's critical dependence on Karachi-Bin Qasim complex for its overseas trade. Chinese involvement in the construction of the port provides them with an outpost at the mouth of the Persian Gulf and is likely to disturb the geopolitical balance in the region. A mega project, which hopes to usher in prosperity in the region, should have been welcomed by the local residents but in the case of Gwadar, the locals have been opposing it vociferously.

The Gwadar Deep Sea Port Project is the largest infrastructural project being executed in Pakistan since its creation in 1947. With a 14.5 metres deep approach channel, it is the deepest port in Pakistan and can berth much larger tankers than either Karachi or Port Bin Qasim can do. The importance being accorded to the project is evident from the fact that Pakistan wanted it to be inaugurated by Pakistan's President and the Chinese Premier jointly. The first part of the project was completed in 2005 and the second phase was to have been completed by 30 June 2006. The port finally became operational in 2008, when the first ship carrying 52,000 tonnes of wheat from Canada docked there.[6] The port was formally inaugurated by Mr Nabil Ahmed Khan Gabol, Pakistan's Federal Minister of Ports and Shipping on 21 December 2008, when a ship carrying fertiliser from Qatar anchored there.[7]

According to Pakistani government, the port when fully functional would link the countries of Central Asia and Afghanistan by a network of railways and roads.[8] At the groundbreaking ceremony of the Gwadar Port, General Pervez Musharraf underlined that the excellent location of Gwadar on the mouth of the Persian Gulf gave it enormous strategic advantage. He also stated that the port would emerge as the regional hub for trade and commerce after the rail and road infrastructure was fully developed. He also hoped that the port could serve as the mother port at the junction of traditional trade routes opposite Strait of Hormuz, and has the potential to provide an alternative access to the sea for export and import of cargo from and to the 'Northern Areas' of Pakistan.[9]

Gwadar is the first major Pakistani port outside the Karachi-Port Bin Qasim complex and removes a critical vulnerability for Pakistan as it will provide it with another option to disembark vital supplies in case of non-availability of Karachi-Bin Qasim complex either due to natural disasters, accidents or naval blockade.[10] The port is connected by the newly constructed Makran Coastal Highway (653-km-long) from Sheikh Raj, approximately 105 kms north of Karachi to Gabd near Pakistan-Iran border. This highway links the ports at Ormara, Pasni, Gwadar and Jiwani with Karachi and has the potential to boost trade between Pakistan and Iran. Another road link in the pipeline is the Gwadar-Ratto Dero motorway which would join the Indus Highway through Turbat, Awaran and Khuzdar. A rail link has also being planned to connect Gwadar to Quetta and Zahidan.[11] The port along with the communication links is expected to kick up economic development in a region that has remained most backward in Pakistan. The port was constructed following the Asian Development Bank's (ADB) Ports Master Plan study, which considered Gwadar to be the best alternative to the Persian Gulf Ports in terms of location to handle mother ships and large oil tankers and "to capture the transit trade of the Central Asian Republics as well as the trans-shipment trade of the region".[12]

The port due to its location at the entrance of the Persian Gulf, some 460 km from Karachi, has immense geostrategic significance as it has the potential to provide the shortest access to the landlocked Afghanistan and Central Asian Republics.[13] "Pakistan was interested in the project to seek strategic depth further to the southwest from its major naval base in Karachi that has long been vulnerable" to the Indian Navy and Indian Air Force. "To diversify the site of its naval and commercial assets, Pakistan has already built the Jinnah Naval Base at Ormara, which has been in operation since June 2000". The port can berth a dozen ships, submarines and harbour craft. The Gwadar port project is destined to make "the Pakistan Navy into a force that can rival the naval forces in the region. The government of Pakistan has accordingly designated the port area as a 'sensitive defence zone'."[14]

Besides its geostrategic importance, the project is the cornerstone of economic development of Pakistan and Balochistan and it could change the landscape of the region and fortune of its people. The major economic benefits that the authorities perceive from the project are opportunities for trade with Central Asian Republics and Afghanistan, promotion of trade and transport with Gulf States and evolution of the port as trans-shipment hub for containerised cargo.[15] The port is planned to be linked with the hinterland and Central Asia and Afghanistan through a network of roads and railways. The development of Gwadar town by the Gwadar Development Authority is also progressing in accordance with a master plan.[16] According to *Khaleej Times*, when fully completed it is expected to become one of the busiest ports in the region and would provide "warehousing, trans-shipment and industrial facilities for trade with over 20 countries including Gulf countries, Iran, Central Asian Republics, India, China and East Africa".[17]

Pakistan government, with the aim of attracting foreign investment in the region, has permitted China and South Korea to set up tax-free special industrial development zones in Gwadar.[18] Pakistan has sought investment from Kuwait and other West Asian states. It has succeeded in persuading Oman to invest $ 80 million in Gwadar, besides the $ 20 million already invested in the project. Incidentally, Gwadar was part of Oman till 1958, when Oman was cajoled into selling 2,400 sq miles of territory including Gwadar to Pakistan for just $ 8.4 million, by UK.[19] The present investment by Oman in Gwadar is not governed by its historical attachments, but a realistic assessment of the economic potential of Gwadar.

## Gwadar Deep Sea Port Project

The Project started on 22 March 2002 and the Phase I, which was scheduled for completion by March 2005, included construction of three multipurpose berths with length of 602m, a 4.5 km approach channel dredged to 11.5m to 12.5m with a turning basin of 450m diameter, as well as one 100m service berth and related port infrastructure and port handling equipment including pilot boat, tugs, survey vessel, etc. Phase I enabled the port to handle bulk carriers of up to 30,000 Dead Weight Tonnage (DWT) and container vessels of 25,000 DWT. Phase I was constructed at a cost of Rs. 14.9 billion (US $ 248 million).[20] Of this China has paid $ 198 million while Pakistan has contributed $ 50 million. China has also offered expertise in the form of technical staff and has provided bulk of the equipment. Phase II of the port was a much more ambitious project.[21] Merchant ships have been entering port since January 2003 to offload hundreds of tonnes of project related cargo even before the Phase I was completed. Pakistan Petroleum, which is exploring offshore gas, has also been using the port for loading and offloading equipment fairly regularly.[22]

While the basic purpose of Phase I was fairly modest to establish Gwadar as a functioning port, the Phase II aimed to establish Gwadar as a major port. It included building of nine additional berths, which will include four container berths, one bulk cargo terminal to handle 100,000 DWT ships, one grain terminal, one Roll on Roll off terminal and two oil terminals to handle 200,000 DWT ships. The deepening of the approach channel to 14.5 m had started in January 2005 and is reported to have been completed by June 2006. The Phase II accordingly envisaged a much higher outlay of around $ 600 million. It also had plans to build additional berths on Build Operate Transfer Basis. President Musharraf had asked all the agencies associated with the project to complete all required infrastructure facilities at Gwadar port before June 2006.[23] It was believed that on completion of all facilities associated with the project, "Gwadar deep sea port would be one of the world's most strategically located port in the region" and would not only emerge as the Gateway to Central Asia, but will also start attracting traffic from other Gulf ports, mainly Dubai. If successful the port could generate enough revenues to change the landscape of Makran Coast and its hinterland.[24]

## Development of Hinterland

The project also includes development of a number of facilities in Gwadar town that include setting up of a desalination plant to provide water in this arid region. The plant will also generate up to three mega watts of electricity. According to authorities, Gwadar city is planned to be developed to half the size of Islamabad City in three to four years. A 350-bed hospital is proposed to be built in Gwadar, besides a fishing town, a fishing jetty, a modern sport complex and a few five-star hotels. "The Gwadar Master Plan envisages development of about 18,600 hectares of land for this project including port development in phase I and II on 400 hectares of land, an export processing zone of 74 hectares located on land adjacent to the port in East Bay", a Special Industrial Development Zone (SIDZ) of about 4,000 hectares located 30 km north of Gwadar, "an oil refinery in 1,000 hectares of land located to the northeast of Gwadar, linked to the proposed oil terminal by an underground pipeline across East Bay and a residential area of 400 hectares stretching north of the existing town of Gwadar along the West Bay".[25]

In order to connect Gwadar to rest of the country a 529 km long coastal highway has been built at a cost of 10 billion Pakistani rupees.[26] The additional development projects also envisage electrical supply of 132 KV Transmission Line from Turbat to Gwadar at an approximate cost of Rs. 360 million.[27] A feasibility report on connecting Gwadar Port with rail track is being completed. The proposed 550 km rail track would connect Gwadar with Dalbandin via Turbat and Panjgur. This would not only help goods from Central Asian Republics and Afghanistan to reach Gwadar but copper from Saindak project and Reko Diq copper gold project will be exported to foreign countries from this port. Rail connectivity with Gwadar would approximately cost Rs 8,500 million.[28] There are plans to upgrade the existing length of runway at Gwadar Airport from 5,000 ft to 15,000 ft for operation of wide bodied jet aircraft, but recent reports indicate that a new site is being developed to construct a new airport.[29]

Gwadar offers enormous possibilities as far as business is concerned; a number of economic activities are possible. These include fish processing, crab processing, cold storages, ice factories, sea water reverse osmosis desalination plants, business development, service providers, oil palm cultivation, marine and automobile repair workshops, renewable energy, wind and solar energy, clearing and forwarding agencies, hospitals, re-rolling mills, shrimp farming, training services in fisheries and aquaculture, port management projects, hotels, restaurants and resorts, date processing, canned food, gravel crush plant, water sports centre and recreation facilities, cluster for internet service providers, warehouses, boat building and naval architecture, oil storage tankers, ferry service for Karachi, Ormara and Pasni as well as for Oman and Dubai.[30] Pakistani elite believes that Gwadar port project would "generate huge economic activity paving the way for the progress and development of Balochistan". This project could also open the opportunities to export natural resources and minerals of Balochistan.[31]

## Regional Interests

Chinese involvement in the construction of the port has led to speculation about China's interest in this vital port. Some analysts feel that China would like to use this port to supply the economically underdeveloped regions of western China. China can use this port to supply energy to its hinterland without worrying about its oil supplies being choked in the straits of Southeast Asia. The port also provides China a toe hold in the crucial Persian Gulf. Though primarily built as a commercial port, the port can be used by Pakistani Navy as well as Chinese Navy and any reasonable naval force at the port can easily interdict any ship leaving or entering the Gulf. The port, therefore, gives significant maritime capabilities to any maritime power using it. According to Pakistani authorities, several countries, including the UAE, Saudi Arabia and Singapore have shown interest in the operations of Gwadar port.[32]

Though China was initially not very keen to provide funds for the construction of the port project because of US troops' presence in airbases in Jacobabad (Sindh) and Pasni (Balochistan), it finally agreed to offer financial and technical assistance for the project, after it asked for 'sovereign guarantees' to use the port facilities to which Pakistan agreed, despite US unease over it. The Chinese aim through Gwadar "to integrate Pakistan into the Chinese economy by outsourcing low-tech, labour-absorbing, resource-intensive industrial production to Islamabad, which will transform Pakistan into a giant factory floor for China". Ultimately, Gwadar will be available for trade and commerce to China through highways and possibly railways that will stretch to and from Karakoram Highway in Gilgit-Baltistan that border Xinjiang.[33]

The movement of energy resources and commerce between China and Pakistan will be enhanced considerably once the proposed highway to connect Gwadar port to the Karakoram Highway is built.[34] China aims to use Pakistan as an energy corridor between China and the Gulf and plans to develop a two lane highway from Gwadar to Gilgit with oil and gas pipelines and optical fibre running alongside. It also intends to use this port to facilitate exports from Chinese factories located in northwestern China. It has accordingly constructed a dry port at Sust, 140 km north of Gilgit, which was inaugurated by General Pervez Musharraf on 4 July 2006.[35] "China and Pakistan have agreed, in principle, to build a trans-Karakoram oil pipeline along the Karakoram Highway to connect the Middle East with northwestern China through Gwadar". The pipeline would facilitate the flow of oil and gas from the landlocked Central Asia to the rest of the world. Like the trans-Alaska pipeline, it should be possible to establish an oil and gas "grid starting from Turkmenistan or

Kazakhstan travelling through Tajikistan and the uninhabited Wakhan corridor and the peaceful Ishkoman valley of the Northern Areas to converge with the trans-Karakoram pipeline at around Gilgit for onward transportation to Gwadar."[36]

This will ensure the availability of Caspian oil to the world market, especially "the rapidly growing economies in Asia, bypassing conflict-prone and politically problematic countries like Afghanistan, Iran, Russia, Armenia, Chechnya and even Georgia. The proposed route also bypasses the comparatively troubled spots within Pakistan like the Tribal Areas and the restive Balochistan province". There is also the possibility to link up Gilgit to Karachi instead of Gwadar, through Punjab thereby avoiding the troubled province of Balochistan totally. The region is endowed with vast reserves of oil and gas. According to reports, "the proven natural gas reserves are estimated at more than 236 trillion cubic feet, and estimated oil reserves range up to 243 billion barrels". As the entire infrastructure including the oil grids were designed during the days of the Soviet Union, they have been so constructed that they feed the consumers in Russia. Russia thus maintained its hold over the production of oil and gas in the former Soviet Central Asian Republics and all export of these energy resources to outside world. However, the 1,176 km-long Baku-Tbilisi-Ceyhan (BTC) pipeline which started transporting oil from the Caspian Sea in Azerbaijan to the southeastern Mediterranean port of Ceyhan in Turkey through Georgia on 28 May 2006, has made "the first serious effort to wean Central Asia away from the Russian clutches". US Department of Energy estimates that the oil reserves of Azerbaijan and Kazakhstan alone are more than three times the reserves of the United States and are believed to be more than 130 million barrels. Given the fast rate of resource depletion, and the chronic political uncertainties of the Middle East, the energy reserves of the Caspian assume greater significance.[37]

Plans are also afoot for a rail link between Pakistan and China by extending the railroad from Xinjiang to facilitate a faster movement of cargo and personnel between the two countries. It also fits in their plans "to seek access to Central Asian markets for energy imports and Chinese exports by developing road networks and rail links through Afghanistan and Pakistan into Central Asia" and "to appease restive parts of western China, especially the Muslim-majority autonomous region of Xinjiang, through a massive infusion of development funds and increased economic links with the Islamic nations of Pakistan, Afghanistan, Kazakhstan, Kyrgyzstan, Tajikistan and Uzbekistan".[38] Moreover as long as Afghanistan continues to be turbulent, Karakoram Highway may emerge as the trade route for countries of Central Asia as well. Pakistan is already considering movement of goods to Central Asian Republics through Xinjiang, thereby avoiding the need to transit through a hostile and unstable Afghanistan.

"The port, by design or by default, also provides China a strategic foothold in the Arabian Sea and the Indian Ocean", and causes alarm in India and discomfort in the US. Being located just outside "the Strait of Hormuz, through which 80 per cent of the world's energy exports flow, the Gwadar port will enable China to monitor its energy shipments from the Persian Gulf".[39] Presently China imports 80 per cent of its oil "through the narrow and piracy-prone Malacca straits. The trans-Karakorum pipeline will allow it to import oil in a more secure and sustainable mode".[40] It would also enable it an alternative option of importing oil and gas from Central Asia, "in case of any hostile interruption" to its shipments, from the Gulf. "Its presence on the Indian Ocean will further increase its strategic influence with major South Asian nations, particularly Bangladesh, Nepal, Pakistan, and Sri Lanka".[41]

According to US Director of Net Assessment, China is pursuing a strategy of 'string of pearls' that incorporates building of strategic relationships along the sea lanes from the Middle East to the South China Sea in ways that suggest both defensive and offensive positioning to protect China's energy interests. It also aims at serving broad security objectives by building bases and establishing diplomatic ties stretching all the way from the Middle East to southern China, including Gwadar. According to him "Beijing has already set up electronic eavesdropping posts at Gwadar and is monitoring ship traffic through the Strait of Hormuz and the Arabian Sea."

## Limitations

Ideally, a mega project that triggers economic development and provides employment should have usually been welcomed by the local residents, but the Baloch people are not happy with Gwadar Deep Sea Project. Although the Pakistani government has ambitious plans for developing Gwadar, and it could be the harbinger of prosperity in the region, the Baloch insurgents have been targeting the work and the personnel associated with the project quite regularly. Three Chinese engineers working for a Chinese construction company in Gwadar were killed and nine others were injured when their vehicle was attacked by the insurgents. Rockets were also fired on Gwadar airport.[42] Authorities claim that local people are being given employment in this project on a preferential basis and have been trained to operate the machinery and equipment installed at the port. Many of them have been sent to Karachi and Islamabad for training but "the Baloch leaders complain that the manpower for the project, which is being run by the federal government, is drawn largely from outside the province".[43] The channelling of funds has mainly been in the hands of the non-Baloch, because the provincial government has been totally dissociated from the project and it has accordingly been alleged that the Baloch plea for control over decisions pertaining to development activities have been ignored by the Punjabi bureaucracy. Added to this is the perception of being colonised by Punjabi real estate cartel. The Baloch complained that Punjabi settlers have been grabbing prime land and property in and around Gwadar.[44]

Pakistani government has tried to impress upon the locals that Gwadar "will provide a lot of opportunities of not only employment but business, trade and investment for everyone", but according to Abdul Hakim Baloch, a former Chief Secretary of Balochistan, "the basic issue is not the construction or the operation of the project but its ownership". The government land around the port and the Makran coastal highway, "which belongs to the province, has been usurped by the land mafia in collaboration with the Makrani underworld and its members who are in government and the legislative bodies". This act of land grabbing, which is the result of the criminal-politician nexus and in complete violation of the existing laws, has deprived the provincial government of Balochistan of a major source of revenue, with a potential to generate trillions of rupees. Besides, Gwadar has been connected to Karachi, but it has not been connected through Turbat, Panjgur and Khuzdar to Quetta, the provincial capital. As a result, the rest of the province will not derive any benefit from these projects. "This is making the people restive as they feel that they are being converted into a landlocked province despite having the longest coastline in the country".[45]

On the other hand the people from outside will not only gain economically but in due course will also colonise the coastal regions. Baloch nationalists feel that fruits of Gwadar will not reach the Baloch people; on the contrary, they feel it will lead to large scale influx of outsiders in Balochistan[46] and make them a minority in their own province. "There are also fears that unbridled foreign investment and development projects will bring too much foreign influence, threatening the indigenous social and cultural patterns".[47] According to former chief minister of Balochistan Ataullah Mengal, "If there are jobs in Gwadar, people would flock there, Pakistanis and foreigners alike. With time, they would get the right to vote". However, if Gwadar ends up with a migrant population equal to that of Karachi, it would turn the Baloch population into a hopeless minority. "Gwadar will end up sending more members to the Parliament than the rest of Balochistan, We would lose our identity, our language, everything".[48]

## Conclusion

Situated at the cusp of the Strait of Hormuz through which most of the world's oil flows, Gwadar Deep Sea Project being completed with financial assistance from China is the largest developmental project being undertaken in Pakistan and has enormous economic potential. At a time when both China and South Asia are experiencing a sharp rise in the demand for energy, which is expected to double in the coming decade, the port along with Trans-Karakoram pipeline "opens more exciting opportunities to unlock the true business potential of the energy resources" being extracted from the landlocked states of Central Asia.[49] The port can become another Dubai and change the landscape of Balochistan. The port and other associated economic activities have the potential to take the Pakistani economy to great heights. Besides its economic value, the port has enormous strategic and defence potential. It not only reduces congestion and dependency on existing ports complex at Karachi and Port Qasim Authority but also serves as an alternate port to handle Pakistan's trade in case of blockade of existing ports.[50] It also provides any naval force the wherewithal to influence the events in Persian Gulf, which is probably the most important economic and geostrategically the most vulnerable maritime zone in the world.

From India's point of view, Gwadar Deep Sea Port poses a long term threat. Most of India's energy imports originate in Persian Gulf region and most of these are offloaded at the Single Point Mooring (SPM) at Vadinar in the Gulf of Kutch. Most of these ships carrying supplies for SPM at Vadinar pass less than 40 nm from Gwadar and would be extremely vulnerable in case of any hostilities with Pakistan. The port would also enable Pakistan to monitor Indian shipping to and from Persian Gulf and will enable its interdiction. It is quite feasible that Pakistan may use it to apply pressure on India to force it to come to some sort of accommodation on contentious issues. Besides, if Gwadar emerges as the Gateway to Afghanistan and Central Asia, then Indo-Iranian project of developing Chah Bahar Port and onward road link to Afghanistan via Zaranj and Delaram will probably not remain cost effective. International trade would shift to the port that becomes fully functional at the earliest. Some Pakistanis do believe that insurgency in Balochistan has been triggered by external powers that are opposed to the development of Gwadar Port.

Despite Gwadar's enormous potential there is no dearth of sceptics doubting its ability to deliver. The underlying reason is that despite its huge potential, Gwadar can not attain economic viability till it is connected to Quetta by road or rail for it to emerge as a bridgehead to Central Asia. Similarly, as far as China or even access to Central Asia through China is concerned, its viability depends on timely completion of Gwadar – Ratto Dero Motorway. The use of Makran Coastal highway to transport goods does not make commercial sense because it almost amounts to taking goods to Karachi by road which could be done much more economically by sea. Gwadar's potential to become the future trade and energy hub for the growing economies of West, South and East Asia and the landlocked Central Asian Republics, therefore, lies in cutting down of transportation costs and time to the port. However, this can not be achieved as long as the restive population of Balochistan does not feel enthusiastic about its potential. As long as violence continues, Pakistan can not emerge as an energy corridor to China nor can a direct road link to Central Asia be established. Not only does violence affect the investor confidence, it also affects the implementation of infrastructural projects, especially the pipelines, roads and rail links, which can not be perpetually defended in their entirety.[51] As long as violence continues in Balochistan, foreign direct investment in Gwadar is not likely to materialise, including from friendly China. If Gwadar has to develop as a future Karachi, it will require a large private investment.

Despite the operationalisation of the port, the successful culmination of the project is fraught with uncertainty. There is, however, no doubt that successful completion of the project will result in emergence of an ideal gateway for the landlocked states of Afghanistan and Central Asia. It will yield enormous benefits to Pakistan and provide China with a crucial outpost in the Persian Gulf. Finally, it is going to be Pakistan's handling of discontentment in Balochistan and to some extent in Gilgit-Baltistan through which Karakoram Highway traverses, which will decide the ultimate viability of Gwadar Port Project.

## ENDNOTES

1. "Gwadar Port as Trade, Energy Corridor", *The International News*, Internet Edition, 20 June 2006.
2. "China sees Pakistan as Energy Corridor", *The International News*, Internet Edition, 17 June 2006.
3. B. Raman, "Let Down by India", from Outlook Website http://www.outlookindia.com/full.asp?fodname=20060616&fname=raman1&sid=1&pn=2 (Accessed on 20 June 2006).
4. "Gwadar's Rich Potential", *Dawn*, Karachi, 13 June 2006.
5. Alok Bansal, "Gwadar – Port of Hope or Despair?", From IPCS Website http://www.ipcs.org/whatsNewArticle11.jsp?action=showView&kValue=1796&status=article&mod=b (Accessed on 14 August 2006).
6. "First cargo ship anchors at Gwadar Port", from http://www.app.com.pk/en_/index.php?option=com_content&task=view&id=32210&Itemid=2 (Accessed on 23 December 2008)
7. Saleem Shahid, "Gwadar port becomes fully functional" *Dawn*, December 22, 2008.
8. "First Phase of Gwadar Port Completed", *Dawn*, Karachi, 4 December 2004.
9. President of Pakistan General Pervez Musharraf's Address at the Ground-Breaking Ceremony of Gwadar Deep Sea Port on 22 March 2002.
10. Alok Bansal, "Implications of Gwadar Port Project", *Journal for Indian Ocean Studies*, vol. 13, no. 2, August 2005, p. 183.
11. Noor ul Haq, "Balochistan: Its Past and Present", *The Kashmir Times*, 8 February 2005.
12. Govt of Pakistan Board of Investment Website http://www.pakboi.gov.pk/News_Event/Gawadar.html (Accessed on 22 June 2005)
13. Noor ul Haq, n. 10.
14. Tarique Niazi, "Gwadar: China's Naval Outpost on the Indian Ocean", Association for Asian Research Website http://www.asianresearch.org/articles/2528.html (Accessed on 22 June 2005)
15. Note 11 ibid.
16. Note 7 ibid.
17. "Pakistan to Decide Operator for Gwadar Port next Week", from *Khaleej Times* Website http://www.khaleejtimes.com/DisplayArticleNew.asp?xfile=data/business/2006/August/business_August318.xml&section=business (Accessed on 14 August 2006).
18. Ihtashamul Haque, "Tax-free zones in Gwadar Planned: Wooing Foreign Investment", *Dawn*, Karachi, 17 June 2005.
19. Alok Bansal, "Gwadar – A Chinese Gibraltar", *India Strategic*, vol. 1, February 2006, p. 53.
20. Ihtashamul Haque, "Rs 16.3 bn released for Gwadar port project", *The Dawn*, Karachi, 1 June 2005.
21. Phase II has reportedly been completed by end of June 2006, though no formal handing over ceremony has taken place.
22. B. Raman, "The Baloch Cause", Opinion, Outlook.com (Accessed on 19 April 2005).
23. "President for completing Gwadar port by June 2006", *The International News*, Internet Edition, 11 June 2005
24. Tahir Rathore, "Pak, Chinese presidents to open Gwadar Port", *The International News*, Internet Edition 27 November 2004.
25. Ibid.
26. Malik Siraj Akbar, "Who leads the Baloch", *The Nation*, Lahore, 29 December 2004.
27. Rathore, n. 23.
28. "Gwadar Rail Track would be completed soon", *The Frontier Post*, 19 November 2004.
29. "Aziz directs acceleration of Gwadar work", *Daily Times* Website http://www.dailytimes.com.pk/default.asp?page=story_5-6-2005_pg7_28 (Accessed on 8 June 2005).
30. Rathore, n. 23.

31. "Expectations from Gwadar", Editorial, *The International News,* Internet Edition, 7 October 2004.
32. Rathore, n. 23.
33. Tarique Niazi, n 13.
34. "Gwadar-KKH link", Editorial, *Dawn*, 6 July 2006.
35. Safdar Khan, "Karakoram Highway's Gwadar link likely", *The Dawn*, Karachi, 5 July 2006.
36. M Ismail Khan, "The Trans-Karakoram Oil Pipeline", *The International News*, Internet Edition, 31 October 2006.
37. Ibid.
38. Tarique Niazi, n 13.
39. Ibid.
40. M. Ismail Khan, n 35.
41. Tarique Niazi, n 13.
42. Shahzada Zulfiqar, "Port of Terror", *Newsline*, June 2004, p 56.
43. "Balochistan's Grievances", Editorial, *The Dawn,* 9 November 2004.
44. Urmila Phadnis, "Ethnic Movements in Pakistan", in Pandav Nayak (ed.), *Pakistan: Society and Politics* – South Asian Studies Series, *6*. New Delhi, South Asian Publishers Pvt Ltd, 1984, p. 195.
45. Abdul Hakim Baloch, "Bringing development to Balochistan", *The Dawn,* 13 December 2004.
46. "Terrorism in Balochistan". Editorial, *The Dawn,* 18 December 2004.
47. "Confrontation No Solution to Balochistan Imbroglio", Editorial, *The International News Internet Edition,* 16 January 2005.
48. Idrees Bakhtiar, "Mega-projects are a Conspiracy to turn the Balochis into a Minority in their Homeland", an interview with Sardar Ataullah Mengal, *The Herald*, August 2004, p. 51.
49. M Ismail Khan, n 35.
50. Rathore, n. 23.
51. Alok Bansal, "Gwadar Port: Economic Panacea or A Red Herring" from IPCS Website http://www.ipcs.org/whatsNewArticle.jsp?action=showView&kValue=2104&status=article&mod=b (Accessed on 14 August 2006).

# 20

# India and Afghanistan: Options for Access and Trade

*Mondira Dutta*

## Context

Afghanistan is considered as the 'Crossroad of Asia' and its mere location became a perfect meeting point for the famous Silk Route. The north led to Samarkand, Bukhara and Khiva ultimately entering into the steppe; in the east it led to China and further on; in the south-east was the undivided India; in the west was Iran, which went on to the Mediterranean Sea and ultimately to Europe. Thus any trade that took place in the region could not have avoided passing through Afghanistan.

The glorious past was a witness to the region of South Asia and Central Asia, mingling and merging amongst itself through the Silk Route spreading religion, trade and culture. Over a period of time, alternative routes were explored discovering new routes. No one even noticed when colonization started and millions became slaves of a few. Finally the heyday of the Silk Route came to an end and its importance started diminishing as new trade routes emerged. The world has changed drastically since then. But the indisputable facts of history, geography and culture have left behind the mangled remains of ancient trade routes which continue to influence much of the region's economic trade and transport linkages even today.

Afghanistan forms the bridge between India, Central Asia and Iran. Today India has come a long way from the period of the cold war when Afghanistan bordered British India's Northwest Frontier Province (NWFP). In fact a significant Pashtun population from the NWFP participated extensively in the Indian independence movement.[1] The significant cultural and economic linkages developed painstakingly over the centuries are under constant threat and are getting eroded and fragmented with divides based on ethnicity, religion, race and color. Tagore's 'Kabulliwalah' days of the late nineteenth century seem to be a fantasy and an unrealistic past in comparison to today's world of political realism. Unfortunately years of violence and conflict have shattered the region's economic and transport linkages. Every regional and global player seems to be engaged in looking out for a smooth access into the 'Crossroad of Asia' in order to deepen their strategic partnership and widen their scope of a stronghold in the region. Most of the country has no roads, no piped water and no electricity. It's a common sight to find miles and miles of dilapidated buildings with few schools and hospitals located in broken buildings or in the open. Unfortunately "the Afghans had done more damage to their own country than had the Soviets."[2] If the security concerns could be addressed in the country of Afghanistan, it would become the "linchpin of a trading network connecting Iran, Central Asia, India and China."[3]

India's relations with Afghanistan reiterate the ancient historical perspective, the reminiscences of which are still visible in Delhi and large parts of northern India which are littered with monuments testifying to the relationship that existed between India and Afghanistan for several centuries. There are libraries in many parts of India such as the Rahul Raza library, the Khuda Baksh library in Patna, the library in Bhopal and many others which contain a huge wealth of details on the quality of relation that existed between different communities in India and Afghanistan. To this date there are communities in parts of northern India and also in Rajasthan, which have distinctly Afghan background and all these factors reveal the strong bonding that existed between India and Afghanistan over the centuries.

The close relationship that once existed between India and Afghanistan soon ended when Taliban came into power. The Taliban controlled Afghanistan was a source of grave security threat for India, such impressions got authenticated through the enhanced terrorist activities in Kashmir during the nineties. The hijacking of the Indian Airlines Flight IC 814 in 1999 to Kandahar and the destruction of Bamiyan Buddhas also occurred during the Taliban rule. It was only in 2001 after the Taliban were thrown out of power that India developed its normal relations once again.

The media discourse has been largely dominated by the security threats in Afghanistan. Such a perspective is important from the national security point of view as Afghanistan is critical to the rest of South Asia. There is a direct connection between the deterioration of internal security environment in India and rise of violence and extremism in Afghanistan.

India came forward along with several global players in contributing towards the reconstruction process in Afghanistan post-9/11. The world community today is engaged in various action-oriented programmes in Afghanistan with the objective of its reconstruction depth and ushering in peace and stability into this war torn region. Even after a decade since the Bonn agreement, peace and stability continues to elude the region. Afghanistan continues to play the centre stage for all the wrong reasons like terrorism, poppy production, drug trafficking and insurgency. India's contribution of $1.3 billion aid package towards the reconstruction process of Afghanistan has made it among the top five international donors making the Indian presence conspicuous much to the annoyance of Pakistan which has been considering

Afghanistan as its backyard. This has resulted in the sacrifice of lives of several Indians in Afghanistan as a result of suicide bombers and target attacks.

Some of the sectors in which India's contribution has been significant are hydro-electricity, power transmission lines, road construction, agriculture and industry, telecommunications, information and broadcasting, capacity development, humanitarian assistance, education and health. These are identified as the priority sectors according to the government of Afghanistan. The Indian contribution may be categorized under six heads.[4]

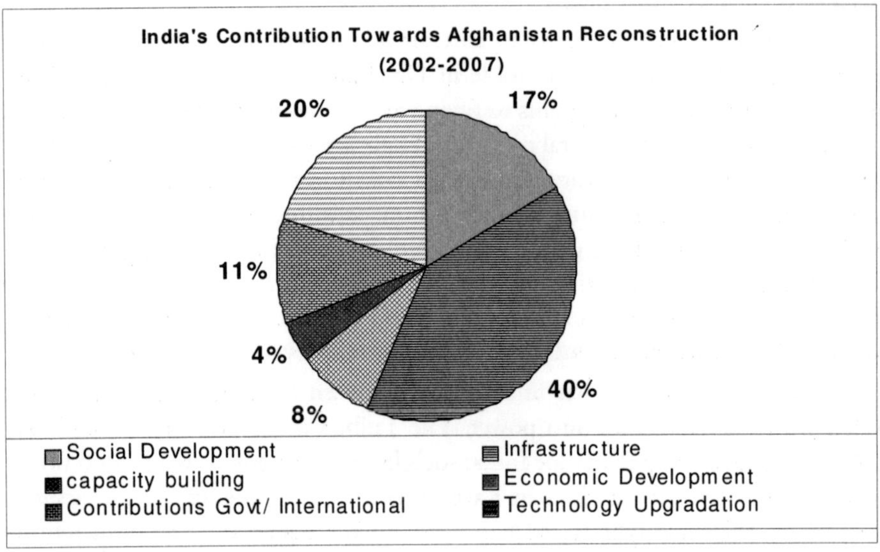


**Source:** Dutta Mondira, 2008 in *World Focus*.

Major thrust of the Indian contribution (40 percent) has been in the sector of infrastructure. This includes the supply of aircraft, buses and vehicles. It also includes the construction of transmission lines and solar electrification in addition to development of roads. In terms of approximate expenditure (in million USD), the infrastructure development involves a large share of the total expenditure amounting to the tune of $39.1 million.[5] Despite threats and suicide attacks on Indian personnel, India has successfully completed some of the major projects in this sector including the construction of a highway of 218 kms from Zaranj to Delaram linking Afghanistan with Iran and curtailing Pakistan's hegemony over the link through the Gwadar port. India has been appreciated by the US and others for having contributed greatly towards diplomatic relations and development activities which form two out of the major three components of international presence in Afghanistan. Defense is the only component where India has restrained in getting involved. A survey[6] was commissioned jointly by the BBC, ABC News of America and ARD of Germany, covering more than 1,500 people. The sample was divided equally between men and women and taken from all of the country's 34 provinces. It clearly showed the Indian preference over Pakistan by the respondents in Afghanistan.

In one of the field visits undertaken for studying the impact of government of India's initiatives by the author in May 2010,[7] praises for Indian initiatives were conveyed by native Afghans from the villages of Balkh province in north Afghanistan. They appreciated the timely help by the Government of India in activating a deep well which had stopped working after being installed and handed over to the community. Each deep well supplied water to six or seven villages. Thus the non-functioning of the water supply implied a lot of hardship for the community.

It would be inappropriate for India to lose its foothold in Afghanistan at this stage after incurring a huge expenditure in addition to the loss of Indian lives. India is aware and shares the same concern along with the US about the expanding role of China in Central Asia. Pakistan is a strong ally of China and both have a vested common interest in curbing the influence of India. Therefore, any void created by India will be quickly replaced by China. Hence a weakened Indian role in Afghanistan will be advantageous for China, which has a larger geopolitical interest in the region.

## Indian Involvement and Project Sustainability

Many of the projects that have been undertaken by India in Afghanistan are either complete or nearing completion. These include the Zaranj–Delaram road, the construction of transmission line from Kabul to Pul-e-Khumri in the north which extends further to Afghanistan, building of Habibia School and the construction of the Parliament for the Afghan government. India has also been involved in a number of smaller projects in terms of electricity generation and also helping in irrigation and related works. Energy is an area where India has concentrated a considerable amount of resources. However mere construction will not help unless the ownership is handed over and run by the local resource people themselves. India has been forthright in ensuring that there is an adequate number of technical manpower available in Afghanistan to run all these projects after they are handed over. If they are not, it would only be a half hearted attempt by the donor agency and the project would not reach its logical end. Thus capacity building has to be initiated with a holistic approach and begin from the school extending up to the universities, people working in fields and the technical capacities which are available with the Afghan government. Accordingly India's capacity building programmes that are currently implemented are promising and ambitious. Among the most visible ones are the scholarships awarded to persons who finish school and come to India for graduate and undergraduate studies. These total to around 675 and in addition another 675 scholarships are awarded to people who are already working either with the government or elsewhere. They come to India for short courses to enhance their own technical skills and technological capabilities. These annual scholarships goes a long way in training the next generation of persons who would be available to the Afghan government for addressing its future needs. There are other capacity building measures imparted to empower the women in Afghanistan through implementing partners such as SEWA, Hand in Hand, Confederation of Indian Industries, etc. The capacity building programme includes a range of other programmes such as the civil servants who are attached to different ministries. These civil servants in Afghanistan are the trainers in building up the capacities of the different administrative ministries and so on. Capacity building is an important component without which it would be a futile exercise putting up the entire hardware for a particular project. It cannot be left without any sustainability programme as regards how to maintain and keep it going for the future. So the aim by the Indian government has largely been to see that every completed project is handed over to personnel who are fully equipped to maintain it and run it in the foreseeable future.

In terms of health sector there are several missions in different parts of Afghanistan where teams of doctors extend primarily to out-patient department services. Attacks by the Taliban have taken the lives of some Indian doctors and development workers who were attacked in February 2010 killing as many as nine Indians. India has been involved in the upgrading of some of the hospitals in Afghanistan – the most important of which is the Indira Gandhi Child hospital in Kabul. There are programme for doctors from Afghanistan coming to different hospitals in India for attachments which range from two/three months to a year. The local Afghans are also permitted to come to India for health checkups and medical consultation.

In addition to security issues India faces the biggest disadvantage for want of a direct road linkage. There is no common border shared by India and Afghanistan. This has forced the Indian government to use indirect routes of transportation incurring huge costs, enormous hardship, time and effort. While India is actively involved in reconstructing the infrastructure within Afghanistan, at the same time it has to look for the via media to reach Afghanistan. The most visible challenge therefore is the spatial location of Afghanistan itself. Although Afghanistan is a bridge, but the fact remains that reaching the bridge is the biggest hurdle for India. This issue of transit through Pakistan dominates the entire programme in Afghanistan because absence of a transit implies that every project or every programme is much more expensive and much more difficult to execute. For example India has assisted in building the construction line from Kabul to Pul-e-Khumri. There is an Indian company which has built this section of the line. There is financial assistance for the same company which will then further build the line from Pul-e-Khumri to Uzbekistan as part of the ADB project. India actually built a substation which connects the transmission line all the way from the Uzbek border to Kabul. The idea was to bring power from Uzbekistan to Kabul so that the power shortage in Kabul is met with. In building the substation the biggest problem faced was the transshipment of equipments. This is due to the fact that there has been deterioration of situation in several pockets. This reflects that the road option that existed for transporting the equipment from India to Iran by sea and thereafter from Bander Abbas through trucks to the Afghan border and from there to Kabul would be extremely risky and difficult due to the rise of Taliban and their attacks on the convoy. The equipment itself was extremely large, costly and too risky to transport it by the road option especially in the absence of a proper transit. Thus the only option available was to airlift the equipment where each part ran into 100 to 120 tonnes.

Similarly many of the capacity building measures and training programme undertaken by SEWA[8] and other NGOs had to airlift sophisticated machines from India to Afghanistan. Therefore transit continues to be a very important component of the challenges. While Afghan products can reach Indian markets through Pakistan but it does not allow Indian goods to be transported through its soil to Afghanistan. Hence the construction of the 218 km road from Zaranj to Delaram has been a major achievement. But how far this will provide an ideal substitute is yet to be realized. The Taliban opposed tooth and nail this project and launched frequent attacks on the construction workers, so that work may be abandoned. A total of six Indians, including a Border Roads Organization driver and four ITBP soldiers, and 129 Afghans were killed in these attacks.[9] However this road has been completed and the road handed over to the Government of Afghanistan.

The present paper attempts to study the possible options of road linkages that lie dormant between India and Afghanistan with the help of Geographical Information System. It also highlights the road linkages that connect the major cities of Afghanistan. However, despite the existence of well defined route linkages, the flow remains restricted and even non-existent due to political barriers. An attempt has been made to analyze the best possible viable routes available before India in the context of present geo-political situation in the region.

## Transport Linkages within Afghanistan

Afghanistan's internal transport system may be studied with the help of Table 1. It suggests the poor connectivity of road infrastructure that exists today with major provincial roads still to be repaired. This would hamper not only the speedy progress of reconstruction process but also in developing trade and developmental activities.

**Table 1: Intra Connectivity of Afghanistan**

| | |
|---|---|
| **Roads** | • Afghanistan had 8,200 kilometres of paved roads and 26600 kms of unpaved roads in 2003. Most of the provincial roads are still in ruins.<br>• Main connections are with the cities of Ghazni, Herat, Kabul and Kandahar to Pakistan.<br>• Commercial and military connections through Salang & Tang-e-Gharu passes.<br>• Major partners towards road construction are US, Germany, Japan, India, Iran, Pakistan and others. |
| **Railways** | • There existed 5 short domestic lines in 2006 including one line passing across the friendship bridge into Uzbekistan.<br>• All lines built from the neighbourhood towards Afghanistan abruptly end at the borders.<br>• Five new freight dispatch stations along the borders in 2006 were developed to link domestic roads with railroad lines from neighbouring countries were initiated. |
| **Ports** | • The main ports along its chief waterway, the Amu Darya constitute the ports of Kheyrabad and Shir Khan. |
| **Inland Waterways** | • The Amu Darya River runs for 800 kms along Afghanistan's border and can ac commodate large scale vessels up to 500 tons. |

| | |
|---|---|
| **Civil Aviation & Airports** | • 46 airports were in operation in 2005 with only three runways of 3,000 meters.<br>• Kabul International Airport, was under renovation in 2005 and did not have international certification.<br>• Airports at Herat, Jalalabad, and Mazar-e Sharif still lack the basic facilities.<br>• In 2003 the first private airline, Kam Air, began operating flights.<br>• After regaining approval for international flights Ariana began regular flights to Delhi, Dubai, Frankfurt, Islamabad, Istanbul, and Moscow in 2004.<br>• Both Ariana and Kam were rated as having poor safety regulations in 2005.<br>• Since 2002, Afghanistan has received substantial foreign assistance; India has trained flight staff and contributed Airbuses.<br>• However the local airports are still under renovation and far from being secure. |

**Source:** Library of Congress, 2006.[10]

It was in 1960s that a 'Ring Road' was conceived to be developed as a highway connecting the country's major cities. Feeder routes were to be developed in order to link the provincial capitals and smaller towns with the 'Ring Road', with assistance from various countries. The United States came forward for the construction towards south of the Hindukush, the Soviet Union helped towards the north of the Hindukush and West Germany for Paktya Province. These roads in turn were to connect the major cities with the principal border crossings such as:

- Herat to Iran and Turkmenistan in the west
- Kandahar to Pakistan in the south
- Kabul through Jalalabad to Pakistan in the east
- Balkh to Uzbekistan in the north

However such a plan was never realized as war broke out in the 1970s even before the northern section of the 'Ring Road' could be built. Subsequently, the 2,700 kilometers of the highway lay in tatters with decades of fighting that followed.

With the collapse of the Taliban regime in late 2001, major focus of the internationally backed reconstruction efforts was to repair the existing highway and complete the remaining part of the Ring Road. Referred to as the 'backbone' of Afghanistan's transportation network, this 'Ring Road' after completion could contribute significantly towards a smooth implementation of international reconstruction efforts – not only in Afghanistan but also to Central Asia promoting an efficient delivery infrastructure system. A total of 5 sub-contractor countries got involved in the reconstruction of the 'Ring Road'.

This is one massive sector that requires immense inputs. Organizations such as the World Bank and the Asian Development Bank have been actively involved in contributing towards this project, but have expressed doubts on the security concerns that daunt the developmental activities. Although the Afghan government has stepped up security along this road, but travelling on this continues to be risky and dangerous. ADB states that "it has confronted repeated security-related delays and cost overruns. The bank has agreed to pay an additional $2.5 million to train and dispatch nearly 500 police to guard road crews."[11] The last part of the road (233 kms) was to be

**Map 1: Ring Road of Afghanistan**

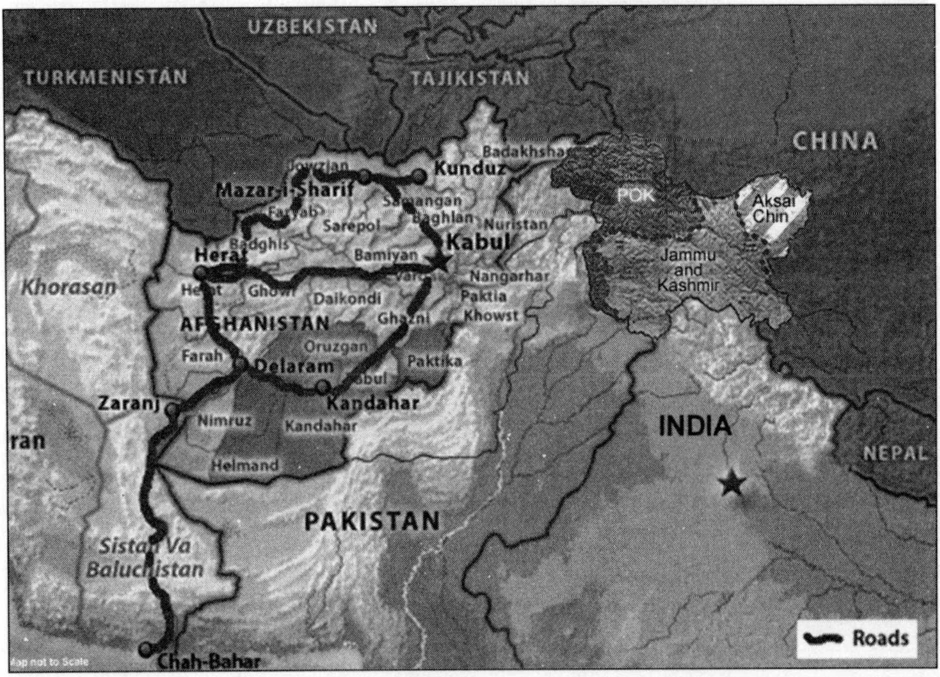


developed by Japan through the Asian Development Bank (ADB) with expenditure to the tune of $ 340 million and connecting the towns of Qaisar, Bala Murghab, and Laman. Although work has been initiated and followed along the original track foundation, but materials for developing the road structure were not available in Afghanistan and had to be brought from various countries. In addition the ADB has also contributed in developing 75 kms train line from Mazar to Uzbekistan, 420 kms transmission line from Uzbekistan to Kabul and so on. No doubt the completion of this 'Ring Road' will forge connection speeding the humanitarian assistance and linking Central Asia, South Asia and the Middle East but security concerns have dominated the scene.

The Border Roads Organization (BRO) from India has completed the 218-km long Zeranj-Delaram highway connecting it to the ring road (Refer Map 1). One cannot ignore the fact that the completed trade route passes through several sections of vulnerable areas within Afghanistan extending southwest to north before entering Central Asia, making it very lengthy and risky. According to the report of International Council on Security and Development, 2009 the southern province in Afghanistan, i.e., Nimroz where India has completed the Zaranj–Delaram road is extremely risky with a maximum concentration of the "Taliban and Insurgent activity" (80%) (See Map 2). Such concerns need to be addressed before the road can be utilized in full swing.

**Map 2: Taliban Presence in Afghanistan (August 2009)**

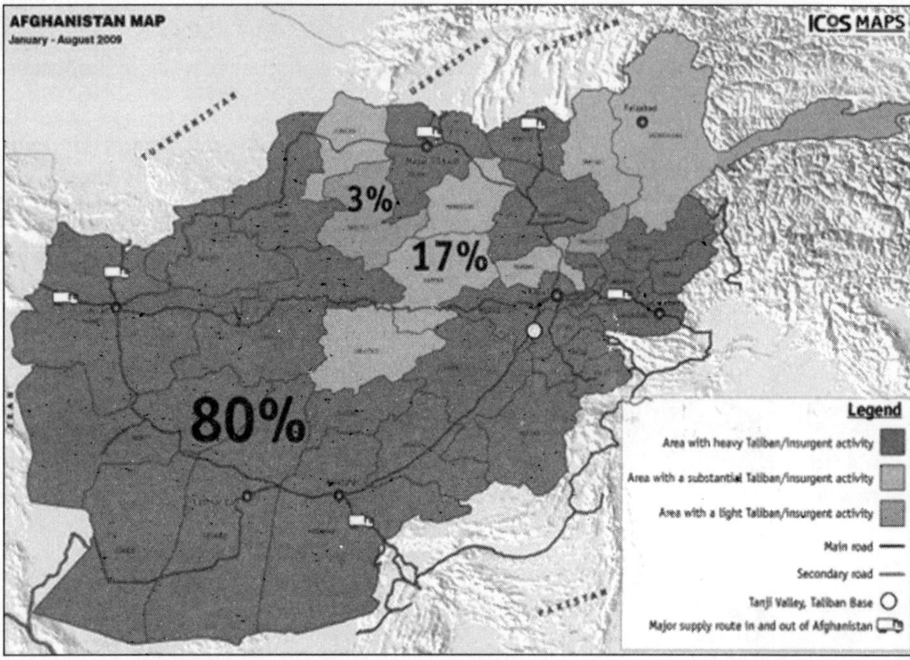


**Source:** http://www.icosmaps.net/taliban_presence/050_map/050_map (International Council on Security and Development).

## Dormant Routes

The dormant routes as identified with the help of Geographic Information System (GIS) and Google Satellite Imaginary were studied in the framework of population concentration, agriculture activities, and resource endowments. On the basis of the data collected through GIS, the partially dormant routes provide some options for route connectivity. A careful study of these nodes were undertaken and an identification of important route linkages were demarcated between India and Afghanistan considering the human habitation, concentration of economic activities and resource distribution of the region.

Some of the possible options on the basis of the dormant routes were as follows:

- India-POK-Afghanistan
- India-Nepal-Tibet-Tajikistan-Afghanistan
- India-China-Tajikistan-Afghanistan
- India-Iran-Afghanistan

## India-POK-Afghanistan

India, Pakistan and Afghanistan have all been a part of the Silk Route and have shared a common history. Remnants of such historical past are left behind in terms of road linkages and cultural uniqueness. The shortest route between India and Afghanistan is via Pak occupied Kashmir (PoK). The route that traverses through Kargil is via Skardu, Gilgit to Khunjerab Pass meandering its way into Tashkurgan in China before entering Murghab and to Afghanistan border at Khorog in Tajikistan. (See Map 3)

The Khunjerab Pass is a high mountain pass located in the Karakoram mountains on the northern border of Gilgit–Baltistan and the Xinjiang region of China. This is the only pass which is motorable and is the highest point on the Karakoram Highway and is about 130 km from Tashkurgan. The highway built by China has been functioning since 2006 from Gilgit in Kashghar of China. Attempts to make a railway connection through this pass are seriously being considered for connecting China with POK. Gilgit, the capital city of Gilgit-Baltistan was an important city during the Silk Route days, along which Buddhism spread to Asia.

The route meanders into Tashkurgan, a very important stop of the Silk Route days. This is strategically located on the borders of Afghanistan and Tajikistan with the majority of the people being ethnic Tajiks. Before entering Murghab in Tajikistan

**Map 3: India–POK–Afghanistan Route**

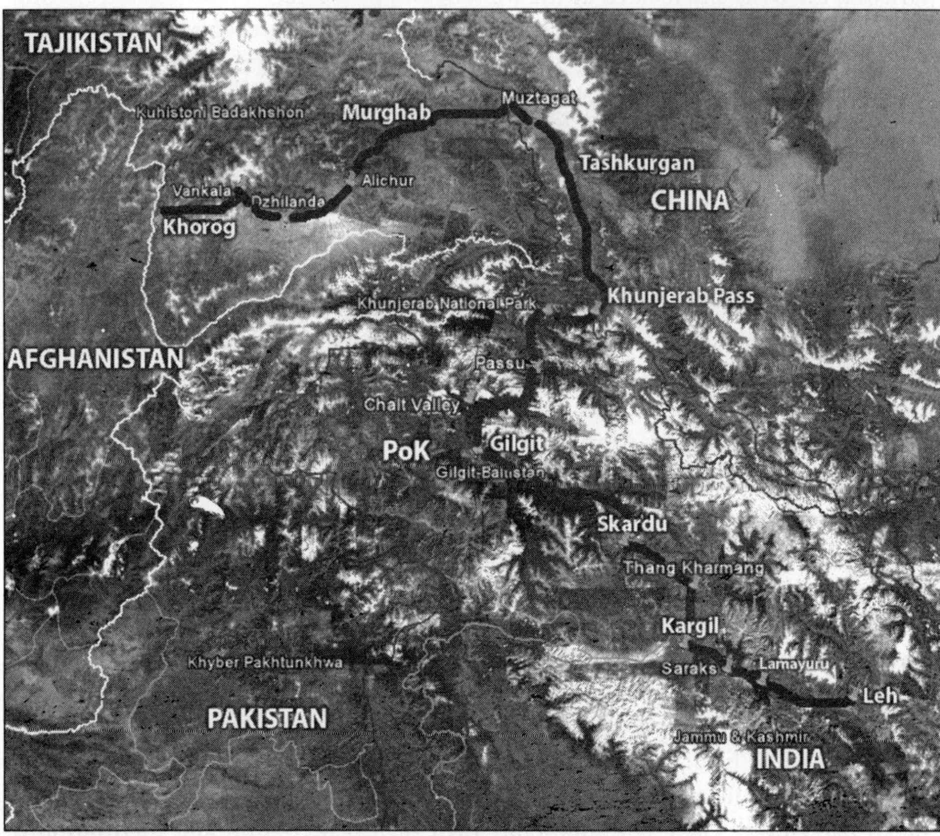

the route enters Muztag which forms the northern edge of the Tibetan Plateau. Murghab is a capital city belonging to Gorno-Badakhshan Autonomous Region of Tajikistan. The population here constitutes a mix of Pamiri and Kyrgyz. Before reaching the capital city of Khorog the route passes through the small town of Alichur which consists of mainly Kyrgyz people. The town of Khorog is the capital of the Gorno-Badakhshan Autonomous Province (GBAO) in Tajikistan. Situated along the Pamir Highway, Khorog also gets connected to the Karakoram Highway of China and Pakistan.

### India-Nepal-Tibet-Tajikistan-Afghanistan

Another option is via Nepal through Mahendernagar, Seti, Nara La to Tibet's Burang, Mansarovar Lake and Ngari. The route proceeds via Aksai Chin, Yarkand, Jiayicun and Tashkurgan in China and finally to Khorog via Murghab and Alichur. The Nara La Pass is situated on the north western border of Nepal. It is located close to Burang in Tibet and has a road which could be accessed on foot. Burang located near the borders of India and Nepal is a very ancient trading involvement. Ngari includes part of the Aksai Chin area and is still under the occupation of China. Uyghurs live in the area because of the trade between Tibet and Xinjiang. The route passes through Yarkand, the oasis city located at the western end of the Tarim river basin. A highly fertile area, it produces a variety of grain crops and the towns produce many handicrafts, such as fine cotton and silk textiles, carpets, and leather goods. The population of the oasis area includes Chinese (Han), Ughyurs, Iranians, and some South Asians. Before entering Tajikistan, the route passes through China's Jiayicum situated in Pamir Knot. Other places such as Keziletaoxiang, Lagan Dadui, Tama Kala Dadui, Plateaue of Tchitchilik are also situated on the Pamir Knot. However many parts of Pamir Knot are uninhabited. There is a short distance from Jiayicum to Tama Kala Dadui which does not have a metalled road (See Map 4). Jiayicum was referred to as Yumen in 1926.[12] A traveler moving towards Turkestan's wilderness from China cannot miss this "gay little town". The route finally reaches the Afghanistan border town of Khorog in Tajikistan.

### India-China-Tajikistan-Afghanistan

The route from Leh to Nubra Valley is located in the Ladakh province of Jammu and Kashmir in India. The Karakorum pass lies to the northwest of the valley and connect Nubra with Xinjiang which used to be very active once upon a time when trade passed through the area connecting East Turkestan and Central Asia. The Karakoram is a large mountain range lying in close proximity to China occupied Aksai Chin, spanning the borders between Pakistan, India and China located in the regions of Gilgit-Baltistan under Pakistan's control, Ladakh (India) and Xinjiang region in China. There is a stretch of unpaved road between Nubra valley and Aksai Chin. The route further enters Mazar through the Karakoram Pass and from there on to Yarkand – Jiayicun via Xilanqi in China. The surrounding areas do not have much habitation. There is a motorable road till Lagan Dadui, and then onwards

**Map 4: India-Nepal-Tibet-Tajikistan-Afghanistan Route**

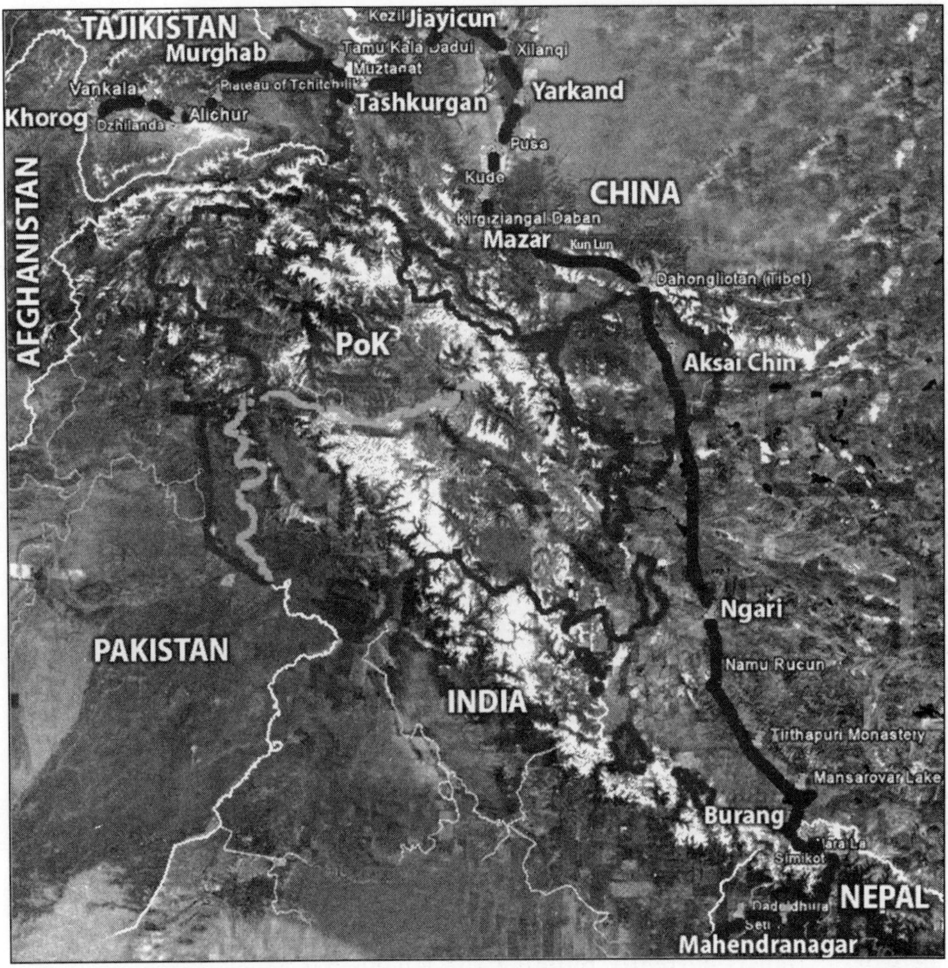


the route can be approached only by foot till Tamu Kala Dadui and further. From Tashkurgam, where majority of the people are ethnic Tajiks, a proper metalled road exists to reach Murghab in Tajikistan via Muztagah and finally reaches Khorog on the Afghanistan border. (See Map 5)

Most of the dominant dormant routes between India and Afghanistan have been identified in Map 6. A study of the map shows the existence of well defined routes barring a few patches in the Karakoram pass and between Jiayicun and Tashkurgan.

## India-Iran-Afghanistan

An alternative route linkage between India and Afghanistan has been developed by India via Iran. This route utilizes the Chah Bahar port of Iran. India is involved in assisting Iran to develop the Chah Bahar port, for accessing oil and gas resources in

**Map 5: India-China-Tajikistan-Afghanistan Route**

Iran and the Central Asian states. Chah Bahar is considered to be the best advantage point for India in terms of access to the Indian Ocean. Chah Bahar's people mostly consisting of Baluchis are very close to the Deobandi school in India, which hosts foreign students from Kazakhstan, Iran, South Africa, Malaysia etc. India is committed to rebuilding the railroad from Chahbahar to link it to the Iranian railway network. "Iran is currently building the Chahbahar-Milak-Zaranj road in Afghanistan. The three countries – India, Iran and Afghanistan – had signed a memorandum of understanding in January 2003 allowing duty free access to Chahbahar port for both Afghan and Indian goods."[13] India has constructed the 218 km highway between Zaranj and Delaram, thereby getting connected to the ring road of Afghanistan. Zaranj is located in south west Afghanistan in Nimruz province constituting mainly of Baloch and Pashtun ethnic groups. Delaram located on the Ring Road in western Afghanistan is a hub with convergence of several major roads.

## Viable Options

The route linkages which display a strong evidence of historical and cultural ties that bonded the region as one single entity once upon a time, can no longer trigger off trade and commerce among the concerned countries. The region today has

**Map 6: Dormant Routes between India and Afghanistan**

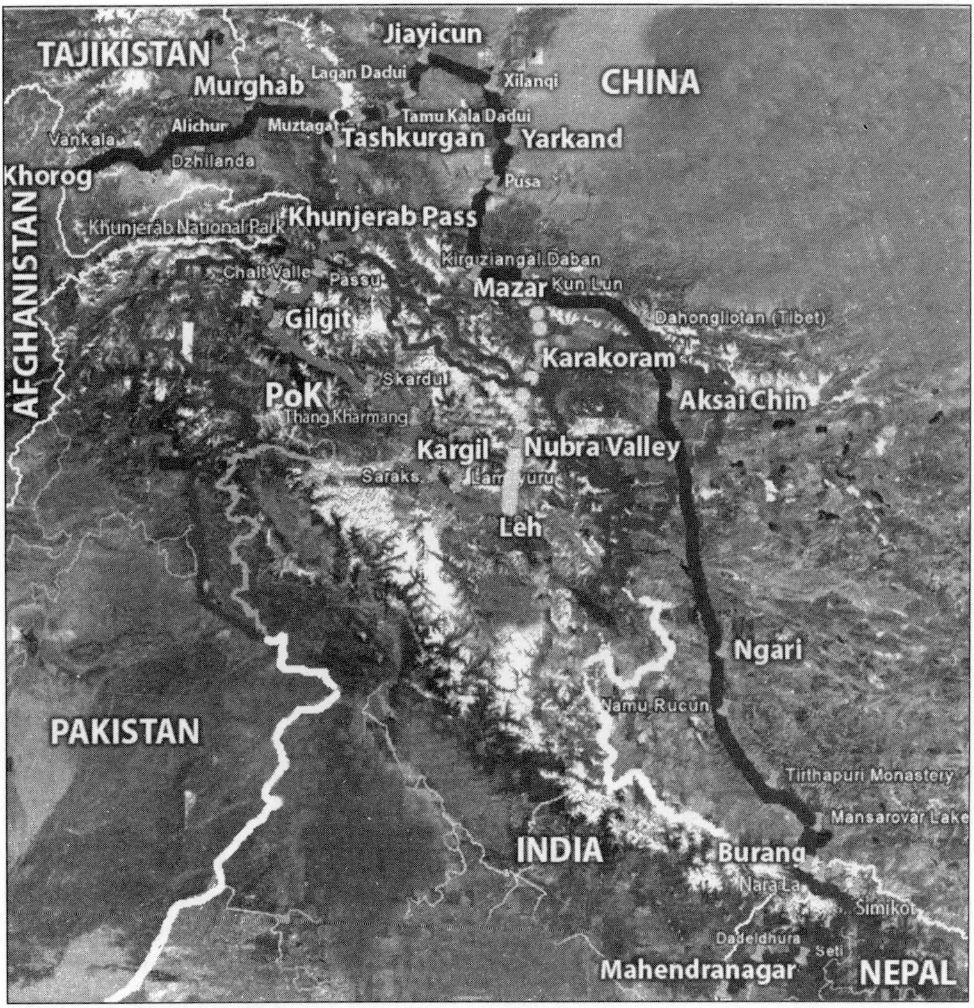


become fragmented on the basis of lines of demarcation forcing the movement of goods and people to become restricted and confined. Trade and transport can no longer be studied on the basis of existing road connectivity but needs to be deliberated within a larger framework of the current geo-political situation prevailing in the region.

Most of the routes pass through one or more of the neighboring countries such as Pakistan, China, Nepal and Tajikistan. Unfortunately the current inter-country relations between India and its immediate neighbors do not seem particularly favorable for India. The most feasible and shortest route between India and Afghanistan is the route that passes through Pakistan. But given the Indo-Pak relations, accessing the route for trade and commerce is a far-fetched dream. The route is full of risks and is susceptible to continuing violence. Currently goods such

**Map 7: India-Iran-Afghanistan Route**

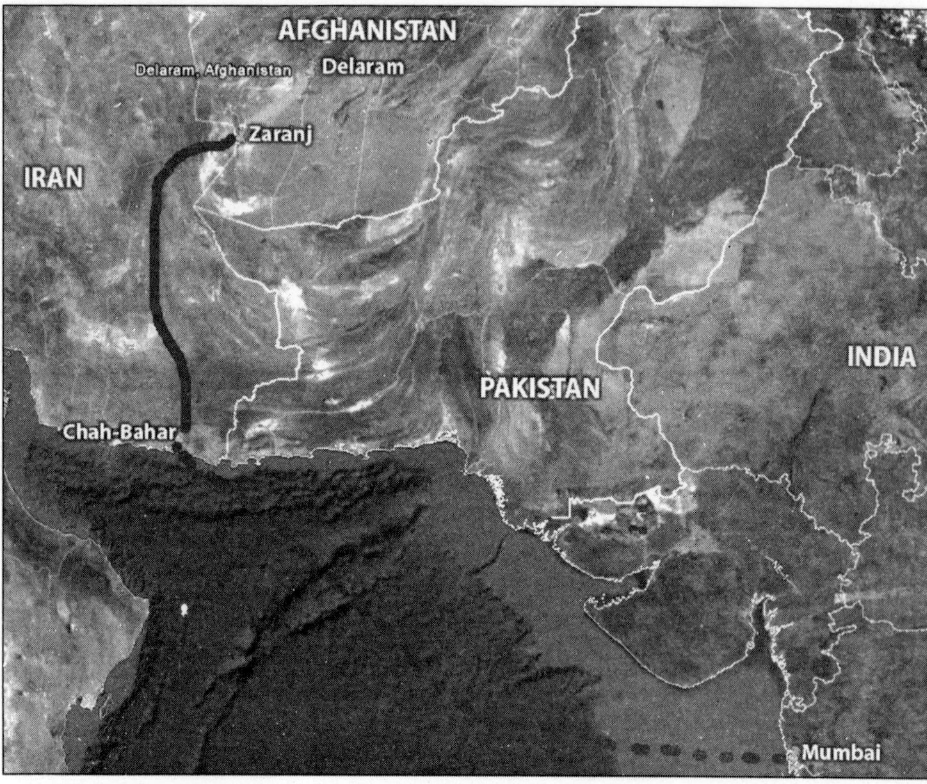


as fresh and dry fruits from Afghanistan are allowed into India for trade through Pakistan but the reverse is not allowed. Even humanitarian assistance such as high protein biscuits for school children in Afghanistan from India are not allowed but need to be transported by other vehicles at the borders without signs such as 'India' or 'Bharat' on the packages. Such a passage for transit and trade no doubt restricts the growth of the economy and hinders in the 'take off' stage of the region's development. Efforts to increase and improve connectivity through the South Asian regional cooperation programme such as SAARC are in process. Some success has been met as regards the movement of drugs in the border areas of India and Pakistan but access and transit for trade and commerce is yet to develop into any substantial direction and purpose. Needless to mention that such developmental initiative would have been of crucial significance in rebuilding the economy of Afghanistan.

The route through China dates back to over 2,000 years. However, the land route between India and China has remained dormant following the 1962 border war. It was with the opening of the Nathu La pass in 2006 that border trade between the two countries by land got activated. Restoring the road connections to Shipkila in Himachal Pradesh and Lipu-Lekh in Uttarakhand[14] are under consideration and may open up avenues for further trade and bilateral co-operations. Although the routes through Ladakh in Jammu and Kashmir via Aksai Chin and Karakoram pass seem to be the shortest in the present circumstances, it is not likely that these routes will ever see the light of the day. Although the route is less complicated, involving only China as a land-link between India and Tajikistan before reaching Khorogh at the Afghanistan border, other routes involve heavy risks and pass through long stretches of vulnerable areas infested with insurgency.

It needs to be borne in mind that India has registered its protest on the current practice of stapled visas that China provides and their refusing to stamp visas into the passports of people living in the Indian-administered part of Kashmir. Moreover, China is against the Indian government providing shelter to the exiled Tibetan spiritual leader – the Dalai Lama, who has been campaigning for Tibetan autonomy and human rights while living in northern India. Nonetheless this route has tremendous potential for both China and India and would no doubt cut down on transport costs enhancing the trade.

India needs to develop a synergy of all major concerned stakeholders by developing regional grouping. Information sharing, defence of borders and close monitoring and developing the capacity buildup among these regional powers.[15] India needs to initiate such a process by involving all concerned players in the region such as Afghanistan, China and Central Asia. All efforts to utilize the existing forums of regional cooperation such as the Shanghai Organization Cooperation (SCO) and the Asia Cooperation Dialogue (ACD) need to be synergized in order to activate the regional transport routes that lay dormant for want of immediate intervention. Simultaneously the regional grouping needs to develop directions for transport linkages within the region in such a manner that these in turn get linked with the international transport system such as TRACECA, ECO, INSTC, Asian Highway Network and so on to achieve greater network efficiency.

India has built a new port in Chah Bahar in Iran, which is closest to Indian shores. This port was developed connecting it with Kabul and beyond. In fact India built parts of a highway originating from Chabahar (in Iran) through Afghanistan to Tajikistan (Chabahar-Kabul-Kunduz-Badakhshan) which would enable India to have a transport corridor to the otherwise inaccessible Central Asian region.[16] The recently completed Zaranj–Delaram road by the Indian government in Afghanistan has opened up new options for India via Chah Bahar to access the Central Asian energy resources. Although the route seems to be a viable option for linking to the southern parts of Afghanistan and Central Asia, but the vulnerabilities that this route poses cannot be underestimated. The proposed trade route passes through the entire length of Afghanistan from south to north exposing itself to a huge number of risks such as its long distance, enhanced taxation and border duties and hassles involved in the multi-mode system of transportation such as waterways, railways and the roadways. Moreover, this route passes through the south of Afghanistan which is considered to be a Taliban hub. While constructing the Zaranj–Delaram road India has been attacked several times and many lives had to be crucified before completing the road. The road in operation has a security issue which needs to be borne in mind. Over and above, India has voted against Iran in the IAEA meet. Given the scenario, India needs to maintain friendly ties with Iran and forge ahead with its regional partners such as China, Central Asia and Iran on an issue based approach.

## ENDNOTES

1. Mondira Dutta, "India-Afghanistan Relations: Opportunities and Challenges", *World Focus,* (Annual Number) November-December 2008, pp. 347-348 and 412.
2. Ahmed Rashid, *Descent into Chaos,* Great Britain, Allen Lane, 2008, p. 172
3. http://unama.unmissions.org
4. Mondira Dutta, op cit.
5. www.mea.gov.in
6. Jill McGivering, "Afghan People Losing Confidence", BBC News, 9 February 2009.
7. Mondira Dutta, "Indian Initiatives for Afghan Women – An Evaluation Study", Ministry of External Affairs, Government of India.
8. Ibid.
9. http://www.dnaindia.com
10. Library of Congress, 2008: Federal Research Division; *Country Profile: Afghanistan,* August 2008, p. 14.
11. Peter Wonacott, "Afghan Road Project Shows Bumps in Drive for Stability", *The Wall Street Journal,* 17 August 2009.
12. Richard B Fisher, *The Marco Polo Expedition – A Journey along the Silk Road,* Hodder & Stoughton, London, 1988, p. 186.
13. http://mathaba.net/news/?x=580583
14. P. Stobdan, "Exploring India – Kazakhstan Transport Linkages", Institute for Defence Studies and Analyses Policy Brief, 22 December 2008.
15. Mondira Dutta, Note 1, pp. 359-360 and 496.
16. *Pakistan Times,* 2009: 'Road to Nowhere', 21st June 2009, http://www.newpakistantimes.com/archives/18179

## Appendix

Recommendations of the International Seminar on ***Energy and Transport Linkages between Central Asia and South Asia*** organised by the Himalayan Research and Cultural Foundation at ICSSR Complex, New Delhi on 25-27 November 2006.

1. The Seminar stressed the need to involve area specialists, economists, sociologists and professionals in order to make detailed studies and put forward policy-oriented recommendations. Working groups of think tanks, experts and academia from the Central Asian and South Asian countries should be set up to initiate dialogues for appreciating each other's view points on proposed energy projects and to prepare workable road maps for energy cooperation. This would also later on help in smoothening the inter-governmental MOUs, agreements etc.
2. The Seminar underscored the need to establish professional institutional linkages between the two regions for sharing of experiences and knowledge on energy sector developments, including development of renewable energy sources, technology transfer and other related fields.
3. The Seminar highlighted the importance of undertaking case studies and field work in the region to study the cultural, demographic and socio-economic infrastructure in the region.
4. The governments and civil society in the region should take into account the future energy consumption rates and re-evaluate the development of domestic energy sector taking into consideration ground realities such as traditional energy sources, under-development of domestic distribution, infrastructures and environmental factors.
5. The determining factor for laying of pipelines should be their commercial viability rather than power projection.
6. Keeping in view the physical obstacles as well as the adverse security situation in Afghanistan and also reluctance of the interested parties to make huge investments, the Central and South Asian countries can look for a reliable alternative option to bring Kazakh hydrocarbon resources via China to South Asia. The existing infrastructure of Atasu-Alashankou pipeline, and in the light of improved India-China Relations and also the prospects of Russian oil to this pipeline, will facilitate energy and transport linkages between Central Asia and South Asia.
7. In view of little progress in regional integration of Central Asia, India needs to promote energy dialogue with both Russia and China thus taking the SCO and Moscow-Delhi-Beijing unofficial triangle forward.

8. India should explore the possibility of establishing joint ventures in Kazakhstan and other Central Asian Republics in petro-chemical industries in order to facilitate and promote the economic development in the region.
9. The governments of the region should facilitate and encourage cross-continental trade and remove the complexities of existing custom regimes and transport tariff systems in the region.
10. Keeping in view that 1/5th of the world population is concentrated in South Asia and that the major infrastructure linkages are already existing in the region, India needs to get actively involved in linking the North-South Corridor through the corridor continuum in South Asia and even beyond to South East Asia. The Himalayan Research and Cultural Foundation should be encouraged to undertake research projects/field studies to assess the status and economic viability of the North-South Corridor to South Asia and its linkage with the land-locked countries of Central Asia.
11. Given the role of India as an observer in SCO, India needs to carry forward its energy initiatives in the region. India should undertake joint projects with Russian oil/gas majors and also work towards joint development of large Vankor deposit and the Kurmangazy project on the Caspian shelf.
12. The Seminar underscored the benefits of interconnections between the South Asian and Central Asian electricity grids. Interconnecting these grids would benefit all concerned, as only small investments are required for the purpose.
13. Ensuring regional energy security in Central and South Asia demands adequate multilateral confidence-building measures and the parallel need for investments to build the infrastructure.
14. The contradictions and competing trends among various countries in the region can be minimized if these countries are made stakeholders in the existing and prospective projects of energy and transport linkages.
15. The Seminar stressed the need to make efforts to explore energy saving and oil conservation technologies that should be promoted while developing new energy sources.
16. The Seminar welcomed the re-opening of the India-China border trade point at Nathu La in the Indian state of Sikkim. This reopening will provide access to the landlocked Central Asian states to the Indian port of Kandla on the Arabian Sea. The Seminar recommends to the governments of India and China to similarly reopen the historical and traditional India-Central Asia overland trade route via Ladakh (Indian State of Jammu and Kashmir) and Xinjiang region of PRC to the Central Asian Republics.
17. The Seminar calls upon both the governments of India and China to accept the proposal of Jammu and Kashmir government to open the Leh-Demchuk

route to western Tibet as an easier alternative route for pilgrimage to the Kailash-Mansarovar across the LOC in Ladakh. This will help not only in reducing the journey time and provide a safer passage to pilgrims, but also revive the traditional India-China trade via Ladakh and Tibet.

18. The Seminar underlined the fact that the problem of connectivity between Central Asia and South Asia can only be solved through a cooperative and inclusive approach as against the competitive and exclusive one. Geo-economics and geo-culture must take priority over competitive geopolitics to address the problem of connectivity between there two important regions of Asia.

# Index